The Humphre

HUMPHREY JENNINGS v   at
Cambridge University. He is recognised as one of Britain's
greatest film-makers. His studies of national life made for the
GPO Film Unit, the Crown Film Unit and the Ministry of
Information before and during the Second World War include
Listen to Britain (1941), *Fires Were Started* (1943) and *Diary for Timothy*
(1945), films which are both invaluable records of their time and
cinematic masterpieces. Part of the richness of the films is attrib-
utable to the wide range of interests and talents which Jennings
brought to the drama of his subject matter. He was a poet and
literary critic, a gifted painter and a leading member of the
Surrealist movement. In 1936 he played a key role in organising
the International Surrealist Exhibition in London. He was also a
founder member of the anthropological movement Mass
Observation. Humphrey Jennings died in an accident in 1950.

KEVIN JACKSON is a writer, broadcaster and documentary film-
maker. His books include *Invisible Forms*, *Pyramid* and *The Verbals*.
For Carcanet, he has written *The Language of Cinema* and *Letters of
Introduction*, and edited the poems of Anthony Burgess and a selection from Robert Burton's *Anatomy of Melancholy*.

Film books from Carcanet

The C.A. Lejeune Film Reader, edited by Anthony Lejeune
The Dilys Powell Film Reader, edited by Christopher Cook
Westerns: Aspects of a Movie Genre, by Philip French

The Language of Cinema, edited by Kevin Jackson

THE
HUMPHREY JENNINGS
FILM READER

Edited by Kevin Jackson

CARCANET

First published in Great Britain in 1993 by
Carcanet Press Limited
Alliance House
Cross Street
Manchester M2 7AQ

This impression 2004

A CIP catalogue record for this book is available from the British Library
ISBN 1 85754 748 9

The publisher acknowledges financial assistance from Arts Council England

Printed and bound in England by SRP Ltd, Exeter

Contents

Illustrations
(between pages 168-9)

Acknowledgements

My main debt is to Dr Mary-Lou Legg, not only for the excellent order in which she has kept her father's archives, but also for the patience and good humour she has somehow managed to maintain despite years of being pestered by researchers with more doggedness than tact. I'd also like to thank Michael Schmidt and Philip French for encouraging this book, David Thompson for his usual generosity with videos, Philip Dodd for arranging screenings of Jennings's rarest films and Martin Rowson for his diplomatic efforts. Thanks, too, to Ed Buscombe of the BFI, Andrew Murray of the Mayor Gallery, Richard Humphreys of the Tate Gallery, and to Peter Carpenter and the masters of the Tonbridge School.

Professors Leonard Leff and Martin Wallen of Oklahoma State University, together with their colleagues in the TSAL (Territorial Society for the Appreciation of Literature), helped confirm that Jennings's work still holds its appeal for cinephiles across the Atlantic. Nick Lezard, Toby Poynder and Claire Preston gave indispensable help during successive computing disasters.

Broadcasts by Humphrey Jennings are published by kind permission of the BBC Written Archives Centre, Caversham, and the BBC's Legal Adviser's Division, Copyright and Artists Rights Department; his review of *The English* in the *TLS* 7 August 1948, by kind permission of the *Times Literary Supplement*. 'Rock-Painting and *La Jeune Peinture*', by Humphrey Jennings and G.F. Noxon, is reprinted by kind permission of G.F. Noxon's estate. 'The Boston Evening Transcript', from *Collected Poems 1909-1935* by T.S. Eliot is reprinted by permission of Faber and Faber Ltd. An extract from 'Colonel Fantock' from *Collected Poems* by Edith Sitwell is reprinted by permission of David Higham Associates and Macmillan.

We are grateful to the following for permission to reproduce the illustrations: Mary-Lou Legg for nos. 1-8, 10 and 13; Andrew Murray for no. 9; Michael White for no. 11; Anna Clarke and Martin Rowson for no. 12; the Bolton Art Gallery for no. 14; Mark Lancaster for no. 15; Jean-Pierre Haik for no. 16.

Introduction

In December 1992, the British Film Institute's magazine *Sight and Sound* published the results of a poll in which some 230 directors and critics from around the world had been asked to nominate the ten best films in the century-long history of cinema. On the whole, the results were fairly predictable. *Citizen Kane* topped both the critics' and the directors' charts, and the names of Renoir, Kurosawa, Fellini, Ray, Hitchcock, Ozu, Bresson and Dreyer were liberally sprinkled throughout most of the individual lists. A closer look at the voting did yield one or two surprises, however, and not the least of them was the number of votes cast for *Listen to Britain* (1942) and *Diary for Timothy* (1945/6), directed by Humphrey Jennings.

There are various reasons why Jennings is an unlikely name to find in this august company. Unlike the others, he did not direct theatrical features – only one of his films, *Fires Were Started* (1943), is of anything like feature length – but instead worked almost exclusively in the unpromising medium of government-sponsored documentaries. His financial and technical resources were tightly restricted, and though his credit appears on almost thirty films, only a couple of them are more than twenty minutes long. In effect, he was just one among many hired hands for the Ministry of Information's wartime propaganda effort; at best, one might say, a minor, poorly paid civil servant. Finally, his career was cut short by accidental death in 1950. He was forty-three, an age at which many directors are just beginning their real work. Why, then, do so many of those who know and care about such matters think Jennings not simply a talented director, but one of the very few British directors of world rank?

As with artists in any medium, some of the answers must be sought in the area which, Ezra Pound maintained, was the test of any man's sincerity: technique. Even some of Jennings's most ferocious detractors (he has always had enemies as well as fans) have conceded the exceptional beauty of the images he achieved with his various cameramen; and the orchestration of those images, particularly when he was working with his gifted editor, Stewart McAllister, is at once singularly graceful and forceful. His innovative uses of sound are possibly less striking today than they were at the time; none the less they continue to influence new generations: the young Scottish director Ian Sellar, who made *Prague* (1992), was happy to admit how much he was in debt to the inventive play of soundtrack against picture in *Listen to Britain*.

Felicities of technique alone, though, would not be enough to win Jennings his place in the pantheon. One of the glories of Jennings's best work is its power to move viewers who have little or no conscious awareness of the manner in which its effects have been achieved. People can respond to these films as 'great' because they have such manifestly great subjects: the lives and deaths of people at war, the strengths and fragilities of a national culture under attack, the spectacle of unremarkable men and women rendered heroic by history. Yes, they are propaganda, but propaganda of an order so high and humane that the word loses its usual pejorative edge.

One way of appreciating their idiosyncratic brilliance is to think not so much of what they show as what they refuse to show. For example, they seldom so much as mention the Nazi enemy, let alone try to whip up resentment or hatred for him, and many of their highest flights are set to music by 'enemy' composers, Mozart and Beethoven, as reclaimed for British ears by Myra Hess. (Since hostilities ceased, these films have been warmly received by German critics.) Their invocations of Britain's military prowess are similarly rare and tend towards understatement. The face and voice of Churchill are not much in evidence, except briefly in *Words for Battle* (1941), and when H.M. the Queen appears in *Listen to Britain* it is not as a figurehead or embodiment of the national spirit but as one among many appreciative members of a concert audience. The British faces these documentaries record are hardly suggestive of ferocious Anglo-Saxon, Norse or Celtic warrior ancestry, but are humorous, patient, shy and sometimes touchingly ugly.

Small wonder, in short, that a contemporary reviewer of *Listen to Britain* thought that its effect on morale was likely to be disastrous, and said he dreaded the prospect of its being seen by our allies. (In fact, it proved a hit with audiences on both sides of the Atlantic.) Since then, Jennings's admirers have gone to what might appear the other extreme, and compared his work to that of Hitler's court director Leni Riefenstahl, such as *Triumph of the Will*. The comparison is intended to add to his stature, since liberal intellectuals are often strongly taken with Riefenstahl's films (see, for example, Susan Sontag's essay 'Fascinating Fascism'). Yet, as the novelist and critic Gilbert Adair recently pointed out, its real effect is not so much to boost the English director as to show up the German one. Melodrama, theatricality, hoarse rhetoric – Jennings's films are as free of these Riefenstahlian properties as they are of their democratic counterparts, ready pathos and glorification of the Little Man.

At the heart of Jennings's achievement is, if not quite a paradox, a productive conflict of interest. He used the most seemingly anonymous of all film forms in which to work out an unmistakable personal language; he was scrupulously honest to his material – more so than directors who thought of themselves as 'realists' – and yet dealt in myth; he tried to speak plainly and directly in public about subjects which had for years occupied his most abstruse private reflections. It has been said (by, among others, the British director Lindsay Anderson) that Jennings was one of the very few people for whom the Second World War came as a piece of good luck. Disaster forced him to focus the energies he tended to dissipate in too many other artistic and intellectual projects. Conversely, a country at risk of invasion became suddenly receptive to the ideas and pictures of a man who had thought more than most about (to twist Henry James) the curious fate of being English. Jennings had written scholarly papers about Martial Laureates; in 1939, he became one.

All of which should help make that *Sight and Sound* result somewhat less puzzling. But Jennings's career was far more extraordinary than this swift resumé of his war service can suggest. Though he may not loom as large in the story of cinema as some of the other names on the 'Ten Best' poll, Jennings is – with, say, Orson Welles and Satyajit Ray – one of the very few whose names would still be in all the cultural reference books if he had never exposed so much as a foot of film. Like Ray (the artist and composer) and Welles (the all-round theatre artist), Jennings was also a man whose diverse pursuits and accomplishments enriched his films, made them what they are.

First of all, Jennings was a painter, and from 1930 until his death regarded the development of skill with the brush as his main artistic aim. (His initial approach to film-making appears to have been rather reluctant, and prompted mainly by want of money; later on, he said that if he had enjoyed a private income, he would have done nothing but paint.) He was born in Walberswick, Suffolk in 1907, and was, inevitably, keenly aware of East Anglia's pre-eminence in British art history. Apart from painting, he also designed sets for the theatre and films, experimented with colour processes on Len Lye's film *The Birth of the Robot* (1936), made collages and took many photographs.

Much though by no means all of this work was surrealist in inspiration. Jennings was not merely an energetic member of the British surrealist group but provided its main personal link with the French founding fathers, including André Breton and Paul Eluard (who wrote a poem in Jennings's honour). Among other activities, he helped to organize the notorious Surrealist Exhibition of 1936 – the one at which Salvador Dali delivered a lecture from inside a deep-sea diver's suit – and exhibited several of his own pieces there; he translated Breton's essay on Marcel Duchamp's *The Bride Stripped Bare By Her Batchelors, Even* and the poems of Eluard; he wrote surrealist prose poems of his own. In one way or another, all of these things cast their uncanny light on his wartime films.

This might seem a bizarre assertion, given that surrealism was a

revolutionary internationalist movement which delighted in staging anti-
bourgeois outrages, and that Jennings's work can be as stirringly patriotic
as the work of any English poet – when he quotes Kipling in *Words for
Battle*, he does not intend to mock. Indeed, the surrealists, who once gave
their imprimatur to Jennings's own minor outrages (such as the photo-
collage *Minotaur*, which was rude about Lord Kitchener) were later to
excommunicate him angrily when he accepted the Order of the British
Empire in recognition of his work with the Crown Film Unit.

For all this, the surrealist aspect of the films is demonstrable: Jennings
had listened to Breton. The war itself could be regarded as bringing out
the latent surrealist dimension of daily life, and as one critic has neatly
suggested, a bomb hitting a big city hospital might easily bring about
Lautréamont's ideal image of beauty from *Les Chants de Maldoror*, a
'chance meeting, on a dissecting table, of a sewing machine and an
umbrella'. Jennings never came across that particular juxtaposition, but he
did show an art gallery with empty frames, a shop being entered by its
smashed window, tin hats clustered around a royal statue and houses
turned inside-out. Some might argue that in recording these freaks and
violent yokings-together, Jennings was doing no more than report the
facts, but their frequency in the films and his curious fascination with
them clearly bespeak a surrealist sensibility. Such pictures can have the
cryptic portent of a surrealist 'found' object, as, in a different way, do the
lines of one his most regularly cited poems, 'I See London':

> I see a thousand strange sights in the streets of London
> I see the clock on Bow Church burning in daytime
> I see a one-legged man crossing the fire on crutches
> I see three negroes and a woman with white face-powder reading
>   music at half-past three in the morning
> I see an ambulance girl with her arms full of roses
> I see the burnt drums of the Philharmonic
> I see the green leaves of Lincolnshire carried through London on
>   the wrecked body of an aircraft.

>   (May 1941)

Surrealism shaped his work in other ways, too, from the effects he and
McAllister achieved with unexpected edits to his day-by-day shooting
procedures. In a review of Herbert Read's *Surrealism* in 1936, Jennings
observes that Breton had said that

> Surrealism has replaced the 'coincidence' for the 'apparition', and
> that we must 'allow ourselves to be guided towards the unknown by
> this newest *promise*.' Now that is talking; and to settle surrealism

down as Romanticism only is to deny this promise. It is to cling to the apparition with its special 'haunt'. It is to look for ghosts only on battlements, and on battlements only for ghosts. 'Coincidences' have the infinite freedom of appearing anywhere, anytime, to anyone...

Especially to a sharp-eyed director. Jennings's fondness for improvisation on the spot (and his concomitant reluctance – often found maddening by his employers – to plan much ahead of time) was not so much a matter of artistic temperament nor, more flattering term, of Negative Capability, as it was a willingness to let such 'coincidences' take place. Those who knew him well recall that his working days were filled with happy flukes and accidental discoveries. Ian Dalrymple, who produced many of the films, noted the importance he ascribed to what others might call chance:

> Once when he went to shoot a cargo ship for a symbolic purpose he discovered, to his joy and amazement, that her name was BRITISH GENIUS. He rang me up from the North with huge satisfaction just to tell me. I said 'Oh Humphrey, you do have the luck.' But he didn't think it was luck, or coincidence; it was the truth that won't be denied. Things like that were always happening to him...
>
> (*Humphrey Jennings, 1907-1950: A Tribute*)

They carried on happening, Dalrymple said, right up until the unhappy chance of his death, when he fell from a cliff face on the Greek island of Poros.

> In his pocket was the book he had carried and dipped into constantly during the short time he was in Greece. It was Trelawney's *Last Days of Shelley and Byron*...And I don't think that was coincidence either. I just think that Greece has claimed another English poet. (*ibid.*)

Obituaries should always be allowed their touches of hyperbole and mysticism, but Dalrymple's really does not require so very much indulgence. If by the phrase 'Surrealist film' we intend something like *Un Chien Andalou* and *L'Age d'Or*, then *Fires Were Started* is admittedly not a surrealist film. Yet without his apprenticeship as a hunter and gatherer of the extraordinary in daily life – that is, as a Surrealist – none of his best films would have taken their distinctive forms. It is striking that when the critic David Thomson speculates about the kind of artist Jennings might have been had he survived his fall, the comparisons for which he immediately reaches are, first, the most famous of all surrealist directors and, second, one of the few English poets regarded by the Surrealists as an unofficial ancestor. Jennings, Thomson suggests, could, in 'the subdued caution of post-war Britain... have become a Buñuel-like figure. His fires were, like Blake's, a condition of the soul and might even have burned down English good manners' (*A Biographical Dictionary of the Cinema*, 1975).

The other main area in which Jennings achieved both distinction and notoriety during his lifetime seems, on the face of it, to have nothing to do with the arts. Rather than as a film-maker or painter, Humphrey Jennings is known to social historians for the decisive part he played in the pioneering sociological movement Mass Observation. This project was launched some time towards the end of 1936, when Jennings, together with the self-trained anthropologist Tom Harrisson and the poet Charles Madge, asked some fifty people from around the country to file detailed reports on how they spent their days.

Press coverage of this novelty caught the public imagination, and by the time of George VI's Coronation in May 1937, more than a thousand Observers – 'coal miners, factory hands, shopkeepers, salesmen, house-wives...' to cite Mass Observation's own list – were helping to construct this 'anthropology of our own people'. Dozens of day reports on the Coronation itself were assembled into Mass Observation's first major book, *May the Twelfth* (1937) – a kind of prose documentary, co-edited by Jennings and Madge. A sober enterprise then, scholarly and almost scientific in its rigour?

Up to a point; and there is no doubt that the fidelity of Jennings's films to the minutiae of working people's lives, and particularly their enjoyments, is one result of his Mass Observation period. *Spare Time* (1939), generally regarded as the first of Jennings's films to bear his personal stamp, tends also to be seen as the cinematic equivalent of a Mass Observation study, especially in its attention to the newer forms of pastime enjoyed by industrial workers outside factory hours. (Jennings did not regard what we now call Popular Culture as any kind of threat to High Culture, and some of the most memorable sequences in his films are edited to pop songs of the day – the factory girls singing along to 'Yes, My Darling Daughter' in *Listen to Britain*, for example.)

But Jennings was never much interested in statistics and averages, and it does not take a very penetrating gaze to see that beneath its would-be scientific pose, Mass Observation – at least as conducted by Jennings – was really a kind of first cousin to surrealism. *May the Twelfth*, with its quotations from Confucius, Shakespeare, Baudelaire and Freud, is actually closer to a surrealist collage than a documentary – it is about the unofficial, 'unconscious' mind of Britain on its most ceremonial day.

Just as the French Surrealists, taking some cues from Freud's *Psychopathology of Everyday Life* and other books, had begun to regard weird little details from their urban surroundings with the same rapt attention with which they scrutinized wooden gods from Oceania or listened to the outbursts of the insane, so Jennings was trying to seek out small but telling clues to the unacknowledged semi-pagan beliefs and idols of his fellow-countrymen. His photographs of the period dwell on children's graffiti, billboard advertisements and so on, and the surrealist flavour of Mass Observation's syllabus is nicely conveyed in an early list of 'problems' for investigation compiled by Madge and Harrisson:

> Behaviour of people at war memorials
> Shouts and gestures of motorists
> The aspidistra cult
> Anthropology of football pools
> Bathroom behaviour
> Beards, armpits, eyebrows
> Anti-semitism
> Distribution, diffusion and significance of the dirty joke
> Funerals and undertakers
> Female taboos about eating
> The private lives of midwives

The strangeness, charm and humour of that list, with its quaint phrasing and internal rhymes – 'the private lives of midwives'! – should be enough in itself to explain why Jennings was regarded with immense suspicion by his dourer colleagues in the documentary film movement, who not only (and wrongly) suspected him of sneering at the masses but also felt that there was something unhealthy about his whole approach. Jennings frequently ran into trouble with John Grierson (the presiding spirit of British documentaries and their most powerful producer) and with his followers, who took a very strict line on how the Workers were to be shot. Documentaries of the Grierson persuasion, such as *Housing Problems* (1935) and *Enough to Eat?* (1936), were, as their director Edgar Anstey later put it with commendable wryness, concerned with 'presenting the norm; and making sure that characters were appropriately heroic in adversity.'

By contrast, Mass Observation in general and Jennings in particular were held to be in pursuit of 'the curious, the eccentric, the inexplicable, the mysterious'. Perfectly true; but the condemnation can be turned through 180 degrees, and helps to explain how Jennings managed to achieve such fresh and persuasive results. He would not turn people into allegories or types, no matter how benign the typing might be, and the outcome was that he was able to show the British at war as nobody else could. Those singing factory girls are neither dupes of capitalism nor Stakhanovite heroines: they are the women Jennings chanced to meet when he took his cameras down on to the shop floor, and their faces are vivid and unforgettable after half a century.

Lastly, Jennings's films derive some of their complexity and scope from the more scholarly of his several short careers. It is entirely possible that, like his undergraduate friend William Empson, Jennings might have spent his whole life as an academic critic and teacher of English Literature. After attending the Perse School, Jennings went on to read English at Pembroke College, Cambridge; he took a starred first in the Tripos, and went on to do graduate work under the supervision of I.A. Richards. He worked mostly on Thomas Gray, and sent an essay on Gray's *Progress of Poesie* to T.S. Eliot at *The Criterion*; Eliot liked the essay, but considered it too long for publication. Jennings also published an edition of the 1593 Quarto of *Venus and Adonis*, and wrote unpublished essays on other Elizabethan poets.

There are one or two obvious examples of Jennings's using his official war assignments to reflect on the continuities of English literature. *Words for Battle* sets pictures of Britain in arms to readings of freshly pertinent extracts from, among others, Milton and Blake, and though their phrases are quite familiar, Jennings would scarcely have overlooked the different meanings *Areopagitica* and *Jerusalem* would have held in the past or the place of their authors in the English radical tradition. Similarly, *Fires Were Started* uses a passage about death from Sir Walter Ralegh to chastening effect. But touches of this kind require no more than average literacy. The real influence of Jennings's literary studies on his films is harder to pin down – it is in his ideas, influenced by Richards, about the function of 'the image', and about the changing relationship of the English poet to his potential audience; to which latter point, I shall return.

The other aspect of Jennings's films which arises from his academic pursuits is their unique perspective on industrialism. At Cambridge, Jennings had participated in the extraordinary student magazine *Experiment*; with undergraduate friends such as Empson and Jacob Bronowski he made vigorous forays into the studies which united The Two Cultures, as other Cambridge men were to call science and art. Jennings was especially absorbed by the early days of the Industrial Revolution, and long after he had left Cambridge continued to amass a copious body of texts for a projected anthology about the Coming of the Machine. He never managed to edit these into a form that was acceptable to publishers; more than three decades after his death, though, a large extract from his notes was published as *Pandaemonium* (1985, edited by Mary-Lou Jennings and Charles Madge).

Both the nature of the materials he collected and the reminiscences of his friends suggests that his attitude towards industry was conflict-ridden.

On the one hand, he was appalled by the wounds it had inflicted on the land, sky and waters, and on the lives of the people who had poured into the cities (and whose descendants are among the heroes of his films). On the other, he was thrilled at the moral energy, ingenuity and physical courage which had made it all possible, and thought that the great practical scientists and technologists were also artists of a special kind. 'When we admire the sunset we are using the eye of Turner, when we switch on the light we are tapping the mind of Faraday', runs the commentary for his last film, *Family Portrait* (1950).

In the wartime films, displaying British industry harnessed to the fight against Hitler, it is generally his sense of wonder which surfaces, as in the magnificent sequence of the Spitfire factory which closes *Listen to Britain*. Yet these scenes too, with their awe-inspiring shots of flames blazing inside giant furnaces, convey the sense of the Machine as something potentially threatening, and not only to the *Luftwaffe*.

Jennings is, in a few words, a man whose place in British culture and world cinema ought to be beyond dispute: 'our greatest documentarist' (Gilbert Adair), 'the only real poet the British cinema has so far produced' (Lindsay Anderson), and 'a true war artist, in the way that Henry Moore's drawings in the Underground and Evelyn Waugh's *Sword of Honour* trilogy transcend war and reassert the primacy of the human imagination' (David Thomson). Add to these the other accomplishments as painter, photographer, anthropologist, actor, poet, editor, scholar, critic, theorist, intellectual historian, and the sum is ... a man who has been more or less forgotten.

His documentaries are hardly ever screened, apart from the three or four which are dutifully programmed each year at the National Film Theatre or in film schools. There is no published catalogue either of his paintings or of his photographs, and they have not been exhibited for more than a decade. There has been no biography, nor, apart from a short item on BBC's *Omnibus* ten years ago, any television programme about Jennings since Robert Vas's tribute in 1970. And however much specialists will deny the point, to the general public his name is unknown.

The full extent of the obscurity into which he has vanished may be gathered by looking at the Penguin Twentieth-Century Classics edition of Waugh's *Decline and Fall*. On its cover is a black and white photograph of a sensitive-looking chap in a smart suit, blowing an ectoplasmic puff of smoke from his mouth and representing, one assumes, some picture researcher's idea of how Paul Pennyfeather must have looked. The photographer, credited, is Lee Miller; the sitter, uncredited, is Humphrey Jennings.

II

One of the intentions of this book, therefore, is to act as a reminder of how much we have lost in permitting this collective lapse of memory. To describe an artist as 'unjustly neglected' is usually cant, but in Jennings's case the miscarriage of justice has been grievous, and the neglect palpable, especially as regards his written works, which are almost all out of print. True, some extracts from Jennings's assorted writings have been reprinted in the past decade or so, notably in the first part of a catalogue for the exhibition of his paintings and films at London's Riverside Studios in 1982 (*Humphrey Jennings: Film-maker, Painter, Poet*, edited by Mary-Lou Jennings for the BFI). But most of the articles and poems in *The Humphrey Jennings Film Reader* have been buried in Rare Books rooms since the 1930s, and a good deal of the other material has never been published before in any form.

The *Reader* has four main sections.

The first and longest tells, in the director's own words, the story of how Jennings made his films. It puts his various scripts, treatments, proposals and other such documents together with the letters he wrote about what became of these plans. Most of these letters were written to his wife Cicely Jennings, *née* Cooper, to whom he was married in October 1929, and to his young daughters Mary-Lou and Charlotte.

Some of these working papers will be of exceptional interest to his admirers, and they help put the completed films in new perspectives: the routine dismissal of *Family Portrait* as half-hearted or bland, for example, will be a lot harder to sustain after reading Jennings's angry accounts of tussling with Grierson over his ideas for the film, and it can be seen how many of the concerns he was working out at the time dovetail with his work on *Pandaemonium*. The letters are more revealing still. It is not by accident that they appear to become most frequent and most eloquent during exactly the years in which Jennings did his finest work. Cicely Jennings took their children to the safety of the eastern United States from August 1940 to November 1944. Even though a number of Jennings's letters were lost in transit when ships were sunk, those which have been preserved give a running account of the business of directing – in its artistic as well as practical dimensions – that is more than worthy of a place on the shelves next to Cocteau's *Beauty and the Beast: Diary of a Film*, or John Boorman's *Money into Light*.

Since he was a man of such wide and intense interests, the letters also range far beyond film-making. They provide an unusually thorough account of day-to-day life on the Home Front, the detail and care of which must also be largely due to Jennings's Mass Observation discipline of writing Day Reports, a habit he kept up long after his official ties with the movement had been cut. They are further testament to his sensitivity to the natural world – to the perennial English conversational staple of the weather, but also to the changes in the agricultural landscape brought about by war and to the unchanging ways of indifferent birds and insects.

Above all, they offer the fullest and most authoritative evidence of Jennings's views on politics, an area which has been bitterly contested by the different factions who want to claim him for their own, or to cast him into the outer darkness. Broadly speaking, he was a man of the left, and once described his politics as those of William Cobbett. The other English radical these letters strongly bring to mind is George Orwell, whom Jennings praises in 1941: 'Excellent analysis... in George Orwell's *Lion and the Unicorn* – still quite a bunch of "intellectuals" here who are afraid of becoming "patriots"...' Jennings, these letters make plain, had no such fears.

Moreover, his reflections on making *Fires Were Started* and *The Silent Village* (1943) should make life a lot more awkward for those who want to brand his socialism as that of a condescending toff. (Nor, although the *canard* is often repeated, was he ever a rich man; one of the constant refrains of his letters, heavily trimmed down here so as to avoid monotony, is the family's chronic financial worries.) The East End firemen, he tells his wife in May 1942,

> have certainly proved one thing to me, but proved it in practice – that all these distinctions of understanding and level and other such are total rubbish and worse – invented by people to mislead. And not merely the famous upper-classes but also those made [by] the grubby documentary boys who try and give a hand to what they call emerging humanity, the common man and so on.

The second section of the *Reader* collects (to the best of my knowledge) every article about films, theatre, poetry, painting and British history ever published by Jennings, from his early contributions to *Experiment* in the 1920s to his catalogue note for an exhibition of paintings by his friend Paule Vezelay in 1948, plus a previously unknown article about Stubbs. It omits, however, the critical pieces he wrote for I.A. Richards as a research student, and his translations. The fourth section does not attempt to be similarly complete, and gathers no more than a selection of Jennings's poetry: in essence, it reprints his posthumous collection *Poems* (The Weekend Press, New York, 1951) but replaces the first five poems published there with their original texts as published in surrealist magazines, and adds one additional piece, 'Report on the Industrial Revolution'. Jennings wrote quite a few other poems, but they exist in so many drafts that to do justice to them would require a different book.

My main reason for keeping the third section apart from the others is because it shows Jennings in a role that has, to date, been unfamiliar even to his admirers: that is to say, expounding his notions not in rather complex articles for the pages of esoteric small press publications but in straightforward terms to the nation at large (and therefore anticipating, to some extent, what he would do with and in his films). It contains the scripts of nine talks Jennings gave on the BBC National Programme and French Service in the late 1930s and early 1940s, including five talks from his ten-part series *The Poet and the Public*. The other programmes in this series took the form of discussions which he recorded with three poets – C. Day Lewis ('A Young Poet and his Public', 31 May 1938), Herbert Read ('The Effect of War', 7 June 1938) and Patience Strong of the *Daily Mirror* ('Poetry as a Best Seller', 21 June 1938) – and with two representatives of the reading public, Mr Joseph Keen ('Poetry and the Ordinary Listener', 10 May 1938) and Mrs Edna Thorpe ('Understanding Modern Poetry', 24 May 1938).

While these latter programmes contain some worthwhile passages, their general effect is somewhat diffuse and they do not greatly clarify or add to the themes Jennings pursues throughout the series. The five scripted talks from *The Poet and the Public*, on the other hand, and the two earlier talks on 'Plagiarism in Poetry' and 'The Disappearance of Ghosts' are even more enlightening for us today than they were for their listeners, since they connect Jennings's academic past with his imminent future as a director.

Despite the occasional fireside chumminess of their tone, which now reads stiffly, these discussions are remarkable, and some of the most direct statements we have of Jennings's views on social history and aesthetics. 'Plagiarism in Poetry' begins as if it will be about nothing much more than a minor literary oddity, but it soon develops into a set of musings on authorship, originality, the workings of the creative imagination and the ways in which the poet's place in England had altered: 'the change in social conditions between 1580 (when Spenser began to write) and 1740 (when Gray began to write) divorced the poet more and more from contemporary life ...' Not the least striking part of these broadcasts is that they make a small gesture towards closing that breach between artist and audience in the very act of diagnosing how it came about. They deserve fuller study, especially when they speculate on the function of the Poet Laureate (here, it is often worth substituting for 'poet' the word 'film-maker') and what he and his kind can best offer his readers:

> You see, however industrialized we may be, we have ancestors – whether we like them or not, and how they come in here is (I think)

best expressed by the French poet (Apollinaire) who said that unlike other men he didn't stand with his back to the past and face the future; on the contrary, he stood with his back to the future, and with his face to the past because it was in the past that he could dis-cover who he was and how he had come to be him.

Jennings is now one of our ancestors himself; no longer one of the living poets who tries to keep the past alive for the sake of the present, but one of the voices we have almost lost. It would be wrong – in fact, an insult – to say that Jennings can only hope to appeal to British viewers and readers these days. On the contrary, when he is shown to audiences from other countries, the result can be astonishment, enthusiasm and demands to know more about this dazzling unknown talent. Jennings is one of the few directors with whom we can seriously hope to rebuke François Truffaut's gibe about the words 'Britain' and 'the cinema' having nothing in common – except, *bien sûr,* in the films of Alfred Hitchcock.

For all this, it remains the British who have most to gain from (as he puts it) turning to face Jennings. The weeks in which this book has been in preparation have been punctuated by yet more reports about the termi-nal decline of the world's first industrial nation, whose origins Jennings investigated so diligently; and newspaper editorials have reacted to the supposedly novel violence and tawdriness of our country by asking the very same question Jennings invokes in 'Poetry and National Life'.

Jennings was not a nostalgic man – 'there is only one occasion when admiration for past deeds may be given full rein', he wrote 'and that is in an epitaph' – and to return to his films from a desire to wallow in the grand old days of what Studs Terkel has called The Good War would be to mis-apply and misread them. Nor was he a jingoist. His patriotism did not blind him to the things about Britain – and specifically about England – which were terrifying or dismaying. The article he wrote in 1948 about the English character uncomfortably stresses its brutal aggression, ruthless-ness, opportunism and almost limitless capacity for self-deception. He gave a more even-handed answer, too, saying that

> The English are in fact a violent, savage race; passionately artistic, enormously addicted to pattern, with a faculty beyond all other people of ignoring their neighbours, their surroundings, or in the last resort, themselves. They have a power of poetry which is the despair of all the rest of the world. They produce from time to time personalities transcending ordinary human limitations. Then they drive other nations to a frenzy by patronizing these archangels who have come among them, and by indicating that any ordinary Englishman could do better if he liked to take the trouble...

There is a sense in which all of Jennings's best films – *Fires Were Started, Listen to Britain* and *A Diary for Timothy* – are nothing more nor less than the most generous and deeply felt answers he could give to the question for which his country felt it needed an urgent answer – and apparently, if for different reasons, still does: who are we? And this is another good reason for endorsing Lindsay Anderson's definition of Jennings as our only cinematic poet. These films meet, and more than meet the conditions Jennings set out in 'Poetry and National Life':

> he [the poet] can't tell the community who they are unless he does ...two things. Unless he talks about the things the community knows about (the things that they're interested in) and unless he also looks at the community's past – at the figures, the monuments, the achievements, the defeats, or whatever it may be, that have made the community what it is.

Half a century on, Jennings's films are 'answers' which have joined the ranks of national achievements, as the enduring works of an artist and thinker who was unusually aware of the complicated ways in which presents are always shaped by their pasts. The art and mind of Humphrey Jennings are resources we would do well not to forget.

Kevin Jackson
March 1993

A Note on the Text

Most of Jennings's letters were evidently composed in great haste: his handwriting can sometimes be hard to make out, and his typing can be a little erratic. I have tried to steer a middle course between correcting nothing and distorting the rapid, off-the-cuff nature of these extracts with too much fussy tidying. A few obvious slips of the pen or the key and his more idiosyncratic spellings have been silently corrected, and one or two punctuation marks supplied where sentences would otherwise have been hard to follow. Cuts have been indicated by square brackets: [...]. Where pencilled annotations on scripts and the like have become too dense to reproduce, I have usually followed the original wording.

The scripts of Jennings's radio broadcasts are also heavily annotated, but much more legibly so; with these, I have tried to give his final thoughts. Where Jennings's quotations in these programmes differ significantly from well-established texts I have made amendments, and indicated them: [*Text amended*]. All other texts by Jennings follow their earliest published versions, except as otherwise noted.

Film-making:
Treatments, Scripts and Letters
1934-1950

Humphrey Jennings's career as a director began when he joined the GPO Film Unit (later the Crown Film Unit). This was probably some time in 1934, but may have been as early as 1933: the only letters which have been saved from this period are undated, except for later notes in his wife's hand, indicated here as CJ.

TO CICELY JENNINGS   *12 Holland Street, W.8*
Monday night [CJ: 1933/1934?]   *[his parents' house]*

My darling,

I don't know where to begin. The job, to begin with, is perfectly real – I have already begun work. I cashed a cheque & enclose £2 for the moment. I am staying here for tonight – after that I am not sure. I feel happy enough to be 'in work' but rather lost without you: and wondering how to exist for the next couple of months – The hours are approximately 9 to 6 – or more like 10.30 to 6.30. Half day Saturday: Sunday off. They are taking me seriously enough – and are treating me as a 'director' at once. It now remains to get some order into everything – to leave time for painting and so on: & to see you & Marie-Lou [sic: Mary-Lou Jennings, their daughter], alas!

It is clearly essential to waste the minimum of time getting to & from work. I will come back Wednesday evening [Cicely Jennings was probably living at 28 Bateman Street, Cambridge, where the family had moved in the autumn of 1933, or possibly at her parents' house, at Duns Tew in Oxfordshire] for the night I think: let me know, to Holland St by return, if that would be best. After that it will have to be week-ends I am afraid – or – I might take a weekly season for the first week or so – perhaps you could think of some way.

I am spending this evening sorting family silver and being given some sharp carving knives & so on.

I hope this plunge into the world won't swamp everything.

Kisses and kisses to you both.

Your loving Humpers.

TO CICELY JENNINGS   *12 Holland St, W.8*
Tuesday [CJ: 1934]

My darling

Just a line to let you know how I am getting on. I have just had such a day: learning to 'cut' film, reading Scripts watching projections in the theatre, visiting the new GPO Studios at Blackheath (very nice) – watching cameramen at work at the Wimpole St Sorting Office (a film about lost letters –) & so on. I am working immediately under Stuart's eye [Stuart Legg] and to some extent 'with' Cavalcanti which all seems promising, & certainly it is very exhilarating stuff. Also not particularly strenuous & the people extremely pleasant.

I dropped in for a moment into a superb exhibition at Tooth's – mainly incredible Renoirs – & Rousseaus. I am staying tonight again here – & will come down for tomorrow night. I do hope you are not too lonely or miserable or helpless my creature. Your boy has so much to tell you. I will be back about 8 with any luck.

Bless you bless you and kisses to Baberum   Humphrey

By the end of 1934, Jennings had edited *The Story of the Wheel*, designed sets for Cavalcanti's *Pett and Pott*, taken a role as an heroic telegraph boy in Cavalcanti's *The Glorious Sixth of June*, and directed his first two shorts, *Post Haste* and *Locomotives*. By the autumn of 1934, his family had come to live with him at Blackheath, so there are few letters to document his life from 1935 to 1939 – years in which, as well as writing, painting and directing for the GPO, Jennings worked with the director Len Lye on *The Birth of the Robot*, an advertising film for Shell-Mex and BP; helped organize London's International Surrealist Exhibition (1936); and co-founded Mass Observation with Tom Harrisson and Charles Madge. In 1939 he travelled to the North of England from his new home in St James's Gardens, London W11, and began to direct a film which drew directly on his Mass Observation work: *Spare Time*.

TO CICELY JENNINGS   *Victoria Hotel, Manchester*
[postmark 21 March 1939]

[...] Then after Derby up into the Peak district – quite new to me – where the pubs are painted like early Ben Nicholsons: coloured lettering LIKE THIS [written in large block letters] and the edges of the houses in pink. And right up on the top of the hills lime works blowing white dust on the moors: not unconnected with BN now. Mixture of mist and hardness. Buxton looking very smug: and then the beginning of Cotton at Stockport. Cotton seems to produce a desolation greater – more extended – than any other industry. From Stockport it is really all *streets* through Manchester, Bolton, Preston – almost to the sea at Blackpool – about 60 miles. The desolation – the peculiar kind of human misery which it expresses comes I think from the fact that 'Cotton' simply means *work*: spinning what is produced or grown elsewhere in America or India. Coal and Steel at least suggest something *produced* on the spot.

At Manchester there was a sort of thin wet sunlight which makes it look pathetic. It has a grim sort of fantasy. And a certain dignity of its own from being connected with certain events in history [...]

TO CICELY JENNINGS   *Victoria Hotel, Manchester*
Friday [postmark: 31 March 1939]

Well, precious, after a day of goodish weather for Manchester we are getting along pretty well. I do hope the flat is alright. We shall be here till Monday morning. We went to the Salford Art Gallery this afternoon which has some heavenly 19th century local paintings: simple views of Manchester & so on. The gallery itself is a kind of Italian palace surrounded by statues of statesmen on pedestals and at the back big mill chimneys [drawn here] in fact pure Chirico.

We were up at 6.30 – very cold – photographing landscapes in the mist. Tonight working at Belle-Vue stadium... [...]
[drawing of a tiger here]

TO CICELY JENNINGS   *Royal Station Hotel, Sheffield 4*
[postmark: 13 April 1939]

[...] This is a vast hot crazy hotel – which [sketch of hotel here] stands right up above Sheffield and certainly has the most wonderful views of

factory chimneys & waste land & railway lines – Railways – I see *La Bête Humaine* is coming to the Paris Cinema in a day or two and is all about railways – how nice to go with you... [...]

TO CICELY JENNINGS　　　　　　　*Royal Victoria Station Hotel*
[postmark: 14 April 1939]

[...] It's now 8.30 & I am just going to bed – as we were up at 4.30 this morning. I hope you get as good weather for your weekend as we got today. Bright sun & huge white clouds and patches of rain – with a rainbow and circling pigeons – We also photographed men buying 6d postal orders for football pools – they sell about 7,000 every Friday at the P.O. here – [...]

> In July, Jennings travelled to the Mediterranean to film *S.S. Ionian* (also called *Her Last Trip*). In August he returned to the GPO Film Unit and, after the outbreak of war, made *The First Days*, *Spring Offensive*, *Welfare of the Workers*, and *London Can Take It*. The GPO Film Unit came under the control of the Ministry of Information, and Ian Dalrymple came into the Unit to replace Cavalcanti. In September 1940, his wife and two daughters went to America, and Jennings began work on *Heart of Britain*, a regional counterpart to *London Can Take It*.

TO CICELY JENNINGS   *c/o Ian Dalrymple,*
21 September 1940   *South Cottage, Chorley Wood, Herts*

[...] As you see I have moved – I am working at the moment at Denham, so its very much more convenient and one does get more sleep! [...] But things began to get hot in town and I expect you were wondering about us. The first few nights were pretty grim but the new A.A. barrage cheered everybody up – any way we're getting used to it all now and feeling fine. Rod [Rodney Jennings, his brother] and Sybil and Mesens [E.L.T. Mesens, the surrealist writer, and his wife] and Brunius [Jacques Brunius, the surrealist writer and actor] are all flourishing. The effect of bombing is very different to anything you imagine: maybe one house in a street gets it but the others go on just as before. The ARP and the Fire people are absolutely superb. Psychologically of course this indiscriminate bombing is the greatest mistake Hitler could make. [...]

Work goes on much as usual – I am also managing to get sorting of papers and writing done here – where I am marvellously looked after. Even some painting [...]

TO CICELY JENNINGS   *The Adelphi Hotel, Liverpool*
20 October 1940

My darling Pip –

At last I have an opportunity to reply to your letters and give you an idea of what is going on. To go back to the beginning: you left you remember on a Friday night in an 'alert' as we now call them. The next morning was quiet enough: very fine & bright. We were working at Blackheath as usual – then quite suddenly at about 4 in the afternoon the blitz began: the studio of course right in the middle of it. The boys of course were terrific – saved the negative from an incendiary on the roof – went out all night photographing the fires... [...]

Well – after the first burst of blitz they decided some of our work could be done out of town and as Dalrymple had come to take Cav's [Cavalcanti's] place & I was pretty tired by the end of ten days of it – he asked me to come down for the week-end to Chorley Wood & in the end I stayed on & fixed up to stay there when I haven't got to be in town: so now I get about 60% of my nights in the country – a good deal quieter [...]. After the first fortnight we began to work on film-reporting of the blitz and are now up to our eyes in it – first pic *London Can Take It* specially for you in the States!

I am in Liverpool just for a moment on a kind of *Spare Time* assignment. Everybody is in good spirits: after one's first bit of bombing one is all right. Some of the damage in London is pretty heart-breaking – but what an effect it has all had on the people! What warmth – what courage! What determination. People sternly encouraging each other by explaining that when you hear a bomb whistle it means it has missed you! People in the north singing in public shelters: 'One man went to mow – went to mow a meadow.' WVS girls serving hot drinks to firefighters during raids explaining that really they are 'terribly afraid all the time!' People going back to London for a night or two to remind themselves what it's like.

Everybody absolutely determined: secretly delighted with the *privilege* of holding up Hitler. Certain of beating him: a certainty which no amount of bombing can weaken: only strengthen. A kind of slow-burning white-heat of hatred for the Jerries and a glowing warmth of red flame of love and comradeship for each other which *cannot* be defeated: which has ceased to think of anything except *attack*.

Maybe by the time you get this one or two more 18th cent. churches will be smashed up in London: some civilians killed: some personal loves and treasures wrecked – but it means nothing: a curious kind of unselfish-ness is developing which can stand all that & any amount more. We have found ourselves on the right side and on the right track at last! [...]

TO CICELY JENNINGS   *Royal Victoria Station Hotel*
3 November 1940   *Sheffield 4*

My darlings –

To go on with the story: I hope first of all that you have seen *London Can Take It* which we (GPO) made for the Ministry – that Harry [Watt] & self directing [*sic*] – plus Jonah [Jones], Chick [Fowle] and MacAllister [Stewart McAllister] cutting – plus of course the terrific luck of using Quentin Reynolds' commentary. We have been seeing a good deal of American war-correspondents here & grand wild fellows they are.

We gather here that *London Can Take It* has been a success in the States: we are also a shade sore that it had no GPO credit – but you know what it is. Certainly it has done us a great deal of good *here*: & we are as busy as can be.

Well after the events in my last letter we spent a fortnight or so filming the blitz as above and a week cutting it – it was a rush job of course. In the meantime I have been round the country. Round the Midlands & the North which are quiet & warmhearted & practically untouched – believe me!

I have seen Kathleen [Raine] at Ullswater: very happy she seemed in the wilds. The country is wintry now after a very beautiful windy golden autumn. The lakes I had never seen before – now I am back in Sheffield & Manchester and the North: astonishing wet streets & grey skies & dim chimneys & patches of flame.

And the war? Well we feel we aren't doing too badly: in fact there is a kind of secret exultation. You know I have always said the war was a moral problem for the English. Mary-Lou must [not] bother too much about my not being in uniform: when the shrapnel is coming down in the streets one is glad to have a tin-hat & there it is. [. . .]

TO CICELY JENNINGS   *Siddles' Crown Hotel, Penrith*
12 November 1940   *as from GPO Film Unit,*
                     21 Soho Square, London W.1

My darling Pip

As you see I am still moving about the North – here at least in a place that hasn't had an Air Raid Warning yet! We are shooting some scenes in the lakes and I managed to see Kathleen for a moment yesterday: she is well settled down & flourishing & surrounded by children as she has other evacuees there.

Well, everything continues much as usual: we have had a few exciting nights in the Midlands but not much else. The hills and valleys of the North are as quiet as ever & the pubs & dancehalls are fuller & brighter than before. Everybody here is very happy about Roosevelt. [. . .]

Work is still at night & day pressure for us: hope you saw *London Can Take It*; Quentin Reynolds the *Colliers Weekly* correspondent who did the commentary is a great guy: Harry and I & others have huge whiskey flasks from him with inscriptions! So you see there is not much wrong with our 'morale'.

[In darker ink:]

Since writing the above there has been the grim attack on Coventry – which I am glad to say we were not in: we had left there a few days before. But we have very many good friends there and I am at the moment on my way there to find out how things really are. The voluntary workers there – canteen girls and others – we had been photographing & had been out at night in the canteen washing up mugs and making tea. A superb group of people: sweet young kids and magnificent women: how are they?

I am afraid this letter is very scrappy my dear – life is pretty hand to mouth & we hardly let up at all: so anything private gets a very second look in [. . .]

TO CICELY JENNINGS   c/o Ian Dalrymple,
14 December 1940   South Cottage, Chorley Wood, Herts

[...] the week at Coventry was not I think as grim as we expected: at
any rate the people really were magnificent. Then after that there was
Birmingham – the trouble is one doesn't know from one moment to
another where one is going to eat or sleep in these jobs. I have been very
well looked after here: we came back from the North pretty dead beat
& no wonder I got flu. [...]

London is looking more itself now: people restoring roofs & windows
& clearing the streets up. It is remarkable what an amount of bombing
a city can take and remain itself. [...]

TO CICELY JENNINGS   c/o Ian Dalrymple,
Christmas Day, 1940   South Cottage, Chorley Wood, Herts

Darling,

Here is 24 hours off and a chance to sit down. [...] We are still
working heroically: less troubled by the Blitz at the moment. Christmas
pretty bright considering but the good things of the world rather at their
last gasp. However the Italian situation has put spirit into everyone, if
they needed it.

Suddenly you all seem a long long way off: but I am sure you are
better in New York than in the misty country which just now sits waiting
dully for the winds & the bombers of the spring. London is tidier, but
other cities less so. As we get deeper into the war we shed past fashions
of opinion and politics and ideas like useless clothes or equipment, and
repose more & more on what we all have in common instead of crying
out our differences: we remember past history and average likes and
dislikes, not for good or bad qualities but because all that is what *this*
has come out of. [...]

We are working more and more at Denham and are getting along
nicely after the success of *London Can Take It*. New GPO film in America:
Christmas Under Fire: last sequence true and moving. It is now 3.30
Christmas afternoon. Bright fire – grey still landscape outside. A Christmas tree in the corner with last year's tinsel. The children here very
excited rehearsing *Macbeth*. The inevitable after lunch country walk. A
kind of deep breath in the middle of war and an unspoken regret everywhere. Tomorrow we shall stand up again and fight and forget. [...]

1941

TO CICELY JENNINGS   *c/o Ian Dalrymple,*
25 January 1941   *South Cottage, Chorley Wood, Herts*

Darlings –
  I think your last letters must have gone astray – nothing since the beginning of December. Your mother says she has had a word from you about sending a photograph but alas, none here yet. I expect you got my cable at Christmas – and perhaps two letters since and I hope you have seen Quentin Reynolds – if not do ring him – and he will tell you all about us. Perhaps you have seen *Christmas Under Fire* – there is another pic. of ours (specially mine) coming called *This is England* [i.e. *Heart of Britain*] – hope you see that.
  At the moment we are sitting still in a lull – I mean these Islands are – but by the time you get this anything may have happened or tried to happen. We follow Wavell in Libya, think a little more seriously of our gas-masks – and agree with the German radio that we are on the verge of historic something or others: we also know that the other day an old lady of ninety-odd by herself tore down the wall paper with her bare hands and put out a fire-bomb – that children playing in the streets lie flat on their faces when they hear bombs falling and then get up and go on playing – that people are singing Handel and listening to Beethoven as never before [...]

TO CICELY JENNINGS   *Etoile Hotel,*
10 February 1941   *Charlotte Street, London W1*

[...] I look very like selling the Industrial Revolution book [i.e. *Pandaemonium*: the reader for Penguin books, the economic historian H.J. Beales, was very enthusiastic about the project, but the deal came to nothing] – and that would produce some ready cash. [...]
  I am sure and certain I have left very many things undone and unthought of – dearest – which would be as bright as day to others. But the real problem as I see it is not simply to make a success of *one* of the infinite number of problems – money, your work, the children, films, the future, our families, our hearts, books, travel, the complexity of work itself – and all, but to make a success of some sort out of them *together* and at once. To be a fighter and to make ends meet. So if and when I appear to neglect any one or more of these things I hope to be forgiven – so long as I am not giving up on the whole life-network. [...]
  [Jennings goes on to describe a visit to the home of Len Lye and his wife Jane:] Old paintings of Len's and mine still on the walls. Len is a

great deal more serious – no that's hardly the word – profounder than he used to be – less fuss about Jazz somehow and more human. Has helped me lately with advice on current films and the book enormously. The Welsh picture seems to be working out well – it is just being cut. Painting I am afraid I have neglected since the summer, but I have the impression of tucking away things for later use, I hope so anyway. Am supposed also to be writing some newspaper articles – but I haven't got to them so far. The book really does promise well – the ancient and bitter problems of art and Marxism, and working-class poetry and poetry and science – but I promise you not as awful and dull as that sounds. Have you I wonder ever read *The Life of Mary Ann Schimmelpennick* – who was a quaker at the end of the 18th century and knew Priestley and Dr Darwin and Wedgwood and others and wrote the most beautiful prose. Also have read (for the first time!) Mrs Gaskell's *Life of Charlotte Brontë*. Some one should have told me about that. Or I should have paid attention. What a great cool depth there is in women's writings – very like the best of Monet and Sisley. Great patience. I think I should notice it too as I see *you* in their pages – either in the characters presented or in the writing itself – nobility and delicacy and discernment – not the virtues of war-time London, believe me. The tiniest white and pink buds of May are just visible in Hampstead now, and in the morning the sun throws long shadows of hurrying people below my window in Charlotte Street, and on clear nights the river is more beautiful today than ever I should think in its history – from the sense of air on its banks where they have demolished buildings and yet with the snug little tugs still hurrying and hooting and the white train-smoke drifting down from strong bridges. All this is landscape – not rationed. The earth and the stars and the sweeping tides. But after Wales in particular I find the people grubby and lazy and noisy and drunk. It was that especially that added to Papa's visit; the sense of another century was stronger than ever. And yet he was describing a low-flying Dornier! [...]

Day Report
Saturday, 8 March 1941

Saturday, March 8th was a pretty astonishing day. We began early with a new job: fixing music, sound effects, ideas for a film on the raid on the Lofoten islands. We had the LPO booked for the evening and they were going to play Arne's original score of 'Rule Britannia' which was essential for the opening of this picture. Then we got a Norwegian flag, to be shot on the top of 20th Century Pictures for inserts and the orchestral parts of the Norwegian National Anthem (which we had heard on disc Sunday evenings) and we rang the pastor of the Norwegian church in Bermondsey to produce us half a dozen Norwegians for sound effects, and we tried to trace the wording of the supposed appeal to the patriots at Lofoten, and a man to speak it. Ken suggested recording this appeal in the Queen's Hall after the LPO session to get an echoing effect like the sound travelling up the fiords and echoing in the hills.

By lunch time we had the job pretty well organized and in the afternoon we had a date with Malcolm Sargent at the Queen's Hall to hear a piano version of Handel's Water Music for another film. Actually Malcolm Sargent did not turn up and we spent an hour or so outside the Queen's Hall in brilliant sunlight listening to bits of Beethoven through the stage door. And then at about 3.30 we picked up Lulu Watt and Mrs Smith who had come up from the country for the first time since the Blitz. Had tea at the Swiss Patisserie and then they went off in a taxi to have a look round the city. 4.30 we got just in time to Kay's to see the first running of the Army Film Unit material of the raid on Lofoten: brigadier and censors all present. Stuff pretty poor: 30% out of focus. Brigadier said: 'There is a fug in here – all officers not sitting keep outside the door – shut the door please.' Show lasted until 5.30. Caught a taxi to the Queen's Hall where the LPO and Malcolm Sargent were waiting – spent the first quarter of an hour going over the piano score with Sargent and then carried straight on into the recording of Handel's Water Music with the Orchestra: the Queen's Hall emptied – the finest orchestra in England playing all for ourselves. After the Water Music, Rule Britannia – including a very soft version for the Fleet going into action at Lofoten (which we had just seen) and then the Norwegian National Anthem, played straight first, then played with a lilt in a dramatic way for the dawn sequence of the men with Brenn [*sic*] guns passing the fishing fleet in the early morning in the harbour. Then after a break we went on to more Handel. And the Norwegian announcer turned up without the original message, but we invented something he could say to record with an echo. On coming out to the truck to listen (it was now about 8 o'clock) we realized for the first time that there was a blitz on. A full moon and the guns going hard and a plane overhead. Finally we recorded the Leonora Trumpet Call with a bomber on the end of the take. Then we let the orchestra go and we had the echoing call to the Norwegian patriots coming out of the speaker in the van and across Portland Place as the bombs began to drop. 9 o'clock we packed up: walked back along Oxford Street with a parachute flare coming down over Kensington, and arrived at Soho Square at about a quarter past. Two fire watchers in tin hats came running up to Burroughs and Watts saying they had seen a parachute coming down on a roof. They were sure it was there. The Army Film Unit car had just arrived and as we stood talking another whistler came down and we lay flat on our faces outside the joint. Then up came the sound van and McAllister with the undeveloped negative of the LPO. Then another one came down and we threw ourselves flat on our faces again – the Army Film Unit, Duggie and myself with the tin of negative in our arms, but the whistler died out and there was no explosion. We waited a minute or two. Moved most of the film into the shelter. Then we decided to go on with projection – running of the Lofoten material in the theatre. Half way through this there was a hell of a crash, and the theatre and the projection lights swayed a bit but we went on with the session. At the end somebody said 'There's a smell of burning' and in comes Hudson in shirt sleeves and a tin hat saying 'It's alright we put it out.' At about 11 o'clock we decided to go out and eat. The planes were still overhead but there was less bombing. We walked down towards the Coventry Street Lyons and came round the corner by the Café de Paris just as we hear a woman screaming in the street. Outside the Rialto and the Café there is a big crowd and line of ambulances and stretcher party cars and men shouting 'Gangway please – gangway please.' There are people kicking glass about in the street. There were Guards Officers in 'blues' in the tobacconist's opposite, watching. There were two Canadians who come and say 'Where are all the people killed?' And we tell them and they take their coats off and go across and they bring out more dead on stretchers. We watch one body carried across right to an ambulance and another left put into a side street – and Mac says 'Do they put any labels on them?' After a bit it gets really too grim and we move along to Lyons, but inside on the unused tables there are wounded lying with their heads tied up and rescue squad men in white tin hats getting them food and drink. Then we go downstairs – there are people all down the stairway sheltering from the raid – but at the bottom the orchestra is playing a rumba and we eat bacon and eggs and the raid is forgotten. Finally we come back at about 12.15 and sleep in the shelter at the joint. Hudson is still fire watching.

TO CICELY JENNINGS   *South Cottage,*
27 March 1941   *Chorley Wood, Herts*

Darling –

This is actually written sitting in a bus at Rickmansworth on the way to work after the first week-end off since Christmas. We were just settling down to some sort of order when the Lofoten Raid produced another rush film. However –

As you gather the blitz seems to be coming back but the supposed invasion not yet here – But the winter was certainly not as grim as one expected – what with a let-up on the bombing and the Libyan campaign to watch.

[...] I am normally down here about four nights a week & the other three in town – sleeping at Rod's – still pretty 'blitzed' – or at the shelter at Soho Square – fire-watching. Almost everybody does fire-watching now. It's a boring job mostly – and sleeping in your clothes not so pleasant but one gets used to it. The blitz is [a] queer thing: it's not the danger itself that bothers one – but the mess afterwards – the smell of death and ruin and ambiguity meeting the daylight again. The gaps in the landscape. The smoking horror. The next morning.

We have of course been reading *For Whom the Bell Tolls*: I must say pretty astonishing. About the best thing since *Goodbye to All That*.

I hope MaryLou got a letter from me: I told her to read a poem of Whitman's after your letter about Brooklyn Bridge – I had just bought a copy of the Nonesuch ed. of Whitman with some of his prose – 'Specimen Days'. I have been writing a series of a kind of 'Specimen Nights' in the blitz – I will try & send you some sometime. Also a little painting. [...]

TO CICELY JENNINGS   *c/o Ian Dalrymple,*
Easter Monday 1941   *South Cottage, Chorley, Herts*

[...] I am still carting books and frames and oddments from Ladbroke Square out here where I have a lovely semi-circular 'study' overlooking the (enormous) garden and endless woods and valleys – very high up – and at night over the tree-tops you can see the gunfire in London.

But latterly there hasn't been much in this part of the country (poor Bristol and Coventry again) – when there is one it's sudden and vicious. The night-fighters seem to be developing: astonishing things – dog-fights at night. From the ground you can see nothing of course – except sometimes when the moon is very bright and it's frosty and you can watch the white vapour-trails of the invisible machines twisting and curling – like gigantic wisps of cotton-wool stretched over the face of the moon and the night. And in patches of silence you can hear the machine guns. Queer life: we were recording Handel's Water-music (of all things) the other night at the Queen's Hall with the LPO – and the sound comes out from the loudspeaker in the sound-truck in the street. Near the end of the session there were 'chandelier' flares overhead – lighting up the sky – the music echoing down the street: the planes booming and the particular air-raid sound: people kicking broken glass on the pavement.

[...] I can hardly object to the kits' prayers as I have just been accused here of 'going religious' for putting the Hallelujah Chorus at the end of

This is England. This of course from Rotha and other of Grierson's little
boys who are still talking as loudly as possible about 'pure documentary'
and 'realism' and other such systems of self advertisement.

Looking forward very much to seeing *Letter From England.* Two letters
back – I think – you asked where we had got to in movies over here: well,
last two possible American ones – *The Long Voyage Home* (London docks
black-out ending pretty wrong) and *Arise My Love* which was something
of an eyeopener as evidence of American opinion. Also *The Philadelphia
Story.* Reading: Leonardo's Note Books, 'Post D' (by John Strachey) – read
it if you can get it – Dream Tales by Turgenev and as mentioned before
Hemingway.

The other day I did a minute piece of broadcasting in French for the
French programmes: there is a series of five minutes-s for foreigners to say
'Pourquoi j'aime la France' [See below, p.285]. After nine months of 'not
thinking about France' it was good to take a deep breath and think of the
France of Corot and Renoir and 'The Man with a Knife and a Glass of
Wine'. The war makes one think not of peace but of well-being: the riches
of the earth and the warmth of the sun.

[...] As I write it is becoming a delicious spring evening outside – the
land shining after a day of drizzle: the birds winging so slowly across the
valley – one's eye is accustomed to planes as the natural inhabitants of the
sky – and the rooks cawing in the big trees behind the house. But the news
is not so good tonight and the one blurs the other. [...]

TO CICELY JENNINGS   *South Cottage,*
9 April 1941   *Chorley Wood*

[...] We are even busier than ever if possible. I have been making a film
which Mary-Lou would like about the Lincoln statue in Parliament
Square. [i.e. *Words for Battle*] [...]

Report
(19-25 April 1941)

'The Spring of 1941'
Byron, whose statue sits in Hyde Park, opposite the statue of Achilles,
died at Missolonghi in Greece on April 19th, 1824. So on the morning of
April 19th, 1941 his statue has a wreath of spring flowers hung on it, blowing in the strong wind which has swept over London every day since the
big Blitz of Wednesday. [handwritten: = 16th]

On the same day – the 19th – the newspaper placards announced

'BRITISH AND GREEKS FIGHTING LIKE LIONS – FULL DETAILS.' But on Monday morning, the 21st, two Greek armies give in in the Epirus. In the London suburbs the spring is shooting up past the wrecks of the October bombing, and some schoolchildren, one of them a little boy with a tin hat, and another a little girl with a bunch of daffodils, are coming back to school for the opening day this morning after their holidays. The school was hit by a land mine in October and many of the class-rooms are still wrecked and the trees on the edge of the playground are torn and some of them dead.

In the centre of the city, St Paul's now stands high and fully visible since they demolished the houses and shops burnt in the fire-blitz at Christmas. In Newgate Street, they are building an air-raid shelter. In Warwick Lane they are burning doors and windows from three centuries. In New[po]rt Court and St Pancras Square, the rescue men are still looking for the dead of last Wednesday, and the spring wind blows in their eyes the dust of broken tenements.

Thursday – the crowds in Piccadilly filing past a new bomb-hole read: 'BRITISH FLANK UNBROKEN: PLYMOUTH BLITZED AGAIN.'

Friday, the 25th, is Anzac Day. The flags are out over Australia House and the Imperial troops are said to be holding Thermopylae.

WORDS FOR BATTLE

Treatments:

IN ENGLAND NOW
[i.e. *Words for Battle*]

General Scheme of Images

MILTON –   opening landscapes
people
recruiting for Air Training Scheme
(and/or Hatfield Air Material)
German Newsreel material
(perhaps bombed house as link)

BLAKE –   Children in the country

SHELLEY –   Man ploughing
                   Man at bench in factory
                   AFS man
                   recruits changing into uniform
                   Army marching
                   Navy

BROWNING –   Panning shot of Convoy near Gib.
                   Nelson
                   Gib.
                   Naval guns before Bardia
                   Bardia Newsreel material
                   Wavell

KIPLING –   last war memorial (Unknown Soldier)
                   people
                   bombed houses
                   Air raid shelters
                   Perhaps Coventry funeral [pencil: ? Guildhall]

CHURCHILL –   shot of Churchill in wind
                   (perhaps Dunkirk material)
                   Anti-invasion defences (Army material)

LINCOLN –   pan across to Lincoln
                   Lincoln material
                   people in street
                   back to landscapes

The following script has been collated from three separate undated
fragments.

IN ENGLAND NOW
Shooting Script

Titles: In England Now   [Deleted: 18th Century
A Film Anthology, Spoken by   Slow March] played by
Laurence Olivier   A Regimental Band…

Produced by the Crown Film Unit.

Sequence I

1. L.S. *Ext. Westminster Abbey*
        Mix:

2. PANNING SHOT *Int. Westminster Abbey, ending on a group of statues.*

COMMENTARY BEGINS (general sense): Among the Nation's most precious memorials now nightly threatened by fire bombs – Westminster Abbey.

3. MIDSHOT *of the Poets Corner*

Here lie the tombs and the statues of the Kings and Queens, of statesmen and men of action – of the English poets.

4. L.S. *Monument of Pitt*

5. C.U. *Tomb of Spenser*

How splendid are the monuments of ancient victory; how simple the shrines of poetry.

6. C.U. *of Wordsworth*

Thought and action are so different to one another.

7. C.U. *of Monument of Wolfe*

But in history both are inextricably interwoven.

8. C.U. *of 'Victory' from Wolfe's Monument.*
        Mix:

The laurel wreath is given both to the poet and the soldier.

9. C.U. *of Wreath on Tomb of the Unknown Soldier, panning to the word:* 'Dunkirk'

10. C.U. *Inscription: 'Beneath this stone lies the body of an unknown warrior'...*

Repeat Phrase of Slow March or Drum Roll....

11. L.S. *of Unknown Soldier*	And often in the past the poet has gone into action and the soldier has been impelled to speak.
12. C.U. *of candle burning beside the Unknown Soldier.* *Mix:*	Then they described for us the England of their day – what it was like to be in England – then.

Sequence II

13. L.S. *Landscape of England in the 16th Century.*	(16th Century description of England, in prose.)

[Later notes:]

For the air is most temperate and wholesome, situated in the midst of the temperate zone – for water it is walled and guarded with the ocean, most commodious for traffic to all parts of the world – the earth fertile with all kind of grain, manured with good husbandry, rich in mineral of coals, tin, lead, copper, not without gold and silver, abundant with pasture, replenished with cattle both tame and wild, plentifully wooded – beautified with many populous cities, fair boroughs, good towns, and well-built villages, magnificent palaces of the Prince, stately houses of the nobility, frequent hospitals, beautiful churches.

[from *Camden's Description of Britain*]

[Revised opening commentary:]

Among the most precious memorials of England, now nightly threatened by fire-bombs, is Westminster Abbey. Here lie the tombs and [word deleted] of Kings and Queens, the statues of statesmen, the monuments of ancient victory. [Deleted: And] here too the much humbler shrines of English poetry [deleted]. You may think of the poet as a dreamer and not a man of action, but they too were stirred by the events of their day – As we look at their graves and likenesses it is their words we . . . we remember what they said and wrote – what they said and wrote about England – Milton –. this was what Milton said of England just three hundred years ago –

Sequence 2

Methinks I see in my mind a mighty and puissant nation rousing herself like a strong man after sleep, and shaking her invincible locks. Methinks I see her as an eagle mewing her mighty youth, kindling her undazzled eyes at the full midday beam, purging and unscaling her long abused sight at the fountain itself of heavenly radiance, while the whole noise of timorous and flocking birds, with those also that love the twilight, flutter about, amazed at what she means and in their envious gabble would prognosticate a year of sects and schisms... [from *Areopagitica*]	C.U. of Milton mixing to L.S. English landscape mixing to L.S. crowds of people. Sequence of Air Training Scheme.

Methinks I see in my mind a mighty
and puissant nation rousing herself
like a strong man after sleep,
and shaking her invincible locks.
Methinks I see her as an eagle
mewing her mighty youth, kindling
her undazzled eyes at the full
midday beam, purging and unscaling
her long abused sight at the
fountain itself of heavenly radiance,
while the whole noise of timorous
and flocking birds, with those
also that love the twilight,
flutter about, amazed at what she
means and in their envious gabble
would prognosticate a year of
sects and schisms...
[from *Areopagitica*]

C.U. of Milton mixing to
    L.S. English landscape
mixing to L.S. crowds of
    people.
Sequence of Air Training
    Scheme.

sequence of C.U.'s from
    The Triumph of the Will
    – bombers
C.U.'s of Hitler and
    Goering and Musso.

Sequence 3

Bring me my bow of burning gold
Bring me my arrows of desire
Bring me my spear – O clouds unfold
Bring me my chariot of fire

Sequence of evacuated
    children shot by Arthur
    Elton.

I will not cease from mental fight
Nor shall my sword sleep in my hand
Till we have built Jerusalem
In England's green and pleasant land.
[Blake, 'Jerusalem']

Sequence 4

Men of England, heirs of Glory,
Heroes of unwritten story,
Nursling of one mighty Mother,
Hopes of her, and one another;

Man ploughing
Man at bench in factory
AFS man
RAF recruits changing
    into uniform.

Rise like lions after slumber   Army marching
In unvanquishable number,   Navy.
Shake your chains to earth like dew
Which in sleep had fallen on you –
Ye are many – they are few.
[Shelley, *The Mask of Anarchy*]

Sequence 5

Nobly, nobly Cape Saint Vincent   Panning shot of convoy
    to the North-West died away;   near Gibraltar (from
Sunset ran, one glorious blood-red,   *Able Seamen*).
    reeking into Cadiz Bay;
Bluish 'mid the burning water, full   Nelson
    in face Trafalgar lay;
In the dimmest North-East distance,   Naval guns before Bardia
    dawned Gibraltar grand and grey;
'Here and here did England help me: Bardia newsreel material
    How can I help England?' – say,
Whoso turns as I, this evening,   Wavell.
    turn to God to praise and pray,
While Jove's planet rises yonder,
    silent over Africa.
[Browning, 'Home-Thoughts, from the Sea']

        Tomb of Kipling in the Abbey.

Sequence 6

It was not part of their blood,   Last war memorial
It came to them very late   (Unknown Soldier)
With long arrears to make good,   People
When the English began to hate   Bombed houses.

It was not suddenly bred,   Air Raid Shelters.
It will not swiftly abate,   Ruins at Guildhall.
Through the chill years ahead,
When Time shall count from the date
When the English began to hate.
[Kipling, 'The Beginnings']

    Shot of Churchill in the wind (from newsreels).

Sequence 7

We shall go on to the end; we shall defend our Island whatever the cost may be; we shall fight on the beaches; we shall fight on the landing grounds; we shall fight in the fields and in the streets; we shall fight in the hills; we shall never surrender. And even if this Island were subjugated and starving, then our Empire beyond the seas, armed and guarded by the British Fleet, would carry on the struggle until in God's good time, the New World with all its power and might steps forth to the rescue and liberation of the Old. [Churchill, speech of 4 June 1940]	Anti-invasion defences (Army material) Exterior of Westminster Abbey, pan across to statue of Lincoln

Sequence 8

It is for us, the living, rather to be dedicated here to the unfinished work they have thus far so nobly advanced. That we here highly resolve that the dead shall not have died in vain, that the nation shall, under God, have a new birth of freedom, and that the government of the people, by the people, and for the people, shall not perish from the earth. [Lincoln, Gettysburg Address]	Lincoln statue. People in street. Landscapes.

Before starting work on *Listen to Britain* in June 1941, Jennings planned and shot a five-minute film of one of Myra Hess's lunchtime concerts at the National Gallery, in which she was playing Mozart's Piano Concerto in G Major, K.453. Later in the summer, the pianist (now Dame Myra Hess) repeated her performance before an audience which included H.M. the Queen; this provided *Listen to Britain* with its well-known climactic sequence.

NATIONAL GALLERY

Rough Shooting Script

L.S. Trafalgar Square and National Gallery from Whitehall.
Sound: traffic and four quarters of the chime from St Martin-in-
the-Fields. Double print main title:

LUNCH-HOUR

Mix to
Mid-Shot dome and portico of National Gallery itself.
Continue above sound.
Double print production credits:
Mix to
Panning shot from roof of National Gallery down steeple of St
Martins to clock with hands at one.
Clock strikes one. (Avoid balloons.)
Mix to
Insert of lunch-hour concert announcement outside National
Gallery: pan across to special lettering
MOZART CONCERT
with
MYRA HESS
and the
RAF CHAMBER ORCHESTRA
People walking past and up steps. Noise of talking and tuning-up.
Mix to
C.U. of printed score of the music
First Movement
Mozart Piano Concerto
in G. Major
(K.453)
Silence.

1. (15)   Music begins with L.S. orchestra from rostrum at back of
audience and over their heads.
C.S. strings.
C.S. wood-wind.
2. (9)   M.S. ensemble
3. (10)   Reverse shot of audience in main aisle from orchestra rostrum.
4. (7)   Track down one of the aisles to C.S. pair of ambulance drivers
in uniform (girls from Station 76).

5. (7) C.S. group of audience including a young girl music student, who is following with a score, a woman air-raid warden and an old man listening by himself with his hand over his eyes.

6. (8) C.S. an [deleted: RAF officer] artilleryman and his girl – two tough looking Canadian soldiers

? (also seen in the audience in these shots a rough looking country parson and a wounded soldier in blue head bandaged).

7. (8) Whoever is in the last close-up is looking at the ceiling and round the gallery: (a) the glass above one of the aisles is splintered and the curtains torn.

(b) On the opposite side to the audience are empty galleries which have a few empty frames hung in them.

(c) C.U.'s artists' names and (d) pictures' titles on frames.

8. (9) (a) End 7 with track to cut to pan of [deleted: artilleryman (L/C)] RAF P.O. and his mother coming from canteen past empty wall to concert entrance at back of aisle; he is carrying two cups of tea and she sandwiches.

(b) Reverse shot (C.S.) attendant at doorway whispers them to keep quiet (c) and piano solo begins. Reverse L.S. of orchestra and soloist from their point of view (i.e., the same set-up as 1).

9. (13) C.U. soloist and hands.

10. (4) C.U.'s audience:

(a) Polish Flyer standing against reproduction of Gainsborough's *Artist's Daughters*.

(b) Sailor with a beard standing against Uccello's *Rout of San Romano*.

11. (3) (a) C.S. [deleted: artilleryman] RAF P.O. and mother sit down quietly with cups of tea at back of audience.

12. (6) On steps in entrance hall people are sitting with their backs to a concert with cups of tea. Pan across to notice of WAR ARTISTS' EXHIBITION: people going past it up steps.
Mix to

13. (10) Slow tracking shot across room of exhibition beginning with two attendants sitting at table with programmes and postcards: one reading paper, other dealing with people – by the table an oil heater:
Track across past man sitting on seat in centre of gallery to people looking at pictures ending on AFS man with tin hat (carried) looking at big Topolski painting of St Pauls. Other C.U.'s: two women pointing at picture of aerial dog-fight. Man with S.P. white tin hat looking at evacuation of Dunkirk. Also shot of blitzed roof and pile of fire buckets and stirrup pumps in corner.

14. (17)   Panning shot following woman from canteen in entrance hall
           through swing door out on to balcony looking down to
           Trafalgar Square and Whitehall.
           Reverse shot from street looking up at line of people leaning
           on balcony.
           Shot on roof of gallery against blitzed windows of Office of
           Works men having their lunch.

15. (8)   What they see: C.S. Nelson, Birds, clouds – avoid balloons –
           pan down to traffic in the Square.

16. (4)   C.S. looking up at one of the lions with sandbags for fire bombs
           between its paws.
           M.S. same location a section of the Grenadier Guards march
           across through pigeons from Admiralty Arch – beyond them the
           traffic. Shots of traffic itself from point of view of lions.

17. (14)   Piccadilly Circus: M.S. traffic passing flower seller in front of
           boarded-up Eros with anti-aircraft slogan HIT BACK legible.
           Also C.U. flower seller.
           Leicester Square: Panning shot of girl with arm bandaged
           walking past Ritz Cinema: *Gone with the Wind* posters visible
           (other people moving in back of shot).
           Strand: traffic passing New Zealand House: two Anzacs
           standing on pavement beyond traffic discussing.
           Soho: tracking shot with barrow of plants and palms blowing
           in wind and beyond it, on the pavement, two French sailors
           walking in the same direction.

18. (7)   Episodes of people in Charing Cross Road and WAAF's in
           Oxford Street.

19. (11)   Shot from moving car of traffic in Oxford Street coming to rest
           at lights and then shots of people crossing, traffic going and
           stopping, and so on.

20. (13)   Shot of traffic crossing approach to London Bridge from Lower
           Thames Street. Shot from a bridge of Thames tug and lighters
           passing under.

21. (23)   L.S. River looking down-stream – shot from tug. Tracking shots
           from tug of river banks and craft. Tracking shot at Barking
           approaching balloon barrage lighters.

22. (18)   L.S. from river of wharf steps at end of blitzed street: at the top
           of the steps the flag of an Incident Officer.
           M.S. street: Incident Officer is sitting at table writing – rescue
           squad men are sitting around eating and reading paper.
           Up the street towards camera comes an old woman with her
           head in a shawl carrying a black American-cloth bag. She comes

up to the Incident Officer – they talk and she points across street.
C.S. damage. C.S. Incident Officer. He looks down at his papers
and then up at her and says something we do not hear. She
smiles and walks away up street again – pan with her.
Shoot cut-ins of rescue men.
Pioneers' fire: men throwing rubbish in it and boiling kettle:
wooden table standing in middle of demolition with metal
tea-pot and cups on it.
Second-hand shop in same type of district (? Princedale Road):
A man comes mooning along road and looks in at window.
C.U.'s pathetic objects in window.
Corner of similar street: newspaper man writing on blackboard
placard: 'RAF OVER HAMBURG – MORE MOON RAIDERS
DOWN'.

23. (12)　M.S. balloon lighter (shot steady from another lighter) – the
crew are loosening the balloon cables and the balloon begins to
rise and sway in the wind.
Longer shots of balloons beginning to rise.

24. (9)　On roof of hospital: A group of nurses is standing at the edge
of the parapet eating their lunch: their caps and aprons are
blowing in the wind.

25. (15)　C.S. balloons rising.
C.S. nurses laughing and pointing.
L.S. balloons in position. (Shot from below looking up.)

26. (16)　Hampstead Heath: Top shot from building looking down on
school-children (with gas masks) running across path to a
Punch and Judy show. This is at a point where the path meets
the road and is next to a brick shelter with the poster: FALL IN
THE FIRE-BOMB FIGHTERS.
C.S. children (from ground level).
C.S. Punch and Judy show.
Same location: a man with a[n] ice cream barrow selling ices
to soldiers.

27. (5)　Primrose Hill: A.A. gun site – pan across to predictors: by them
a group of ATS girls having their lunch. C.U.'s girls.

28. (6)　M.S. balloon crew lying full length on their metal lighter,
patting the hot deck and eating their lunch. C.U.'s (top shots)
faces looking into sky.

29. (6)　C.U. spade of man digging in an allotment. M.S. allotment:
man in foreground and over his shoulder a by-pass with rapid
traffic. (Shoot also cut-ins of his coat and gear hung up on
fence and of his face.)

30. (7)   Tracking shot from car along by-pass – past more allotments
          and over-taking cyclists on cycle path.
          Note: cyclists mostly have tin hats on their carriers.
31. (7)   Tracking shot continues and goes under railway bridge
          (Denham) just as enormously long goods train crosses the
          bridge.
32. (7)   Tracking shot reaches the outskirts of a fighter station and
          catches a glimpse of a squadron of Spitfires. C.U. man cranking
33. (8)   Spit. with a mouth full of chocolate: air screw turns and cut
          back to tracking shot passing Dora notice: DO NOT SLOW
          DOWN FOR NEXT TWO MILES.
34. (8)   Tracking shot: fighters take-off and cross bonnets of the traffic
          on the by-pass. Shot of by-pass from point of view of fighters.
          Shot of distant balloons and factories from the air. *Mix to*
35.   L.S. fighters shot from Anson. *Mix to*
          Clouds above London. *Mix to*
          Vapour trails of fighter squadron very high up (shot from
          ground). *Mix to*
36.   (a) L.S. soloist in National Gallery (top shot from dome –
          avoid showing hands – non-sync).
          (b) C.U. pianist and hands (sync)
          (c) C.U.'s of Polish flyer, music student, Canadian soldiers, etc.,
          as before, but now more settled down and happier – very
          intent on music – ending with C.U.'s of [deleted: artilleryman]
          RAF P.O. and mother who have put down their tea and
          sandwiches. The [deleted: RAF Officer] artillery officer and
          girl are holding hands.
37. (12) (a) Extreme L.S. audience, orchestra and pianist (from
          rostrum in gallery behind audience aisle). *Mix to*
          C.U. dome of St Paul's.
          L.S. St Pauls from Warwick Lane.
38. (9)   Extreme L.S. St Paul's from River – pan down into the running
          water and double print: THE END.

TO CICELY JENNINGS   *South Cottage,*
10 May 1941   *Chorley Wood, Herts*

My darling Cicely,
    I have delayed writing you immediately after getting your last letter
(about *This Is England* [. . .]
    Your last letter was lovely to read: it is good to know that one's films

really do get on to American screens and better still that you see and like them. The same pic. had a pretty good success here.

[...] Life is much the same here for the moment. Sudden savage raids on London – most of which I seem to miss – much more going on North and West which I seem to miss altogether so far. The spring cold and windy – very beautiful days and moonlit nights. We have a better regard for the moon now as it allows our night-fighters to go up. Greece we all took pretty philosophically I think. Difficult to hold all the reins of life together today. Here this afternoon as I sit typing and thinking of America and Crete and Tobruk I can hear a cockoo [sic] in the valley and see a plane way way up in a hazy sky.

Your remarks about Wellington and Waterloo and the last twenty years very good. Excellent analysis of same thing in George Orwell's *Lion and the Unicorn*: still quite a bunch of 'intellectuals' here who are afraid of becoming 'patriots'. [...]

TO CICELY JENNINGS   *South Cottage,*
15 June   *Chorley Wood, Herts*

My darling,

I am afraid there has been the most enormous gap since my last letter and in the meantime we have had Hess and Crete & the Bismarck & Syria & all sorts. I seem to have been busier if possible than ever in the last few weeks: mainly photographing the lunch-hour concerts in the National Gallery including Myra Hess – tremendous screen personality and of course enormous audiences – & then [...] the Queen! All part of a film about music in wartime: quite a possible subject. In one way and another the British cinema seems to be looking up: our pictures really go down extraordinarily well now – & the film version of *Love on the Dole* – just out – is a miracle: really a miracle to reconstruct the hunger-marches of 1930 & put them on the screen at this moment –

Harry Watt has deserted us (permanently I think) & is working at a vast salary for Walter Wanger on an Eagle Squadron picture: I suppose he knows what he's doing – but it's dangerous I feel: difficult not to become the big-shot and make bad pictures – but we shall see.

Cav. still at Ealing. In the meantime Jack Holmes has suddenly blossomed: has *Merchant Seamen* running in London: voted best war short & since has finished *Ordinary People* of which Grierson has a copy: he & Stuart & others sent raving telegrams about it: maybe you have seen it. Lovely picture. So Jack Holmes steps up into Harry's place as the old maestro of the unit.

[...] I met the other day Robert Capa the photographer who has come over a few weeks back – marvellous person –

[...] What a game also politics & economics & the rest: but I don't find that the war makes me take a greater interest in them really: on the contrary. I agree our foreign policy is a [illegible] joke and our home organization a cruel farce; but I still think that the real world is the world of Uccello and Mozart.

[...] This late afternoon I sit & think of you & hear for you the sounds of English summer: the buzz of the fly against the window pane – the bees in the sun – the curious whine of the Spitfire high up in the blue – the children shouting away down the valley.

The Sunday papers look much the same. It is a great year for lupins all colours – white pink, purple in vases on the piano. The leaves are full out now on all the trees & the wind is rocking them fiercely. The lawn has already a slightly *white* look meaning that June is here & the spring forgotten –

[...] I begin to be able to deal with people a little better I think & to keep my temper & remember to be as pleasant and thoughtful as possible. Curious what war teaches one! Now a big bird passes the French windows & the Spitfire returns and goes away up towards London. The sun is dropping & the birds beginning to sing for evening. The Dalrymples are out. In a minute I shall turn on the news. [...]

TO CICELY JENNINGS   *As from: South Cottage,*
2 August 1941   *Chorley Wood, Herts*

My darlings –

Actually as you see from the postmark I am writing from near Glasgow: Wishaw is a small town on a hill above the Clyde – near the celebrated falls of Clyde & Robert Owen's New Lanark – mostly apple & plum orchards & fruit farms with the smoke & chimneys & tips of Motherwell & Clydeside on the horizon. What am I doing here? I am having a few days holiday after work that really hasn't ceased since you left eleven months back. [...] It is raining & I am sitting by the fire in the home of McAllister – who cut *This is England*.

[...] You have probably heard of *Target for Tonight* Harry Watts' new film about the crew of a Wellington: terrific technically – a bit soul-less. Did you by any chance see a little picture called *Words for Battle*?

[...] The war & the feelings of war change so much week to week and even day to day that it adds to the time-lag & break between us –

If our official reaction to the invasion of Russia was a surprise to a few people so should be the feeling for the USSR here at the moment. Britain whether she likes it or not is being forced into historical honesty. It only remains to become the allies of China & the Spanish Republic & we shall really be in a position to expiate our sins.

The trouble about us is that when the danger is not immediate we relax & gather a little strength – which looks so bad – but is probably an excellent way of living – as honestly two years of war – most of the time fighting *alone* find us stronger – happier – not yet really underfed – not more so than in the days of unemployment – and on the verge of a victory for common-sense. The way in which people have been misled about the USSR is dawning on them – since the Red Army's resistance is a *fact*.

[...] In the meantime I am pretty tired of films – still paint and write a little. Read Turgenev – Lawrence's poems – A week or so back I was in Suffolk – at Martin's [i.e. Martin's Farm] where we shot *Spring Offensive* – down there for about a week. It was magnificent – superb summer weather: the new corn three quarters up. The country has really been transformed these last two years. So rich & deep & good to see & hear & smell. [...]

TO CICELY JENNINGS   *South Cottage,*
13 September 1941   *Chorley Wood, Herts*

[...] I have since been up to Blackpool – making a dance sequence for a new film and to Manchester and Bolton and – new to me – the country – farming country this side of Chester: Alderley Edge – sudden very beautiful patch in the suburbs of Manchester and Warrington. The trip to Blackpool was very successful and at least as good results as *Spare Time* Lancashire material. Film is about music. Getting back to people. Dal [Dalrymple] has been a tremendous help in a quiet way about tackling people and not straying off into landscapes and trick ideas. *Words for Battle* wasn't distributed in the US I think but I know Selznick saw a copy in Hollywood as he called us. It was a very short (7-minute) pic. with a commentary spoken by Laurence Olivier (and pretty good too) consisting of quotes from Milton and Blake and Abraham Lincoln and so on applying to the present situation with of course contemporary shots of RAF and bits from German newsreels and sounds very highbrow and queer but although it might have been we chucked ourselves into it pretty deep and the result turned everybody's stomach's [*sic*] over and was a huge and quite unexpected success in theatres here...

[...] We have been working *very* hard lately and everything everywhere seems to be at a kind of turning point. The break-up of the Russian-bogey illusion and the years of trickery and dishonesty which produced it are now becoming really clear to the nation here as a whole and producing a new kind – or several new kinds of people who wish the USSR well. People who cannot be bothered with politics and who regard newspapers as rubbish and arguments as propaganda are yet tremendously impressed by Russian newsreels and by the simple fact of Russian resistance – one of these days this is going to come back on the people who have misled everybody. Yet another stage in the stripping bare of British illusions. Not well put I am afraid.

Thanks to the Russians, thanks to the RAF and the Navy, thanks to Roosevelt and thanks especially to luck the situation here – I mean the civilian situation after two years of war – is really remarkably good. By and large good food – good wages – people healthy and feel they have a useful job to do – only grumbling because we aren't doing more – there is a good deep reserve of energy and resistance which no doubt we will need alright but it is there.

Reading *Fontamara* [by Ignazio Silone] and *Moby Dick*. Painting a picture of Walberswick. Making a film as I said about music (Mozart and Roll out the Barrel). Feeling a little more confident – or grown up – or tired: whichever fits at the moment. Thinking of you all with a queer mixture of regret, necessity, love. Knowing you alone in the whole world understand and stand firm and reach out from Uccello to the people at Blackpool. I only regret I have never been and really am not anywhere near good enough for you. [...]

TO CICELY JENNINGS   *[Paper headed:*
19 October 1941   *Royal Victoria Station Hotel,*
                                                     Sheffield 4]

[...] The smoke curls up from the autumn fires & the pithead chimneys: the guns get louder: the stars shine clear & the winter settles in. Luminous nights & long thoughts of New York and Moscow: two worlds away.

I wonder if Hitler thought he was dividing this country by attacking Russia. Slowly – how slowly – but clearly enough England & Scotland & Wales are beginning to look at *life*: the way they did in 1400 – the way they have been unlearning for so many centuries. But looking at a life of what possibilities and what disasters. There is a kind of malaise in the air now like the wind worrying the leaves: ideas turning over: self-criticism: parties dissolving: the clouds changing –

I imagine by the time you get this you will have seen *Target for Tonight*. I wonder what you think – here it already seems out of date but of course the facts remain true night & day. We all have now strong moments of revulsion from just making films – as we did at Dunkirk – and then return to hard work. I think I have changed a great deal lately – perhaps the influence of Dal – he and Megan [Mrs Dalrymple] have been unrepayably sweet now for a whole year – perhaps through increased responsibility – anyway more confidence and less fuss I think – [...]

Post-production script:

LISTEN TO BRITAIN

U certificate
Length – 1685 feet.
Produced by the Crown Film Unit (Producer, Ian Dalrymple).
Directed and Edited by Humphrey Jennings and Stewart
McAllister. Photographed by H.E. Fowle, Recorded by Ken
Cameron. Assistant Director – Joe Mendoza, Production
Manager – Dora Wright. (RCA Sound System.)

'The music of a people at war – the sound of life in Britain by night and by day.'

(Titles designed by Barnett Freedman. The background contains symbols representing music in war – the violin and
55.   bow with a few notes of 'Rule Britannia', the shadow and flash of a gun.)

Britain in summer. The waving tops of the trees and corn. The sound of larks from above the corn drowned by the roar of two Spitfires. Land army girls at work and Observer Corps men on duty. The sound of the squadrons flying far overhead is interrupted by the busy clatter of a tractor drawing a reaper. A rich harvest landscape. Strong forces of RAF fighters in the evening sunlight. Now the blackout curtains are drawn in a house from which is heard the voice of Joseph McLeod as he
130   reads the six o'clock news. News from overseas or from men in uniform? Some are on leave, contemplating the sunset, – others don steel helmets and prepare for night duty. The strains of a dance band are coming from the Tower Ballroom in Blackpool where members of HM Forces dance at half price to the tune of

'Roll out the Barrel – for the gang's all here!' Hundreds of them in uniform enjoying themselves with young ladies evacuated from Government Departments in London. Outside the fire-watchers are ready.

272   The clanging cage at a pit-head where the men are going on night shift is a sharp contrast. In the clear light of the moon the night traffic on the railways is shunted about – holding up a

370   passenger train on which a bunch of Canadians are engaged in telling stories of the old days back home and singing 'Home on the Range'.

The line is cleared and the train puffs on into the night.

523   A bomber factory. The whine of machinery and the clinks of metal as rows of aircraft are assembled.

The lights in the roof of this great factory are like stars in the night sky.

Outside another machine takes off.

The women on night duty in an ambulance station are listening to the 'Ashgrove' sung by one of their colleagues.

Her voice echoes through the big marble hall, one of the many famous buildings put to new and strange uses.

622   Big Ben rings round the world as the BBC Overseas service
638   gets into its nightly activity. The British Grenadiers March
664   plays triumphantly from London to the countries all round the globe. Dials and valves quiver with the voices in dozens of languages. A woman announcer in the Pacific service gives greetings to all serving in the armed forces and in the Merchant Navy.

715   The most natural sound in Britain so early in the day is the sound of the birds, but not long after come the people to the
778   factories.

Coleman Smith wakens up the others with his morning P.T. song and a new day is in full swing.

830   A housewife watches her child dancing with others in the school playground below and thinks of the man in a foreign land.

900   Bren gun carriers come crashing through the village street – shaking the plaster and timbers of 'Ye Olde Tea Shoppe'.

940	A bugle call – calling all workers – the BBC programme of
960	'Music while you Work' every morning in the factories
	[deleted: Gillettes] – the girls sing 'Yes, my darling Daughter'
1012	[deleted: and machinery seems the brighter for it].

Uniforms on a station platform, Canteens for rescue

1028   squads in a street. Painter on a ladder covering a factory with camouflage.

'And when the storm Clouds all roll Over'

Inside Flanagan and Allen are singing 'Round the back of the Arches' to a thousand workers at their lunch.

Menu – Scotch Broth, Fried Cod and chips, Grilled Sausages, Greens, Boiled Potatoes, Lemon Pudding, Jam Sauce, Damsons and Custard.

1170   Another lunch time concert is in progress in the National Gallery. Here office workers and shop assistants listen to the RAF Orchestra playing Mozart's Piano Concerto in G, with Myra Hess at the piano. The ceiling and windows above are cracked by bombs like most buildings in London and the Galleries have been cleared of their treasures, yet in one of them there is an exhibition: War Artist's Paintings. A sailor on leave looks at one of Dunkirk. The place is thronged with lunch hour Londoners – mostly civil defence workers – the Queen is there listening with the others to Dame Myra Hess.

1456   Outside in Trafalgar Square where Nelson stands, the traffic of London moves on. The factories are making tanks for this country to fight with.

1512	The noise of the factory drowns the Mozart and out of the
1554	din comes the thumping of the drums of the marines [*sic*]
1600	'A Life on the Ocean Wave'. The thump of the drums is
1638	taken up by the thud of the steam hammers, forging arms
	from red-hot steel. Listen to Britain. The fire in the heart
	of our people, the music in their voices, swells into the air,
	out of the factories, over the fields of grain, and up over the
1686	land.

TO CICELY JENNINGS   *South Cottage,*
3 December 1941   *Chorley Wood, Herts*

My darling
There have already been two false starts to this letter – which has been
hopelessly delayed by the rush-finishing of a picture (*Listen to Britain*)
and a second lot of flu. Finishing a pic and flu always seem to coincide.
[...]
    In the meantime we are working harder than ever. Very lucky to get
Sunday – the country as a whole is doing a sixty-hour week – plus fire-
watching. *Listen to Britain* is the music film I mentioned I think. Two reels
– no commentary – highspots Flanagan and Allen and Myra Hess playing
Mozart. Saw George [Reavey, the surrealist writer] and Gwyneth [his
wife] the other night back from Spain. Kathleen is down from her Cumberland exile – working in London. Bill Empson married – to a ravishing
Africaans girl. I hear [André] Breton is in New York. We are beginning
to get large quantities of canned American food over here – especially
Spam and that sort of thing. Pretty good – but in any case I must say –
other complaints about the war-organization apart – the food situation has
been remarkably well handled – we really feed magnificently considering.
As for the Russians our enthusiasm is nobody's business. But then you see
– we have been misled for 25 years and in a sense enthusiasm now is our
revenge on the newspaper peers – since they have now *got* to be enthusiastic to keep going at all. Then there were two excellent things from a propaganda point of view that happened together. One – the USSR resisted as
her admirers said she would – and two – even so she had to retire as anybody else would have had to – which in a sense proved the Russians were
human beings. A ridiculous thing to have to prove if you like and a
wretched way of proving it but never mind – very necessary here. Since
the *Human* side of the USSR has always been forgotten by its supporters
who have done nothing but talk economics. Anyway there is a hell of a
warm feeling around now... [...]
    [Added in handwriting:] Since the above bombs have been dropping on
Pearl harbour and [phrases deleted] we are waiting to see what happens
next. Here everybody is really too busy to be surprised – at least so it
appears. For me I just feel it's another ancient crime of ours – Manchuria
I mean – coming home as Abyssinia & Czechoslovakia & the rest have
done... Good to be on the same side as China anyway.
    Have started reading Gorki and also the short stories of Turgenev.
Reading & painting & music extra-popular everywhere here. People really
fighting for coloured reproductions of Breughel & Renoir for Christmas.
[...]

Today it is bright icy sunlight & the Pacific Ocean unknown, undisco-
vered. In winter, even in wartime, the world seems to go back in time.
Today looks like 1600: H.G. Wells unborn.

This is all very snappy – I am afraid: systematized picture of existence
pretty difficult. But out of the snaps there seems to be developing a great
sweep of human energy and determination like the sound of a plane
linking little farmsteads miles apart in a momentary gust. 'Space-time'
seems to have come into its own with a vengeance: all the fronts facing
different ways like the tank-battles in Libya. [. . .]

1942

FIRES WERE STARTED

There are many more documents for the making of *Fires Were Started* than for any of Jennings's other films. These include cast lists, various anonymous accounts of air raids, Unit lists, briefings on fire-station procedures, dialogue suggestions and other contributions by Maurice Richardson and so on. Among these papers are a number of Jennings's successive treatments for the film, under several different titles:

N.F.S. [i.e. National Fire Service] – earliest treatment 25.10.41
N.F.S. [i.e. National Fire Service]: a report on Jennings' visit to the
    Chelsea Sub-Station 11.11.41
Counter-Attack: Rough Treatment of National Fire Service film,
    22.11.41
Counter-Attack (undated treatment)
Untitled treatment, marked 'December 1941'
'Bare Outline of N.F.S. story' 16.12.41
Re-write of outline of N.F.S. story 19.12.41
N.F.S. Re-write 2.1.42
'The Bells Went Down!': 'Bare first treatment of National Fire Service
    story': 4.1.42
N.F.S. Second Treatment 12.1.42
N.F.S. Third Treatment 17.1.42
Fourth Treatment 17.1.42
N.F.S. [in pencil; 'To Be a Fireman'] Fifth Treatment 27.1.42

Many of these treatments run to at least ten pages, and the whole file is far too long for this collection. Here, then, are the first two documents and the latest of the treatments. The early pages of the latter have been heavily (and often illegibly) annotated in pencil by Jennings; any attempt to reproduce these notes would make them hard and confusing to read, so I have, for the most part, simply followed the original typescript.

N.F.S. 25.10.41

The film might begin with a fireman feeding some rabbits, and talking to the rabbits and he would be the man who was going to get killed in the film. And then in the same station, or sub-station, there would be some girls making toys for bombed-out people, and also an artist fireman painting a picture of a fire, and perhaps a dialogue scene with him reminiscing or other people criticising or both, and there might be a chap playing some music in the background. Some kind of a very long tracking shot all round these activities might very well be the opening to establish the human beings as distinct from the routine.

Probably the next thing to establish would be the night shift of the factory coming to work and maybe – especially if they were girls as they probably should be – they might be coming to work past one of the fire stations which are going to be involved, not necessarily the main one, but a group of them passing a trailer pump unit and having a bit of back-chat with just a wee hint of danger in it. Then you come back to the more serious side of the firemen, actual description of the machinery and introduction to some of the higher-ups. This as the evening comes on. Then you have got to go back for a moment to the factory with the girls actually at work because it is going to be essential to get a good kind of invisible link between the firemen and the girls, and it is at this point that you would be able to emphasize the danger of the work that the girls are doing. So that from this establishment of danger you can go crack into the siren or other device for opening of the raid.

Well, you have the raid and you probably take it from the point of view of the spotters on the factory roof, and also on the adjacent roofs – maybe you can have a scene of spotters on the factory roof whistling to the chaps on a warehouse roof the other side of the street. Well, the roof of the warehouse gets alight and it would be the spotters on the factory roof who would tell their manager and their manager would report to his own fire brigade, but especially to the station we saw at the beginning.

This station would send out its crew as described in the Woolwich report, and everything would proceed very much as in that report except that it would be the warehouse which would be alight and the curtain of water would have to be thrown in the narrow street between the warehouse and the factory. Of the procedure inside the factory we know nothing at the moment, but obviously there are two principal things to be considered in it:

(1) The sheer danger from explosion of the dumps, and

(2) the safety of the workers in the factory and the relation of production to their safety. In any case, they can hardly go out of the factory, so even if they are in shelters they will be in danger and so of course will be their machines which, with them, are responsible for production. Well, the firemen, to begin with, get on pretty well – the fire should not be represented as being of such a devastating nature as the Woolwich one actually was, but should follow much more the pattern of the fire at the beginning of *Fire over London,* and very much of what happens there should happen, i.e. a high explosive would fall between the pump crew on the top of the building who are principally dealing with the fire and with the

curtain of water, and cut them off from their comrades, and also exaggerate the fire beyond the capabilities of the personnel at the spot. So the Station Officer who would be presumably on the ground, would call for reinforcements and it is in the story of the bringing up of reinforcements that the whole organization of the NFS can be shown. Well, next comes the central incident to involve the pump crew we have seen right at the beginning of the picture. It can be of one of two kinds. Either (a) the rescuing of another fireman or (b) a man doing a job such as the shell stories in the Arsenal Memo. But in any case it will end with one man definitely giving his life to make sure that the curtain of water is kept up between the fire and the shell dump.

Well, the fire is put out, the various units go home. The procedure of checking, cleaning equipment and so on should be emphasized, i.e. the job is not done when the fire is out. In the factory production is restarted and here again we need information of the change of shifts after a blitz. The end of the film consists very simply of a sequence to match the opening sequence beginning perhaps with the pumps being repaired, cleaned etc, the artist continuing his picture, the man who was playing music switching on the radio to announce the news of the raid with an emphasis on the failure of the bombs to disturb production. Cross-cut this with the production in full swing in the factory, with the gap in the pump unit caused by the death of the man with the rabbits and perhaps end with another man, a man with a different voice, bringing the rabbits their food.

N.F.S. Tuesday November 11th, 41

The recreation room at 6W – Chelsea Sub-Station is a large, high-ceilinged, beautifully proportioned room in a house in Cheyne Place, Chelsea. Over the fireplace there is a modernistic frieze painted on brown paper – and on the wall facing it there is an amusing parody of monkeys engaged in human recreations. Both these friezes are the work of a sculptor fireman – Loris Rey. In the room there is a ping-pong table and a quarter-size billiard table.

Upstairs, one of the bedrooms is numbered – Room 504 – incidentally this is the best-kept room in the place. This room belongs to a fireman called Davies, who is also an artist in his way. I saw examples of his work – a type of work I had never seen before. He cuts individual flowers from coloured reproductions of flower paintings, mounts them on cork so that they stand out slightly and so makes a flower portrait against a black background. It sounds awful – but the composition and combination of colours are really lovely – and a most surprising hobby for the little short fat fussy fireman Davies.

Loris Rey – tall and thin with a gentle pointed face and large blue-grey eyes was busy on a Watch Room Board of his own design. It's nearly finished now – and it's the first of its kind – and so good that it has been accepted by the Fire Brigade as the official design from now on. Movable wooden slats with the men's names on fit on to wooden ridges – showing at a glance the disposition of duties and personnel.

The Watch Room which receives calls was a temporary one, the permanent one having been put out of action in the last raid. Two W.A.F.S. are on duty there. Station Officer Goddard in charge there told me that the normal attendance at any fire during a blitz on a first call was one trailer pump only. His full equipment consisted of one heavy unit, four trailer pumps and a Mobile Scout. The Mobile Scout is an emergency water supply car for small fires. It carries 500 gallons of water in a canvas tank.

6W is also in charge of six river pumps. Loris Rey looks after these and he has to man them as soon as a warning comes through. These pumps are on a floating raft moored to a wooden pier. Yesterday there was also an Ambulance ship moored to the raft and a mine-sweeper was anchored alongside. There are three pumps at each end of the raft. When the order comes through for river water – suction pipes from each pump are dropped in to the river – the engines are started up with one turn of the crank handle – and pressure according to instructions from the shore is given. The firemen on shore run down the wooden pier and lay hoses from the pumps to an emergency water tank on the bank. On shore by the emergency water tank – the water officer takes over and it is his job to see that the water is relayed from there to the fire.

The girls on the ambulance ship made us a cup of tea which was very welcome as I had a sore throat from talking so much.

At the Local Station – No. 6 Brompton, the Watch Room was on exactly the same lines as the one at headquarters with ticker-tape machine operated by smash-and-pull fire alarms. Very good double garage doors open out on to a pleasant square. The firemen do all the cleaning of equipment in the morning. Control room in basement run on same lines as headquarters control room. Here, direct lines to sub-stations are marked by letters not names, e.g. 6 W, 6 X, 6 Y. The WAFS and mobilizing officer at this station have had plenty of experience of operating in blitzes. In the last blitz two land mines fell on either side of the Station straddling it. The front door was blown out – lights went out – dust and dirt filled the air and the whole house rocked. They carried on by candle light.

In one of the girl's bedrooms I saw samples of the toys they made for bombed-out children and the children of workers in munition factories. This girl told me that she will never forget the experience of distributing

these toys. At one nursery school the children must have been told that
the toys were coming and when the firemen in the lorry with the toys
arrived they rushed out and swarmed over the lorry. The girl said 'I shall
never forget their little faces.' In other places the children were having
their tea – or had just been put to bed.

More toys are on exhibition now and will later be distributed. Miss
Thomas is going to let me know when and where so that we can go along
too if we want to.

I met Victor Haffenden – the producer of the firemen's Revue. He composed the music and designed the dresses. The firemen rehearse in an old
church hall in Church St. It has been bombed and is all patched up and
has notices saying 'Danger'. The stage is so small – it is only big enough
for the piano – so the men have to rehearse in the auditorium.

Their big show was given at the New Theatre on Saturday – May 10th
– can you beat it. Imagine the firemen climbing out of their ballet skirts –
and going straight out to fight the biggest fire in history.

I went up on to the roof and up a steep iron ladder to the watch tower
– and had a good view of the raid damage all round.

N.F.S.
Fifth Treatment

27 January 1942   *Crown Film Unit,*
                                                     Denham Studios,
                                                     Denham, Middx.

NOTE:
Generally speaking, the terms of rank, command, area and so on, used
here are those of the old system. This has been done simply for temporary
convenience and does not stop the use of the new terms in the film itself.

PROLOGUE TITLE:
Today Britain is protected by a unified National Fire Service which has
been created in the heat of battle. Commands, areas, methods have been
constantly modified by experience. This story is designed as a picture of
average occurrence and as a tribute to the firemen and firewomen of those
heroic years.

Begin with a close-up of the bas-relief on the Firemen's Memorial at LFB
HQ – old-fashioned firemen in curious helmets. Obliterate this image
with volumes of oil-fire smoke. Out of the smoke comes a big close-up of
a modern rubber-tyred wheel – one of the wheels of an up-to-date heavy

unit marked 14 Y HU1. It is early morning on a riverside road – the night mist still on the water. The pump has no crew, only a driver. From time to time its bell clangs as it chases through lumbering dock traffic, and echoes under a railway bridge. Then it turns a sharp corner – scatters pigeons, sets a dog barking and sweeps past the fireman on duty at the gate of a school playground. Here it pulls up and the driver dismounts and goes up steps through an arch marked 'Infants' to a door with the notice '14 Y Watch Room'. Inside the watch room are Mrs Townsend and Edna.

(Mrs T. AFS woman Section-Officer in charge of Watch Room. Slightly masculine type, cropped hair, possibly spectacles. Makes maternal impression in spite of masculine appearance. Age about 30. Edna, the other girl on duty in the Watch Room. Pretty, trousers.)

Mrs T. with tea-pot in one hand, Edna sitting at a phone facing a map of the sub-station's ground. The driver comes in and reports H U 1 back from repair. Mrs T. looks out of the window and says: 'Oh, hasn't she got a nice new coat?' Edna yawns and picks up the phones: 'Hullo Local – Y here. Reporting Heavy I back from workshop. Yes.' Looks up at the clock. 9.30. Mrs T. offers the driver a cup of tea and then says: 'Edna, dear, make out a ticket for the new recruit. Coming in this morning. His book's down there somewhere.'

Edna: O.K. Which Watch is he going in?
Mrs T: Blue.

Edna croons 'In the Blue of the Night' and sorts papers: 'Name of Barrett, that right?' 'Yes.' Grunt from Edna – she makes out ticket. The driver says: 'So long, girls' and exits. Mrs T is still looking out of window at Heavy 1: 'Might be good to put him on Heavy 1 right away.'

Edna: Who?
Mrs T: Mr Barrett. I was trying to think of the old crew. There's the Sub. – Johnny Daniels –
Edna: – Walters –
Mrs T: Oh, Mr Thomas (this to a section officer in the yard) – see who's back? . . . About the crew, would it be alright to put up the Old Blue gang – plus a new boy?
Thomas: Yes, I should think so, as long as you've got the sub. It's his pet pump, you know.

Sub-Officer Dykes is a Regular fireman, ex-Merchant Navy. 42. Clean-shaven. Firm, but quiet. At the moment he is standing at a street corner talking to a sailor: 'That was June the third, nineteen seventeen, mate. We was in the drink for sixteen hours before we was picked up, and I remember

Pincher Martin, he says to me he says, "When we gets out of this, I'm going to join the Fire Brigade"...'

Inside a small fishmonger's another fireman (B.A. Brown – Liverpool Irish. Real clown.) He is holding up a kipper by the tail: 'Once upon a time he was an innocent young herring – one of a family of three million herring-folk – but now he's been cured of all that, see...'

Another shop: 'S. Jackson, Newsagent and Tobacconist'. Fireman Jackson (a comic-pathetic saintlike character) is leaning over the counter giving his wife a long last kiss: 'Take care of yourself, old dear.'

Mrs J: It's you that need taking care of. (He gets his bike into the doorway). Now don't do anything silly, Jacko.

Jacko gets on his bike looking back at her and nearly hits a customer.

A row of rabbit hutches, each labelled: 'Spitfire', 'Hurricane', 'Joe Louis', etc, in large chalk capitals. In front of them a huge Cockney ex-taxi driver (Johnny Daniels) is on his knees sparring with a little boy of 10.

Johnny: Come on Carnera! Let's see that left. That's better. Keep that right hand up.
Voice Off: Twenty to ten, Johnny. Time you was off.
Johnny: O.K. sis. – coming along. And don't forget to feed the rabbits this time...

Along the road to the station some other firemen. Among them a Giant and a Dwarf walking side by side. Marching briskly by himself is A.F.S. S/0 Walters – tall, dark and handsome, whistling a phrase of 'Humoresque', his signature tune. Then Joe Vallance (a big lazy-looking, fair-haired man) getting off a tram with a bunch of daffodils. Glimpse of 'Jacko' biking along the riverside. At the traffic lights a lorry driver shouts down to ask an address: 'Alderman's wharf.' Jacko points down to the river front where huge cranes are swinging boxes into this hold of a grey merchantman.

At the Station the man on the gate gives an impressive salute and says: 'Morning Colonel' to a tough little Scots fireman (name of Rumbold) who takes it dead seriously. Then says: 'Morning Sub.' in a quiet and respectful way to the Sub. himself as he arrives. Now 'B.A.' and Johnny come in together. Now the Sub. enters the Watch Room – greets Mrs T – looks at the pump. Now from the Watch Room they see the others arriving (including Walters and Vallence). (The total number in Blue Watch is 23.)

Vallance comes up with his flowers and presents them to the girls in the Watch Room. Jacko gets a cheer as he swerves into the yard, and with the Watch Room clock at 10, the Fire Bell begins to give an intermittent buzz, and the Blue Watch assemble for Roll Call. At the same time comes the change-over of the girls in the Watch Room: Rose taking over from Edna. A crowd gather round the notice board reading the riding order. On the outskirts are Dwarf and Giant.

> *Giant:* That's the fifth time running I've been on Number 4 and we've had a working party every bloomin' morning. What you riding, Tich?
>
> *Dwarf:* Dunno yet – can't see.
>
> *Giant:* (Leaning over heads of crowd) You're riding 5 with Solomon Isaacs and Tiger Tim. Heavy One's back. She's got her old crew.
>
> *Vallance:* (Jerking thumb at board) Just like old times.
>
> *B.A.:* Get her cracking there Johnny!

(Wink from Johnny.)

> *Rumbold:* Who's Barrett? (Pointing to new boy's name.)
>
> *Walters:* (Who has just come up with a Roll Call book in his hand) New bloke. Recruit from the Training School. Now then, fall in.

Inside a docker's café the racket of talk is broken by the ping of the door bell, and the slightly bewildered face of a young fireman in clean uniform looks in from the street. 'Can anyone tell me the way to Number 14 Y Fire Station?' – 'Yes, mate...' Half-a-dozen people start giving directions at once, but the little Chinese proprietor shuffles forward from the back and very kindly and charmingly takes the new boy back into the street and gives precise details in pidgin English.

In the yard our crew now detach themselves from the others and walk over to HU 1. Jacko is discussing a domestic scene with Vallance.

> *Jacko:* I was just toasting me toes when a great red hot coal jumped out of the grate and fell plonk in the middle of the rug. Gave me quite a turn.
>
> *Vallance:* And what did the wife say?
>
> *Jacko:* Well, yer don't expect to find a blinkin' conflagration on your own hearth rug first thing after breakfast!

Passing the Pump are the last of the Red Watch going off duty. Rumbold is finishing an argument with one of them: 'If it wasn't for the fact that the Fire Service was in urgent need of my services, I could stand here for eternity supplying you with arguments...'

> *Voices from the Pump:* Come on Colonel!

At the gate a Red Watch man is talking to the man on duty.

> *Red Watch Man:* You'll be in the limelight tonight. Full moon.
>
> *Man on the Gate:* Who says so?

At this moment the new boy arrives with a suitcase.

New Boy: This 14 Y? Can you tell me where the Watch Room is?
Man on the Gate: Straight over – up steps.

The new boy feels a bit self-conscious lugging his suitcase across the yard with the Pump Crews watching. As he goes up the steps a man washing the floor floods the top step with a bucket of water. He steps over a squeegee mop at the top then sees the watch room door.

The Sub. is leaning out of the Watch Room window looking over the yard. He has, in fact, seen the new boy walk across. Mrs T. is arranging the flowers. The new boy enters.

New Boy: Barrett, T.P., reporting for duty.
Mrs T: Ah, you're the boy we've all been waiting for!
New Boy: Sorry I'm late, but they kept us quite a time at 14.
Mrs T: Hey, Sub. – here's Barrett.

(Sub. turns his head, sees recruit and comes over to him.)

Sub: (Shaking hands) Hope you'll like it here, Barrett.
Mrs T: 'Course he will. This is the best Sub. Station in the whole ground.

(Sub. turns back to window and yells for Johnny).

Johnny: (On pump, looks up, points fingers at his own chest) What, me?
Sub: Yes, you I said!
'B.A.': (Standing up on back of pump, screwing on delivery caps). That means a working party for us, my cockers! You see if it don't. (Imitates imaginary orders) 'Heavy One. Pump out flooded sewer.'
Mrs T: Where's he going to sleep?
Sub: There's a spare bed in the 'Monkey House'.

Johnny enters the Watch Room.

Sub: Johnny – this is Barrett. This is Johnny Daniels who is driving Heavy One. He'll put you wise to things.
Johnny: Pleased to meet yer, chum.
Sub: Johnny, show Barrett the 'Monkey House', and when he's stowed his gear take him out and politely introduce him to those other perishing geezers.
Johnny: O.K. Sub. (to Barrett) You come along o' me, chum.

The Sub. returns to the window and tells off the others for not working hard enough.

'B.A.': We didn't ought to have the Pump parked right under the Sub.'s nose like this! It's asking for trouble.

Jacko and Vallance are stowing a suction. B.A. and the Colonel are squatting down stowing lengths of hose in one of the side lockers. Johnny and Barrett come up to them.

> *Johnny:* Here we are Barrett – meet the boys. This is Joe Vallance. This is B.A. Brown – he'll try and sell you a pair of braces in a minute! This here bagpipe goes by the name of Rumbold, but we calls him the 'Colonel', and this is 'Jacko', our little ray of sunshine.

Each of the men in turn shakes hands or salutes and says 'Pleased to meet you' in his particular fashion. Then the whole party set to work again.

Now Rose, the new telephone girl, rings the Control Room at 14, the Local Station: 'Hullo Jane – Y report call. 2 HU's, 3 TP's, fully manned.' Local control. In the foreground a row of telephone girls and behind them the Mobilising Officer with his board and gadgets. The first girl is just taking Rose's call. The other girls are taking similar calls from W, X and Z. 14 W used to be a garage. By the old garage pumps men are working on a trailer pump unit. 14 Y used to be a school – a curious inconvenient 'gothic' building. Men scrubbing hoses and drying hoses on a hose tower. 14 Z is a place similar to the real 28 K, i.e. an old Customs House in the dock area. The Mobilising Officer hooks up the appropriate discs on his board. A similar report call from a river station to its own headquarters. Men cleaning Diesels on a fire float. Then at Local Control a girl begins dictating to District (Divisional) the total of appliances 'on the run' from these stations: 'Hello, Divisional, 14 here. Plenty for you this morning: 2 DP's, 1 P, 8 HU's, 18 TP's, 25 ATC's, 1 IIL, 2 TT1's...' During and leading from this dictation, a 'documentary' sequence of men and appliances. Men cleaning pumps. Men unloading a hose lorry. A classroom full of faces at a lecture. River drill being directed from a pontoon bridge. Hook ladder drill. Jumping sheet. A course of turn table ladder instructions ending with the ladder zooming up and locking into place section by section.

Now someone turns on the radio in 14 Y canteen: lunch time session, with the mighty wurlitzer. 'B.A.' gives a 'hog call' and the men begin coming in from the yard. In the kitchen a fat and genial woman cook. In the canteen the men beginning to sit down – the food coming through hatches. The 'colonel' has impaled a sausage on the end of his fork.

> *'Colonel':* If we examined this object under a microscope, we should find underneath the skin a world of animal life...controlled

by the same electric currents that control the destiny of man.
(He pushes sausage under the nose of the man sitting next
him.) For what resides in this sausage resides in us also and
what we recklessly consume contains a superabundance of
vitality that would be safer left upon the plate.

Another Man: Trust the 'Colonel' to vivisect the grub.

'Colonel': Only fools and ignoramuses shrink from the mysteries of
matter. (Cuts sausage in half and masticates slowly and
contentedly.)

As the Blue and White Watches are settling down to table, the Sub.
comes up behind Johnny and Barrett who are sitting together, and
suggests that after lunch, if they have nothing else to do, it would be a
good idea if Johnny took Barrett round the Station ground.

The Sub. then sits down at a separate table with the S/Os, Mrs T. and
the girls. The group round Johnny look across at them and somebody says
the Sub.'s looking a bit queer. He doesn't like it when the Sub. looks queer
– always means trouble. – a blitz for example.

Next thing we see is an old taxi-cab painted grey with 14 Y on it, trund-
ling along between high dockyard walls. Johnny driving Barrett and talking at the top of his voice. He remarks that this is not a good place to pick
up a fare late at night. Reminiscences about his old taxi driver days: turns
his head over his shoulder and carries on burlesque conversation with
imaginary fare. Barrett says he used to be a plough-boy. Johnny says:
'You'll be alright at Y – you've only got to use your loaf.' Barrett asks about
fire fighting. Johnny says no need to worry about doing it by numbers. All
the men of the pump's crew muck in together. As the taxi passes a tall narrow house with a girl leaning out of the window, Johnny makes a crack
about a hook ladder. Barrett asks if hook ladders are used much in practice. Johnny says he has only seen a hook ladder used once and that was
when the Station cat wouldn't get down from a tree overhanging the yard
and the hook ladder nearly pulled the tree down, etc.

Johnny points out the Alderman's Wharf and remarks on peculiarities
of riverside fires – never enough water, etc. After a word at the gate they
go through to the water front. Here is the big grey merchantman we saw
in the morning still being loaded. Cranes, swinging great white boxes
marked 'To the Officer in Charge'. From a small office window at the back
of a wharf, out pops the Wharf Manager's head, shouting to the chief
stevedore and popping back to his phone to tell somebody they were well
ahead with loading – that they will knock off at seven tonight and that with
the morning shift coming on at eight they should get her off on tomorrow's
tide in time to catch her convoy.

The taxi drive continues. In his office the Dock Master makes the routine afternoon call to Brigade Control on the state of the tide for tonight: 'Low water at 21.58'. (This call always comes in about tea time and allows us to introduce some of the higher-ups and to suggest some of the strategical machinery involved.) For example, another call to Brigade which we can follow through to the office of the Fire Force Commander (a pleasant mannered, white-haired officer) who is having tea and talking to his assistant. This call comes from Home Security (or from the Air Ministry?) and indicates that there is pretty likely to be a raid on this area tonight. Hint of radio location.

14 Y. The man on the gate. The taxi turning into the yard. Then Johnny and Barrett tiptoeing along a long corridor. 'Sh – they're supposed to be asleep!' On each side the men's rooms are numbered and also have comic notices on them – 'Water Rats' – 'Monkey House'. The 'Monkey House' is where Jacko and Johnny sleep: seven or eight beds line the walls – some of them camp beds: one or two mattresses on the floor. One man has rigged up an elaborate iron bedstead with sheets. Jacko is asleep, snoring. (He has fixed up a tube from the gas to the side of his bed where he has a gas ring and kettle.) One man is sitting at a table writing a letter. Another is lying on his back, reading. Another is asleep. Another sitting on the side of his bed rummaging in a suitcase under the bed. Johnny throws a paper ball at Jacko's open mouth. Jacko wakes up. Jokes about Jacko's bedside tea-making apparatus. The man on the gate pokes his head round the door and yells for them to wake up his relief, who is one of the sleepers. In other rooms introduce other characters. For example, an artist painting a picture of a fire. Dwarf and Giant playing chess. 'B.A.' comes up behind and gives a burlesque broadcast commentary.

'B.A.': On my right we have the chess champion of the 'Water Rats', Tich Potter, and on my left by special arrangements with the authorities at the Zoo, that sagacious beast Jumbo Cunningham. He ought to be ashamed of himself taking on men half his size. This is the battle of the century. They've been sitting here like a pair of Egyptian mummies for half an hour. We are now taking you over to the field of play. Square four. Tich has taken his hand out of his pocket. He's going to move. No, he isn't.

A man polishing his axe carefully and laboriously with emery paper.

Vallance: You been a long time titivatin' that chopper of yours, Sid.
Sid: I'm on the gate tonight.
Vallance: Well, no one'll be able to see if it's rusty or not in the dark.
Another Man: Remember the time old Jacko painted his axe handle

black and got told off by the superintendent. Told off
proper, he was. (He turns to recruit.) You can't have a
black handle to yer chopper until yer a Station Officer.
Recruit: Yes, we had to learn all that at the Training School. All about
how to identify Officers at a fire and all.
Other Man: Now, there's something I never been able to understand.
How can you recognize a black axe handle in the dark?
Vallance: You're forgetting your drill, Wally. Seen from the back at a
fire, a Station Officer and a Superintendent looks alike, see?
But a Superintendent has a white axe handle and a Station
Officer has a black one.

'B.A.' in the kitchen organizing tea.
Clock strikes five. (Tea nearly over.) Some of the men beginning to play
cards. Two are playing ping-pong. Billiard room scene with Rumbold and
several other men. 'B.A.' selling a pair of braces to Barrett.

'B.A.': You alright for braces, my cocker? Something special these are.
(Stretches braces across his chest.) They're so strong you can do
your daily dozen with them. They'll keep your pants up for a
lifetime and if that's too long, you can hang yourself with 'em.
The whole pair for half a dollar and no coupons or questions
asked.
Recruit: Daresay I could do with a spare pair.
'B.A.': Spare pair indeed. Let me tell you that once a man has worn
these braces...
Johnny: He's tied himself in such a ruddy knot he can't never stand up
straight again.

At 6 p.m. the canteen opens and some of the men drift towards it. For
the first time now the Sub. comes down among the men, down the middle
of the room to the canteen. On one side of the bar is a tank of fish – the
station mascots. Rather dirty, bloated-looking fish – for some reason
treasured by the Station. On the other side of the bar is the station cat. The
ping-pong game at the far end of the room comes to an end with a smashing shot which ricochets over the men's heads and finally into the fish
tank. Some confusion during which the cat goes across to inspect. Johnny
says the cat can tell the difference between A.A. fire and bombs, knows
his hook ladder drill and is authorized to make the pumps up to five.

Someone begins to strum a piano and a woman comes in from the
kitchen to organize supper which is a pretty irregular meal. In the corner
near the piano, Walters and one of the girls are doing a mock adagio-
dance. The barman is having an endless argument with the Sub. and
others about rates of pay, compensation, etc.

Sub.: He's right there. When you're in the dirt, half the worry is wondering what would happen to the wife and kids if you copped it. It's not so hard on regulars. We know where we stand as regards compensation, but if one of you geezers cops it, and he's disabled for more than thirteen weeks he's discharged. Why, I reckon some of you blokes has done more fire fighting in the last year than a whole Fire Brigade would do in peace time.

The men at supper start beating on the table with spoons in time to the piano, making the salt cellar and mustard pot do a dance of their own. At 6.45 – blackout. The heavy vehicles in the yard are moved into convenient positions. At 7 o'clock the purple.

With the purple warning the men begin putting on their boots. The piano continues playing. General feeling that a raid is coming. Outside the moon is rising. The dockers are going home – a snatch of conversation between them and some fire watchers, especially a street arab called Mickey. A silhouetted cat with its tail in the air stalking through the roll of danet wire at the top of a dock wall. Man climbing up to an Observation Fort looking down on the river. The observers plot the direction of the wind and ring up Brigade Control. In the Brigade Control, message for the O.P. Officer. The wind is blowing strongly across river. On the other side of the river somewhere among the dark houses, Jacko's wife is having supper alone. Back in the canteen the men are preparing to go out: the piano playing loud – someone with a concertina – the men singing. *Warning:* a momentary pause to listen. The sigh of the concertina. On the roofs outside and above the warehouse the fire watchers are ready. Rumbold is giving Barrett a lecture.

Rumbold: It says here…(he reads aloud from a book)…'we feel our way towards the light like earth worms. Man is a midget obeying mysterious forces which drive him relentlessly forward to glorious triumphs or to fearful disasters. This mysterious force is generated from innumerable electric currents in the stratosphere…'

Searchlights down river. The beginning of plane sound. The first thud of A.A. fire. The men on the Observation Post can see a big fall of incendiaries further down the water front. This is checked by another O.P.: both reported to Brigade Control and plotted. Now the curious clatter and isolated shouts of men on roof tops dealing with incendiaries. A moment's silence and then the earth-shaking crump of the first H.E. Billiard balls giving a little jump with the explosion. Now a fire watcher telephoning to Local Watch Room. The Mobilising Officer in Local Control. Now 14Y Watch Room gets its first call and rings a bell. First pump away. Shout of address. Quickly followed by a second call and the second pump. Another much closer H.E. Mickey telephoning Local Control. Girl at 'fire situation' board writing 'Trinidad Street'. At 14Y the bell again and call for 'Heavy 1 – Trinidad Street'. Our crew. The pump outside the station with the crew in the dark jumping on. The Sub., Jacko, – somebody looking after the new boy. Heavy unit on its way to the fire: Johnny singing and bouncing up and down in the driver's seat. The Sub. shouts: 'Do you know Trinidad Street, Johnny?' Johnny says yes he does. He was right there this afternoon with the new man, next to Alderman's Wharf. The tyres crunching over broken glass. The crew as a Unit.

Shout from Johnny. 'This is Trinidad Street.' The pump stops at an alley corner to a big warehouse. As they jump off they are met by Mickey (the street urchin from the warehouse roof). There has been a fall of incendiaries and then an H.E. Part of the roof is on fire. This from Mickey to the Sub. while the crew scatter to look for a hydrant. Broken glass and bricks have covered the hydrant covers. We follow the new boy along the side of a wall – through patches of darkness from high buildings which cut off the glow of the fire – finally kicking aside broken glass and going down on his knees to find what he thinks is a hydrant.

Up comes 'B.A.' with a torch, and the hydrant turns out to be the manhole of a sewer. 'B.A.' begins to tell off the new boy but away behind them someone shouts 'Hydrant!' Johnny backs the pump to the hydrant and 'B.A.' and the new boy rejoin the crew. A glimpse of Mickey showing the Sub. an inside staircase to the warehouse roof, then back to the crew coupling up to the hydrant. (All above in rapid action.) The Sub. tells the new boy to stay with Johnny and look after the pump – orders the crew to get a branch to work on the ground and then goes off to inspect the general lay-out of the fire, taking Jacko with him. They go up the inside staircase and through a sky-light. The roof is well alight. But it is clear that the real problem is not so much to save the warehouse as to stop the fire spreading over the dock wall to the transit sheds and Alderman's Wharf. And in any case to stop the merchantman becoming too much of a target.

On the ground, Walters, Vallance and 'B.A.' are holding the first branch. The water is through: When the Sub. and Jacko come back, he directs this branch on to the dock wall. Then he explains to Jacko and Rumbold how to work on the roof. They and the new boy run out hose lengths from the second delivery and then get a branch ready for hauling up to the roof.

The Sub. goes to a phone box (the one used by Mickey) and phones Local Control. He gives his whereabouts and asks for pumps to be made up to 5 and will they send a fire float down to Alderman's Wharf to get water ashore.

Jacko and the 'Colonel' are now on the roof and are just pulling the branch and hose up from the ground with a line. The Sub. comes back to the pump and says to Johnny he hopes the hydrant will hold as the tide is going out and he has a hunch there is going to be a shortage of water.

Now come to Local Control. Two girls telephoning simultaneously. One asking for pumps to go to Trinidad Street, and the other calling District (Divisional) ordering a fire float.

The water front at river station: the roar of Diesels being turned over. Clattering down the pontoon bridge from the shore come the crew. Cast off.

Trinidad Street. The Sub. is now on the roof and as we come to him and Jacko and the 'Colonel' the jet comes through. Both deliveries are now working and Johnny sends the new boy along Trinidad Street to try and find an emergency water supply. Halfway along a particularly close H.E. comes down. The new boy throws himself flat. At this exact moment a terrifying noise comes down the cobbled street close to his head. Out of the darkness a man running towards him leading three dray horses whose frightened eyes reflect the fire and the gun flashes. The two crews go on fighting the fire irrespective of H.E.'s. The new boy comes running back to say he has found a sunk barge used as a dam at the top of a Cut. As he is explaining where, the water gives out and the two jets die. That H.E. must have hit the main. On the roof the fire takes advantage of this stoppage. And then about three streets away they hear the fire bells of the reinforcements and the new boy is sent back to the Cut to stop them there and explain the situation. The fire is burning, the fire floats are chugging down river, the new pumps advancing down Trinidad Street. After being nearly run over by the pumps and cursed by the new officer in charge, the new boy manages to explain the situation, and the officer orders the pumps to lower suctions into the barge and couple up for series pumping to HU 1.

At this point appears the Wharf Manager. (Should this be the skipper of the vessel?) He is worried. A cross-river breeze is blowing sparks and bits of timber from the warehouse to the transit sheds. In the sheds lie piles of precious boxes: 'To the Officer in Charge...' The tide is now too low to move anything and the fire is beginning to make the ship an ideal target. The officer reassures the Dock Master that the fire float is due at any moment. He also sends a D.R. back for a turn-table ladder and orders the new boy to tell the Sub. to hang on until the ladder arrives. By the time the new boy gets there, the series pumping is under way and the two branches (reinforced by other pumps) have got the new water through.

Now we follow the D.R. back to 14 Watch Room. At Local Control all the lights have gone and the windows have been blown in, but the girls still manage to pass the D.R.'s message to District by candle light.

The fire float is now in sight of the warehouse and the vessel, but it is now nearly low water and they have to tie up to a buoy or anchor out in the stream and get the hoses ashore by dinghy and over the mud. When this is done the fire float can go on filling the sunk barge which is now nearly empty. From the roof the Sub. sends Rumbold down to report that the fire is very fierce but they will hold on as long as they can.

The arrival of the TTL is the beginning of the climax of the picture. It sweeps down Trinidad Street, gets a cheer from the men doing series pumping at the Cut and goes straight to the fire, i.e. at the foot of the warehouse below where the Sub. and Jacko are working. While it is being manoeuvred into position the officer in charge shouts and signals to the Sub. and Jacko to come down. They don't seem to hear, so he sends the new boy up with a message. He has to fight his way through the smoke in the staircase and arrives on the roof just as a piece of wall begins to collapse. There is a crash – the Sub. is knocked unconscious – and the inside staircase is blocked with burning timbers. But the turntable ladder is now run up to their level and Jacko tells the new boy to carry the Sub. down while he deals with the branch. The new boy picks up the Sub. and just manages to make the ladder – Jacko automatically pausing to try and lower the branch. On the ground below are upturned faces watching Jacko. Another piece of wall begins to give. The man on the ladder yells 'Come on, you fool!' – the new boy carrying the Sub. pauses on the ladder, looks through the rungs and sees the rest of the wall going – collapsing inwards away from the ladder and carrying Jacko with it. There is a moment of darkness and then a burst of fire and sparks which fly out over the wharf wall and the transit sheds. The new boy reaches the ground and the man at the top of the ladder phones to the pumps below. The chain of water is now complete: from the fire float on the river to the barge, to the pumps in the street, to the branches at the fire. At the top of the ladder the jet comes through.

At Brigade Control the Fire Force Commander is discussing the Trinidad Street fire with the Mobilising Officer. The latter is just allocating stand-by crews to the empty stations of 14. In answer to a question from the Fire Force Commander he says 'Trinidad Street reports that have now got enough appliances and are doing alright. Afraid there was a bad fall of wall there, sir.'

The First Aid Post. Mickey (or one of the First Aid men) is talking to the Sub. who is lying on a stretcher: '...poor old Jacko. Would be him! Fussing about his branch, I suppose, instead of watchin' out.' At the warehouse Walters' branch on the ground is still working: Rumbold and the new boy are both dead beat. Observation Posts report the fire under control. 'All clear.' Safe in the river below the Observation Post lies the grey merchantman. Firemen look up and grin and give a great sigh. Down Trinidad Street comes a canteen. Groups of firemen struggle across to it: pick up mugs of cocoa. One of them says to the canteen girl: 'Bless your beautiful face.' Someone else to the fireman: 'You look pretty beautiful, too.'

He looks like a nigger minstrel. 'B.A.' meets an old pal. Reunion. 'B.A.' breaks the bad news to the group at the canteen. The Sub. is moved into an ambulance. A superintendent comes over to Walters and says: 'Crew of HU 1 to make up and go home.' Rumbold and the new boy, who have been sitting on the edge of the pump, pull themselves together – the others go across from the canteen and begin making up hoses in inches of water. Following out the line of a hose in among the wreckage the new boy comes across a dented tin hat with 14 Y on it: Jacko's. In the front shop Jacko's wife is sorting out the morning papers. She has the radio on – the 8 o'clock news – 'Last night there was a sharp attack...' She clears her face as the first customers arrive. Now down Trinidad Street the first dockers arrive too. Heavy 1 begins a slow journey up the street in the opposite direction bumping over rubble and hoses. Exchange of shouts and greetings and news between the crew and the dockers: the dockers will find their work and their ship still waiting for them. Now the sun begins to shine – the tide rising over the mud flats. The dockers swarming on to the water front. People flooding back to work along dockside roads. All over the city, life reasserts itself and the day's work begins. In 14 Y Mrs Townsend produces endless cups of tea. The men just flop in helpless positions on their beds or sit with their heads in their hands.

In his little office the Wharf Manager is telephoning: 'Oh yes, sure, we can make it – she will be there!'

The final sequence of the film takes place a couple of days later. The big grey merchantman dropping her pilot and nosing out into the open sea – into wind and weather – and contrast it with a scene in a small churchyard on the edge of a great city – the fireman's funeral.

Jacko's tin hat surrounded by white chrysanthemums – the coffin wrapped in a Union Jack carried by the other seven – Sub. with his head bandaged. Other members of the Blue Watch. Mrs Townsend. Mrs Jackson. The bugles blowing 'The Last Post'. The bows of the great grey vessel hurrying to join her convoy.

THE END

TO CICELY JENNINGS   *South Cottage,*
11 January 1942   *Chorley Wood, Herts*

[...] I find now I just work and think of you three. Really nothing else at
all. The picture about music called *Listen to Britain* is now finally finished
and everybody likes it very much but I don't know when it will get on the
screen – some pretty deep battles developing here between Ministry and
big business: although in fact the Government have been carefully good
– much too good to them. Now beginning a biggish picture about the Fire
Brigade – now called the National Fire Service – story pic. with characters
etc. So far so good. And of course smashing chaps – the firemen. On all
this we are roughly lucky if we get Sunday off. Food situation remains
really remarkably good. But anything like luxury – including cigarettes,
drinks, cinemas – either very expensive or rare or both. But the standard
of living is still pretty astonishing considering and compared – very
uneven and unfair need I say. [...]

Today it is bright winter sunshine – and pretty cold. I am writing a
detailed script of the fire film, arguing about fire-watching tonight. Planes
drone, birds cheep, a blue-bottle has woken and is buzzing against the
window. Singapore and Mojaisk seem worlds away until one opens the
Sunday papers. The other day we came across a Canadian broadcaster
called [Leonard] Brockington [who reads the Foreword to *Listen to Britain*] – a pal or enemy or both of Grierson's: I wonder if you have come
across him. Ex-lawyer and devotee of Whitman. [...] And I find myself
reading Kipling.

Jan 12 – before work. A misty frosty morning – the rooks cawing.
Trucks shunting away down the valley. Streaks in the east and the great
red-helmeted sun pushing up through fog and mist as I write. Chinese
vermilion. In a minute Dal will shout 'Humpers' and I shall make a rush
for my shoes – which want repairing and I see no more rubber for shoes
this morning. Then find my coat, get into the car – go five miles or more
to Denham on icy roads: the top end of the valley. Now the sun is fully out
of the mist and an express is throwing out clouds of white smoke which
turn black as they drift over the red disk. In ten minutes I shall be cracking
into work again. Dictating yesterday's script – arguing about the ending.
Above the sun now there is a patch of illuminated cloud – very intricate
lace-work of orange and grey-blue: as intricate as the future. Sebastian
(one of Dal's children) has just been stopped from putting 'Yes my darling
daughter' on the radio-gram for the millionth time. Now there is a great
black line across the sunface like the war that divides us. Now another
train – going other way – 'Humpers'...[...]

My darling

It is alas weeks and weeks since I have written to you, and I have had
such lovely letters [. . .] All this time I have in fact been away from here
and away from Pinewood which is our new HQ in place of Denham – in
Stepney and Wapping on the Fire picture. We have more or less taken
over a small district, roped off streets, organized the locals and so on. It
has been exceptionally hard and tiring work. A difficult film anyway, then
a lot of camera trouble and no Chick [Fowle, Jennings's cameraman] and
everything – film, petrol, supplies of all sorts very short. But of course the
place and the people illuminating beyond everything. The river, the
wharves and shipping, the bridge in Wapping Lane smelling permanently
of cinnamon, the remains of Chinatown, the Prospect of Whitby and
another wonderful pub called the Artichoke which is our field Headquarters. Reconstruction of a fire in the docks. A charming Fire-station at a
school in the centre of Wellclose Square which for all the world looks like
Vermeer's view of Delft. Ridiculous plaster rococo cherubs on the front of
a blitzed house, an old man who comes in and plays the flute superbly well
on Fridays, Mr Miller who owns a chain of antique shops and specializes
in Crown Derby, Jock who runs the sailors Mission, Wapping Church
mentioned in Pepys which we are using for a fireman's funeral. And the
people themselves, firemen and others – T.P. Smith ex-international ban-
quet waiter – Fred Griffiths ex-taxi driver – Loris Rey ex Glasgow School
of Art – Sadie the girl at the Artichoke – Mr C. at the warehouse who upset
a precious bottle of Soir de Paris all over the safe and then insisted on
drenching everybody's hankies in it – and what the Sub-Officer's wife said
when he came home smelling like that. For the last two months we have
been working at this down there for twelve hours a day six days a week:
we are now roughly half way through and pretty exhausted: the results
peculiar and very unlike anything I have had to do with before: popular,
exciting, funny – mixture of slapstick and macabre blitz reconstruction.

[. . .] Rodney I have seen occasionally at the 'Players' which is a kind of
highbrow night-club – on the lines of Victorian music-hall – not unlike the
'Cave of Harmony' that Laughton and Elsa Lanchester used to run –
sounds awful but in fact it is extremely good – the turns really brilliant –
it has been for two or three years a kind of first appearance place for revue
'finds'. The atmosphere quite a reasonable compromise between Bohemia
and Mayfair and Services on leave. But honestly in London winter a god-
send after dark. I met there about a month back Eric Knight – American
film critic and his wife who were particularly enthusiastic about *Listen to*

Britain (now on at the Gaumont Haymarket) and who promised to look you up. *Listen* has had very violent notices one way and the other – three stars in the *Sunday Express* with tremendous popular boost – and of course Mr Anstey [Edgar Anstey, the documentary film-maker and critic] in the *Spectator* thinking of every gag to damn it. But in fact a success and very popular.

To continue: it has now become 14 hours a day – living in Stepney the whole time – really have never worked so hard at anything or I think thrown myself into anything so completely. Whatever the results it is definitely an advance in film making for me – really beginning to understand people and not just looking at them and lecturing or pitying them. Another general effect of the war. Also should make me personally more bearable.

[...] I get to Pinewood roughly once a week – I might just as well be in Glasgow. Film still going pretty well. Saw Mrs Goring [the mother of Jennings's friend Marius Goring, the actor, who had also attended the Perse School in Cambridge] for a few moments the other night. Very well. Brought up a curious idea – probably correct – that the queer mixture of art-theatre stuff and militarist training at the Perse is doing its stuff now – at least as far as I am concerned ... I know by the way that *Listen to Britain* has been seen by the boys in Ottawa – so maybe you could see a copy from there. I gather that Sidney Bernstein (M.O.I.) and a good friend of mine is coming over to see you – I hope you see him – has done an enormous amount for our unit.

Painting etc. I am afraid I haven't touched for months now – but maybe when this pic. is finished I shall get back to a little. Reading nothing. Life concerned with a burning roof – smoke fire water – men's faces and thoughts: a tangle of hose, orders shouted in the dark – falling walls, brilliant moonlight – dust, mud tiredness until nobody is quite sure where the film ends and the conditions of making it begin: a real fire could not be more tiring and certainly less trouble. But what one learns at midnight with tired firemen ...

You must believe we really are working night & day now & people – the people – & things are having a tremendous effect on me at the moment. Only for the good believe me – making me much simpler and more human – but somehow making it very difficult to concentrate – [...]

TO CICELY JENNINGS   *South Cottage,*
29 May 1942   *Chorley Wood, Herts*

[...] We are at last getting to the end of shooting the Fire picture which has certainly taught me a thing or two. A great deal more confident – happier dealing with people – capable – apparently – of directing funny scenes as well as pathetic ones – capable of working inside a studio as well as outside.

The spring and early summer here have been extraordinary – long weeks of endless sun – a burst of rain and then the same again – but the winter was pretty rough and we deserve it we consider. Smashing for pictures anyway. Find myself thinking of two painters almost only: Rousseau and Rembrandt: being close to human beings I suppose. The country as a whole is fairly happy I should say – the RAF and the Commandos buck it up from time to time. Amazing in fact what has been done since Dunkirk. But you know how we take things for granted. Quite a number of American soldiers visible on London streets. Anything connected with Russia a wow.

And then what a longing to see you all again. We have got so into wartime habits of work and sleep and eat what you can and keep working that one's ordinary feelings get dulled – and then when you rest your feet or wake in the morning – it all comes back. The shout of a child in the street sounds like Marylou – the back of a girl in the Underground looks like you – I see Holland Park and Blackheath and others on notice boards and signs. And then sometimes it all seems so natural – that one forgets not only the personal past but what a real danger we were in two years back. It is all helped – or confused – by this country, I mean countryside's trick of looking just the same.

Apropos *Words For Battle* and *Listen to Britain* – get Sidney Bernstein to show them to you at the Library of Inf. I hear *Listen* was well thought of in Hollywood – also among the troops in the Middle East. A toughish Commando officer was raving about both those films to me yesterday – which was really very gratifying – shows it's worth taking trouble and not underrating people. But as you say in your last letter we are just as responsible as the so-called non-intellectuals for everything. In any case my (I say my but) firemen have certainly proved one thing to me, but proved it in practice – that all these distinctions of understanding and level and other such are total rubbish and worse – invented by people to mislead. And not merely the distinctions made by the famous upper-classes but also those made [by] the grubby documentary boys who try and give a hand to what they call emerging humanity, the common man and so on.

For the first time since the first winter of the war I personally begin to find it a bit tiring – there seems particularly no time to do anything – just work[,] and believe it or not I am better at relaxing than I used to be[,] but there are fewer chances now. Also of course at the end of a film one is always apt to be tired and bad tempered etc. Reading the *Memoirs* of Herzen [see *Pandaemonium*, pp.267-8] – ex-aristocrat born at Moscow in 1812 – became a friend of Humboldt and was exiled to Siberia – a sort of link

between the Russia of *War and Peace* and *The Cherry Orchard.* Parallel to
Stendhal's *Journal.* Very difficult at the moment to read anything with a
story in it – necessity for actual human beings.

Of us I find it very difficult indeed to speak. You are so completely and
entirely and utterly the only person in the world – but of course it is only
this certainty that makes separation possible – every standard I have,
every emotion goes back to and turns on you and you are nearest when
least expected. You will say I still rely on you too much – but in fact it is
now part of life and nature. To be without you is like having lost one complete sense – to be deaf or to have lost one's memory.

I have just been told by Megan [Mrs Dalrymple] that I look extremely
well and non-tired for the finish of a picture – so you mustn't worry about
that.

Lately I have seen nobody. If I'm not at work on location I am at [place
name cut by Government censor] which is miles from anywhere: a film
factory. Takes an hour and a half to get there from London and practically
all travelling has to be by train and bus now – rigid cutting down of petrol
and production [of] cars. [...]

TO CICELY JENNINGS   *South Cottage,*
28 July 1942   *Chorley Wood, Herts*

[...] Here the news [is] getting steadily grimmer. Work much the same.
The Fire picture finished. I am going down to the Rhondda next week on
something new. [i.e. *The Silent Village*] That goes back a long way, too. I
am finding more than ever that the chief problem in all times is to fit in
all the worlds that exist together. The world of the day to day war – the
world of the past (Suffolk, Cambridge) – the great landscapes of the USSR
and the USA – the rich nostalgia of France and Italy – the constant struggle of poetry and economics – the alternate claims of man and nature – the
sudden long-term reminders from Greece and China – how to fit all in ...
– To shift rapidly and easily from Tobruk to Courbet – from the momentary shaft of six o'clock sunlight to the local politics of the Welsh valleys
– Handel, Moscow, Vermont ... you alone combine and do not separate.

Your description of the Bisbee's farm [in Vermont] cool and deep and
moving. We are really very lucky.

London – to look at – has settled down to a big village-like existence.
Most of the damage demolished and cleared up. Endless allotments –
beds of potatoes, onions, lettuces – in parks, in the new open spaces from
bombing, tomatoes climbing up ruins – trees and shrubs overgrowing
evacuated and empty houses and gardens – in some places shells of

eighteenth-century cottages with black blank windows and Rousseau-like forests enveloping them, straying out over the road – no railings – climbing in windows. Elsewhere the utmost tidiness and care in lines of planting on AA gunsites, aerodromes, fire stations. The parks and squares open to all – all railings gone, shelters overgrown – but now with increasing alerts and bombings in the Midlands some stiffening up of nerves and care of where to sleep.

There is of course very widespread exasperation about the second front – partly political but more unspoken impatience and shame – the more so because the country realizes that it *has* been working hard and sacrificing. Americans everywhere. Absolutely no petrol. Cigarettes and beer better but much more expensive. Food still remarkably good. Vigorous campaign for saving light and fuel.

Continuing at the office – I should say camp – as that's what it's like: miles of uniforms, camouflage & barbed wire. I have been seeing the material which Sid Stone shot in the States: one sequence of trucks driving at night across Broadway & Brooklyn Bridge to the waterfront – very exciting. The lights always romantic and thrilling to us –

I may get a day off before going to Wales & am thinking of going to Cambridge; it's been two years or nearly since I was there and that was in Blitz-time. The famous statue of Newton was sitting encased in sandbags. I remember Kate was still thinking of France and Hugh was still anti-war. Ah well – I hope the backs are as leafy as ever. I remember sitting under the trees with you there once when Mary-Lou was young. But in the end I expect I shan't get there...

I should theoretically be very tired at the end of a picture but I don't think I do – at any rate everybody, including your mother, says how well I'm looking. On the other hand, I have only to lay my head on the pillow to fall fast asleep. I don't think it's work – so much as war: one just hasn't as much energy. Or maybe it's middle-age – but I don't feel middle-aged, on the contrary – younger than ever. There is nothing so exhilarating as seeing even a few ideas one has had coming into being on the screen – [...]

TO CICELY JENNINGS   *26 Lluest,*
10 September 1942   *Ystradgynlais, Swansea*

My darling one

I am writing as you see from the depths of the Western Vallies of Wales, where I shall be I think for most of the next two months: making a mining story. [...]

Your description of the Lexington Avenue apartment being one of our kind of places reminds me – alas – that I was looking at Round Church Street [in Cambridge] for a moment in a day's flying visit a month or so back only to find our home that was destroyed by a bomb the night before ... always a noisy and dusty place you remember!

Down here I am working on a reconstruction of the Lidice story in a mining community – but more important really than that is being close to the community itself and living & working inside it, for what it is everyday. I really never thought to live to see the honest Christian and Communist principles daily acted on as a matter of course by a large number of British – I won't say English – people living together. Not merely honesty, culture, manners, practical socialism, but real love: with passion and tenderness and comradeship & heartiness all combined. From these people one can really understand Cromwell's New Model Army and the defenders of many places at the beginning of the Industrial Revolution. The people here are really Tolstoyan figures – or is it a place where Turgenev's 'Lear of the Steppes' could have taken place –

Well we are photographing them as honestly as possible – neither like *How Green* – too theatrical or *The Grapes of Wrath* – too poverty-stricken. No one seems to have emphasized yet the *double* image of wicked conditions and real zest for life – parallel perhaps to town & country – worker & peasant – hammer & sickle.

[...] I am very well fed – especially down here – where the working-class traditions of warmth & hospitality and too much to eat still hold – but otherwise there is nothing to buy except books – one instinctively now wears one's clothes to rags: I don't smoke cigarettes at all – drink very little, get my haircut half as often and so on. But of course compared to life in Russia we are still having a holiday [...]

TO CICELY JENNINGS   *actually from*
14 November 1942   *Ystradgynlais, Near Swansea*
                                                but still at South Cottage,
                                                     Chorleywood, Herts

My darlings,

A very long silence I am afraid – I have as a matter of fact been ill but am better now and have been in very good hands: combination of abscess from a tooth and general cold in the face and overwork and so on all hastened by working in the coldest and draughtiest places in a coal-mine here. But it is very much better now so don't worry: the people I have been with here the last two months – Dave Hopkins (collier) and his wife have been perfect angels to me. A miner's home is the warmest place in Britain now: here at least there is coal.

Two lovely long letters from the kits unanswered I am afraid. It is terrible how time goes and how work keeps one at it now. Absolutely nonstop in this valley for nearly three months. On this I feel at least however that we have really begun to get close to the men – not just as individuals – as we did in the fire film (which is now about to be shown as a first feature) – but also as a class – with an understanding between us: so they don't feel we are just photographing them as curios or wild animals or 'just for propaganda'.

The Egyptian and Algerian news has certainly bucked people up here – in the sense that it at least looks like the first glimpse of the end of the tunnel. Being down here I really haven't seen a soul and have little idea of what is going on in London – which to me is just an incompetent office-premises.

As you have probably seen, a large number of people – especially archbishops and bankers – have started telling us what the country and even the world is to be like after the war – and many of their suggestions surprisingly 'left' or 'socialis*tic*' – at first glance – but all equally sure that private profit must stay – nationalisation must be avoided and so on. One can only hope that the people will not be bamboozled the ninetieth time.

Have you ever read a Russian novel translated as *Lone White Sail* – do if possible.

The final occupation of France makes one think and look back and hope – no? Fervently hot nights at St Tropez – the cicadas in the brush going up to Petite-Afrique – the wild quarries and white rocks at Cassis – the limitless blue and distant drums of Algiers in the picture-postcard shops at Marseilles – the deep breath of the *pinède* by the morning wayside station, the great hot engine panting, the shadow of the smoke curling across the sand. Curious how some parts of the earth have a 'unified' feeling like the fragments of a broken vase.

Here at this moment – how different and yet also a part with a central motiv of its own: a brilliant afternoon – the wind blowing long low black and white clouds over the hills (the Black Mountains) the white smoke and steam from Tireni pit and the steelworks down the valley steaming across with them. Strong clean winter sun on the washing in hundreds of back-gardens – the chapel standing up white and looking newly washed – the men in blue with white silk scarves and brown shiny shoes squatting on street corners – three lads home 'dirty' from the morning shift almost lying on the pavement waiting for the Neath bus. The children in red woollen hoods coming out of school and walking some of them far up into the hills to little pink-washed farms and lonely cottages. A horse in a front garden. Three geese at the top end of the village. The blacksmith's baby girl with no front teeth – who says 'Hullo Jennings' very aggressively. Dave now back and bathed (he comes home dirty and pops straight into his bath) lying half asleep in front of an anthracite fire. Tonight before turning in Mrs Hopkins will roll back the mat and put out his boots and working clothes before the same fire banked up with cinders – so that they shall be warm to put on at 6 tomorrow morning [. . .]

The pic. Chick [Fowle] and co. were shooting in New York last winter has just had a great success here – which by the way is more than I can say for the Hollywood movies which have been coming over for the last year or so – picture after picture *terrible* – either so slow and dreary – usually adaptations of novels – with all the faults English pictures are supposed to have – or else the flimsiest flag-waving nonsense. Maybe we have become more serious but even so. There has been a really great musical revival in this country in the last year or two – I mean in concert-going – absolutely any night of the week – and all the weekend – choice of really smashing programmes of Haydn, Mozart, Beethoven, Chopin. Really no picture galleries of course. Tremendous book-buying. Luxuries have absolutely disappeared (naturally you can still buy melons at Fortnum's at a guinea a time!) but chocolates, or decent cigarettes, or drinks other than beer or whisky absolutely not. Down here in the country eggs and bacon still appear perhaps twice a week but in London no one would believe that. Transport completely hopeless everywhere. Clothes – well we are managing now by using old ones – but there is a strong feeling that the time will come when clothes bought in the 1930s will be past patching – and the coupon allowance doesn't possibly allow one to catch up.

In the mean time take Mrs Hopkins as an average worker today: she is doing no official war-work – doesn't belong to the WVS or run knitting parties or day any of the things you see in newsreels and *Mrs Miniver* – all she does is this: she gets up at 5 to see her man off to work – his breakfast and collier's box and so on – then she gets up at 8 – then she has her own breakfast and begins shopping and cooking for herself and at least two other families – for Jack's family because he has silicosis and his wife works in munitions – for her brother Len's – because he works in the Seven (Seven Sisters Pit) and his wife is in rooms – then her sister-in-law Nan comes home from night shift from munitions and wants food and sleep. Then lunch for me. Then after lunch Dave comes home – wants bath food and sleep. Then tea for all of us. Then Mary comes in to cook and wash *here*. Then Nan gets up and is off to night shift at 8 (two hours journey there – two hours back – ten hour shift). Then supper and she gets to bed about 11. Fortunately they have no children – some people are doing this with four or five children and/or evacuees!! Then the local authorities announce special priority food cards for people working in factories – Mrs H.'s comment!

At the same time the Wales-England international at Swansea is the most important thing for weeks and Mrs Hopkins and her sister manage to get to Swansea to see *Gone With the Wind* – the Morriston United male Voice choir can still collect 70 men on a Saturday evening to sing Handel's *Sound an Alarm* and to send *All Through the Night* in Welsh go crying and dreaming out along the valleys – a tragic people fundamentally the Welsh ... life in the minor key. In the dark streets now the children are skipping with ropes made of knotted coloured rag – and calling down the hill. At the bottom of the hill runs the river Giedd over huge stones and talks all night. Inside the kettle is singing and Dave and Mrs are playing cards – a peculiar game whose score is written down on the back of Co-Op order forms. Nan is making up her sandwiches for tonight's shift. On the mantlepiece two enormous china dogs stare out at nothing – permanently warm from the tremendous anthracite blaze below them.

Since writing down the above I have learned by frantic phone from London of camera trouble and I have to rush back there by car as soon as possible. Oh dear.

One of these days I hope to be able to sit down quietly for a few weeks and write down a kind of diary or report or something of the past two years and the astonishing things and people I have seen – the surges of ideas, the undertow of disappointment, the waves of nostalgia, the iridescent moments of excitement and clarity. Tomorrow all this will I am sure feel very far away – even further than the years before the war; they will remain a sort of moment of stupidity and reaction – but in the future I think we shall look at the years 1940 onward and wonder why we were so hesitant – why we were only hopeful. [...]

TO MARY-LOU AND CHARLOTTE JENNINGS   *South Cottage,*
18 November 1942   *Chorley Wood, Herts*

My dearest Kits

I am afraid it is months since I wrote to you which is very naughty of me – this moment is really the first little rest for nearly two years and so I am sitting down in the sun to send you a letter. It is cold but very sunny – the rooks are cawing in the trees, rising up in a great cloud and circling round and then settling by their nests again – you know how.

I came back here from Wales two or three days ago after living down there for nearly three months – living and working with the coal-miners, going down into the darkness underground with them and coming back looking like a collier myself and making the bath all black. In the mines it is very dark to begin with but one has a little lamp to see by and after a short time one's eyes get used to it. You can walk for miles and miles underground in a long tunnel called the 'road' before coming to the coal itself.

By the coal where the men are working cutting it out it is often quite hot but very damp too and some men have to work lying on their sides in the wet because the roof is very low. But in the 'roads' it is very cold because of the draught – like the ventilation in the Underground – the 'subway' you call it don't you. So you have to look out you don't catch a cold – I did and was in bed nearly a week. But the miner and his wife that I was staying with were very very kind and soon got me well. They live in a house with only one big room to cook and live in but very cosy and warm – with plenty to eat and everybody very happy and cheerful, although it is not fun being a miner really – they work much harder than anybody else and get paid much less and they are always getting hurt in the mines because of explosions of gas, or the roof falling on top of them. But they keep each other's spirits up and are extremely good and friendly to each other.

I wonder if you are going to be in New York for Christmas – I shall probably be here – it is not much fun going up to London in the winter because the black-out begins so early – about half-past five every day now. Do you have the same now? I am afraid I haven't done much painting the last year or two – one big spotty one of a horse and a picture of London after the Blitz and one or two others but not much. I haven't any time and it is difficult to get painting materials now. Difficult to get clothes too – one thing for working in Wales with the miners, one could wear very old things they way they do – because the coal-dust gets on everything and blackens it. After one has had a bath no matter how hard one has washed there is always a black line round the eyes – so anyone who sees you can tell that you have been 'underground' today...

I expect you hear a great deal about the American soldiers over in Africa now – we see a great deal of them here too – some of them are astonished at London because they had never been to New York or any big city in the States but had lived on farms before they were called up and then came here. Down in Wales there are children who have been evacuated from London and Liverpool who have lived there in the country for two or three years and now speak Welsh perfectly and behave exactly like Welsh children – they get jobs delivering papers and taking the milk round and helping on the farms just like the miners' own children. But I don't know that any of them want to become miners. All round the pits it is very dirty and dismal but away from them in the hills and valleys very beautiful and clean – clean air and clean water running in between the rocks – little waterfalls and deep pools. Trees full of nuts in the autumn and bushes with wonderful blackberries – no wonder the evacuees prefer it to Liverpool. [...]

Radio Talk: *The Silent Village*

[Text taken from a rough transcription of a broadcast on the BBC Home Service, 26 May 1943.]

Well, the story begins exactly a year ago today, on the 10th of June 1942, when the German and Prague radio put out an announcement which ended in the following terms: 'Since the inhabitants of Lidice have flagrantly violated the laws that have been issued,' etc. etc. etc. ... 'the buildings of the locality have been levelled and the name of the community has been obliterated.'

That was in June. Just a month later, I got a typed page of paper with a note on it in the following terms: 'A village in Bohemia: the first draft of a synopsis for a short film on Lidice.' The synopsis begins: 'This is the small village of Lidice somewhere in Czechoslovakia, and this is the village of X in Wales. It is not so long since these two villages were exactly like one another', and then from that the draft develops the idea of a short picture paralleling these two villages and showing the difference in their two fates. This draft came from Mr Fischel [?], a Czech poet in the Czech Ministry of Information. It was brought to me for my comment and I said immediately that I thought it was really one of the most brilliant ideas for a short film that we'd ever come across. This was also the opinion of one or two other people, and the Ministry gave the sanction for preparatory work to be done on the film immediately.

Now the preparatory work on this film, as far as I could see, was bound to be different from that you normally get; for example, it wasn't the faintest good just sharpening a pencil and sitting in an over-heated room somewhere and trying to think something out. After a short discussion we found that the thing to do was to find this village, that is to say, not the village of Lidice but the village of X. We had in our minds X – a village in Wales, and this village we wanted to be an actual village: we didn't want to reconstruct it in the studio and we didn't want to take bits of several villages and put them together. We wanted – as it was explained to me – to find a village in Wales which was predestined to play the part of Lidice, and we proposed to ask for the co-operation of everybody there in the making of this picture: they were to represent Lidice. And I thought that when we had found a village, and we could talk to them and got their ideas on it, then we could start writing the script, but not do it the other way round. So the first problem was to go down to Wales and find this village.

We considered that it might be an important picture from the point of view of Wales as a country and also obviously from the point of view of the miners. So instead of just going down to Wales and looking round in a picturesque tour frame of mind, we decided to go to the South Wales Miners' Federation. This was arranged through Arthur Horner, the President of the South Wales Miners' Federation and he bore out immediately what one or two other people had said to me. Don't go to the Rhondda. Don't go to the well-known industrial part of Wales which everyone connects with [gap in text.] Go to an unknown part of Wales. Go over the mountains into what are called the western valleys. The western valleys are the western end of the Welsh coalfield – the anthracite end of the western coalfield. They're much more Welsh-speaking, they're less industrialized, and they have an agricultural population as well as a mining population, and very strong peasant traditions and roots and so on. Also it's extraordinarily beautiful country.

We went over the top from the Rhondda and down into the western valleys which is absolutely astonishing country, and we said immediately this looks exactly like Czechoslovakia because it has The Black Mountains on one side and the long shallow valleys which run down to [gap in text] and Swansea and so on. And in these valleys there are dotted about little villages, and the pits – unlike the Rhondda – are on the sides of the mountains and even on the tops of the hills, and very often the pits are some distance away from the villages. Now that was very important. because before going I had made some enquiries from the Czech authorities as to what kind of a place Lidice actually was. Lidice, as you gather, was a mining village; but apart from that I was given a very beautiful description of the village of Lidice itself, written by a man in this country who had lived there, and his beautiful and romantic account begins: 'Southwards from [gap in text] leads a road two kilometres long, lined with tall nut-trees. The road slopes down gently into the valley in the hollow of which Lidice was situated.'

So we had to find a valley with a little village situated at the bottom, and it had to have the following characteristics: a village in a hollow; it had to be near a big mining centre with preferably no mine in the village itself; it should have some farming – agricultural work – nearby; it should have a church and a cemetery with a cemetery wall for the shooting scene; it should have a school; it might have a pub near; it should have, if possible, a brook running through the middle of the village or down the valley; it should have rows of miners' cottages and a square; there should be a cinema in the next town; it should have a grocer's shop or a general store where the people could meet; it should have a smithy, and so on.

That appeared to limit our choice. But actually Arthur Horner made a suggestion – not that we should go and look immediately for a particular village, but that we should go and think of it in terms of people. He said, 'Now look, go over into the western valleys – go to a place called Ystrad-glynlais and ask for a man there – a miners' agent – called D.D. Evans. Ystradglynlais is a small town – it's the place where a year or two back Sybil Thorndike played the *Medea* and *Macbeth* with enormous success in front of a miners' audience. It's a place which has always had a tremendous cultural interest and potentialities. It's a place with a photographic club which gives exhibitions; it's a place which has organized a pageant in the last two or three years and so on; and D.D. Evans' – D.D. as we came to know him – 'is the central spirit of all this organization.'

So we went over the hills down into Ystradglynlais and stopped at the corner of the street and said 'Can you tell me where D.D. Evans lives?'

'Oh just up at the top, No. 26.'

We go up to No. 26 and there is D.D. grubbing about in the back of the garden with his potatoes, in his shirt-sleeves. I come up to the front gate and I say: 'Are you D.D. Evans?' He says 'Yes.' And I say: 'Well, I've come from Arthur Horner.' So he said, 'Oh yes, are you the German comrade?' Well that gave me a sort of feeling of international solidarity which is one of the basic things in the picture. Anyhow, D.D. takes us into a little front room which is full of books and the papers connected with his work as a Miners' Agent – the cases of men who have been out of work or who are involved in silicosis or some type of industrial disease or some sort of trouble – and with a portrait of Budenny, the Russian Marshal, as a young man, up on the wall, which had been brought back from Murmansk on a convoy and given to him; and a great mass of lovely books and D.D. sitting on the edge of a chair in his shirt-sleeves and saying, 'Well now, what can I do for you?'

So I spent about ten minutes outlining the idea of the film. D.D.'s a person of great enthusiasm and tremendous physical strength – sort of Tolstoyan figure of a man – used to play rugger for Swansea at one period, and with all the blue in his face that shows that a man has been cutting coal all his life – little bits of coal that fly off and embed themselves in the skin. There hs sits with his face lighting up and saying, 'Yes, well I think we can do that.' So I say, 'Well, the next thing is to find a village.' He said, 'I think if you walk down the valley down towards Swansea' – you can see Swansea from D.D.'s house, actually, about twenty-five miles away, with the smoke drifting up from the pits and the steel rolling mills half-way down; and he said, 'You go down the valley and have a look round. I'm sure there are several villages down there; you're bound to find one which will correspond more or less to your requirements, and then we can discuss it.'

We said 'Thank you very much' and we walked down to the village square and there was a small stationer's. We went to the stationer's to buy some envelopes or a paper or something, and on the side there was one of those little racks with picture postcards which turns round and creaks as you look at them. I had a look and there, among the picture postcards, was one – very, very beautiful; even though picture postcards are usually colourful, this one was a very striking photo of a beautiful little white chapel with a long wall and a little cluster of miners' houses round it, and a little stream, and a hillside in the background, and underneath it, the magic word, the name CWMGIEDD.

So I said to the man in the paper shop: 'Tell me – where is Cwmgiedd?' 'Oh, it's just round the corner – it's only a quarter of a mile away.' You see we were on the edge of the town and this was up in a cul-de-sac. Well, we go down to see Cwmgiedd. You get to Cwmgiedd by crossing over – out of the town, straggly houses and so on – round the corner you come to a coal canal – one of the old canals that they used for getting the coal down to Swansea and Cardiff before the railways came in and there was a bridge over the coal canal; and the coal canal sort of cuts the village off from Ystradglynlais and from the rest of the country. Up in a narrow little valley, there is the village of Cwmgiedd, with a little straight street that goes up into the hills and on each side charming little stone houses, and down the middle, parallel to the street, is a mountain stream that comes running down with a little water in the summer, as we saw it, and then as we got to know it in the autumn and the winter with floods coming down when the snow is on the Black Mountains. And half-way up is a grocer's shop on the right – Tom Powell, Family Grocer – and on the left, a beautiful white Methodist Chapel – the Chapel of Yorath, the name of the original village. Because Cwmgiedd isn't really a village name – Cwmgiedd means the Valley of the turbulent river. It's a very turbulent river running down this valley and this extraordinarily beautiful group of cottages and then the rest of the street going up, beyond the school and so on, up into the farms and mountains, and way, way up into the woods at the top.

And we were, admittedly, knocked pretty silly by the first view and I said: 'Well – I'm sure that a place that has the unity of look that this place has must have a tremendous community spirit. And honestly, silly as it may sound after only being here ten minutes, I'm sure this is the place.' So we took our courage in both hands and went back to D.D. and said: 'Look, I'm sorry, we haven't been away long enough I know, but what about Cwmgiedd?' 'Cwmgiedd?' he said. 'Yes, that's right.' 'Very independent place – strong Welsh-speaking people. [The following lines have been struck out by pen: In the last war, Cwmgiedd was called the neutral country.' So I said 'Why?', and he said, 'Because there was not a man who volunteered. They were all Pacifist.' I said, 'How did that occur?' 'Well, you see, there was a man down there who had great power with the villagers and he was a reader of Tolstoy and Tolstoy was a Pacifist.'] It is a place [deleted: like that] which has a tremendously strong community sense – only a few families. It has a kiosk at the top end of the village which was presented to the villagers for their part in the rescuing of a crew of an RAF plane in 1939. There are stories about the way in which they defended a gypsy who had been prosecuted under the game laws, and that they put up money for his defence and had got him off, actually, and had made the mountains and the woods above the valley, free for everybody instead of being closed. Surprising – with a tremendous sense of liberty and freedom and so on. And the majority of the population are miners; they work in pits which are anything up to ten miles away, up to Ystradglynlais and over the other side in the next valley called the Dylais Valley.' 'Well,' I said to D.D., 'all this is charming and lovely and ideal, but we have after all to get the co-operation and agreement of the people.' 'Oh well,' said D.D., 'that's not difficult – we'll call a public meeting.' I thought, well this is too good to be true, but still I said 'Well look, I'll tell you what we'll do – I want to go back to London and I want to tell them what I'm doing as I don't want to let the thing get completely out of hand – and I'll be back in a day or two and see how we're getting on.'

I go back to town and almost before I'm back, I get a letter from Doctor Fischel at the Czech Ministry of Information saying that he has already had a letter in the following terms: that the village feels deeply honoured at having been chosen to re-enact the splendid story of your people's wonderful resistance etc., on behalf of the Provisional Film Committee, Yours faithfully, D.G. Williams.

Well, I said it was to be a co-operative film, but we felt that as my immediate boss said, 'If you don't go back to Wales, they'll be making a film without you.' So I went back and was just in time to find D.D. Evans handing round the last circular which had been drawn up to invite people to the public meeting: 'It will be necessary to depict the whole life of the village – social, cultural, religious, trade union, political etc.' Well, I needn't quote all that, but we did have on the 21 August 1942, at 6.30 p.m. in the Welfare Hall at Ystradglynlais, a meeting at which about a hundred people were present, representatives and delegates of all the groups of feeling in that part of the world, particularly from the village itself – to hear, as they put it, what was required of them. I explained to them approximately what I was trying to do, what the Ministry wished to do, and what we wanted of them. I said that we were going to be a nuisance; I said we were going to turn their houses up-side-down; that they might think it was going to very exciting to be on the films to begin with, but by the time we had been down there four or five months, they'd begin to regret it.

But, they were very, very sweet about the whole thing – a vote of confidence was taken and a film committee of twelve people was elected. So the thing was put on a democratic basis and if I wanted something or wanted introductions to people, wanted corrections on ideas, help on the script and any other types of co-operative effort, I could go to the appropriate member of the Film Committee and our kin. And then after that, when we started shooting, we had meetings of this committee once or twice a week in the Sunday School at the top end of the village in which I read out to them a sort of report – usually on the current version of the script – and told them what we were doing and asked for criticism. Because there's an important point here: we didn't want the film to be an inch out – to the village, to Wales, to Lidice, to the miners and so on. I said advice, because it's always easy to make a thing with even the best intentions in the world, and you end up by insulting them – representing them as being other than they are.

Then again, we wished to use the cultural bodies and different types of organizations to help us – the scenes at the pit were organized by the Pit Lodge Committee, that is to say the 'Miners' Trade Union'. The school scenes were organized through the school and the Chapel scenes were organized through the Deacon's meetings. And this brings us to the next point which was, of course, that we wished and we did in fact have all the people to play their own parts – not only no actors but to have them be themselves, playing with their own names, their own ages, their own addresses and so on. And that was really quite important because there is one scene, for example, in the film where there is the registration of the people in the village, where they come before the Germans – the 'protecting' power – to give information about themselves. And they co-operated completely on this and described themselves as themselves exactly. In other words, not only were we not having any actors, but it wasn't in fact acting. They were playing themselves and themselves as the people of Lidice – that's to say, making an imaginary transformation of themselves which I must say they did supremely well.

The next point is that we proposed not to show any Germans. Now you may think this is very, very difficult: to make a picture about an occupied country without showing any Germans – but not entirely, because the whole film was to be an imaginative picture and not exactly a realistic picture. We have the documents recorded by the BBC of the announcements and so on made by the Germans to Czechoslovakia, to that part of Czechoslovakia and to the people of Lidice itself. These were transposed into terms of Wales, so that you have an announcement, for example:

As from today, the districts of southern and western Wales stand under the protection of the greater German Reich, and so on. Then it became possible to make the film not simply another horrifying story of a massacre, but a picture of the reaction of the people – not the people of Lidice only, and not of the people of Wales only, but the reaction of people – of ordinary, nice, common people – working-class, warm-hearted people represented by the miners of Cwmgiedd – their reactions to fascism. At the end of the picture, after the people have been represented as being shot – being taken away to the concentration camp and so on – we say: 'Yes, that happened in Lidice – it did not happen in Cwmgiedd.' Well, at the end of the picture, the people of Lidice [*sic*: Cwmgiedd] say what they think about their comrades in Lidice and they say it in a speech which is made by the person who's responsible for all the organization in the making of the film and who, if the Fascists came into Wales, would be the type of person in that area to organize resistance to them – I mean, D.D. Evans, the miners' agent. His last words being: 'The name of the community has not been obliterated; the name of the community has been immortalized; it lives in the hearts of miners the world over,' etc.

[Section cut from transcript here]

Well, there are one or two other points that perhaps should be clear – one is this. We were not asking the people of Cwmgiedd to pretend that they were Czechs – we were not asking the village of Cwmgiedd to be the Czech village of Lidice. We were using Cwmgiedd and the country round it as a country under the 'protection' of the greater German Reich, and this meant that we had to take the story and the incidents of the Nazis in Czechoslovakia and in Lidice and find the equivalents to them in Wales. For example, the Welsh language. Much of the film has been recorded in Welsh – not that the audience is expected to understand it, but it is the sound made by the people who live in the country. To a certain extent it may even suggest that it is Czech, but there are more important things that go with it. One is this: the teaching of Welsh in schools. Now the teaching of Welsh in schools is a matter of very great consequence to the Welsh people: the existence today of the teaching of Welsh to young children is regarded by the Welsh as a conquest of theirs; it is a thing they have insisted on and now have captured. Just as, in Czechoslovakia, one of the first things that was done under the so-called 'protectorate' of Heydrich was the suppression of Czech culture, so in the picture we have shown the suppression of Welsh teaching in schools, but we've also shown that Welsh – precisely because of this – is the language of the underground movement in this film. An illegal newspaper is produced in Welsh. The children speak Welsh when they're playing in the street, even though they're not allowed to do so in school.

Then, a wider point: the guerilla warfare, which is represented in the middle of the picture, takes place as indeed it might in the Black Mountains, in one of the most romantic and historical parts of Wales. For up in the Black Mountains there is a most magnificent and wonderful castle, the castle of Carreg Cennen, an enormous ruin which stands about 300 foot up the top of a valley and from which you can see practically down to Swansea. This we've used in the picture as the centre of the HQ of the guerilla resistance. There were many things like that that we found when we got down there and which we obviously couldn't have thought up by ourselves in London. This brings me to the next point, which is that we were down in Cwmgiedd and in those valleys from August until January: we came down in the marvellous weather, with leaves on the trees and bright sunlight, and we left in the middle of snow and rain and floods and so on. We saw the village and we saw the people in every kind of mood. There are no hotels of any kind there; we – the whole unit, up to twelve or thirteen people – lived in the miners' cottages and lived with them. And I think that on both sides it was a great success because, for example, some of our chaps from the Unit – one of the electricians and one of the camera men – were allowed to bring their wives and families down to live with the miners' wives and families, and I think that those people were genuinely sorry to see us go.

That might just sound sentimental or silly, but in fact it has a great deal to do with the making of the picture. Because when it came to directing the people, when it came to getting into the hearts of their feelings – remember that this story of shooting men and taking away children from their mothers, taking away men from their womenfolk in Lidice, when you get right down to that moment in it, it is a tremendous human, tragic story and it would have been impossible to portray that without our having something more than the confidence of the people down there. It was necessary to be able to ask them searching questions about how they would behave under those circumstances, and I think that was really only possible because we lived with them for a long time and were welcome – more than welcome – in their homes and houses, and tried to understand their point of view. And the result was that we were able to portray not only what life in Wales is like at the present moment, but what life – their lives, reactions would be like if they were placed in the situation that the people of Lidice were placed in.

There are one or two other points. One is the representation of the Germans. I've said that we didn't actually show any Germans; we show one or two tin hats, a swastika, a loudspeaker, things of that kind. But the main feeling of oppression, the existence of the invisible Germans, is carried in the film by a German speaker; sometimes he's speaking on a loudspeaker, sometimes from radio sets, and so on – one voice. We used for this purpose the original documents but – this is an important point – these documents are perfectly accurately monitored and they do say the most astonishing and hair-raising things; we have not invented any of them. They will announce, for example, the shooting of half a dozen people higher up the valley – then in the same breath make an appeal for the German Red Cross.

Now, that which occurs in the picture is perfectly genuine and it was done through the help of anti-Nazi refugees in this country who know the mentality of the Nazis and the mentality of Nazi propaganda. So in this picture you see not only the reconstruction of the Lidice story, but also the clash of two types of culture: the ancient, Welsh, liberty-loving culture which has been going on in those valleys way, way back into the days of King Arthur and beyond, still alive in the Welsh language and in the trad-itions of the valleys; and this new-fangled, loudspeaker, blaring culture invented by Dr Goebbels and his satellites. And it's through the clash of these two cultures that the mechanism of the film, so to speak, is pre-sented and not simply as a blood-and-thunder story of some people marching into a village.

Expenses Invoice, November 1942

Statement of clothes totally lost or spoilt during location work – 1942

Note: I have been working on location on two films – *I Was a Fireman* and *Lidice* for nine out of the eleven months of this year. Both these productions were distinguished by the dirtiest locations imaginable – i.e. the docks during a blitz fire and a Welsh coal-mine both below and above ground. In both cases the dirt and smoke and fire were part of the story and were treated in the most realistic way possible.

It would not be in any way an exaggeration to say that the following clothes have been totally lost as a result of the above work.

One pair of walking shoes (value £2.10)
One good suit (value £6.6.)
At least three pairs of socks (these get ruined particularly when wearing wellingtons – value approx 3/6 per pair)
One pair of flannel trousers (value £2.2.)

Also spoilt with tar, fire etc – but now repaired – one overcoat (value £8.8)

The above would definitely not have been lost and spoilt but for work on location.

(signed) Director 24.11.42
H. Jennings

1943

*at the Etoile,
Charlotte Street, London*

My darling Pip,

When your cable arrived I had a letter for you in my pocket which I have now torn up and re-write. Oh, the confusion of the last six weeks – but I think it is all straight now and I can give you some account of it. The trouble began about three weeks before Christmas over the Fire Service film – which although adored by almost everybody did not go down well with the commercial distributors – at least that was the story. They said it was too long and slow and so on. Quite likely from their point of view they were correct. In that case there was a little recutting to be done and that would be that. But no. All sorts of people – official and otherwise who had not had the courage to speak out before suddenly discovered that that was what they had thought all along – that the picture was *much* too long and slow and that really instead of its being the finest picture we had produced (which was the general opinion till then) it was a hopeless muddle which could only be 'saved' by being cut right down and so on. Well, of course one expects that from spineless well-known modern novelists and poets who have somehow got into the propaganda business – who have no technical knowledge and no sense of solidarity or moral courage. But worse – the opinion of people at Pinewood began to change – Ian of all people suddenly demanded what amounted to a massacre of the film – all this arising out of the criticisms of one or two people in Wardour Street – who had other irons in the fire anyway and who fight every inch against us trespassing on what they pretend is their field. In the meantime [C.A.] Lejeune of the *Observer* had seen it and said it was easily the finest documentary ever made and that to touch it would be like cutting up Beethoven! Well, at the time I was in bed in Wales with a swollen face trying to get the Lidice picture finished and trying to keep it from being dirtied by this mixture which was brewing in London. Needless to say Mac (McAllister my cutter) and most of the Unit were on my side – but it was not pleasant having a real battle with Ian with whom I was living and who has been so exceptionally good to me and whom really I trusted implicitly. Add to that Mac was ill too and much more bad tempered than me even! All of us overworked and tired of the picture by then anyway. Then I was due in any case to leave Chorleywood as you know. Well, for some time it looked as though the only thing to do was to get out of the unit – particularly as there were other pieces of stupidity (or so they seemed to me) which were letting pass. But against that there was the fate of the Lidice picture – by now far more important to me than the Fire one – and important not just to me or to the unit but for the miners in South Wales and as a real handshake with the working-class which we have not achieved before. Further there was money and the eternal problem of uniform or not and so on. That was why I found it at the time impossible to answer your queries about future money – well, after a really desperate fortnight or so round Christmas I had to go back to Wales for some final shots and I went down feeling very sick at heart and as we came into our beloved valleys and villages there it really was nauseating to compare the two Nations (as Disraeli called them) and to feel that precisely what had happened to the Fire Film was only too likely to happen to the Lidice one – if not worse. Well obviously I could not go on with the people down there without mentioning the situation to them – as we have always been absolutely frank as between ourselves and I have no wish to delude them in any way. So I had a day or two previously written a short account of the situation to Dai in Wales, asking particularly for his advice. He after all has been fighting these battles with the bosses for the last twenty-five years. I came into his house I remember about three weeks ago – and found he was out but had left a letter for me replying to my queries. The most astonishing and magnificent document. Talk about the culture and understanding of the working-class:

'As miners we have known this from experience for the best part of a century. We have seen the product of our labour produced in the most haphazard manner, lending to the miner no desire to develop pride of craft. We have seen mother earth hitting back at us with relentless precision, killing and maiming a small army of men in a few years. The result is that we have no interest in the final outcome of our collective labours, but rather in the standard of life we are able to wrench from our masters. Whilst our very work develops in us a grandeur seldom found in men in other industries, our beings are completely divorced from the product – coal.

'Not so in your industry. You not only work for wages or salaries – you produce a thing that can express your own personalities. You have a very deep interest in the final product of your collective labours, but in the main the ideas of one or at the outside two individuals, hence your strong personal feeling when that work is to be mutilated, and Mac's strong objections to doing the mauling of your creative effort... This frustration is no new thing. You will find it in every aspect of the productive, social and aesthetic relations in this society. What of the thousands of scientific workers that meet it at every corner. What of the hundreds of artists that meet it in the same way. In fact every man meets it in some form or other in his particular mode of expressing himself. Strangely enough, the people that grow most in stature are those that meet it on the greatest number of occasions. Therefore, Humphrey, whatever your intensity of feelings on the matter you should not leave Pinewood. You would only be leaving the scene of battle...it is quite possible that Directors will endeavour to cut out altogether films that tend to show this old world as it is, but despite their heavy hand of censorship, men will express their creative ability, just as working-class women make miniature palaces of hovels...'

And so on – as you see a tremendous letter from an outstanding man. Well apart from settling my own personal problems it settled the problems of agreement with the people down there. So we took up again the battle of the Fire picture – got a certain amount more sense out of people and ultimately have got a sort of minimum re-cut which is at least not the massacre it was before. This is in the last three weeks during which I have managed to get flu. On coming back from Wales I should have started to look for a flat – but there are only twenty-four hours a day and two other sorts of work have also re-appeared on the horizon so I had the idea of seeing whether Madame had any room back here at the Etoile – which astonishingly enough, she had: no more expensive than ever and the same service. [...]

In Wales we had snow – the snow on the hills looks very much like snow on hills everywhere – but snow on a coalmine – in the smoke and black dust – the men with black faces and white boots: what a vision ! Well, the flu is a bit better and I am managing to tackle the cutting of the Lidice picture and also voluminous write-ups of the story of making the picture in Wales for the English and Russian press and elsewhere – which is really an excellent idea of somebody's. Then I have got out again as a result of talking to Dai the material assembled years back on the Industrial Revolution [i.e. *Pandaemonium*] and he has asked me to go down to the Swansea valley and give a series of talks to the miners on poetry and the Industrial Rev. which really is a golden opportunity – so doing some work on that I have got as far once again of thinking of it as a book and looking for a publisher and so on. Masses of new material – but again no time or very little. However, Ford was over the other day and gave a really sensible talk I thought on the propaganda situation in America – although the films mentioned by him as some sort of successes (including *Listen to Britain*) quite belied his recipes for what films should contain. Better to stick to one's hunches I suspect. [...]

TO IAN DALRYMPLE
[No date]

c/o The Etoile,
Charlotte Street, London W1

Dear Ian,

Let us get it straight for goodness' sake. I confess to being discouraged, but I do not want it to take the form of being ungrateful or disgruntled or just bad-tempered. I know very well that you have many more things to criticise, and justly, in my performance during the last two years than I have in yours – and what is more it is not my business to criticise. So please let me apologise for any unhappiness and worse that I have caused you, and please try to excuse any particularly gross pieces of rudeness you may remember against me. I owe you in the office and Megan at South Cottage more than I can thank you for – more than you are aware of I think – but I am not good at saying thank you and worse still at giving any formulated explanation of behaviour – I am afraid I just tend to 'disappear' when it comes to it. But I do thank you both very very sincerely for all that you have done for me – all the more so as it was all the time so utterly disinterested and direct. As regards film you gave me I know tremendous backing and freedom – and I suppose it was so unexpected that I came to take it for granted and when I seemed not to get it disappointed me with equal intensity. Quite illogical I know but perhaps excusable. However, whatever the origins of the feeling I do sense that something has snapped in our understanding and I have learnt that that kind of thing is usually my fault. I have also learnt that it is not much good trying to be someone other than oneself – so I suppose it is up to me to try and find a way out. In the meantime Ian, please try and put up with me and I will try and be reasonable.

Yours very sincerely,
Humphrey.

TO CICELY JENNINGS
29 March 1943

The Etoile,
Charlotte Street, London W1

[...] In the meantime all kinds of things happening here: to begin with I have actually managed to sell the book [*Pandaemonium*] to Routledge – through Herbert Read – Agreement all signed and delivered. To come out in the early Autumn. Really very good terms. Second, the famous or notorious fire picture – now called *Fires Were Started* – has at last reached the screen – and (no doubt to the amazement of the timid officials in charge) has received honestly a tremendous press. Which – vanity apart – is extremely useful. Anyway it's playing in two West End cinemas at the moment. [...]

Lidice – I mean the Welsh film – is going fine to date. The book really going to be something & we are all *so* looking forward to seeing you, my darlings.

Oh I also had the privilege – because that's what it is – of going down to Wales – to the villages we have been working in – and giving them readings from the book – which went down astonishingly well. With an invite to come back. After the press show of *Fires Were Started* we all went down to the pub in Stepney which had been our Head-quarters last year – with great success – very sweet people – but so they all are everywhere once the barriers are down.

How really delicious MaryLou's letter & poems: I think when you come back you will be surprised at the *drive* in things here and nothing *now* I think could be better for the kits to lap up. No doubt the antique pessimism still huddles in smoky corners in Chelsea and even Birmingham but I don't come across it any more. To meet as I did [the writer] John Davenport rather drunk a week or two back was really like a ghost at noonday – and just as fleeting. [...]

TO MARY-LOU, CHARLOTTE AND CICELY JENNINGS   *Hotel Etoile*
24 May 1943   *Charlotte Street, London W.1.*

My dearest sweet children,

[...] the Welsh mining film is done and I am going down to the miners' village on Thursday to show it to them before anyone else sees it. Then I am supposed to have a day or two's holiday but I have my book about machines to finish and I think I shall work on that – there is masses of typing to do: clean copy without mistakes! I am still living very comfortably here – in a little top bedroom surrounded with books. I am also supposed to begin at once on a new film, a very exciting subject which I will tell you later when it is all settled. So I have plenty to do. I wonder have any of you seen the Firemen's film yet? It was a great success here in the end, after waiting about for months and months. [...]

I am feeling especially well and happy and energetic – at the moment everything seems to be going very well – people say I look thin but I think I always did. Someone said yesterday – 'Do you direct films – you look too thin for that – you look like an assistant!' I suppose directors are always supposed to be fat like cooks. We have had a few air-raids lately – on clear moonlight nights – but nothing much: a tremendous noise from our guns banging but very few bombs. From making my book I have collected here all sorts of funny books about machines and about English history – which I shall keep so when Marylou has done with the Greek gods and goddesses and the Chinese emperors and philosophers she can learn about the English inventors who had even more wisdom than Minerva and cheated even worse than Juno. I have also been thinking of doing some more painting but it is difficult to fit it all in with work and fire-watching and home-guarding and all!

Darling Pip – [...] The Lidice picture – called *The Silent Village* – is now finished passed sold etc. without any cuts or horrors I am glad to say – coming on in London about June 10-16. I am supposed to be broadcasting about it in the Home Service June 10. Welsh première tomorrow in the village where we were working. Everybody seems very happy about it. New pic. already lined up. [...]

Life in general pretty hardworking but full of excitements and promise. Dal has been full of help on *The Silent Village* and very sweet in many ways. My relations with the Ministry etc. seem to have improved almost out of recognition. Have also been elected to rank-and-file production committee at Pinewood – so there is real hope of getting people to work together. [...]

TO CICELY JENNINGS   *as from: Crown Film Unit,*
26 June 1943   *Pinewood Studios, Iver Heath, Bucks*

My darling Pip,

You will by this time have received a very scrappy letter addressed to the children and nothing else for weeks: this for official reasons which will appear later. [...] Since writing, the Welsh-Czech mining film – finally called *The Silent Village* – has had a pretty successful presentation. Amazingly enough no trouble in the final stages with ministries and suchlike. Mr Edgar Anstey of course does not like it but the miners themselves do, including Arthur Horner himself who wrote the most flattering review of it – really much nicer than anything from the critics. We had a 'world-première' (so-called) in the village itself and spent a blindingly moving final week-end in the Swansea valley: really, I think, achieving the thing long-wished-for – that of showing the people on the screen to the same people themselves – and being able to say 'Look we have done it for you' – 'We have not betrayed you' and getting their real agreement to this. Difficult to say goodbye to this mixture of coal-dust and clean brass – warm hearts and grim faces. Very kind words from Cav. on this picture. There is a copy at the British Library – hope you may see it. Also radio version to America by the BBC. [...]

The book has been advancing very well but rather slowly: I feel I am really beginning to get a sense of British history, specially the history of

science: ideas started in queer corners like Papa's book of mediaeval science and Charles's [Charles Madge] books on Darwin. [...] Papa I have
seen again: he seems to have begun working again for the Bloises and has
been turning out their family records going back to 11 or 1200! What a
country! Have been re-reading Homer – tell Marylou. Also some naval
history mostly about the East Coast in the days when Yarmouth & Dun-
wich & Harwich were great ports. Today only the same sounds & the sea
on the stones. [...]

TO 'PROF. PITMAN'   A L'Etoile,
[i.e. Allen Hutt, Night Editor of the   30 Charlotte Street
Daily Worker and historian of newspaper design]
Sunday [no date]

Dear Professor,
   A line a propos the review in Our Time – first of all it is too much – but
beyond that can I convey to you my thanks, not for the personal write-up
but for two things: 1. Because Allen you are really the one person from
whom such statements are precious in this country (Professor Jennings
has after all also had his eye on looking up for many years) 2. Even more
important the surge of comradeship that comes from this final meeting of
intellectual and worker. It was to begin with – do I have to tell you – the
greatest privilege as well as pleasure to work with the people in Wales; it
was the greatest ratification of hopes and promises to have their acceptance of the thing finished – both at the Cwmgiedd show and in Horner's
article. I wonder if they realize what that means to one of the artist tribe
– so long, all of us, in ivory towers. Now your words complete the circle
of intellectual – workers – intellectual and take the energy latent in one little film towards the future. You talk about moving to action – but that is
what their acceptance and your words do. Sorry to be so pompous, but so
moved. [...]
   ... it is going to be necessary in the next years to build up film units not
from a reshuffle of the 1920s (including self) but from youth.
   Becoming pompous again so will stop. With deepest thanks Allen
                                                          fraternally,
                                                          Humphrey.

In July, Jennings began to make notes for a possible film about the history of the Royal Marines, but his research was interrupted by a 'special
mission' to film the invasion of Sicily. Jennings's unit shot commando
training exercises in Scotland before joining the Sicilian expedition.

TO CICELY JENNINGS   *Etoile,*
3 September   *Charlotte Street, London W1*

My darling Pip,

A long letter after so many gaps and silences. To begin with, most of the time I have been away from the country – going out with the expedition to Sicily. Away in the wilds, first living with a Commando unit, and then going out in convoy, the Mediterranean sun (surprisingly one felt) just as it always was, then watching the landings – the first at night and then by day, and then returning again by sea, via Algiers and Oran and Gib. Some Focke-Wulfs on the way back and a few bombs but otherwise nothing – and except for submarine scares nothing at all on the way out. Very exciting really, and prodigiously skilful – really and truly thousands of ships coming up through the narrows to the Sicilian coast – keeping their time and station to a matter of minutes – watching even the moon set just before the landing craft were dropped!

The chaps themselves – the unit we (Jonah and I) were with were really tremendous. Young and on their toes – not at all the popular conception of Commandos as roughnecks. The officers principally ex-intellectuals – a landscape-painter, a writer, a man with the Oxford Book in his pocket – chaps extraordinarily like the old GPO boys. The imagination of the type said seriously to be better when it comes to it than the military order-obeying mind, the men violently anti-propaganda ('flannel' they call it). Small wiry fellows mostly, with very strong unit-sense. Everyone including Brigadier under 40 – mostly under 30.

We ourselves had a really lazy time apart from going on exercises. The food first-class. The stomach turned-up a bit by anti-malaria doping. Came back with the hair white and the face brown and as strong as a horse. We did some pretty good shooting I think – but as ever the most exciting and moving stuff quite unphotographable – as the night landing itself (very dangerous, as it had been blowing a gale all day and the sea was swamping landing-craft) as the last night in port – the chaps singing 'Goodbye ladies' and – astonishingly enough – 'Who killed cock-robin?' and a miraculous little song beginning 'Ohhhh! the little humming bird...' Then the church parade held simultaneously by the whole convoy – including lessons from the Revelation – the vision of the White Horse. As someone remarked afterwards – 'the chaps who come out of all this the best are the Elizabethans.'

I hope by now you have been shown either *Fires* or *The Silent Village.* I met Frank Capra the other day who was very enthusiastic about *Silent Village* and *Listen to Britain.* But I gather the distribution of our stuff in the States is just a joke. It isn't exactly a picnic here. The Trade has now decided off its own bat that people don't like War films and that the time is now right for the old pre-war doping to re-commence. However.

I saw Cav. the other day who was asking very sweetly after you. I am sure the kits had a lovely time: I wonder if you have had any holiday yourself? I have also been up in Suffolk on a job – Bury and Diss. Incredibly beautiful country still. I have also been reading about it in the 18th cent. for my book which got rather held up by the Sicilian trip – but resumes now. Bury was a stronghold of resistance to the manufacturers and poor-law Commissioners and other miseries of then. Really knowing something about its history and seeing it in place after ten years (it is) of town and machine life, makes Suffolk a great deal more human and less landscape than it used to be, if you remember.

I don't know if I told you Dal. had left the unit to go back to work for Korda. I suppose he knows what he's doing – but I can't say the effect on the unit has been very brilliant. Jack Holmes is now 'in charge' which is the right word as he is hardly a producer. There are dozens of people organizing and beaurocratizing [sic] and accounting and fussing around inside a huge machine but totally without reference to production. Not a good situation and I doubt if the group will survive it. Seriously, the old GPO group and sense has practically disappeared – the whole thing has become too big and too mechanized and official and actually less efficient. I wonder very much what to do and think of resigning at least once a week. Theoretically I have nothing to complain of – certainly nothing they can understand. It is a pity – a great pity – the unit has been a remarkable institution – a really democratic and anti-beaurocratic group with great influence and still greater possibilities – but it needs a Dal or a Cav or a Grierson to lead it. Then again as the war becomes clearer so do the true colours of the people in it and particularly the people with whom one has been collaborating. Ah well...

I am sending you some photos and magazines with *Silent Village* pictures under their own cover.

I myself very tired (work on script of new film) but pretty gay – dominated really everybody is here by the thought of the future – what is going to happen? Both personally and generally. [...]

I am still under the roof at the Etoile – very cluttered up with books but very comfy and well looked after. We took a packet of bombing in London once upon a time – but at the end of the four years we are extraordinarily lucky – compared to anywhere in Europe itself. What happens in German (and Italian) cities I do not like to imagine. I suppose we shall sort it out sometime. Do not, dearest, in the next year as things get confused and rougher, forget me or let me get further away: the confidence we have got must be there when the fighting stops – sententious as that may sound.

No, but I say that because England has you will find, changed a great deal: not so much any one person is different but the young coming up are pretty determined – and people in general if they have the same character have had a good think. The man and woman in the particular job – the ploughman and the coal-cutter and the commando are very definite as to what was wrong five years ago. The present resilience of Russia – the sheer performance – from Stalingrad to Kharkov and beyond has had an effect I think even greater on us than the original heroic resistance and scorched earth. We ourselves were good at taking a beating. But with all due respect to our great 8th Army – the dazzling Russian advances of this summer: done by mere sheer military means – invoking neither winter nor mud nor snow nor heat not terrain nor poor allies nor internal collapse – but by the art of war – this has really opened our mouths. I do not think it has been sufficiently appreciated publicly – but in our hearts we know now that not only have the Russians saved us from the Nazis, but also that they are beating them for us all. I hope and trust we shall not forget.

My reading (midnight and after) has been mostly Cobbett and Arthur Young – who came from near Bury in Suffolk: *The Annals of Agriculture* and other writings on the decay of the English peasant. I find great numbers of good East Anglians moved from Suffolk and Norfolk and Essex to America and especially Canada not only in the 17th Century but also in the 19th – under disgusting new Poor Laws – people from villages I know to what are now towns that you have seen and been near. [...]

This is a restless time in England – combined wish to let up a bit after the African successes and the four years of it – and to get on with it before another winter is upon us. [...]

> The Royal Marines film was never completed. In October, Jennings began work on a film about 'Lili Marlene', the popular German song which had been adopted by the Eighth Army. The commentary for this film was read by Jennings's friend from the Perse School Cambridge, the actor Marius Goring.

'LILI MARLENE'
Final version of Marius Goring's Commentary
13 December 1943

1. (Opening shot of film – Marius Goring in front of map)
'Lili Marlene' is the name of a song. The story of 'Lili Marlene' is really a modern fairy story. Only it's a true story as well.

In the homes of Britain today, people are already hanging up trophies and souvenirs of the Second World War. But among them there is one trophy which you will only find in the homes of the Eighth Army – the disc of the German song of 'Lili Marlene'. *This* trophy was captured in the Libyan desert in the autumn of 1942...

2.   (On the scene of the souvenirs on the wall, and the sound of the German disc.)
      ...But the history of 'Lili Marlene' takes us back to the year 1923, to the time when the men of the Eighth Army were still children...

3.   (Children playing on captured guns)
      These captured German guns commemorate the devotion to duty and the achievements of those who fought for their country in the Great War of 1914-1918.

4.   1923 was the year in which Hitler began to persuade the German people that the German army had never lost the First World War and it was in 1923 also that there occurred in Hamburg the birth of Lili Marlene.
      (Now follows interview with German Refugee leading to the writing of the words of the song.)

5.   That was in 1937. The music was written the next year, in 1938 – about the time when the Nazis marched into Austria. (Similar interview with German musician and sequence of Lale Andersen singing the song.)

6.   In the autumn of 1940 after the fall of France, the Germans formed the famous Afrika Korps. It had its own battle song: 'Tanks over Africa'. 'Lili Marlene' and Lale Anderson were still unknown. Their first real appearance was in the spring of 1941.

7.   In that spring the schools of London were re-opening after the winter blitz and in Germany Hitler was planning an easy conquest of Yugoslavia. Then at the last minute the Yugoslavs began to resist and Hitler lost his temper and ordered the destruction of Belgrade...

8.   ...Among the first Nazis to arrive in Belgrade was a so-called Propaganda Kompanie consisting of war correspondents, newsreel cameramen and particularly radio engineers. The German bombers had contrived to leave the Belgrade radio station more or less untouched. The Nazis' idea was to use it as a Deutchensoldatensender – a radio station for programmes for the German troops. But first of all they had to be sure who was in charge of the station – patriot

guerillas or the fifth column? The Propaganda Kompanie had
tommy-guns issued to it as well as radio apparatus...

9.   ...Fifth column: But even with their help there was a rush to get
going. There were no lights but the station had its own power for
transmission. Just before leaving for Belgrade someone had packed
up some gramophone records. They might come in useful.

10.   From the first moment 'Lili Marlene' was a smash hit with the
German troops. From Africa, from the occupied countries, from
the U-boats, they wrote in asking about that song with the girl and
the lantern and the sentry. And this enthusiasm was immediately
exploited to build a programme round the song – a Messages from
Home programme for the troops at the front – a programme
moreover extremely useful at the moment, as in the same month,
June 1942, the Nazis had begun the invasion of the USSR.

11.   Night after night at 8.40 the record of 'Lili Marlene' was broadcast
to the German troops. Not just once a week, but every night at 8.40.
(Mixing to scene of BBC engineers recording the song on wax. No
dialogue.)
It had other listeners too. Listeners in Britain. People to whom the
famous song was just one more piece of enemy propaganda to be
taken down and analysed in sober quiet. The BBC.

12.   And the singer? The little Swedish night club girl? What had
become of her? While the Nazis battered at Moscow and retook
Benghazi and besieged Tobruk, she had become a national figure
touring the home towns of Germany.

13.   But on July 4th 1942, the Eighth Army held the line at El Alamein,
and it was here that Dennis Johnstone of the BBC found our men
also listening to Lale Anderson. (Dennis Johnstone's dialogue and
scene as in original script.)

14.   (A farm in the Highlands. A cottage in Wales. A newspaper shop
in the London Docks.)
Home...home...home. It's a funny thing the way the Germans
of all people are sentimental about home. But they forget other
people have homes too – the Eighth Army, the Russians, the
oppressed peoples of Europe – they all have homes. We will see
whose home thoughts serve them best.

15.   (The Battle of El Alamein)
Rommel has not taken Alexandria. The Afrika Korps is in retreat.

The Italian infantry – the Trieste Division among them – has been
cut off and surrounded – but it is still singing 'Lili Marlene'.

16.   (The Battle of Stalingrad)
Von Paulus surrendered before Stalingrad on the 2nd February
1943. That night the German radio announced a three-day closing
of all entertainments, theatres, and variety halls and the tune of
'Lili Marlene' which had been played for five hundred consecutive
nights by the Belgrade radio was stilled into silence.

17.   The next day, the 3rd of February, something even more astonishing happened. From a neutral country there came word that Lale
Andersen was in a concentration camp. She had been sending
messages home – to Sweden: 'All I want to do is to get out of this
terrible country . . .'
      Now was the BBC's moment. Now it was their turn to broadcast
a message from Lili Marlene to the German forces. To send the
tune *back* to Germany – but with new words and a new singer: the
famous German actress Lucie Mannheim. (Lucie Mannheim
sequence)

18.   But that is not the end of the story of 'Lili Marlene'.
(There follows an interview with a Canadian about the increased
popularity of 'Lili Marlene' in the Mediterranean and the way the
Eighth Army are using it as an actual marching song)

19.   I told you it was like a fairy story. 'Lili Marlene' was born in the
docks in Hamburg, and then she went to Berlin and then flew to
Belgrade, and was sent to the desert and was captured; and then
she was transformed and marched with the armies of liberation
into the heart of Europe.

20.   How will the story end? I think it will end as it began with the
dockside hurdy-gurdy.
      I think that when the blackout is lifted and the lights of London
are re-lit and the shining domes of Stalingrad have been rebuilt,
then the true people and the real joys of life will come into their
own again. And the famous tune of 'Lili Marlene' will linger in
the hearts of the Eighth Army as a trophy of victory and as a
souvenir of the last war – to remind us all to sweep Fascism off
the face of the earth and to make it really the Last War.

TO CICELY JENNINGS   *The Etoile,*
30 December 1943   *30 Charlotte Street, London*

[...] There has been pretty good confusion and trouble at the Unit – and
I have been slogging to re-arrange my position completely – which I think
will come off – only it has muddled my money situation for the moment.
I have of course had flu – and have also been up to the eyes in *Lili Marlene*
– current picture which we have just finished shooting. Also I was contemplating moving – partly for more space and partly to save money –
only you know what a move is – and of course transport of trying to get
anything done or bought or made now is hopeless. All this sounds depressing I am afraid but is not really. Just a bit muddled. I myself am very well
now and full of energy and ideas. [...]

Here – confusions and stupidities apart – I have I think begun to make
a real impression and hope very much to do two things – to assist in putting the *British* cinema a little more on its feet – and to give you and the
kits a real chance financially. I can just see that in the distance – and will
have to watch like mad that it does not slip away. It is difficult I think to
know at what moment one should sit tight and just work at whatever is in
front of one and when one should take a long chance and break out into
something new – or go and get some totally different experience – as one
would in the States – ideally combine the two.

This is all very abstract I know – but for the present it is very difficult
to think of anything definite or clear . . . I feel so long as I am learning and
you are not too dependent on others and the children are geting a good
schooling – that is as much as one can hope for. When the moment comes
a big switch over may be possible. In all this Ian has and is being the
greatest possible help. The work on *Lili Marlene* (the song of the Eighth
Army) has been greater than I expected when we started on the film in
October . . . and has really kept me up night and day for three months . . . I
have been working without a producer and very much on my own (except
for Chick [Fowle, Jennings's cameraman] – thank goodness) and have felt
rather out of my depth – with professional actors and so forth and a very
theatrical story. The book still staggers on – but too slowly really. I need
a 48-hour day or two pairs of eyes or hands or something.

All the same, for the first time in all this I have begun to feel like having
something to say – both in print and on film – instead of being merely a
reporter. The work on the book has opened my eyes very wide about history and the reception of *Silent Village* has made me think inevitably about
personal style and ideas and so on. One gets to the moment of having if
possible to *be* something more than *promising* –

Then again, I want very much to be someone for the kits to come back to – who really is someone – and not in a vulgar way – but you know I often used to feel about my parents and indeed their generation – well they always might have been something terrific and didn't really manage it and were got down by the world and this – at least to my idealism of those days and even of now – seemed a wretched compromise and disappointing and disheartening. We must I feel – without being blinded by the lights – try and be really successful – really good at our work – and that will be the finest model for them – otherwise we are just talking at them like all parents and then they will have to go through the whole school themselves again...

Again very abstract I am afraid – but for a so-called intellectual really to do his own work and feed and clothe his family and make good in the ordinary sense and really work *in* the world in a common sense way and marry all these together – without writing book reviews for the *New Statesman* – well [it] has never really been done yet – and it would be something to do it I think.

The *Lili Marlene* story is a true one about a German song which the desert Army picked up from the German radio at El Alamein and made their own and took over. We have reconstructed the history of the song going back practically to the last war and ending the film in the future – the song is the hero of the story – mixture of actors and real people – dialogue partly in German partly in English. Have been working with Marius among other people.

Here of course everything is full of the Invasion (whenever) – Christmas was I think very happy everywhere – but the winter – the English winter has been at its most deadly...flu and cold and misery – that wet penetrating cold so typical – the food system still remarkable. A little time back people gave the impression of being very tired – now they are just as tired probably – but have decided not to mention it or something – or maybe they can begin to see the end and feel better.

It has been really very encouraging to see the N.Y. press-cuttings on *Silent Village* & *Listen to Britain*: minority criticisms certainly – but very warm-hearted & understanding & on the whole more intelligent than the (good) press-notices here. Thank you so much for sending them – others I have seen through the Ministry. I hope you did *not* see the American potted version of *Fires* – of which they sent back a copy to us some months back & which really is disgraceful – even the stupidest people here thought so. [...]

1944

TO CICELY JENNINGS   *8 Regent's Park Terrace,*
16 January 1944   *London N.W.*

My darling Pip,

Note the new address – actually I am not at the time of writing 'in' – but I shall be in the next fortnight. It is the ground floor of a lovely 18th century house taken by Allen Hutt and he is letting me have three rooms. I have got some of the furniture from Downshire Hill [E.L.T: Mesens's house] & moved the books and things from the Etoile and from Pinewood. O the horrors of moving – but it is mostly done now. [. . .]

I am really delighted you like the photo – I thought it was fairly good considering how difficult I am to photograph anyway and everybody here liked it. I certainly have felt most of the time as you say young & more like my original self: actually I think I rely much less on other people now & have learnt by sheer necessity to prowl round on my own as I used to at Cambridge when we first met – only without the social 'malaise' of those days and without feeling too alone. Much better at talking to people & seeing their point of view – more tolerant. [. . .]

TO CICELY JENNINGS   *8 Regent's Park Terrace,*
14 February 1944   *London N.W.*

[. . .] My film-life has been or is being completely re-organized – I hope to be able to say fully how next letter – and finance will be a great deal easier. I am so glad you liked the photo – Lee Miller also has taken some of me which I have not seen – for *Vogue* of all things – they should be good though. [. . .]

I was up at Cambridge for 24 hours a week or so back – principally trying to get a rest from Pinewood which to me at least is a complete madhouse. I have had the normal second or February dose of flu and have been absolutely dead beat at the end of *Lili Marlene* which in any case I don't think is a good picture – but that can't be helped. . . I am now trying to go a little slower. Cambridge was I thought dismal and no help to the over-ticking brain. [. . .]

Met up with a grand man from NY two or three weeks back – Marc Blitzstein – the playwright and composer – had long talks about New York and London and films and all . . . but a really lovely person. A little uncertain what he is up to here or at least he had a nice crack: *It depends on the General see – one General says 'Symphonies is O.K.' – another General says 'Latrines is O.K.'* . . .

Put my head yesterday into a Bond Street picture Gallery – Redfern or something – O dear what has happened to my eyes – or is it the pictures or the times or what – found I couldn't bear anything – not only not bear the pictures (admittedly only Matthew Smith – Sickert – Rouault – Braque) but couldn't really stomach the idea at all. Yet I love the few Old Masters – Velasquez – Renoir – or Quentin Massys which they hang in a corner of the National Gallery every so often... at the same time I have found myself reading *Manhattan Transfer* [John Dos Passos, 1925] with great pleasure. I don't know...

The Americans here I find really a bit much in the mass standing on street corners chewing – but individually they never fail to be charming and original – and what a delicious dry sense of humour – met a man yesterday looking of all things for *Yardleys*... bored – bored with not getting on with the war and over with the war: *'I wanna LIVE see... here I am marching up and down saluting people I don' even know!'*

Very happy you liked the calendars – I found a similar one for your mother with a bunch of flowers and one for Papa with a map of Suffolk... Papa is extraordinary – when I was down there at Christmas he said would I like to look through some old papers up in the attic – you know any house of Papa's has an attic with papers – so I had a look and of course found a complete set of uncut large paper Cotman etchings and lithographs of Norfolk and Yorkshire churches – terrific stuff – then I had to make Papa promise not to have them cut or bound or stuck...

As you see I was interrupted – but the sun has come out and it is a nice warm day for a change.

How curious you should mention that muff of yours of 1930 – I was describing it to someone only the other day and saying what difficulty you had getting it made – I remember it and the coat with it so well – I even looked up Bradwell's Yard the other day at Cambridge – just the same – builders' yard and all... only the buildings don't have that childhood shine on them that I think they had then. I suppose one always has at least one Castle Perilous that one carries about – chock-full of romance – today for me I suppose the London docks – somewhere between the Tower and Wapping... where the streets still smell of cinnamon and the piano plays in the pubs on Saturday nights.

What a contrast to the shiny – unbelievably efficient – still luxurious American magazines I have lying in front of me... two worlds.

Ah well – in time we will unite the two. [...]

In March, Jennings was seconded from the Crown Film Unit to the independent production company Two Cities to write a treatment and script for a documentary which he had proposed to them in January.

Proposal for 'Two Cities'

There is a subject for a film to be made by Two Cities which, to my surprise, seems to have escaped everybody, a film of the two cities themselves – London and New York – living simultaneously through twenty-four hours.

There have been quite a number of films about the life of a single city. They have usually been vivid, symphonic or generalized studies, but there is no doubt that it was found difficult to get drama into them without bringing in a story in an unnatural way. But to make a film about two cities and give each of these cities its representative (its ambassador, so to speak) in the other one, and any human story that you like to play around with each of these characters will appear perfectly natural. [...]

It would be a picture of propaganda for humanity. Remember that we love people not only for their likeness to us but also for their differences. [...]

Do not mistake this paper. What I have suggested here is an idea only, with suggestions for background for the story. A month's work with an American writer will bring to the foreground the four main characters and their adventures. These however must be related to the background and grow out of everyday life. People have often asked for the fusion of the realistic school of film-making with the fictional. Here it is. A small group of actors in the foreground and the vast double canvas of the two great cities beyond them.

[*13 January 1944*]

TO CICELY JENNINGS   *8 Regent's Park Terrace*
12 May 1944   *London N.W.1.*

[...] At the moment I have been allowed by the MOI to take up a one picture contract with *Two Cities* for which I am being reasonably well paid ... although with the income tax as it is it is easy to reach a ceiling of what you can actually receive ... the picture in question is as I write very undecided ... but I have been paid for an original idea and for three months of script writing ... hence the money.

Regent's Park is a great success ... it is a couple of great white 18th cent. rooms very bare in themselves ... I have got the writing bureau from Hampstead and some book-cases and chairs and table and bed ... and *all* my books from various sources and all the pictures which are not at Duns Tew so I am pretty well ensconced ... I have a delicious drawing of Marylou's on the wall and some 18th cent. industrial engravings with it. Regent's Park Terrace is just by the Primrose Hill railway cutting – rather noisy at times but extremely romantic...it is in a private road with trees back and front and endless birds – particularly now. It is a minute from the park itself (near the Zoo end) and a couple of minutes from the working-class area of Camden Town...the rooms are on the ground floor and get morning and afternoon sun in the summer and suit me fine... [...]

I have been working with a grand New York chap on this script... name of Marc Blitzstein...maybe you know of.

You can't think how lovely it is to have all my books and papers and paintings together in a house of my own again...makes me long to have you all back more than any other thing I think. I have even begun to think about painting again. There a terribly few you haven't seen but nice ones I feel. And the old ones seem to wear well. More poems than paintings. [...]

Sunday I was lucky to be able to see US Army Theatre Unit perform *Our Town*...Sergeant Sweet who has made a great film hit here playing the lead...a really astonishing performance...the play for some reason is not allowed to be acted out of the States except by special permission like this. Now it is being performed by the Army for the army – no ordinary public admitted. Great pity – it is terrific American propaganda – indeed I had the impression that we liked it better than their chaps. There was a film made of it some years back I gather which I never saw and which sounds mad as the whole point of the play is that there is no scenery and that it is everybody's home town and not a particular one. However, Sweet is a grand person...a lanky slow-moving Sergeant-Clerk from Ohio... father a minister...has developed a great weakness for listening to the Hyde Park Orators – particularly the more idealist ones. Actually looks and talks as one imagines Lincoln in youth (remember Henry Fonda?) a peculiar kind of belief in life which in any case I think most Americans have and most of us haven't got...something to do with 'opportunity'. I have been seeing a great deal of the Americans here of all sorts and am more and more impressed. Anyone in England will tell you that the 'Yanks' collectively are a pain in the neck...but question them closer and you will always get the answer that of course the actual individuals whom anyone has met or seen something of are 'charming...charming'. They have a curious combination of (on their own admission) not being grown up and at the same time being better informed than we are...clearly different education. Basically they give me the impression of not being afraid of anything...I suspect we have a bogey inside us about *they* – meaning an indefinite figure of power represented by 'the authorities' 'the government' 'the boss'...from centuries of struggle with it...and being gotten down. The American is still confident that *he* runs America. So Margaret Mead in her book on the American character... given me by Morris Ernst the NY lawyer whom I met over here for a short session. [...]

TO CICELY JENNINGS   *8 Regent's Park Terrace,*
9 June 1944   *London N.W.1.*

[...] The invasion was I think taken here with 'customary British phlegm' ...but I must say the BBC seems to be doing a first-class job. As for the Jerries – either the All-Highest has something very special under his trenchcoat or they just can't take it [...] ...have been working hard at my book and also a little painting... it has become clearer (the painting I mean), less tricky I think but not yet being 40 I suppose one can't be considered to have begun... at least that is what the Pundits used to say... the *Vogue* article came out but copies were so limited even I didn't get one or haven't so far...but I am trying to get copies of Lee's photos anyway which everybody thinks pretty hot. Allen [Hutt] has also been writing some stuff about me (that looks pretty awful), mostly I gather about Suffolk as he also comes from there. It was he who wrote the Prof. Pitman article on *Silent Village* – I agree with you that the end didn't quite click but I think they were crazy just cutting it off like that – makes the film meaningless... or at least pointless... but there – film-making is a pilgrimage and a 'supplice'... a propos the Academy is open again (after being Blitzed early on) and runs excellent old-type programmes – such as *Les Bas Fonds* (Jean Gabin) and Kline's *Forgotten Village*...the mind turns more and more I think to the old simple cinema we loved together...[...]

TO CICELY JENNINGS   *8 Regent's Park Terrace,*
20 August 1944   *London N.W.1*

My darling love,
    I have I know been very bad – even worse than usual – about writing lately – but history or rather Gen. Patton's tanks have been outstripping work and thoughts and plans and all. First let me thank you from the depths of my heart for your very sweet letter about *Marlene*: here it has been very popular in the cinemas, particularly in working-class ones (and got or is getting good distribution) – Caroline Lejeune gave it a crackingly good notice but everybody else including many 'intelligent' friends of mine sat hard on it and complained – between them – of almost everything in it. They have for years criticized me for being high-brow and over

people's heads – now the fault is apparently the opposite. I confess to being upset, particularly as when we finished making it I was tired out and could not 'see' it any longer and was prone to think them right. The people who like it – like it enormously: ordinary simple & charming people mostly: American soldiers, policemen, charwomen I know of. Also a nice note from my mother.

The famous flying bombs or 'doodlebugs' continue but not too badly: I at any rate have got used to them now & manage to sleep through night alerts. They are not really like air-raids – because either they hit you or they don't – & that's all there is to it. So far nothing worse than windows blown out. [. . .]

Well, the *Two Cities* plan ended up with our finishing script only (very good one I think) and my returning to Pinewood: where I have been since July 1: and where I have been given more responsibility for actual super-vision than before & have had to work even harder than ever. But the unit has recovered a great deal of its lost fire and enthusiasm and I am enjoying being back enormously which I would never have thought. I am beginning also a new picture of my own in the next week or two. [. . .]

I have also been working like a nigger at my book – still alas – far from going to the publishers – but without the old fears: H.J. much more confi-dent and grown-up I think than he used to be. I hope so at any rate. [. . .]

It is still very pleasant here (at No. 8) – Allen very kind and good to me. I have really a great number of good & sweet people whom I know who have helped me in one way or another through the camping-out – as it has been really – of the last few years. Now at any rate I have some order in my books & papers & have even (in the depths of the night) got round to some painting – only materials are terribly short – specially brushes. Allen's books on social history & politics fit in very well with mine on sci-ence & industry & poetry & between us we have an encyclopaedic house-ful. [. . .]

Location work on *A Diary for Timothy* began in the autumn. The follow-ing is a transcription of rough, hand-written notes made by Jennings in a grey notebook.

A DIARY FOR TIMOTHY

Dark waves fill the screen: the sea before dawn –
On the wall the BBC signal light flashes –
The face of Frederick Allen turns to the microphone: 'Good morning everybody – this is the seven o'clock news for Sunday September 3rd,

read by Frederick Allen. The fifth anniversary of our entry into the war sees the Germans retreating in the South, the East and the West...'

Big Ben in silhouette

The first flare of the sun on the Thames

The shining face of the Sphinx on the Embankment listening also as Allen's voice continues –

Now the voice spreads out over the country this bright September morning

- along trim little streets
- among V1 wreckage
- out across the fen levels where the wind ruffles the water, past the cathedral towers, the turning windmill, the new pumping station

to be drowned by the roar of Forts and Lancasters wheeling overhead.

As people are going to church the hands of Big Ben touch eleven o'clock – the exact anniversary hour.

Do you remember that same moment – from the same Big Ben – on Sunday September 3rd 1939: 'I am speaking to you from No. 10 Downing Street...this country is at war with Germany...for it is evil things we are fighting against...but in the end I am certain the right will prevail...'

and today challenging the tired voice from the past comes the wail of the new-born babe – as the camera swings across the row of cots to the pillow of TIMOTHY JAMES JENKINS, the hero of our picture, born today September 3rd 1943.

[page torn from notebook]

On her pillow Tim's mother lies dreaming. Father an RAMC sergeant out in West Africa.

Tim opens his eyes and blinks – of the work & worry, of the grandeur & beauty of the world he knows as yet nothing –

Of the roar of town traffic and the clamour of country markets – nothing –

Of that good soul filling her buckets at the pump and that farmer fretting over his harvest – nothing –

Nothing of history either:

of the American invasion of Britain

of that convoy leaving for the far east

of the newsreels of the liberation of Paris

of the latest Hamlet questioning the first gravedigger: 'Why was he sent to England?' 'Why because [he] was mad...'

>of the milk-bar rumours of V2: 'Tom says it's a kind of flying
>refrigerator – come down and freeze everybody...'
>of all this, nothing.

He has never tasted the blackout or seen the Londoners sheltering from
V1 in the Tubes.

But all this is the world which he inherits: whose people – whether they
know it or not – are working for him, helpless as he lies in his cot:

>the airman, peering through the perspex windscreen
>the engine driver leaning out of his cab
>the farmer looking over the years accounts
>the actor holding up Yorick's skull: 'I knew him, Horatio...a
>fellow of infinite jest...'
>the miner combing the coal dust out of his hair.

Tim will have his individual place in the world, as they have. What is it
to be?

*

Tim and his mother came home from the nursing home on September 17.
This was the anniversary of the Battle of Britain. It was also the day of the
Arnhem airborne landing, dramatically announced at three o'clock in the
afternoon. The weather was still fine, the winter far away, V1 nearly
defeated, the allies on the borders of Germany and no reason at all why
the war shouldn't be over by Christmas...It was moreover to be the first
night of the dim-out. For weeks previously the street lamps of Britain have
been cleaned & tested for a modified 'lights-up'. Tonight it would not be
necessary to put a blackout on the window unless the siren went – only
curtains.

Tim safe in the country is having his first bath in his real home – from the
nursery wall his father's photo looks down on the skinny soapy figure.

The farmer's children have their eyes fixed on the screen of the home-
cinema. *Their* father is commentating his 16mm pictures of the farm's war
history; what was for centuries marshland and fen has in five years been
made to produce food.

The sun sets. In London the engine-driver and his wife are listening to the
radio version of *Dr Jekyll and Mr Hyde*. It was a nervous evening – people
were sure *he* would try something! Mrs Enginedriver pulls the curtains to,
and as she does so, the siren goes. 'What did I say?' On the radio Mrs
Hyde's victim is singing 'The Last Rose of Summer':

> I'll not leave thee thou lone one,
>   to pine on the stem;
>   Since the lovely are sleeping,
>   go thou sleep with them...

Mrs Enginedriver puts up the blackout once again, and once again towards London comes the familiar drone of the flying bomb. Engine-driver & wife stand up & listen. Mr Hyde is approaching his victim. The bomb cuts out. The human pair are under the table. Mr Hyde's hands are around the victim's throat. Then crash! 'Pretty close!' they smile weakly. And as they crawl out from under the table the smug voice of the announcer says; 'That was the second instalment of the radio version of *Dr Jekyll and Mr Hyde.*'

And with that episode began the English winter.

Now the low sun stretches out the shadow of the engine chuffing towards Crewe: hauling a long train of box-carriages through the autumn landscape.

Now the same sunlight just touches the black chimney stack of the pithead where the surface-workers are sorting the coal on the screens. Coal, the head of Industry.

In the fens the black earth is being thrown up by the deep-furrow plough: and the farmer's eyes search for an outcrop of the clay that lies underneath.

Searching the earth even more patiently, much more dangerously, are the sappers with mine-detectors – yes in Britain too – searching *our* fields & beaches for the mines we laid down in 1940. These soldiers are also fighting for peace.

And Tim's mother is searching too: searching in official figures and tables for the exact demobilisation number of Tim's father:

> When was he born?
> When was he called up?
> When will he be demobbed?
> What is his group number?

Then the news breaks; the miner coming off nightshift finds the evacuation of Arnhem in the headlines – Arnhem. The radio takes up. Groups listen to the war-report. Tim's mother. Mrs Enginedriver. The farmer. Faces transfixed in the night by the war report.

[Fragment ends here]

1945

Work on *A Diary for Timothy* continued until the late spring of 1945.
Jennings was then assigned to make *A Defeated People,* about the state
of Germany under the Military Government.

TO CICELY JENNINGS   *War Correspondents' Mess, 5 PRS,*
1 Sept [1945]   *British Army of the Rhine*

My darling family,
    This is a combined letter to you all three to tell you I got here safely –
'here' is a place called Herford in the middle of Germany – and that we are
very well looked after and very hard at work. [...]
    Well I have been quite overwhelmed by Germany in the past few days
and can't really say anything sensible yet – it is quite unlike anything one
has been told or thought – both more alive and more dead. I think I will
keep the long descriptions for when I am home – I shall have seen more
by then. We had the simplest and nicest plane journey and have been
given every help and facility here: and I can say already that our chaps –
'The Army of the Rhine' as they are all now called – are doing miraculous
work in running the country and specially in giving the Germans an example of how to behave. That really is so. There is of course much too much
to photograph – ugly and beautiful – life and death – one can only choose
bits and hope they are the right ones. I have never had to record a *people*
or a country before. Of course really it's impossible – specially as so many
things really don't seem to make sense: one can only go on looking at them
until they do. I have working with me besides our boys an Army Film Unit
Lieutenant who was at Belsen and did most of the films shot there: exceptionally nice chap.
    So far the weather has been poorish. The food good. Only one is con-
tinually surprised by the simple things one sees that no one told us of.
Well darlings I hope the moves and the travels and transplantings are not
too much of a slog. (I was this afternoon photographing a German family
piling all their goods & chattels into a railway van and then getting into it
themselves...)
    Monday we are going down to the Rhine itself and I will write again
from there – [...]

TO CICELY JENNINGS   *As from War Correspondents' Mess, 5PRS,*
[undated]   *British Army of the Rhine*

My darling PIP

It is Sunday Afternoon or late teatime and I am sitting down to what you will see is a 'liberated' German typewriter in the Park Hotel, Dusseldorf, and the end of a week's rushed work in the Ruhr. This is the main Mess of MILGOV HQ (Military Government Headquarters) in the Rhineland – we have been attached here this week and are going back to the address above tomorrow or Tuesday. I am still unable to give any sort of reliable picture of Germany – even of the bits (Cologne, Essen, Hannover, Hamm) which we have seen – for the moment the contradictions are too great. At lunch-time today we were photographing a family cooking their lunch on campfires in dixies on the blitzed main stair-case of the Palace of Justice at Cologne – one of the few buildings still standing in the centre of the city – outside apparently deserted – surrounded by miles of rubble and weed-covered craters – but inside voices, cries of children and the smell of drifting wood-smoke – of burnt paper – the sound of people smashing up doors and windows to light fires in the corridors – the smoke itself drifting into side-rooms still littered with legal documents – finally adding to the blue haze in front of the cathedral. The cathedral now with all the damage round immensely tall – a vast blue and unsafe spirit ready to crumble upon the tiny black figures in the street below – permanent figures: Cologne's Black Market – a 13-carat gold nibbed fountain pen for 40 cigarettes dropping to 20... and then returning to Dusseldorf – much less knocked about – blitzed but not actually destroyed like Cologne and Essen and Aachen – still a beautiful city, returning here to tea we met sailing through the park-like streets a mass of white-Sunday-frocked German school children standing tightly together on an Army truck and singing at the tops of their voices as they are rushed through the empty streets (where?) the inevitable chorus – 'Lili Marlene'. In Essen they still fetch their water from stand-pipes and firehose in the streets and the sewers rush roaring and stinking open to the eye and the nose – seep into blitzed houses into cellars where people still live. Look down a deserted street which has a winding path only trodden in the rubble – above the shapes of windows and balconies lean and threaten – below by the front-door now choked with bricks you will see scrawled in chalk 'IM KEELER WOHNEN...' and the names of the families who have taken over the underground passages where there is no light (or once I saw one bulb crawling with bees – they too must live through this winter in Essen) no water – no gas – a ray of daylight from the pavement level airhole – and down here they have brought a cooking stove which has a flue of its own whose wisp of smoke indicates to the stranger that there is life still in this city – beds (very clean – all the clothes and linen exceptionally clean – washed mostly in the street at the water-points) – and a few bits of furniture. The Life Force is certainly strong. Then again there are country towns and villages and farmsteads that look as if they have never heard of war – the evening queue for the cinema, the haymaking in the orange sunlight – the soft sweep of the Weser through the Westphalian Gap... once no doubt Germany was a beautiful country and still remembers it on summer evenings in the country. For the people themselves they are willing enough or servile enough or friendly enough according to your philosophy of History and the German problem. They certainly don't behave guilty or beaten. They have their old fatalism to fall back on: 'Kaput' says the housewife finding the street water pipe not working... and then looks down the street and says 'Kaput... alles ist kaput.'

Everything's smashed... how right – but absolutely no suggestion that it might be their fault – her fault. 'Why' asks another woman fetching water 'Why do you not help us?' 'You' being us. At the same time nothing is clearer straight away than that we cannot – must not leave them to stew in their own juice... well anyway it's a hell of a tangle. For ourselves we have superlative co-operation and facilities and some real enthusiasm from the MilGov characters here. It is much too much of a rush and very liable to be a superficial runaround. The film material is just on every street corner and every station platform (returning empty coal-trucks full of passengers... returning Wehrmacht, ex-evacuees, Displaced Persons, and people who just live on the stations as they did in the London tubes and move from place to place when the Police get tough) – but getting even a small percentage really on to film... ah well.

Then again there is here the Dusseldorf Symphony Orchestra run by the Oberburgomeister which shows that not only Beethoven survives Fascism and War and Famine and all (which we knew) but also the capacity and the wish to play Beethoven... or perhaps the two are unconnected since the playing was encouraged by the Nazis or what? difficult points... at any rate we are encouraging it and at the same time quite rightly arresting the ex-Nazi orchestral players however good as players. We have by the way with us one Lt Martin Wilson – Army Film Unit and ex-documentary film maker who was the first photographer in Belsen concentration camp and took most of the famous film pictures there and who has been all through the last German campaign and a great deal of the desert and Italian fighting. He is our 'conducting officer' and is really terrific. For this job the ideal assistant director. [...]

I found under the jeep outside the Essendorf Hotel Essen where we were scrounging lunch the other day a great purple coloured moth caterpillar – not quite the same as the green and purple one we found on the hedge at Ponds' [Pond's Manor, Clavering, Essex, which the Jennings family rented for six months in early 1945, and from where Jennings and his wife worked for the Labour Party during the General Election campaign] you remember before I left … but just as exciting and beautiful. We and one or two straggly Germans who had come up for the eternal cigarettes gaped at it and then I took it across the road and once again dumped it in the hedge. Essen curiously enough although the most heavily bombed town outside Berlin is very green … has hedges and trees and weeping willows growing finely in between the ruins and up and down what were once streets … so it has its caterpillars just as Cologne which is a real grey ruin has not trees or caterpillars but rabbits … I suppose there were some who survived the bombing and the fighting and being left to themselves really started increasing – now I believe they are quite a menace as in Australia. The Life Force again. (Which is no doubt what keeps Beethoven being played.) […]

TO CICELY JENNINGS   *c/o* PRS BAOR, *Germany*
Sunday 30 September [1945]

My darling

A drizzling Sunday in Hamburg – the lake opposite the Hotel Atlantic where we are, a grey-white sheet – no meeting line between water and sky. But until today the weather has been pretty good. It was a lovely day when I flew over – leaving at 5 or 6 in the morning – landing in icy cold sunshine on the airfield here – how different and superior to Croydon. Since then we have been up the Elbe and seen the U-boat pens and the blitzed U-boat assembly lines – down into the still-used air raid shelters – used for people who have no houses – into a superlative concert by the Hamburg Philharmonic, playing Beethoven's Choral Symphony – meeting Cavalcanti, on his way back to England from making a film near here – meeting Lale Andersen, the original 'Lili Marlene' who lives here and is appearing in a show.

Have I think been getting nearer the problem of the German character and nation – and a grey, dust-swept character it is: seeing, watching, working with the Germans en masse – terrified, rabbit-eyed, over-willing, too-friendly, without an inch of what we call character among a thousand. Purely biological problem – almost every attribute that we strive to make grow, cultivate, has been bred or burnt out of them, exiled, thrown into gas-chambers, frightened, until you have a nation of near-zombies with all the parts of human beings but really no soul – no oneness of personality to hold the parts together and shine out of the eyes. The eyes indeed are the worst the most telltale part – no shine, often no focus – the mouth drawn down with overwork and over-determination – to do what? Terrified of the Russians – cringing to us. Certainly there is a difference between the SS or the Nazi party in the sense that these are the dupes of those. Yes they can laugh and cry and do almost every thing that so called normal humans can and do – yet there is that something missing – helpless now, untrustful of any thing most of all themselves – precisely not 'The Triumph of the Will'.

In a day or two we shall go back to the Ruhr – do about a week's work there and return to England and Tilty Hill [the house at Duton's Hill near Dunmow, Essex, where the Jennings family lived during the winter of 1945-46] some fortnight from now. How is the house? I hope the artistic temperament [probably a reference to the painter John Armstrong, who owned the house, and to his paintings, which Jennings disliked] or whatever it is, is not too troubling – and the move not too difficult. I am really longing to get down there. I had a word with Allen before leaving and we are agreed on a plan for shutting up most of my part of no. 8 – which fits in their plans perfectly. And the kits? Cavalcanti was asking sweetly after you all. Has just got a house on Blackheath – on the heath itself. Very gay and friendly here.

The Belsen trials are going on at Luneberg – not far from here – so there are the most extraordinary array of international journalists, lawyers, interpreters etc. in and out of this hotel – well-known Russian playwright – Chinese war correspondent – French girl war correspondent of *La Voix de Paris* – a Norwegian who has himself been in a concentration camp for 18 months – Jewish Commando Intelligence Officers – American newsreel cameramen – all in addition to our own Military and Naval and MILGOV personnel – and today an outpouring of UNRRA speaking all languages – and weaving in and out of the United Nations the German waiters – 'the dwarfs' as we call them – scurrying like Black Beetles – listening apparently for the crack of the whip – pathetic and beastly...

Food and drink here pretty good – hot water rare – boot-cleaning poor: this part of Hamburg – the old town by the lake relatively untouched – still beautiful on a fine day – the more industrial parts towards the shipyards flat – really flat – the devastated spaces sometimes cleared for an enormous 'bunker' – concrete air raid shelter – looking like a nightmare German mediaeval castle – but extraordinarily strong and round it a cluster of chicken houses apparently with stones to stop the roof blowing off – in which people are living.

Well love and kisses to you all dearest – I don't think I shall be so long now. Take care of yourselves.

Your loving   Humphrey

My dearest love,

A long gap I am afraid since I last wrote at Hamburg. [...]

At Hamburg we did extra good work I think but then some of our transport was (quite unreasonably) taken from us and some things from England have been delayed and so we have been working rather slowly and
disjointedly in the last week or so. However I had an enthusiastic and
heart-warming letter from Basil Wright yesterday about the rushes and
we are now pulling ourselves together for the last few days' slog. At present progress we should finish here in a week's time – i.e. about Monday
the 22nd (I think it is). We should actually get home during that week
unless delayed by transport. Exciting as it is here I am really longing to be
back now. Impressions of Germany deepen I suppose every day – one
adds things: a conference of secondary schoolteachers – a talk with an ex-
Hitler Youth kid at Julich – unable to make up his mind whether to declare
war on us, America or Czechoslovakia! A really delightful lunchtime visit
to Luneberg on a superbly sunny Sunday – the only town in Germany so
far without a filthy smell – absolutely untouched: grand Vermeerlike
houses and courtyards – curved brick pillars and wildly painted coats of
arms – deep cellars and clattering staircases: another world...

It is beginning to get cold here – long avenues of trees leading to the
French and Belgian borders are being cut down for fire wood – hillsides
stripped and the fragments gathered up as though they were food. Julich
Aachen Duren – the places where the armies spent last winter – what a
desert: a place that has been fought in you can tell from one that has been
bombed – I was going to say *just* bombed – Julich has still endless strands
of American telegraph-field telephone wire layed over and under the ruins
– it really has not one house undamaged or even mildly damaged – but it
has 4000 odd inhabitants – who put on their best on a Sunday – the girls
with white rolled near-football stockings and plaits in white silk bows.

Then I have attended a British Military Government Court – the Judge
a Wing Commander in uniform – dealing with theft and curfew breaking
and false statements and so on – very well handled. We are back in the
mess (Park Hotel) where we were on our first visit to the Ruhr a month
ago – extraordinarily comfortable – with excellent drinks and food and hot
water and countless little German waiters ('Dusseldwarfs') longing to be
ordered about – I must say after two or three hours on straight roads towards
Aachen in an open Jeep one needs all of them. Military Government has
quite rightly taken over the best of everything and keeps up – particularly
I think here – a very polished turnout and manner – simultaneously strong

and 'correct' – the only trouble seems to be that the Germans are really incapable of doing anything *for themselves* – so long as someone is there to give them orders well and good. Only our job is to make them capable of behaving sensibly without instructions from us – at least otherwise we shall be here indefinitely...

Martin Wilson and Gamage continue to be pillars of wisdom and good work. Martin ran his jeep into a 15 cwt the other day but came out untouched. Fred (Gamage) was quite rightly pretty pleased to be told by Basil that the rushes reminded him of early Pabst pictures. Of course the whole set-up looks back again and again to the 1920s.

The country – I mean England – appears from the belated papers – nearly all Kemsley productions – which ones sees here – to be standing on its head in gloom and confusion – I dare say all rubbish. And of course all the fault of the Russians. [...]

... remarkable how pro-English being abroad makes one – at least being abroad in Germany. [...]

It is now a quarter to nine at night and astonishingly enough (as Martin is not going to play the piano – which he does exceedingly well – as Mr Ewer of the *Herald* God save us – is entertaining a party in the bar and I have learnt to avoid war correspondents and to dislike intensely being taken for one myself) I am going to bed... the German bed cover consists not of sheets and blankets but of a single kind of washable quilt – the blankets inside the sheets so to speak – which is sensible but rather hot. We are parked in the 'bridal suite' at this one-time hotel – and spread ourselves over two rooms and a bathroom. Tomorrow we photograph the German people watching the Welsh Division changing Guard outside the Stahlhof (the Steelhouse Milgov HQ)... now I go to find an envelope... [...]

1946

In March 1946 Jennings went to Workington, Cumberland, to direct
a film about the modernization of the mining industry for the Crown
Film Unit; it was completed by the autumn, and released in 1947 as *The
Cumberland Story.*

TO CICELY JENNINGS   *Commercial Hotel,*
7 April [1946]   *Workington*

[...] The food here is dreadful – there is absolutely no decent hotel for
miles – the ones in the Lakes are too far off – but as my mother used to
say – we all 'look very well on it'. However there is plenty of Guinness
from Dublin and plenty of pipe tobacco (!) and so far I am managing not
to get too tired or irritable... at least I don't think so. [...] Was up at 4
a.m. this morning and yesterday morning. Must get some sleep – we have
a night session tomorrow – dance sequence – [...]

TO CICELY JENNINGS   *Commercial Hotel,*
[undated: late April? 1946]   *Workington*

[...] The weather here is appalling – [...] As far as we can we are doing all
right. A bit slow. [...] By the way I discovered when I got back to town
that *Timothy* was actually playing at the London Pavilion – without the
Ministry knowing anything about it – if you can believe that. It was a week
ahead of supposed release date – but they knew nothing of dates anyway!
Ah well –
    We had a car stolen last night and so are in rather a flap this morning...
[...] Outside it is grey and rainy and very cold. When we were doing
interiors we had cracking sun of course – now we could really do with it.
[...]

In the Birthday Honours List of 18 June 1946, 'Frank Humphrey Sinkler
Jennings Esq., Director, Crown Film Unit, Ministry of Information'
was admitted to the Order of the British Empire. For accepting the honour, Jennings was expelled from the International Surrealist Movement.

TO CICELY JENNINGS   *at the New Crown Hotel,*
[postmarked 3 July 1946]   *Workington*

[...] We have been unendingly busy – and are all really tired out – I am
longing for a few days rest with you. I think we shall just stick it out – but
only just. Things are going quite well I think – it's just we are working
against time. [...]

At the moment I am really just getting up, working and falling asleep
every day. There is always a period like this in a film – at least in a big one.
The food continues to be very good at this new hotel – so that's something. The weather has been extraordinary – gales, thunderstorms, driving rain, moments of intense heat. Sometimes the wet running down
through the roof of our 'coal mine' making it even more realistic.

Everyone has been very charming about the Honours List I must say –
the Unit seems to realize it included them. [...]

> Once the post-production of *The Cumberland Story* had been finished,
> Jennings left the Crown Film Unit and joined Ian Dalrymple's new pro-
> duction company Wessex Films. Among the projects he began to
> develop in his early months at Wessex were a documentary based on
> R.J. Cruikshank's study of the years from 1846-1946, *Roaring Century*,
> and films of two novels: Hardy's *Far From the Madding Crowd*, and H.E.
> Bates's *The Purple Plain*, about the struggles of an airman shot down in
> the Burmese jungle. In February 1947, Jennings set off to Burma on a
> reconnaissance trip with a small unit.

1947

TO CICELY JENNINGS
1 March

c/o F.W. Benton,
Public Relations Department,
Government of Burma, Rangoon

[...] Our relations with the Burmese have been first class so far – but whatever the outcome of this trip there is no possibility for many reasons of our doing any shooting here for at least 15 months from now – if then – so you needn't worry about my disappearing. I have written this to Ian Dalrymple suggesting that in this way, whatever the final decision on Burma I could make his 19th century film [*Roaring Century*] on returning. [...]

TO CICELY JENNINGS
6 March 1947

c/o Department of Public Relations,
Government of Burma,
22 Phayre Street, Rangoon

[...] I enclose a semi-realistic description of what we saw out in the wilds of the delta about 70 miles from here. I often write detailed or poetic descriptions of scenes here as a kind of photography or painting to bring back. A propos your remark about technicolour I had already sent a note to Alex Shaw seriously saying any picture here must be shot in colour – which was one of the reasons why I told you there was no hope of beginning anything in under 15 months. [...]

TO CICELY JENNINGS
25 March [1947]

c/o the Department of Public Relations,
Government of Burma,
22 Phayre Street, Rangoon

[...] There are two very definite types of British out here – (1) the adventurous soldiers – an Irish colonel of the Chin Rifles called Flanagan who spoke Chin to all his own officers – or the present Governor who was on Mountbatten's staff – or come to that Mountbatten himself who as far as one can see is almost solely responsible for the relative quietness of Burma (I mean compared to Indo-China) – this type speaks the language, mixes with the Burmese and everybody is businesslike and straightforward. He has nothing to be dishonest about.

Then (2) there is still a percentage of old-world Administrators – super Civil Servants who would be intolerable in England and are doubly so here

– even when they are graciously condescending to 'Johnny Burman'. They spend their time informing us that 'ah but it's different out here' and always have nasty little tales about Burmese individuals. The *Passage to India* mentality but applied to a small, cultured, sensitive people, with an acute perception of manners and motives. Of course the result has been disastrous. The Burmese have (compared to us) a peculiarly classless society and (compared to India) an extraordinary religious unity. Anyway there's no stopping them now, which is something. In a year's time there won't be any British administrators to speak of. [...]

> Incidentally, Jennings pinned his hopes on Aung San, leader of the
> AFPFL, who was elected PM in April 1947 but assassinated shortly
> afterwards. Jennings returned to England in June, Wessex was never to
> make *The Purple Plain*, though the American director Robert Parrish
> filmed a version of the novel in 1954, starring Gregory Peck.

Day Report

The weekend of Sunday 17 August 1947

It had been hot – heat-wave hot – for weeks. The country looked really wonderful. After that fearful winter whatever else we lacked we were really getting some sun into our systems.

But there was the crisis. There had just been a tremendous argument in both Houses about the so-called Dictatorship Bill – giving the Government in peacetime powers which were only reluctantly given in time of war. Alas for those old-fashioned distinctions!

The House of Commons had just gone into recess.

Both Attlee and Churchill were making radio speeches and both were disappointing.

And then – round about this weekend (with a glut of lettuces and Compton making centuries daily for Middlesex and England) three events came crowding together which really shook the nation –

(i) the William Pit disaster – at Whitehaven – in which one hundred and eleven miners working in the Six-quarters out under the Solway Firth were trapped – crushed – suffocated by a tremendous explosion.

(ii) the last remains of the vaunted American loan which had been designed to last us till 1951 – were being drawn day after day – not simply to pay our own bills but because of clauses about the convertability of sterling. Other banks in other countries suddenly appeared to take away from us the very means of buying food.

(iii) from India came extraordinary messages of the mobbing of Mountbatten – the raising of the two flags of Pakistan and India – of the troop ships leaving Bombay decorated with Indian flags – bands playing the dance-tunes of Indian barrack dances – the Union Jack at Delhi which flew night and day since the Mutiny finally dipping – the children dancing in the streets – Hindus and Moslems fraternizing – Aeroplanes in the night sky writing Jai – Jai Hind – Victory.

Ah! if this story has been rightly told how clearly will these three events stand linked together. Not as cause and effect – the links of History are subtler than that – but as a final statement of our problems – industrial – financial – Imperial.

The Cabinet huddles together to halt the drain on dollars – to plan at long last that we in this Island shall try to grow the food we eat – the rescue squad hacks its way through a hundred yards of fallen rock – the troopship roars out 'Bless 'Em All' as the engines begin to race. From now on – we are all – all of us – on our own.

1948

DIM LITTLE ISLAND

(Working title: *Awful Old England?*)
A Third Treatment, 10 June 1948

Dark clouds moving across the screen – thunderflashes – gusts of wind and rain... these are the background images to the titles in staring white letters:

AWFUL OLD ENGLAND?

A question from a poem by Kipling,
and four answers to it by:

OSBERT LANCASTER
JOHN ORMSTON *of Vickers Armstrong*
DR VAUGHAN WILLIAMS, O.M.
and JAMES FISHER *the Naturalist...*

...the rain beats down on the pavement – the sombre title-music dwindles until we can hear the raindrops in the puddles and see in one of them the reflection of a man's silhouette – an average looking chap in mac and hat – the camera moves swiftly to his feet and then up the whole length of his figure to his head, as it looks restlessly right and left. A rough determined voice (not his, not expressing him) speaks to the world at large:

> 'Me that 'ave been what I've been –
> Me that 'ave gone where I've gone –
> Me that 'ave seen what I've seen –
> 'Ow can I ever take on
> With awful old England again...'

An extreme perspective of the wet street as he turns to move down it – he is carrying a kitbag – the voice continues:

> 'An' 'ouses both sides of the street
> An' edges both sides of the lane,
> An' the parson and gentry between...'

the silhouette now trudging down a long dark country lane with overhanging trees – like a dream...

'An' touching my 'at when we meet –
Me that 'ave been what I've been...'

we are in close up again and the images change to visions of power and
romance and excitement – the voice and music rise – flashes from the
XIVth Army – the face of the soldier in the jungle – the bouquets of flowers and kisses for the liberators of 1944-45:

'*Me* that 'ave gone where I've gone –
Me that 'ave seen what I've seen –
Me!'

'Awful old England...'

The clouds again, and then as though looking through them a face
being drawn on a piece of paper – a chap with handlebar moustaches, with
something of Much Binding about him, and then we are looking into a
mirror and can see the reflection of the face – I mean the reflection of the
real face, for in fact it is a self-portrait of Osbert Lancaster. As he sits
drawing, his voice (thought-voice) begins to speak. He begins with a
repeat of the key words 'Awful old England' which, when you come to
think of it is, in fact, the subject of his cartoons. Lancaster proceeds to
talk about two things: the country itself and the peculiar power of the cartoonist or satirist to record and transform the everyday world. He isn't *trying* to be funny. He looks at the same things as other people, but he sees
something extra. For him, Life and 'Awful old England' are full of
curiosities. Nothing is absolutely black and white, good or bad.

Of course, the wording itself should be absolutely colloquial, and the
images should jump from the sketch book to reality and back again to the
style of the self-portrait. And also, each time developing a bit so that the
scene becomes a bit wider and that instead of talking about the cartoonist
he ends up by talking about the whole country. Or rather, the curiosities
of contemporary English life. The way we live. And at this point we
should actually reconstruct one or two complete cartoons with dialogue
showing both the cartoon and the reality. In all this, the essential thing, I
think, is the extreme contrast between the official life that everyone is supposed to lead in the 20th century ('This is my Target – What's yours?') and
the unofficial life which they do lead – (I am thinking particularly of the
curiosities of English architecture on which Lancaster is an expert).
Because, after all, so long as we can all manage to live unofficial lives, we
are not completely lost.

The second answer to Kipling comes from the world of absolute reality
– the ship-building yards on the Tyne, and in particular the Vickers
Armstrong Naval Yard which built the *George the Fifth*. The energy,

noise, size and power of the job are by now clichés. We can take them for granted. The thing we are after is rather subtler. It is the supreme tradition of British invention and skill – what the Americans call 'know-how' – and which we can honestly say have not been lost down the years, and which no matter what happens in other national fields will be essential to us, for the simple reason that 'Awful old England' is an island. All of this, we should present through the eyes of a ship-builder – I mean an engineer – who looks on his work rather with the same imagination as the artist looks on his.

So this sequence is partly a sop to those who would expect a film of this sort to show some really good hard work going on on the screen, and for the rest of us can act as a contrast and a parallel to the sequence about the artist himself – I mean Vaughan-Williams. That the present tremendous drive on the Tyne and the Clyde and the Mersey will have its effect on the areas of despair, Jarrow and the rest, I take for granted.

All right, on the purely material side you may say that 'Awful old England' is really trying to keep her head above water. But then there are the legends that compared to the Continent, we don't really have any fun here, or we have no taste, the statement that 'the English are not musical'. And here we will appeal to a man whose judgement and performance are beyond dispute. Do you think, says Vaughan-Williams, that the English of Shakespeare's day weren't musical? Or as late as the time of Samuel Pepys? Of course they were. The secret was that in those days they made their own music for themselves. Pepys was rowed down the Thames in a boat decorated with green boughs and in which all the company were expected to play and sing. And then what happened? The real villain curiously enough is Handel. In the 18th Century, music came to be a foreign luxury to be enjoyed by the rich, but to make music himself was unworthy of John Bull. In the 19th Century the folk song and the church music were destroyed – yes – by the Education Act of 1870, and by Hymns Ancient and Modern. Why try to make your own music when it can be obtained much cheaper and nastier from the popular press?

Perhaps the darkest hour was before the dawn. The 20th Century has seen a great resurgence of music here, in 'Awful old England'. How did this happen, and why? The Elizabethans experienced a great revival of national consciousness which expressed itself in their poetry and music, and it is no mere accident that during the last war when our national consciousness became very vivid when everyone was keyed up to greater and greater effort, the need for music became greater and greater. It has been said, 'Masterpieces are not single and solitary births, they are the outcome of many years of thought in common, thinking by the body of the people.' You can picture it as a pyramid, at the top is the single solo musician, and below him the quartets and the orchestras, and widening out below them again the particular mass of the people who today feel in their bones the need for music.

The actual visuals for this sequence will consist in the main of two groups of shots:

1. The illustration of the pyramid which really should come first in this sequence, and

2. A demonstration with sound of the types of melody that people have made and listened to since the Elizabethans. I mean a snatch of Purcell, a few bars of 19th Century church organ, the unchanging pub sign swinging in the wind, and on it the stupidities of the American musical, and then like a breath of fresh air, the folk song which is the link between the Elizabethans themselves and the great composers of modern England.

The sound of the folk song takes us across the country and up into the rustic area of the Western Highlands. The camera sweeps down from the peaks and across the loch to a tiny figure... His voice announces:

'I am a Naturalist – for me Britain – Kipling's "Awful old England" – is an exciting place which I would not leave for worlds. For its size, it has the most varied wild life of anywhere in the world, the most varied climate (which we all know), the most varied rocks and trees and wild animals and birds. There [are] some parts of Britain like the Western Highlands which are really no use to anyone except the naturalist, but contrary to what you might think wild life exists more in the industrial areas of the North and the Midlands than it does in the Southern farming areas. In Wales the peregrine makes its nest within sight of the pit-head. The Clydeside crane operator looking out of his cabin can see the salmon leaping below him. From Sheffield a 2d bus will take you into the country and 1/- into a National Park – to the Peak, to Gordale and to Malham Cove. But if you live in London it will cost you 15/- and you will have to spend the night. Of course, the National Parks exist only on paper as yet, but we shall have them, and, in fact, we must have them, because a nation which destroys its wild animals and scares away its birds and pours chemicals into its rivers, can't be really healthy or really happy. Now, in the good old days, which we all lament, that was what we did, but today we really are learning to treat the country properly.

'In fact, there are some places from which we shall try to keep you out to give the birds a chance. On the coast of Suffolk lies a piece of marsh called Minsmere. During the war it was flooded on purpose, the beach mined and the trees blasted by shell-fire. Minsmere was the rehearsal place for the Dieppe landing. Today only the dead trees and the tangles of wire recall the war. The marsh there and the surrounding woods are today one of the few places in Southern England where birds can nest in peace – some of them so rare that I shan't give you their names. But this is only because since the war Minsmere has been protected by naturalists. Hidden in the woods is the camping place of two bird watchers – one of them still in the battle dress of the Observer Corps – the other in a tattered RAF uniform... From here they are peering (not at Heinkels and Dorniers) but at the wings on the marsh – all through the spring and summer keeping a log of the birds' movements, noting arrivals and departures, telephoning top secrets to Headquarters, and also keeping away anyone with a gun or an egg collector's box. Today, there are something like half a million people watching birds, amateurs most of them who give their spare time to it. It is nearly as good as Soccer, and as clean a sport as Dirt Track Racing... "Awful old England" indeed!'

Undated Memo on 'Awful Old England'

Shooting problems for music sequence

1. What we call the 'lute in the boat' i.e. reconstruction of close-up of Elizabethan character playing a lute possibly shot on the river to cover VW's words 'when people of necessity made their own music...' I suggest that this might be shot on the lot at Denham ideally with sun but if not with lights. The music played by the lute would be an accompaniment to the folk song to be post-synched. Of course the tempo must be worked out to match the track of the song.

2. Wild track recording of the folk song itself. V.W. had a suggestion of a man who could do it.

3. For the reference to 'the great virtuosi' Muir [Muir Matheson] suggests close-ups of Sargent, Boult, Beecham, of which the first Sargent should match roughly the long-shot of him at Haringay already shot.

4. Similarly for the latter reference to composers we would discover three engravings or paintings of Byrd, Purcell and Arne (look at the illustrations in the *Oxford Companion to Music*) and then for contemporary composers shoot actual close-ups of Walton, Bliss, Bax, possibly Benjamin Britten and if possible V.W. himself. This last point would be discussed with V.W. by Muir. All these contacts with celebrities should be fixed through Muir who will be recording at Watford every day during the coming week.

5. Perhaps we should add to this list of celebrities Dennis Brain if in fact we need to cover the orchestra playing V.W.'s Variants in synch.

6. For the words 'devoted musical practitioners' and the reference to

schools, choral societies and musical amateurs, Muir's suggestions are as follows:

> a. Boris Ord and his choir boys at Kings. Exterior good sunlight.
> b. The celebrated music room at St Paul's.
> c. Contact Marcus Dods (Shepherds Bush) who runs a village musical society somewhere near Denham. This sequence is most complicated technically needing lights and I think a veloscilator but not synch as we would only cover the assembling of a meeting of his people. Perhaps at the end of this sequence there should be a post-synching moment of someone playing a few chords on the piano which would lead into the repeat of the folk song.

7. For the reference to the Elizabethans' and our own 'national upheaval' we might find a striking shot from *Fires Were Started* and reconstruct a silhouette shot of a couple of Elizabethan soldiers on a high point overlooking the sea such as Beachy Head with an Armada Beacon.

8. For the last paragraphs of V.W.'s commentary we should come back to one of the extreme long shots of people coming into Harringay plus perhaps some material from the National Gallery and the Huddersfield Choir (from *Crown*), and for the extreme end of the picture itself collect some existing material shot for the other sequences of this film – the most striking shots.

> After completing *Dim Little Island*, Jennings spent several months researching and preparing a documentary about the London Symphony Orchestra. The film was never made, but in 1954 a version of his notes was published as 'Working Sketches of an Orchestra' in *London Symphony: Portrait of an Orchestra*, edited by Hubert Foss and Noel Goodwin for the Naldrett Press.

TO IAN DALRYMPLE   *8 Regent's Park Terrace,*
4 December 1948   *NW1*

My dear Ian,

When I say thank you for your letter I really mean it – because you know you have no call to make me any offer in the present situation. I think the best thing is to say £40 to the end of February or whenever 12 weeks is up from this week.

I delayed answering until after the L.S.O. meeting because I would prefer to take my chances under you rather than do anything elsewhere.

I put this very badly – sentiment and business jumbled!

Yours ever   Humphrey

Working Sketches of an Orchestra

6 December 1948.   Albert Hall.   10 a.m.
Rehearsal of concert for same evening under Josef Krips.

> Mozart Symphony 39.
> Mahler *Kindertotenlieder*.
> Brahms Second Symphony.

9.40 a.m. The horns in the bandroom practising in the dark (or that is the impression). The bar – a table of workmen. The gas lights in the passages (curving away into nothing: 19th-century image). The bell in the bar. The latecomer.

Lewis (the orchestral manager): 'Now, boys,' clapping his hands. Exciting view of the conductor through the square glass panel in the door leading from the artists' room to the platform; the word SILENCE above it.

The conductor singing with the music: 'Strings – strings' – 'basses – come with me.' The emotional moment (last movement of the Brahms – the theme) when the conductor, having criticized and gone back to letter H, turns to the first violins humming and says as they play: 'That's *nice* – that's good...' Criticizing the finale: 'Excuse me, please – *ta-ta-ta* – not la-la-la – that's too *cosy!*'

Kathleen Ferrier comes in in large hat and heavy coat – gets chair from up behind 'cellos – orchestra have given slight applause on music-stands at her entry – she begins singing sitting – ends without hat, coat, and standing. At emotional moment Krips says 'wait – wait' to orchestra – leans over to soloist as though to pull the notes out of her mouth.

At this moment of quiet one can hear the inevitable 'men working on the roof' and see the cleaners in the boxes. Krips singing again: 'Seconds' – 'now firsts'...

*

12 December, 1948.   Albert Hall.
Rehearsal with Krips for afternoon concert.

> Weber *Oberon* Overture.
> Mozart Symphony 39.
> Beethoven Arias.

At 9.10 a.m., a grey winter morning; puddles of night rain. Kensington looks misty and deserted. The front of the Albert Hall closed, at the back the night watchmen's lights in the street still burning. A 'decorative florists' van outside door 12; two cars already parked outside the artists' entrance; three tiny figures (two carrying violin cases) come past the Albert Hall Mansions; a taxi and then another. A milk can belonging to Express Dairies and three empty milk bottles outside artists' entrance.

Inside the 'decorative florists' are putting the flowers in position in boxes along the platform, men are dealing with chairs, the conductor is discussing the layout of the orchestra...

9.20 a.m. Basses coming into position in their covers. Odd members of orchestra on platform and in amphitheatre stalls; one calls up to the back of the timpani: 'Friday?' – 'Yes, Friday...' Cleaners. The horns begin tuning up before the others; violins form a group in the front of the amphitheatre stalls H, carrying their instruments. One working light above the organ and two in the dome. (Note that the orchestra look neatly dressed this morning because they have an afternoon performance and will not, most of them, get home to change before 3 o'clock. Morning dress.)

There is always a spread of coats on the block H seats and it is here that odd visitors, friends, relations, sit during rehearsals – but shoo'd back by Mr Lewis out of the conductor's vision. Perhaps an illusion that the basses tend to keep overcoats and even hats on?...

The battens go on, the orchestra assembles. Mr Lewis clapping his hands, carrying a sheet of paper, facing the orchestra, but not on the rostrum. Stage-hand with pipe and apron talking to drummer. A youth brings in a bucket of water and gives it to a man who pours it in the flower boxes.

Slight applause for conductor, who comes in briskly, waving baton and smiling and bowing slightly; says a few words about phrasing to firsts, to basses, to cellos...

Weber. – Krips: 'Pa-pa-pa *pa*! Yes?' 'Letter D. Tempo. No, slower' (talking to the brass). 'Ah, ah, ah, ah! Strongly – yes? 14th bar – whole orchestra except first violins *subito mezzo* – otherwise I can't hear – te-yum pa-pa! then the – one, two, three – fourth bar, the whole orchestra... Yes?' And so on through the *Oberon* Overture – not actually playing but explaining. Then a moment of tuning and silence. A break off after two bars and begin again... 'Tempo... *one* and *two* and *three* and *four*, tempo!' Break off to talk about the horns of Elfland blowing: 'A little lighter – elfs! What is called elf here?' (i.e. in English). The orchestra: 'Elf!' 'Elf? Yes?' Restart the brass entry three times: 'Ta-ta-ta – *without push*... please is it possible to play pa-ya not pa-pa?'; 'without any ritardando – I told you – only diminuendo' (leader writes on score); 'I hope you remember it... much better... tempo – *tempo*...' (with a little stamp). Extreme pianissimo – then 'tempo': bang from drummer – 'sorry, that's too much – yes?' Pianissimo again: 'Elfs!... Ha pa fi-ya-fi-ya – basses, tempo!' (Into *Allegro*) 'more *soul* – Elfs – ti-ya...' Insistence on breadth and warmth of playing...

Beethoven: The same drill (i.e. instruction first), plus question of repeats. The emotional effect here of very well-known passages suddenly appearing as fragments in a rehearsal – broken off before completion and just as one warms to them: 'Will you remember that?' 'Now let us start,' pushing away score and desk. Speaking and chanting as usual during playing: 'Sing – sing!' to the strings – shouting out 'Basses!' with cupped hand. The problem of turning pages at a moment of tension – for first violins especially – reminding them that after all they *know* the score and can wait and turn over later... There is a nice warm laugh at the end of the first movement: 'Life is too short.' A photographer takes a flash and produces a series of extraordinarily dramatic effects by taking flashes from between seconds and timpani which punctuate like lightning the increasing drama of the scherzo and finale.

*

13 December 1948.   Albert Hall.
Rehearsal for concert same evening under Sir Malcolm Sargent.

> Lennox Berkeley Concerto for two pianos and orchestra.
> Mozart Concerto for two pianos and orchestra.
> Beethoven 4th Symphony.
> Stravinsky *Firebird.*

The curious shape of smaller brass-instrument cases – as a trio, their masters have tea, 9.30.

Talking to a 'cellist, I find he has an extremely high opinion of Krips – 'so childlike – so appreciative – such a good musician', quoting the turnover problem of yesterday; few conductors would have fussed about that, yet it is important – to have to turn over does take your mind off the work for a moment.

BBC men stretch a mike across the arena.

Sir Malcolm enters; Phyllis Sellick shakes hands with leader; there is a query over the parts of the Berkeley Concerto from Mr Lewis – some of the brass have none; discussion between Lewis and Berkeley himself. Meanwhile, Sir Malcolm calls for what is evidently a new arrangement of the National Anthem, which is extraordinarily impressive.

Berkeley comes back and Sargent begins corrections from the previous rehearsal (this is the second). BBC men are writing in their box; Berkeley himself sits in the front of the amphitheatre stalls with small group of friends and MS score.

Sargent has his own punctuations – 'good... good' instead of Krips's 'Yes?... Yes?'; but Sargent's has no question-mark.

The mike is being slung throughout the Berkeley rehearsal – piano mikes lowered also. Notes are continually checked in copies – 'first bar before H, has anybody got B natural?' and so on. How quiet, military, refined, gentlemanly the English conductor! Saying to the composer 'Tempo's right, isn't it?' rather like the skipper on the intercom in a documentary aircraft: 'I suppose we *are* on the right course?'

For aligning the chairs in the arena the workmen have a cord stretched across the floor. The orchestra noticeably unquiet during any pause for discussion. The slow, rather gruelling speed of a rehearsal of a new work – 'which bar do you mean?. . . oh, F *sharp*;. . . now let's go ahead. . . one bar before' – the glance (to his colleagues) of the trumpet-player, who has continued solo after the orchestra has been halted; the pencil stubs continually coming out of waistcoat pockets, correcting wrong notes and marking expression; voices coming up from the orchestra – 'the – er – fifth bar of that variation. . .' – 'Sir Malcolm' from the basses – 'Sir Malcolm'.

At the end Sargent calls for applause for the composer.

Mozart: 'I shall stop beating in many places – until we come together again', i.e. in solo piano passages. . . The smile between the conductor and leader on the tempo of three chords. 'All right – go straight on.' Sargent *conducts*, directs, but does not appear to interpret; the criticisms are technical, not emotional.

*

14 December 1948.
Recording Session at EMI, Abbey Road (Studio 1) for Columbia under Sir Malcolm Sargent.

Dohnanyi Orchestral Variations.

9.30 a.m. Piano-tuner just finishing (piano will not actually be used); men setting six or seven mikes – cables on floor – not unlike film-music recording session but quieter. One second violin is sitting working with his score. The larger instruments, i.e. brasses, 'cellos, timps., harps, etc., are handled by LSO porters.

The bass leader, George Yates, possesses four instruments, one at home, three in concert halls; given a slack period after Christmas, he says he will play some golf and go round cleaning them, especially removing the tacky bass rosin which collects on the 'table' or 'belly' of the instrument, and needs scraping off with a knife without touching the varnish. This morning, if he had had time, he was going to go over the strings with sandpaper. Always practises at night on his home instrument; 'must keep practice up'. Smaller instruments are, of course, brought by the players themselves. Gordon Walker (flautist) recounted the other day how he had left his case in a taxi – had gone to Scotland Yard and just saved it from being thrown on to a heap of 'lost property'.

George Eskdale was talking yesterday about early sound-film music sessions, and Yates this morning had a fantastic account of early HMV gramophone recordings at Hayes before electrical recording came in, when double basses were not called for orchestral sessions because they couldn't record them. Out of this developed a sound-box and horn machine called the 'Catastrophone' constructed to Yates's specifications – he has a photo of it.

9.55 a.m. Orchestra complain among themselves about new seating arrangements for recording – on the flat except for the brass, timpani, and basses right in a corner ('the Cinderellas of the orchestra': Yates). Yates also remarks about the height of stools provided for bass-players – of course, he has short legs! At one time at Columbia the bass-players each had their own cut down to their height.

10.0 a.m. Sargent enters with 'mixer' (or corresponding official) and discusses orchestral layout while they practise – this is a relatively new piece and they are working, playing over from score, reading, discussing it . . . Sargent runs through figures 1-12, which will make one side.

Question of position of horns playing straight into back wall in a cramped position – Sargent pooh-poohs the objection, which has come from the horn-players themselves. Leader says 'sh' to wood-wind during this discussion. Some smoking: two basses smoking pipes. Coats coming off – it is warmer in a recording studio than in the Albert Hall.

S. says he would like a 'test' straight away; he has a 'phone by his desk to speak to the mixing room. Orchestra give an A before the test signals by buzzer and red light; one buzz for ready, two for running, red light for go (and kept on throughout recording).

Clearly Sargent's absolutely soundless and precise conducting has advantages for the microphone.

'Very nice playing' from Sargent; 'listen very carefully to play-back . . .' Question of strings changing bows at 2nd bar. Recording crew (five of them altogether) come in for play-back, which starts on buzzing signal and comes down from speaker on floor by the harps. Comment by Sargent at one point. Odd remarks between Sargent and leader about playing and then discussion of balance. Now they return to the question of the horn-players' position; they are moved to behind flutes (centre of wood-wind). Comment for the strings generally: 'It keeps too level . . .' 'Winds, I want to ask you – at 2, don't breathe – 4th before 3 . . . try No. 2 please . . .' 'Stop us when you are ready with the wax.'

'Next variation excellent – we will do a quick test of this – whole thing please . . .' Buzz, light as before . . . Before play-back to wood-wind: 'I think you'll find there are two places where you are unhappy – one is 6 . . .' (A player later criticized Sargent for finding fault *before* play-back was heard.) During play-back flautist asks 'Is that the one?' 'That's the one . . .' Flautist at this point is smoking a pipe – extravagant as that may sound.

A man comes in and fiddles with a mike. Coming to the horn-passage in play-back Sargent puts up his thumb to horns. General comment: 'Very good . . .' 'Settle down for master-record, please!' Final fiddles with mikes by men in white coats – man looks at connection on floor. Final word: 'First violins – you have got to be really sensitive about that . . .'

There is a noticeable tension (not necessarily artistic) in the playing for wax which you don't get in the concert hall – no coughs, no squeaks, extreme attention to no wrong notes and to page-turning – also important to note the reactions of the players when not playing.

Red light off – drop in tension – grin from the leader! Further fiddle with mikes.

It is now 11.0: 1. rehearsal, 2. tests, 3. wax. 'O.K., one more!' Still further mike-adjustment. Sargent: 'Good – now we are ready – just let's try the first note, everybody – good!'

Note during this recording the smile of Gordon Walker to Edward Walker, the flautist, at end of E.W.'s tricky passage. Rehearsal for next side: 'Don't smoke while you rehearse . . .'

In passing, notice the varieties of solid 'cello cases standing like statues watching their masters from the far end of the studio.

Tea break: both here and at the Albert Hall there is a dash for the canteen by dignified orchestral players (perhaps half the orchestra) very similar to Cumberland miners coming off shift or the break for lunch in a Tyneside shipyard – it includes, for example, George Stratton, the leader, who is nearly always in a dark suit.

The lady viola-player who wants to make a note on her score has to look in her bag for pencil, which makes her a moment or two behind the others.

Sargent, of course, does call for vibrato effects and so on with singing and hand imitation, but not during playing – separately during break – and addressed to each section: 'Violas – ti-ya, ti-ya . . . !' 'Bassoons and horns – la da di da-*da* – all yours – take your time . . .' To 'cello leader, 'Just play it to me, will you?' . . . 'Clarinets, just let me hear pa-pa at the start . . . That's too short . . . pa-pa . . . perfect!'

'Very well – master-recording.' Difficulty of hearing on conductor's 'phone with orchestra tuning. False start – 'Didn't you get a foreign noise on that?' (to recordist).

As the red light goes off Stratton has a fit of coughing – which he has been controlling!

*

15 December 1948.   Central Hall, Westminster.
Rehearsal for concert same evening.

> Mozart *Figaro* Overture.
> Brahms Double Concerto for violin, 'cello, and orchestra.
> Haydn Trumpet Concerto.
> Mendelssohn *Italian* Symphony.

10.5 a.m. 'Right, everyone, can we have an A, please?' The orchestra are late and gay. Straight into the *Italian* Symphony without discussion.

The artists' room is not easy to reach – up three flights of stairs, past Methodist offices; and the Central Hall platform is a difficult place to come on to late, as a cellist and flautist find. A few moments later George Eskdale walks in and says, 'What time?' (he is the Haydn soloist). 'Do you mind much later?' (Conductor is looking at the clock.) 'Well, they should have let me know.' 'Well, since you're here we had better do it now...' Continues Mendelssohn until Eskdale enters with his trumpet and score.

Conductor calls for applause for soloist with a smile – orchestra give some straight applause and some in mock derision (boo! etc.) – he is one of them! Straight into the Haydn with a glance from conductor to soloist checking tempo...

During a discussion between Eskdale and conductor, the LSO porter comes in in shirt-sleeves with pipe in his mouth – judges this is the wrong moment to intrude and exit...

There is a discrepancy between the letter or figure numbers in the conductor's score and the orchestral parts: result – 'ten bars from the end – no, nine bars from the end – two bars of *forte*, then *piano*...', etc.

During the heavenly slow movement the fat and untroubled cleaner mops her way along the stalls. George Eskdale waiting during the string passage at the opening of the third movement, beating time on his instrument with the fingers of his right hand. Note the very young drummer who is 'standing in' this morning. At the close the orchestra give Eskdale really genuine applause (on their stands) without being asked. Eskdale shakes hands with the conductor and leaves.

'Will somebody just see if the other two (i.e. violin and 'cello soloists for the Brahms) are there? Would you mind, Mr Lewis...?' They are not:

back to Mendelssohn. The orchestra are not really taking things very seriously; those at the back, especially the younger ones, are fooling around a lot – dropped pencils and even a dropped bow – and then from ragging they slide on, though without realizing it, into a real performance of the first movement of the *Italian* Symphony...

'Jolly good'...

Coming to the end of the slow movement, Mr Lewis goes out again to the band room to see if the soloists have arrived – actually we can hear them practising...but the orchestra want to finish the Mendelssohn – 'What about the two horns?' notes the conductor (meaning the two extra horns who have been sitting reading, waiting for the Brahms). At this there is a low anti-horn murmur from the others.

The Mendelssohn third movement – again going into it without discussion. 'Warmer – warmer...very clear now the horns...'

11.5. 'We'll do the finale and then have a break.' 'Hear, hear...'

A player came up in the interval and talked about conducting. *A propos* the Krips concerts, he said the Master was 'the last word' in perfection. 'Krips is a musician – he wants you to *play* – he just moulds you – and you want to play...'

'Ah, well, we have our moments...'

In the Brahms, Harry Dugarde goes to the back of the hall to hear what the balance is like – one solution is to cut down the number of strings in certain sections. Some of the 'reduced' strings – i.e. the last desks of first and second violins – immediately start smoking.

*

5 January 1949 (morning). Camden Theatre (BBC).
Light Programme 'Concert Hour' under Trevor Harvey.
9 a.m. Rehearsal of:

> Mozart *Figaro* Overture.
> Wagner *Siegfried Idyll.*
> Fauré *Masques and Bergamasques.*
> Mendelssohn Scherzo from Octet.

9 a.m. Yet another atmosphere: a converted old-time music-hall, the boxes, circle, and gallery still with plush seats, plaster Hercules and painted 'gods'; but the stalls and orchestra and stage are thrown into one, with functional BBC clocks ticking away every second, replacing Dionysius...

9.7 a.m. 'Good morning, gentlemen – can we start with the Fauré, please?'

Six mikes. The usual man hammering on the roof, cleaners, two men in grey coats and smartly dressed girl (in charge of balance) moving mikes, but fiddling with them less than at EMI or at Denham Studios. Small orchestra this morning; before we begin, George Stratton was still wishing people the compliments of the season. Trevor Harvey: 'Just the start – very light and busy...' 'That's nice – bassoons? – good.' 'Shall we go to 1 2 3 4 5 6 7 8 before one? – a slight change in mood'... 'staccato – otherwise it doesn't tell – *crisp*' (evidently Harvey's favourite word); 'very *legato*, wind' – 'just broad bows in this section without accents – that's much nicer.'

At the back of the pit the control panel, listening room, etc. The extraordinary capacity of orchestral players, especially on an unimportant occasion like this, to talk and smile across at each other and then pick up exactly as the conductors says '2 before 6' or wherever it is.

Note: being a BBC building, the theatre has air-conditioning and is rather stuffily warm – some are working in shirt-sleeves.

Fauré, 2nd Movement: 'We have lost our trumpets.' 'Most of the thing could be a little more *precise*, I think, on phrasing – just at the end we lose the precision – a little more *espressivo*.' It is noticeable this morning how much the string sections depend on their leaders for interpretation and method.

3rd Movement: 'Right – we go on...'; 'right – very crisp'; and just as he says and they play '*pianissimo* but *espressivo*', two women cleaners with buckets come out of the back of the stage and down the wings, and remind us of the discrepancy between Fauré and Camden Town.

4th Movement: At this point the oboes give an A on request from first violins. An elderly man in a grey coat comes in and cleans the glasses used for announcers, which are sitting on a tray near the conductor. Does not the air-conditioning and the consequent central-heating atmosphere have an effect on the playing? The trumpets are yawning.

9.46 a.m. 'I think the safest thing to do, gentlemen, is to take no notice of all these pencil marks', i.e. in the orchestral parts (query: who owns the parts?). A long discussion about the playing of one or two 'danger notes'. '2 again, please.' The rehearsal is slowing down into a discussion: 'What I would like to do gentlemen, is – this is new to you, isn't it?' (i.e. the Fauré) – 'is to do the *Figaro* Overture now, and then come back to it.'

'Quiet, please,' to an unseen person talking right at the very top of the gallery.

Figaro: The contrast is, of course, very great – the confidence both of Mozart and of the orchestra – the conductor's sudden turn to control: 'Bassoons – are you all right there?'

'Now will you play the Fauré right through?'

It is agreed to rehearse the Mendelssohn next, to let members not required for the Wagner to get off early. In the scherzo we arrive at one of those moments where the firsts and the wood-winds cannot hear each other; the orchestra say they are too spread out, i.e. they have been placed according to the different mike positions. The BBC balance-girl comes in Discussion. Stratton: 'We can't hear anything and they can't hear us, that's all there is to it'; but the desks can't be moved for one item only so late in rehearsal; BBC wins.

10.35 a.m. *Break.* Three fiddles and one bassoon spend part of the break practising; Mr Lewis distributes papers, letters; Gordon Walker and Francis Drake sitting discussing; Mr Lewis gets people to sign the attendance register. The Walker-Drake discussion continues, accompanied by one bassoon playing over the Mendelssohn. To the right, a player is eating sandwiches out of a paper bag and drinking milk out of a glass half-bottle labelled brandy. Otherwise, deserted chairs; instruments laid carefully on them replacing their owners who are having coffee. A man hammering in the roof; coats, hats, and violin cases like coffins. Mr Lewis rolling a cigarette. One can just hear the roar of traffic outside by Cobden's statue.

Mr Lewis claps his hands for re-assembly; the conductor is sitting waiting; Mr Lewis is distributing yet more pieces of paper; 'settle down, please, gentlemen...' Heath carries his 'cello, twanging it as he goes. The hammering gets louder. Tuning commences. George Stratton is still shaking hands with members he hasn't met since the New Year.

10.57 a.m. The *Siegfried Idyll.*

*

5 January 1949 (afternoon).   Cheam Baths Hall.
Rehearsal for evening concert under Edric Cundell.

> Beethoven Violin Concerto – Soloist Max Rostal.
> César Franck Symphony.
> Beethoven *Egmont* Overture.
> Mozart *Magic Flute* Overture.
> Sibelius *Finlandia.*

3 p.m. The orchestra broadcast at Camden Town at 12.30, had lunch, and got down here (Cheam) before 3, bringing with them their evening clothes. Some have changed by now, others will later; some wear a mixture, keeping their collar and tie to be changed later.

The difficulty of finding the Cheam Baths Hall in the grey winter wilderness of Sutton, N. Cheam, and Epsom has already exasperated more than one. We start late. The Hall, which is a municipal swimming bath in the summer, is pleasant but very cold.

Members complaining about the use of the *Siegfried Idyll* this morning as light lunch-time music. Discussion of light music so-called, including Johann Strauss. Lewis says he is the only member who has played the *Blue Danube* under Richter. Someone else's opinion: 'We don't let ourselves go. Our conductors don't feel it. Too much tension and precision, and at the same time they exaggerate the hesitation in the waltzes...'

As the conductor comes on to the platform Mr Lewis, as usual, has some things to announce. The seating is very crowded: three brass-players who came in after rehearsal had begun have great difficulty in reaching their places (as in the Central Hall).

'Ladies and gentlemen, shall we play the trombone works first?' No discussions – straight into the *Magic Flute* Overture; only occasional stops. '... that very spot, do we know it? – *piano*, no *mezzo-forte*.' Sheet flies off conductor's desk – picked up by viola-leader – smile – all during playing.

What are this evening's audience doing at this very moment, when this is preparing for them? Quite an important question. Why is each of them coming? Their faces now, and the same faces in the evening – their wishes – and the orchestra's wishes?

Splendid gesture by conductor at end of one run-through – one break only (the impassive face of the cymbalist standing in his overcoat ready for the clash – like the executioner). A moment's rest after this exertion; minor discussion with leader; leader and 'cello leader compare parts – 'after K' – for bowing.

César Franck Symphony. 1. Again and again one notices the extraordinary capacity of orchestral players to be apparently lost in something else right up to their entry and then to come in without fuss.

The conductor's baton used for the accentuated passages, hands for the smoother ones. The empty seats: in the tumult of the rehearsal one imagines again the face of the person who will hear this this evening; who will see such and such a player from *this* position. 'If you make a diminuendo in your last bar – that's what he wanted – I feel'; the first time I have heard a conductor refer to the composer's wishes. No comment at end of movement.

2. The empty seats again: how many of them are taken?; who is buying one now? where? Then the thoughts of the players when playing and especially when not; the brass and timps have long waits and look down from on high.

Cundell as a conductor lets them play with the minimum of fuss and interruption – trusts and compliments the orchestra without saying so. At the end of the second movement he says: 'Those two bars at the end soft – to me the cream of the whole music.'

3. (A figure in the street with a pram passes the poster 'LSO Cheam Baths Hall...' The winter sun is descending – the houses fading into the mist.)

At the end of the César Franck Mr Lewis announces meal arrangements at café by roundabout at 7 o'clock. Cundell says, '*Egmont* please, for five minutes' – i.e. sections only – 'right-ho!'

As so often at the quiet wood-wind movement after the opening chords, a workman tip-toes down the hall – break off – 'Are you all right now?' – a few more bars – break off: 'E – letter E' – (back row of brass put on their hats and coats and leave for break). 'F – to the end.' Question to horns: 'Have you got it filled in? I like it filled in.' 'Thank you, gentlemen.' Tea.

Discussion during tea-break with Gordon Walker about 92-year-old John Solomon, last remaining LSO founder, and about Kathleen Ferrier: 'The best contralto for fifty years. She really sings what is written and it is so much better like that – Elgar would have worshipped her.'

Beethoven Violin Concerto. 1. 'Gentlemen, you don't know Mr Rostal, do you?' 'No!' in derision, plus some tapping on desks.

Before his first entry Rostal beating tune with his 'vibrato' fingers – worrying about the platform flooring. 'Less – still less': R. playing snatches of their violin parts with orchestra. One feels perhaps a little something between him and the strings: 1sts, 2nds, violas – behind him, watching him. One senses the world of the theatre.

Someone smashes a cup in the distance, clearing up tea-things; conductor peers behind him. Cadenza cut in rehearsal. Conductor says to drummer: 'Mr Rostal will have a word with you after the rehearsal about the cadenzas.' Discussion between soloist and conductor.

2. People keep dropping things – in orchestra as well as in hall; school-like giggling; cadenza again cut; during pause Stratton says, 'No noise with mutes'; calls across to 'cello leader, 'Bill, tell 'em no noise with mutes.'

3. Cadenza cut again slight applause at end from orchestra. As they put on their coats conductor, soloist, and drummer begin to run through the cadenzas. A viola-player says: '...found them in Vienna – says they are Beethoven's original – nobody else plays 'em.'

*

Saturday, 8 January 1949. Albert Hall.
Rehearsal with soloists only of *Messiah* under Sir Malcolm Sargent.

10.30 a.m. Splendid opening picture – a totally empty Albert Hall. We are looking from the steps up from band room; we can see the lights in the battens and beyond them, in the gloom, 5000 vacant seats. In the fore-ground the desks are in position but the platform is also bare except for the aged figure of the librarian, who is slowly distributing the orchestral parts, section by section (the librarian and Ernie the LSO porter are, of course, key figures in the early stages of a rehearsal or concert).

The orchestra assemble (afternoon performance – they are dressed already): two violins, coming as usual from their camping-ground in block H, discuss 'what that flower is', pointing with bow to flower-border along platform edge – a similar gesture to that of a player pointing with bow to note in score. As this is a choral work the orchestra are nearly all ranged on the flat; men are straightening seats as usual – soloists enter – slight applause – Sargent enters.

'May I wish you a happy and successful New Year!' – applause. '8', i.e. 8 in a bar – and straight into overture, taking short sections only – open-ing, section in middle, and letter F to end.

The two women soloists (Isobel Baillie and Kathleen Ferrier) are sitting muffled up in really arctic-looking furs.

Fragments of each section: 2 – opening leading to 'Comfort ye' – break off – then on to four bars before C (soloist singing sitting), and so on. Opening of 5 – opening of 6. The 'two-in-bar' section, i.e. 6 D *prestissimo* – then line before I, i.e. the end of 6 and so on; 'that's it – not really *ritar-dando* – should be *deliberamente*'.

Men in the roof swinging and raising lights: 'In 10 I want special atten-tion to double-basses.'

'All right, now we start No. 11'; 'beginning of 12.' 13: 'Now may I remind you that you do not put on your mutes 2 bars before B but 1 bar...'

During the Pastoral Symphony, men in the roof shout 'Wo!' '2 bars before B' – 'Wo!' 'Ti-ya da – ti-ya da. Wait for it, there's no hurry.' S. in his element in Handel. 'You don't listen – I want the outside players to put on their mutes and start playing one bar before B, the inside players stop playing one bar before B – keep the violins up – then you all come in – dur-ing 14 you quietly take off your mutes.'

The soloists just indicate their parts – sitting like monks. Roof: 'Up on that one, Harry!' Soprano singing angel's recitative without music in 15. 'Up, Harry! Wo!' '17, please.' '2 bars from the end – really have a short bow at the end then it doesn't go on.' 'Good.' 18: In the gloom under the dome the unlit lamps swing and clank. 'Up!' Imagine the LSO seen from the point of view of Harry in the roof! '21 is out' – everyone marks this.

As with orchestral players, so with soloists. Kathleen Ferrier comes in '20 – 6 bars after B' without a book, bang on. 23: The opening bars – 'all right'. Kathleen Ferrier slips out.

Sargent to chorus-master sitting in block H: 'We are not doing 25, are we?' 'No, sir,' i.e. 25 is out. 'And with His stripes we are healed.' 'Start of 26, please.' 27: 'di-ya dai-ya dai-ya – da!' 6th bar. 'Scorn – staccato!' 'Tempo!' 'That's it.' The transition from 31-2. 37: Discussion with chorus-master. S. singing odd choral lines: 'The Lord gave the Word.' Cut to 30: 'nice steady tempo!' 'No *rallentando*, please, and no *da capo*!'

So on – 'You don't stand for Hallelujah Chorus' – this to the orchestra, of course. Discussion of introduction to 45, 'I know that my Redeemer...' 'Normal playing – there – everyone can hear the difference – I assure you it's very seldom heard played well – you play exactly what's there – 1 2 3 4 – 1 – 1 2 3 4 – 1'. 48: Discussion of where George Eskdale shall stand for 'The Trumpet shall sound'. The string sections in the Amen: 'Strings, that's the real sort of music – it's a joy to hear it clear like that.' Instructions to drummer for end.

The whole of the above rehearsal took one hour and showed what a pro-digious stage-manager Sargent is.

*

Albert Hall.
Rehearsal at 10 a.m.

It is freezing in the Albert Hall these mornings; the boilers below ground are hissing away, no doubt, but are quite inadequate for the size of the Hall and the weather. The timpani, who are standing about with lit-tle to do, keep stamping their feet like horses; the double-basses are abso-lutely not paying attention, their leader audibly talking – they sit, of course, much more in a row and more spaced out than any other section, and any comment or joke has to be passed along.

Curious effect of *pizzicato*, as in Brahms 1st Symphony, 3rd Move-ment, 6 before A, this morning in the huge empty hall. The sweat on the conductor's face in the artists' room in the break, alone in empty room puffing a cigarette, with glass of water on the table. Agent comes in: con-ductor: 'How's the house?' 'So-so.'

Why, after all, should people come? Timpanist says it's snobbery pure and simple. We have now some little idea of musicians' motivation (as we call it) – what is the audience's? Bach: 'To the Glory of God, and pleasant recreation...' 20th century: 'Pleasant recreation (and, to the Glory of God...)'?

The timpanist (sitting this morning with his son next to him, who sometimes deputises) explaining things in the score (both with overcoats on): he of all members of the orchestra overlooks the scene – sees the con-ductor far off, and beyond him the empty seats or the audience.

*

12 January 1949.   Kingsway Hall.   2.30 p.m.
Recording Session for Decca under Krauss.

Brahms's Hungarian Dances.
Dvořák Slavonic Dances.

Individual tuning and warming up, especially brass, is a fascinating thing: there are definite systems – remember particularly the squeak of the wood-wind's reeds on their own.

One of the seconds said: 'Dislike Kingsway Hall. Bad ventilation. Sloping floor. Over-warm. Depressing place.'

Note: H. carries his own 'cello always – 'they get knocked about in the van – not his (i.e. Ernie's) fault, but they do'; practises on same instrument.

Several of the orchestra, including Soutter and Dugarde, were talking about the splendid day's golf they had yesterday. George Eskdale said that tomorrow he would be playing from nine in the morning until midnight. 'Not this kind of music.' Where?

Some confusion over seating; orchestra have not been told what they are to play – originally operatic arias? – then it was non-vocal Wagner; but the first piece to be distributed is Brahms's Hungarian Dances!

Warm applause for conductor, who appears in white jacket and dark blue, scarlet-lined, short cape slung over his shoulders, like a Hussar: 'Very happy to meet you again.' Trombones are told they are 'safe for an hour'.

Hungarian Dances I: having played it once through – 'Number D – pa yum da di, pa yum da di.' Letter E played by sections: wood-wind, then brass – 4 bars; then 'tutti, letter E, *molto piano* – da di da da di didididi da da'. Letter F: each time singing the tune of that letter very expressively. '*Piano – un bar*, one bar *forte – subito piano*.' Krauss is an adept at imitating the tunes, accents, instruments, in sing-song.

Ghoulish voice from play-back speaker says: 'Test, please – take it easy on the percussion, please, and basses, don't force the tone, please!'

Test: conductor, who has been sitting, stands up at *ritardando*, takes off his glasses (he is further from his score), conducts an instant with glasses in hand. At one burst ('*un bar forte*') from brass, he puts his hand over his mouth as much as to say, 'Oh, dear!'

'Save time – No. 2,' i.e. rehearse 2nd Hungarian Dance while waiting for play-back of test. 'Ta-yum pa-pa – staccato – letter A': same drill. 'The upbeat staccato.' 'Letter E, letter E – pom pom pom.'

Play-back of test in listening room. After this, the recordist says: 'Triangle, where are you? That's no good over there – come over here by your father' (i.e. the drummer). Recordist makes further criticisms: '*piano* not anything like pronounced enough – pizzicato – second fiddles – bring it out – *piano* again at 13, make it *pianissimo* – 4 bars before is one *f* and not two *f*'s and so on.

Now back to rehearsal of 1st Dance again: opening – 'in this passage a crescendo: tio tio tu tu tu tu...' (Krauss): 'letter B – first *piano* good – second *piano* no good – *mezzo forte*.' 'Sh-sh-sh' for *piano*, and smiling and pointing with approval to 1sts – every expression of face and hand and stick used – tapping with it on desk – using his baton – waggling hand from wrist – singing 'ra po po po pa!' at end.

The wax of 1st Dance: tension before recording; someone comes in – creaky chair – distant trams in Kingsway – basses continuing conversation by lip-reading, waiting for red light.

'Red light on?' 'No.' 'Not satisfied.' – 'False start – somebody broke the tape' (i.e. too loud) – 'triangle probably', from recordist.

Clarinets have a little case of reeds like a fisherman's flies – carry them in their mouths and so on; they squeak like bats.

Slavonic Dance No. 8: Same drill, i.e. piece played right through once. Horns playing around – one using horn as though it were an old-fashioned movie camera and turning imaginary cranking handle photographing next horn.

Recorders' music language: 'It's too hefty'; 'not gracious enough'; 'all much more delicate'; 'triangle, play it and play it higher up'; 'wood-winds, very *dolce*'; 'always have to play grace notes slower in recording'. 'Dynamics all the time' – from play-back.

After violent *fortissimo* passage by trombones played with enormous gusto, they smile and bow to each other.

Extraordinary effects and voice from play-back box – 'fiddles and violas, 2nd repeat, diddle diddle diddle, too LOUD'; 'bass drum and cymbals still sluggish.'

Clearer and clearer becomes the connection between the temperament of the player and the instrument – brass, horns, trombones, both behave and look like fighter pilots or clever street salesmen. In comparison, the basses are philosophical comics.

'*Forte* needs to be *mezzo forte* for recording. Pull it down a peg. Mark all *f* down one half – *ff* = *f* and *f* = *mf*.' 'Basses, you can mess the whole record up – *pianissimo*.' 'Repeat at E, outside players only.' 'Should be a dotted quaver – is it marked?'

The human interpretation of music by Krauss and Krips: 'fat music' – 'thin music' – 'graceful music' – 'funny music' – 'singing...' etc.

NOT programme notes on technique: all this conveyed with face, as well as hands, body, etc.

*

Albert Hall.

A violinist heard to say: 'It's curious how different conductors can produce actual and different sounds from the same orchestra.'

Looking at forthcoming Beethoven programme (Symphony 5 and 4th Piano Concerto): 'We shall be through by twelve – he can't spin it out longer than that; they all say the same things, as if we had never played them before...'

Men bringing in flowers. The conductor starts with the last movement of Beethoven 5, amid protests from orchestra – this is to let the trombones go. Letter C, 1st movement Beethoven. Men continue to move flowers. Question from drummer, 'Pa pa pa paaa – do you want a pull up?' 'That clear? That clear, that last one?' 'All clear, I think.' 'Exactly as printed.'

During the pathetic second movement the 'cellos lean across for a joke. The orchestra cannot take the Beethoven 5 quite seriously: *più moto*, the wood-wind for some reason not entering, then the basses, and then others, actually sing the tune!

One does not feel that transforming touch that Krauss had even in the gloom of Kingsway Hall. The conductor seems competent, muscular enough, everything – but not, I think, making or letting the orchestra play really. One can see clearly this morning that whereas Krips and Krauss think of music in human terms, today's conductor for example is interpreting and thinking of its effects on *him* – a critical attitude; this contributes to the gap between him and the orchestra – who *are* the music.

The rehearsal ends as prophesied at twelve with some applause for the pianist, in Beethoven's 4th.

On the bar of the artists' canteen is a pile of dark green cricket caps with a badge: the words 'LSO' on a shield. These are distributed to the cricketing members of the sports club, the energetic and younger members of the orchestra of course – Eddie Walker the flautist, the youngest and most enthusiastic of the 'cellos, etc. They hold an informal meeting prompted by Harry Dugarde and barracked by Gordon Walker. There are the usual comedy effects of trying the wrong-sized caps, putting them on unsuitable people – they put one on Gordon, who is in morning dress and who looks just like Tweedledum. The main purpose of the meeting, however, is to separate the funds of the cricket and golf societies and to collect for the cricketing season in advance: 'so that we can oil the bats, otherwise they won't last a week.'

*

20 January 1949.   Mitcham Baths Hall.   3.0 p.m.
Rehearsal for evening concert.

Mendelssohn *Fingal's Cave.*
Mozart *Eine Kleine Nachtmusik.*
Handel *Water Music.*
Beethoven Seventh Symphony.

I was telling the man who was shaving me in the rush to get to Victoria that I was going to an orchestral rehearsal in the suburbs; he asked which orchestra, and said: 'I think they are coming to Hackney on the 30th.' It turned out that he was a member of the Hackney Civic Entertainments Committee; discussed recent Hackney Symphony Concerts. The hall there holds 1200 or so, but the last time they only got 300-400 people. The committee held a meeting immediately after the concert; he had told them, 'You are offering the people a sandwich made of bread, bread, and bread. All Beethoven. Now if you were to put a bit of Tchaikovsky or Rimsky-Korsakov in the middle of the sandwich, people might come. After all, they're suburban people – Hackney isn't the Albert Hall.'

The train to Mitcham Junction sweeps out of Victoria, over the river, right under the chimneys of Battersea power station, and into the grey landscape of industrial streets, railway yards, and back gardens with washing and struggling trees. Then the train gets into more open country – lines of prefabs, nissen huts, allotments, Tooting football ground; rows of seagulls sitting on flooded furrows.

Mitcham baths hall is like Cheam, but less successful – the orchestra, though of only forty-five players, is going to be cramped, and is placed right under the stage, which won't help the sound. Ernie is there by 2 p.m., having fixed the Denham film session this morning – it appears the timps want a rostrum at the back; some of the orchestra have come from Denham.

The four horns are late – march in with a wink, carrying their cases. (Note: horns usually travel in the same car.)

3.6 p.m. 'We do the symphony – then we'll have tea at once. Horns, please, no repeats in the first movement.' Very business-like. (Note: the librarian has come down here. Talks to Ernie.) 'Right through with the bow – right through.' Strings sound sharp. Kisch conducting without score. 'That fortissimo about three bars back – 2nd and 4th bars, strings down, wood-wind come through.'

2nd Movement: 'Singing tone, please.' 'More strings – crotchets a bit longer.' 'No crescendo – sing out, sing out, on this.' 'Let the oboe through.' 'Lengthen the crotchets, please.'

The conductor has a severe, doctor-like, scholastic manner.

3rd Movement: 'First two repeats – no others.' The orchestra play resolutely compared to the intensity of the conductor. 'Lighten up, gentlemen

– lighten up – nothing heavy for the brass at all.' A tiny smile flicks across
Kisch's face again and again.

4th Movement.

Tea.

Handel, *Water Music*. The conductor suddenly not so tense. 'Sing out
– very nice'; the orchestra less tension, better playing.

*

Sunday, 23 January 1949.   Albert Hall.

  Mendelssohn *Hebrides* Overture.
  Borodin Polovtsian Dances.
  Beethoven Fourth Symphony.
  Rachmaninoff, 2nd Piano Concerto.
  Arias.

The full percussion trio are here this morning, troop in and put out
their boxes of tricks – glockenspiel, cymbals, tambourine, gongs, etc. –
and with little to do, they stand there hands in pockets and cigarettes
drooping exactly like the well-dressed street salesmen one sees in Camden
Town – or, again, secondhand booksellers, one with a scarf round his neck
and no overcoat.

Borodin 2nd Dance: The percussion are in their element here.

As the Beethoven opens, four women cleaners come up as though from
nowhere and begin to polish the chairs – to me, looking down on them
from the timps, they look like cotton-pickers bending over the infinity of
white-labelled chairs. The percussion climb over the side of the platform
with difficulty. The conductor is being fussy over the Beethoven. (A violinist said the other day that, frankly, he didn't like playing Beethoven and
much preferred the *Water Music* – 'has some good tunes in it'.)

During the tea break a group was admiring a fantastic model violin
three inches long – not an imitation, a model – made by Bertram Lewis.

At the Albert Hall, it is in the narrow little corridor between the band
room, the staff canteen, and the platform, just opposite the entrance to the
artists' room used by the leader and the conductor, that Mr Lewis puts the
attendance register for signing and also the dates of future engagements.
Today they are noting a February engagement for recording Vaughan
Williams' Sixth Symphony for Columbia under Sir Adrian Boult. A whole
list of February dates and film engagements at Denham, for pencilling in
diaries.

It was here in this corridor in front of such a notice that the famous line
of dialogue referring to films was heard to occur: 'Raking money out of hell!'

*

24 January 1949. Queen's Westminsters HQ Drill Hall (Territorial
Rifle Battallion). 7.30 in the evening.
George Stratton conducting the first of two rehearsals for the Sibelius
concert under Sargent.

This is a fantastic location. An enormous room decorated with the regimental shields, trophies, rolls of honour, and the more temporary charts
of 2-inch mortar bombs, Bren-gun parts, etc.; weapon-training posters; a
six-pounder covered with tarpaulin in one corner. It is freezing cold and
draughty, the horns in overcoats and duffle coats. Sibelius 5 is, of course,
dead in mood with the extremely sombre, cold, and warlike location, from
whose roof hang six huge gas lamps. Partly for Sibelius and partly from
being on the flat, the orchestra looks enormous. The 'cello cases are
ranged next to ammo-boxes and beer crates. The double basses huddle in
their overcoats in front of 'Grenade, Anti-Personnel, Hand, No. 70 Mark
3', an enlarged colour section.

This is, of course, the first of two rehearsals for one of the orchestra's
own concerts, the one for which the agent said the receipts were £89 so far.
The acoustics are appalling, the echoes infinite. It is very difficult to make
oneself heard. George Stratton uses the usual N for Nobody, M for
Emma, and also E for Elephant! The horns are baffled from time to time
by their parts – 'That right?' to each other with a smile.

8.25 p.m. Sir Malcolm arrives – 'Very sorry I am late.' 'I would like to
start all over again. No. 5.' There has been a great deal of discussion of
parts, etc.; Someone says they don't play it often, maybe some of them
have never played it, very difficult, very bad print.

1st Movement: 51 near D. 'I want accent here – tickerty tickerty tickerty…' 3 before G. 'One two er, one two er, ticker ticker tum!' Letter I.
'…the winds are on the beat, you are before it. One, two three. One two
three.' Smile of success. 'Put *mezzo forte* in a bracket – then you'll know
that's where you've got to.' Letter J. '…think it! three, *one* two three…' to
the firsts and seconds.

At this point, in place of the usual cleaners or man in the roof, a lad in
uniform and a green beret comes in carrying three rifles, and goes through
into the armoury.

Sargent: 'Pai *ya*, pai *ya*,' to the 'cellos. 'L!' to the horns. 'Aiya, *aiya*,
attend with your breath, very strong breath, attend – very well, we are at
Emma!' 'Newcastle' (= N).

At end 'Bravo', out handkerchiefs, horns pour water out after climax.
'Next movement, please.'

2nd Movement: 'This time always *legato* – and stress the bar time, *ta ta ti
ya ta*, letter C.' 'Always diminuendo from the bar line – makes the phrase.'

3rd Movement:

Note: usual place for lighted cigarette during playing is on desk by clip holding. First horn gets lighted cigarette in his mute! Full of smoke! The other horns are convulsed.

The 'cellos and double bass playing their part alone. Sargent asking for *ff*. Last two bars – 'One two *three*'. In the silence – 'long not short'.

Second Symphony, Sibelius: only the better known sections. Letter H. The excitement of a horn sitting with his own single desk, turning over rapidly as he is playing. 'You're bad fellows,' to the winds. Then the smile next time through. 'One bar before the *tempo primo*.' 'Do it once more.'

2nd Movement: "*Forte, forte*" to the 'cellos at opening. '*Mezzo*, mind that B flat.'

Horn: 'Where are we going to now?' Another: '*Andante*.'

3rd Movement (sections only): opening, 'This effect is important... ticker der, ticker der, ticker der *dum*.' Letter E. '*Lento* – next *lento*.'

Then about 9.45 (i.e. well before closing time), Sargent suddenly says, 'Well, I expect you all want to go home; I do', and calls it a day. The orchestra cheer like schoolboys.

*

25 January 1949.   Royal Albert Hall.

Second rehearsal, Sibelius.

The orchestra are tired. They have to go to Denham this afternoon for a film session – 'we should be sleeping this afternoon'. 'Terrible hall that – waste of time – you can't hear anything – you can't get a balance. It's the only place we could find. All the other halls were full.' *A propos* the cold last night: 'We killed that with three rums" (horn-player).

9.30 a.m. *Second Symphony*.

1st Movement: 'Good.' Letter H; looks round for entry – and then remembers with a smile it is a drum solo. Letter I. 'At the moment it sounds like a bassoon solo. I want the basses.' To the drums, 'It is a continuous trill with accents.'

2nd Movement: Note again the curious poetic effect of *pizzicato* in a huge empty hall – visual and aural effect.

At the drill hall last night Sargent changed into and out of his rehearsal coat on the spot, there being no artists' room. Sargent gives the impression of being really at home in Sibelius – sings and mimes the phrases the way Viennese conductors do Brahms and Weber – treats it humanely.

To strings, '*Andante* – ta...ta...ta...' 'Bassoons, play it – wood-wind – can't be slower – you will all play in the right key, won't you – F sharp?'

Listening to the rehearsal in Block H are a fairly constant group of students.

This morning again the influence of Sargent on the orchestral players is clearly established in this Second Symphony – no talking in the double basses and brass except about the music, constant peering at other people's scores, checking of marks, rubbing out, and so on, fingering phrases silently when not playing.

One of the young students – young man, age 20-ish – is following Sibelius and Sargent like a spectator at a fight, conducting with his hands, blowing imaginary brass with his cheeks, anticipating phrases and smiling at them as they come up.

Just as Sargent is saying, 'Three from the end – this is the value – pá-pá-pá', a violinist runs out to the dump in Block H to get a new string from his case – sits there fixing it; Sargent's voice in the background of his hurried work.

3rd Movement: A girl student beats time as though conducting the rapid opening of the 3rd movement – two others studying score – crashing of teacups, etc., behind – repeating of the conductor's rhyme, 'ticker der, ticker der, ticker der *dum*' especially to the trombones.

One sees more and more the point of a whole Sibelius concert – by the LSO for themselves – especially in view of the difficulty of the 5th.

Letter H. Sargent is saying, 'Gentlemen, the tempo is always pushing ahead. Yum pa hum, hum, hum – now we must pull it back.' At this point a hammer in the roof begins a sort of drum roll and the drummer instinctively looks up – smiles – imitates without sound with his sticks – looks across at the basses and indicates the man in the roof with his sticks.

*

7 February 1949. Again at Iverna Gardens, i.e. the London Welsh.

This is a Monday morning, so during the first bars of Strauss's *Don Quixote* there pass across the back of the orchestra three Russian-looking characters in blue peaked caps and old battle-dress with boots clattering on the wooden floor, bent beneath two ack-ack dustbins and a gigantic stack of rubbish, presumably military papers, and so into the infinitely gracious string opening of Strauss.

Previously the strings had gone over and over a *Brandenburg*. George Weldon had, I remember, remarked how we all come back to Johann Sebastian Bach in the end, and Taylor, the drummer, had immediately after stated emphatically his distaste for Beethoven – 'elephantine'.

At a moment during the Strauss, Navarra, the 'cellist, comes in to have a word with Cundell, the conductor, and the orchestra give him an extremely warm welcome with their bows on desks. Cundell is, in fact, deputising for Kubelik – this is one of the orchestra's own concerts; Kubelik's cancellation after announcement is a great pity. This is the first of two rehearsals.

A propos Strauss. Cundell: 'I'm sorry to bother you with all this expression, but with music like this you must make it fantastic.' 'There are points in this work where you hear four things going on at the same time. Someone asked me about trying out one particular part. You cannot try out one particular thing. The *music* is the point. You must be prepared to chuck away lovely music.'

During the second section of *Don Quixote*, at the moment when the tenor tuba is playing against the solo viola, Ernie comes in with a wind machine to add to the fantasy. It is made of wood and canvas but is pretty rickety, and as Navarra, the solo 'cello, is playing, an extraordinary pantomime takes place between young Taylor, who has to play it, his father, and Ernie, who both indicate how easy it will be provided it doesn't fall.

Cundell: 'I think it must go faster – you know the point, don't you. He suddenly sees the dust on the road – the flock of sheep, and the charge is on – make it more exciting.' End of Var. 1.

Confusion of nationalities; Navarra is speaking in *French*; the expression marks in the score being in *German*, '*Etwas schneller*'; Kubelik, who was to have conducted, was a *Czech* refugee; the *London Welsh* W.O. in uniform marches through with a bag; Cervantes, *Spanish*.

At the end of the solo-'cello passage the orchestra instinctively applaud and say, 'Bravo'. At the end of all this the wind machine is, of course, inaudible, and as for the *pp* and *ff* markings, he is winding redfaced and smiling as hard as he can to make himself heard above the din.

After the break Bertram Lewis stands up and says, 'Hands up anyone not going back to Denham.'

*

8 February 1949.   Royal Albert Hall.
    Cundell. Navarra.

Dvořák 'Cello Concerto.

Warmer this morning. 'Sun looks a bit watery.' Schwiller comes on to platform about 9.45, looking around. Lewis and Mr Sanders arranging scores. Schwiller says, 'I was trying to see where I am today.' Sanders with some ironic fire: 'Leave the platform – you will be told nothing – leave the platform.' Schwiller, 'Leave it? I will take it with me.'

During the Dvořák this morning Ernie is in shirt-sleeves repairing the wind machine on the platform.

This being one of the orchestra's own concerts, leaders of sections, i.e. George Yates, Gordon Walker, Bill de Mont, step across into the auditorium to listen to balance. As a result of Bill de Mont's walk round listening, the number of desks is reduced in solo-'cello passages. Harry Dugarde and Bertram Lewis go out and listen.

One immediately forms the impression of serious music-making; it is *their* orchestra, and they are particularly impressed by Navarra, whom they have invited. During the slow movement a drill begins to work on the roof. At this point, where the number of instruments is not great and desks are reduced, quite a number of musicians go and sit in the hall. Then hammering and sawing are added to the drill. The stray members coming back – George Stratton even running – for the 3rd movement.

This morning there is almost no stopping or discussing. The work is played, after all, for the mutual understanding of soloist and orchestra. There is the old difficulty of strings (in this case the solo 'cello) and the wood-wind hearing each other. Play over one or two difficult spots, e.g. bar before 8 (2nd movement).

Note: the soloist, particularly in the accentuated 3rd movement, throws himself into the *whole* performance, following the orchestral passages with emphatic miming, and so on. One is conscious of music-making (Bruno Walter: 'Gentlemen, we are here to make music'), and not the solo boxer sitting in his corner which we saw in one conductor's rehearsal the other day. Someone is brought in to see Gordon Walker and Dugarde, who are sitting in the amphitheatre stalls.

At the end of the Dvořák there is really warm applause, including clapping for the soloists. This is followed by private discussions between Navarra and Cundell and Stratton: Navarra walking from one to the other, cigarette in his mouth, and playing them little fragments instead of talking, George Stratton making notes on score, Cundell looking at watch, while N. and Stratton play a section of the last page over together.

At the beginning of the Strauss, or rather while the strings are rehearsing a section of Var. 9, Navarra goes into the auditorium, wiping his neck and hand and face from sweat.

Always when a section of the orchestra play like this, the others watch them intently and applaud or even hiss in mock derision.

The Performance.

It is clear that the 'moment' may occur, thanks to a soloist as well as or instead of a conductor: the moment of overflowing emotion occurred, I suppose, immediately after the Dvořák, in the interval when they were drinking beer in the bar and George Stratton was making his way through a crush of wives, sweethearts, and autograph hunters, in full evening dress, with two cups of coffee for the conductor and the soloist.

'What an artist!' – that is the word used. If the orchestra often seem to be hard in their judgments, it is because they reserve their enthusiasm for a moment and a player like this.

The emotional and cathartic effect on the orchestra of an evening like this is very great – it influences their playing for weeks.

*

20 February 1949.   Albert Hall.
    Gaston Poulet.

Beethoven Programme.

The horns warming up alone in the band room. Three Welshmen discussing Newport, Swansea Town, Cardiff City. (It is a Sunday; they are looking at the Saturday afternoon notices.) An oboist blowing his reed at the canteen table.

'Mesdames et Messieurs. J'ai à vous dire la joie que j'épreuve de me retrouver parmi vous pour ce beau concert…Bonjour' (applause on desks).

Then Beethoven: exceptionally moving effect of going straight into the Beethoven Violin Concerto.

Gaston Poulet had previously come into the bar with George Stratton and shaken hands with old members of the orchestra…George Stratton translating, 'No, it is I who offer' (Non, c'est moi qui offre) re the coffee. Ida Haendel in very simple girlish clothes with absolutely no chi-chi, standing like a novice, violin under arm; just standing waiting for entry – what a contrast to some we have seen!

Though this is not an LSO concert, Gordon Walker and George Yates and Bert Lewis stand out in the amphitheatre listening to the balance.

This morning's rehearsal consists in playing the pieces straight through by the baton without comment.

Earlier today the timpanist and one of the percussion squad (that is the expression used) discussed the apparent confusion over percussion parts and instruments; said, in fact, there were often too few parts to go round, partly due to printing percussion parts for several instruments on same sheet when, in fact, the players could not stand together, partly due to the vanity of the modern composer (lack of real experience of the orchestra from the inside?).

Leonora. 'Je vous demanderais, messieurs – pas trop court le son' – singing the violin phrases – and then to the wood-wind, 'Nous sommes d'accord, n'est-ce pas?' singing to them. 'Voilà,' as they play. Then singing again. 'Je vous demanderais, messieurs, encore un crescendo supplémentaire – compris? Za-za-za-za-za-pa-pa-PAH!' Extraordinary imitation of the crescendo. Stratton turns and says with a little twinkling voice, 'Understand?' 'Voulez-vous, messieurs, prendre neuf. Voilà – accent. Encore, messieurs.' Here we have the sweet French singing contrast to the German of Krauss. 'Permettez, (singing): da da da di, da da da da.' The theme of Leonora, and then they play. Crescendo, near P: 'Ta re tum tum tum pom, a la da da, martelé à la pointe.' 'Une, deux, treize, quatorze, seize, avant P,' singing with them. 'Permettez, *sostenuto expressif!*' Here we have the singing musician again as opposed to the mathematicians' 'Di ya, di ya, da da'. 'Comptez, où nous étions là, au dernier fortissimo,' singing with a delicious voice.

The trumpet call from the artists' room. 'Très émouvant ceci, beaucoup d'émotion dans la sonorité' in the strings' entry after the trumpet call. Poulet says again, 'Est-ce que je peux voir?' runs out to see where the trumpeter is playing off; comes back. 'La deuxième sonnerie,' i.e. the second trumpet-call off. 'Second time,' says George Stratton. 'Piano, mais beaucoup d'émotion' to the strings.

(Note: the French intrusion is a welcome relief from the Anglo-German struggle, cf. Navarra.)

'Je voudrais encore la lettre G.' 'Letter G.' 'Expressif, messieurs, *chantez*' (cf. Krips, 'sing . . . sing'). '*Molto legato* et puis *expressif.*' '*Presto.*' 'N'est-ce pas, messieurs, aussitôt *a tempo*? Il y a plus de pressé. Gardons le tempo!' 'Trois mesures avant' holding up three fingers. 'Voilà, Ha!' laughing. 'Excusez – excuse me – votre *crescendo* – retenez.' George Stratton: 'Hold the crescendo back.' Poulet: 'Allez, *crescendo.*' Shouting, 'Piya, piya, mya, mya, sans presser.' To horns (cf. Krips, 'Not push'). Letter Ka K. 'Voulez-vous supprimer les dernières mesures' 12 bars before end.

Coffee: 'Seule condition, cette fois c'est moi' – Poulet to Stratton. Break: orchestra very happy. 'It does make a difference having a conductor.' 'He knows music from the inside.'

Debussy, *La Mer*. 'N'oubliez pas que dans cette œuvre les nuances sont exagérées.' 'Toutes les couleurs plus que vous ne croyez' (Poulet was a friend of Debussy). 'Mr Stratton sera bien aimable de traduire.' 'Alors, sept – seven – allez, chantez, messieurs.' 'Attention, messieurs. Ah, pa pa pa *pom*. Ah, pa pa pa *pom*.' 'Cinq avant neuf'; Stratton: 'Five before nine.' Trouble with cymbalist: 'non, non, laissez vibrer.' '*Nove*, neuf, nine – permettez, parce que je vais en Italie, en Allemagne, je confonds tout.' 'Onze – a-leven.' Swinging his arm like a fisherman steering his boat in the swell. 'Fourteen – *molto expressif* – fagottes' (international language).

Wonderful percussion parts at 15. Into the classic Anglo-German conflict comes the sweetness of Dvořák and Debussy – Navarra, Poulet – the international language.

'Dix-huit.' Eighteen – eighty – eighteen – eighteen – dix-neuf – nineteen – this becomes a gaffe! 'Deux mesures avant 22 – prenez bien la parole' to 1sts, 'nous allons prendre 2 avant vingt quatre', '2 before 24'.

He has all the violas and front rows laughing with him, and the orchestra as a whole really working, swinging in and out of the waves of sound. To trumpets (near 28) 'pum, pum, pum, pia di di di, détachez.' 'Permettez, permettez, permettez, premiers violons, bien spiccato.' Really he has a happy family atmosphere – smiling faces. At the end of the 1st movement, 'Bon, bon.' 1st clarinet says, 'Sept avant trente-six.' 'Ah' from the orchestra. Applause.

The opening of the 2nd movement, 2 before 43, terrific! – like a magician, pushing the sound back and back into more mysterious origins. 'Voilà, c'est ça; très bien.' 'Fagottes – oouah! oouah! tout c'est soufflé. Dixième de 42.'

He has steadily taken off his overcoat, coat, and jumper – the last while making them laugh with the translation of a number. 'Allez, allez, crescendo, crescendo.' Like the waves rushing in – 'une petite seconde; avant 48 – six mesures avant 48. Deux.' 'Tout le monde, messieurs.' After a section rehearsal, 'Voulez-vous me jouer le cinquante-quatre?' The glockenspiel player looks a little worried – it involves moving from one instrument to another: 'Glockenspiel – horn – 2ᵉ clarinette. Ta ta ta ta ta – tala tala.' (Cf. Krauss, calling out their names.) 'A la double-barre' (but mesures = bars). 'Les deux plateaux' (both cymbals). 'But, sir, I don't know if it's nine before 54 or nine after.' Stratton translates.

Coming to the performance itself, about 2.45 p.m. a group of the orchestra are sitting in the canteen drinking coffee and telling curious stories. It began with comment on the sudden disappearance of a player's beard. He explained it was due to letting a barber trim it too close; it was then so silly he had to cut it off altogether. Then they looked at Mac, the second oboe, who has a fine square beard (it was he who addressed Poulet in French this morning, to the astonishment of the orchestra); they say if he grows it longer he won't need to wear a collar and tie. Gordon Walker then produces a story of a flute-player in Glasgow who grew a beard and became a moneylender on the side: 'good double, that!' And then the story about another flute-player who was 70-something and had a small bald patch on the back of his head, and in spite of his age was so sensitive about it that before appearing in public he touched it up with boot-blacking.

This morning the seating or layout of the orchestra had been rearranged to get better balance and to let the double-basses play nearer the other strings. It may, Walker says cunningly to George Yates, stop some of the talking at rehearsals in the back rows. George Yates says he said nothing all this morning – in which case, says Walker, the Empire must be safe (Yates' well-known asides being usually political). *A propos* the word Empire, Walker produces an extraordinary true story about the wife of a horn-player who was rung up by an engager when her husband was out and asked if he would be free for an engagement on a Thursday at Winchester. Looking at his book, she said 'yes' and took a message. When the horn-player came in he reported he was wanted for the Empire at Winchester – or something like that; she had been flustered and hadn't got it quite right. 'The Emperor, perhaps,' he suggested. No, not that, she said. Then it must be a concert at the Empire Theatre. Anyway, he rang up the engager and was told no, not the Empire – he had said the engagement was in the Guildhall to play in *The Kingdom*.

The audience during the concert: note the number of opera glasses trained on Ida Haendel. A girl nearby (admittedly not English) at the end of the 1st movement has tears in her eyes as the last violin note is heard. This is a 'moment': the audience waits on the conductor's final beat, then rustles itself into new positions and lets go of its coughs. And then the opening of the 2nd movement swells up.

*

21 February 1949.
Vaughan Williams – Walton concert; rehearsal.

Walton conducting *Scapino*.
Once again notice the fascinating sounds and sights of tuning – the three horns standing apart playing with a definite ritual, a trumpet going off into a separate corner to blow, the strings coming in after that (trumpet says to one of the horns, 'I see you've joined the London Welsh.' 'No, London Irish.' Trumpet gives a brisk impersonation). Young Taylor fixes xylophone. George Eskdale arrives with a bag and umbrella looking like the doctor. Walton is here early – stands, pipe in mouth, talking to George Yates and Stratton. George Eskdale settles himself down at his desk with his umbrella hitched on to his chair, not to lose it.

This being the London Welsh Hall, the conductor's rostrum is a rubber-wheeled truck with wedges on the floor to stop it running away.

Drake is vice-chairman and, Gordon Walker being away, he introduces Walton 'who has done us the honour to become President. Please give him a real hearty LSO welcome.' Loud applause; Walton responds.

Scapino. There is a last-minute rush to fix percussion stands and find parts – the more one sees of the percussion squad, the more respect one has for them; interesting complex problems including the mere counting of bars; there are five of them this morning over and above the timpanist.

The trumpeter's feet before his entry after 7, the heel just rising and falling. The xylophone player is beating time with the toe of his left foot – changing with incredible dexterity to two claps of wood, a cymbal crash, and back to xylophone.

Walton is quiet and firm. No musical curiosities, at least in his beat. 'Cornet, 2nd bar after ten, I think not so loud. Figure 9 once more.' Then the trumpets are beating bars with their left hands – I mean when not playing. During momentary breaks the xylophonist tries over phrases very quietly. 'Percussion, I suspect always too loud, but impossible for me to say in here' (looking at the roof with a smile). 'This *pizzicato*' – taking Lionel Bentley's fiddle, and indicating with hand and centre fingers how to play it; Bertram Lewis gets up and says ahead of him, 'Would someone tell us what it is? We haven't the foggiest idea.' Word is passed back. After the most tremendous racket c. figure 25, Walton says quietly, 'Wire-brush, it's marked.'

At the end, after an hour of repeats and complexities, Walton blows out his cheeks and grins and says, 'Once right through if we can.' Bertram Lewis: 'Dr Walton would like an hour's extra rehearsal tomorrow afternoon – could we make it five – five – yes?'

Press photographers.

Vaughan Williams, who has arrived earlier with near laryngitis, 'has lost his voice, so please be very quiet,' says Lewis.

A London Symphony. The orchestra give Vaughan Williams a great round of applause. Adored by musicians, the majestic grey figure – old, bowed, but immensely impressive – begins to conduct the symphony of the old grey city. With Vaughan Williams there is absolute humility, humanity – following his own sure company without bravura. The gestures absolutely economical. One can understand what the orchestra means by saying that Weingartner 'just looked at us', if the figure is impelling, real enough (and here we are face to face with genius): then the love created is sufficient to light the playing.

The first run through of the 1st movement has only one break off. Then at the end, with George Stratton's aid, he asks for 'letter C' and waves a wild left hand to stop when he has gone far enough. 'S.' Stops, then says just audibly, 'That's much clearer now – not clear before.' At the end of the 1st movement: 'Is there anything not clear? It is just as important for you to be satisfied with me as me with you. It's your reputation and not mine.'

2nd movement: 4 before B. As with Walton, no particular musical phraseology. 'Less detached, I don't want to hear between notes.' A mistake somewhere over in the bassoon area makes Vaughan Williams look up without stopping and say 'All right?' and smile. Stops the orchestra after violin solo, to query the percussion's use of bells. 'More vim, you are in a hansom cab!' for this is the London of thirty – forty years back.

The economy of gesture and small movement is such that when near the end of 3rd movement he crumbles his left hand for a heavy percussion accent, it is like a facial expression, and then the same hand steals up to his lips, which just say 'hardly anything at all – extreme *pianissimo*' to the 'cellos. The repeat of the viola solo at the extreme end of the movement, Vaughan Williams simply watches Gwynne Edwards playing, and as he finishes, bows to him: 'I am here to help you.' During all this, orchestra just show what can be done for discipline – absolute quiet and attention.

3rd Movement: The wonderful fair-music reminds one that there is more understanding of popular music and realism in this one figure standing on the truck in the drill hall than in all the cultural committees and manifesto concocters of the whole of Europe and as far as the Urals.

'All right – now the last movement.' The last march – audience come in with the London Welsh. 'A countryman's view of London.'

A rush of warm applause at the end, a bow, 'Are you satisfied with me?' 'I have an awful cold on me, and I see no reason for rehearsing again tomorrow morning.'

The Performance. I must now record a faint image of the evening's performance. The audience was not large – a fine group of music students at the back of the arena, a general scattering of real music-followers in the boxes and amphitheatre, some people high up, and an extra number of smart art-cum-film-cum-music-cum-socialites for the occasion of Walton's return to England. Not very many of them paying for their seats, I should say: photographers everywhere, and some evening dress (people going on to a party and so on).

The loudspeakers announced that the directors of the LSO regretted than the 'Fanfare' could not be included in the programme. Walton came on and conducted 'The King', then *Scapino*, which I have heard so many times recently that I could not say whether it was good, bad, accurate, or not. It did not, I thought, make much impression. The Viola Concerto, on the other hand, got more applause – Riddle's playing much more poetic than at rehearsal, and if the evening had ended there, one would have gone home with the last solo in one's head. But with all the goodwill in the world, what happened after that altered everything.

The tension in the orchestra as they took their places after the interval was something like stage fright. After all, Vaughan Williams was 77, was ill, had lost his voice: possibly this was the last time he would conduct them?

Then, the *London Symphony* is not just a piece of great music in the

abstract – it is of us, written for us, written about us: this makes a performance in London a social event in the real sense (cf. the social stuff above).
All this one felt.

And after all the curious and different and interesting and uninteresting
conductors, here is the composer with the gift of the spirit as he alone sees
it and imparts it. And here he is – a great silver-haired figure, slowly
appearing from the artists' room. Silver hair (as I say), the most splendid
countryman's head and shoulders, huge arms and hands that in past generations held the axe and the plough. The orchestra sweeps to its feet. He
is their god: yes, a god! His particular attributes – his creative fire and with
it his tenacity and above all his humility – are all that they reverence in the
world. He hesitates, bows to the audience, bows to the orchestra, and
slowly (how slowly!) climbs the rostrum to open the huge score (for his
sight is not good) like a Bible; spreads his arms like a tree, and with the first
four bars we know that we are in the Presence.

The first crash of the cymbals that breaks the quiet comes as though we
had never heard it before. The listener shivers with emotion; the Presence
is not on the platform only – it spreads like incense all over the hall ... The
sound delights us as music, but with it goes reverence for the man himself
and the deepest of all feelings, that we are part of it all: it is not a concert
at all, but an act of music-making.

Here let me record that among the small audience, I don't think there
was present one of the LCC officials in whose hands the great city is supposed to lie, nor any of the propagandists who are always crying for social
realism and such like, though here, if ever, they might find it, written
before some of them were born.

Let me record also that at the end of the 1st movement, with the spell
tightening its grip on us, a mid-European film producer, celebrated for his
wastage of other people's money, who had spent the interval in the artists'
room and had sat in a teddy-bear coat visibly eating oranges, stood up and
left the hall.

For the rest, I cannot emulate the writers of programme notes or the
notices of the next morning. I can say that what the music says, we as Londoners had all been through: I remember our worry as the conductor's
hand occasionally stole back to the rail to steady himself, that his fingers
fumbled in turning the pages, that once the orchestra carried on as he was
lost, that there were tears in our eyes, that Richard Capell said to Gordon
Walker: 'I say, you chaps backed him up splendidly,' that George Stratton
came off the platform really crying and said: 'You can't help playing well
– he doesn't show off!' – that of all the minutes of one's life, we can say that
those spent this evening *were well spent*.

*

23 February 1949.   E.M.I. Studio, Abbey Road, N.W.1.

Recording of Vaughan Williams, Sixth Symphony, under Boult.

I cannot describe in detail all today's session, but the scene was this. The EMI studio – the exact orchestra fresh from the Vaughan Williams concert, still moved from their own performance of the *London Symphony*. Boult conducting, Vaughan Williams listening (he had received tremendous applause on entering the studio), sitting slumped in a chair near the conductor, the score on a stand in front of him.

A morning of extreme tension for all. Boult himself, the 'mathematical mind' of the BBC ('think in semi-quavers, one two three, one two three'). Vaughan Williams, as they said last night, so humble since 'he doesn't show off' – his warmth and his abundant personality had created their playing last night. But then add to this contrast the exceptional difficulty of the Epilogue: setting aside the balance problem, ranging from a muted string quartet to a brass band fortissimo – setting this aside, the tension of continuing over long stretches the sustained, slow, rhythmic playing required, especially in the famous fog-horn passage (muted trumpets) and the muted trombones (after V). After the break, when it was about clear that the orchestra felt they were facing an ordeal for several days, there was a critical ten minutes when Boult tried to solve the muted horn-playing by sheer mathematics. 'Fill in the gaps with semi-quavers, think in the semi-quavers – it's the only way.' Over and over again, 'One, two, three, One, two, three, ... No, early'; Vaughan Williams also complaining the trumpets are early – 'That's just what I am saying.' But it is not just a matter of being simply early or late or even dead on. 'It's funny, I shall have to put somebody to stab him (the second trumpet) in the back, with semi-quavers.' But we know, don't we? that problems are not to be solved by making accurate measurements on the bank of the river, only by jumping in.

Occasionally Boult comes down from the rostrum to consult an actual score-marking and note, 'I say, 14 and 18 –'. Don't let what I have said above suggest that Sir Adrian isn't a delightful character. He makes little jokes at the right moment and so on, which is charming and what is called 'very English'.

'That's going very well; oh, what happened?' to muted trombones at 5. 'We must all get together on that B natural, mustn't we?' 'Once more, just to confirm it – once more.' 'Best just look at the diminuendo in 2 before G.' 'Once more, just make quite certain of those semi-quavers – that's early, ti-ya, four and one.'

Stratton makes a series of gestures to the conductor and turns to the firsts and shows them a piece of bowing. Marking and comments are being passed back and queries passed forward between the back desks and the section leaders. Some of them use the tic-tac system.

The turnover problem and the mute problem arise together, exactly before the strings' 'ghostly' entry. This is interesting. Boult complains that he has conducted this symphony all over the place and strings are always late here. They have plenty of time to turn over. But, points out Stratton, the *mutes* are marked on the far page, and so are not looked for and put on until after the page turning over, and this makes them late. There is always a reason for these things.

Tests from the speaker on the floor of the studio sound terribly mechanical and throttled.

Recording itself begun after lunch – three waxes of the first side – three of the second, which overrun into movement two. Then at 4.20 p.m. we have another take of disc 1. Josephine clicks her bow at her desk, but no one notices and are best satisfied with this take. Then begins work on side 3. Test: George Eskdale in trouble again with semi-quavers of trumpet parts – bass drum comes in late. George Stratton has a fit of silent coughing.

Comedy of listening to these things in play-back. Boult very good humoured. Comments from Vaughan Williams in listening room.

Finally record third side. Record three again. Rehearsal of side 4. Test of 4 (it is 5 o'clock). The quality of these tests is really dreadful.

The orchestra were pretty whacked after yesterday. The cor anglais, Cruft, was so tired at his final solo, they may well have to do that again. Immediately after making a test of end of side 4, and while listening to the test, Bertram Lewis sings out, holding up a card, 'Police want driver of car HPV 649'; deputy leader Lionel Bentley stands up amid the cheers of the orchestra.

Needless to say there is no inter-com. between conductor and listening room. Boult just claps his hands and shouts, 'Oi!' 'All right, now we'll have a whack at this, shall we?' At 11.30 a.m. we are still re-recording this side – minor alterations in side drum.

In the tea break, Bill de Mont talking about his jeep, says there was a member of the orchestra in the old days who used to arrive at the Queen's Hall on a white horse which he tethered to the railings.

After the break begins side 5, which takes us into the last movement – George Stratton has already stressed the extreme difficulty of this movement, i.e. the tension of string playing. The remainder of the scherzo and the last movement are broken up into two sides, making six in all.

*

27 February 1949.   Royal Albert Hall.

> Rachmaninov No. 3, Moura Lympany.
> Litolff. Scherzo from *Concerto Symphonique.*
> César Franck Symphony.
> Tchaikovsky, *Romeo and Juliet.*
>   Walter Susskind.

Wind players tuning: 'Draught in here this morning – blowing the paper away – always was a bit of an out-house.'

Susskind conducting in shirt-sleeves the theme in the 1st movement of the César Franck Symphony. The horn entry and then the *crescendo* following: 'More, more, more, more, *more.*' 'Please, please, please' (to talking players); 'let's play letter K a bit slowly.' Fine effect of the conductor bursting into a smile to the leader as he brings in a very strong violin-entry (after repeat of the theme).

3rd Movement: Round P – Q, long discussion of bowing, with 'high, strings', 'again up!' 'There are one or two spots where they are not playing *legato* – playing pa-pa-pa – letter I, for example – nice, long, long, notes.' 'Now, gentlemen, *cantabile*, please.' 'Put down your bow for the *pizzicato.*' Letter F: discussion with Stratton on string-playing again. Stratton demonstrates suggestion, which is accepted. Nice warm nod from Susskind to Stratton during the revise to show he agrees with the effect.

*

3 March 1949.

What we do on a Sunday morning: three horns in a black saloon car hurtling up Parkway; three hikers on bikes passing the Albert Hall. You may go to church, hiking, stay in bed, but we go to the Albert Hall, wet or fine.

Krips coming out of Q Battery Office. 'Before we start I will tell all the accents in this Overture (*Rosamunde*).' 'Brass *more* – not "ugh" but "ooah"!' Some members of the orchestra are not here. 'Yes – Charing Cross.' George Eskdale arrives late – Krips opens his arms: 'Ah!' 'Nice, please, like in our record we made.' Hand on heart. 'Sing, please.' 'I hope in our concert tonight we do the same.' Conducting the strings alone... '*Vibrato.*' '*Subito.*' 'Yum-pum-pum.' 'Without any pause' (shouting to back desks). '*Vibrato.*' 'Sh-sh-sh.' 'Nice.' 'Have we a letter? – letter C.' Very quickly before the *élan* drops – 'more *vibrato* – less accent' to flutes. 'Every note – small accent.' 'More tension – with me – echo.' 'And now!' 'Just in tempo – now flute and *now*, sh-sh, basses' (walking in and out of sections).

Schubert 6. 'First movement without repeats – as before, all accents more *vibrato* than noise.'

To get silence: 'Master Record.'

'Where are my friends, the Library?' 'What is the matter with the double-basses? Sunday morning mistake, yes?' '*Lento*, they are Austrian dances.'

3rd Movement: 'I don't want to hear the orchestra *going*, the orchestra must be *flying*.' 'That's not so classical, that's like a *caroussel*, like the boys whistling in the street' (last movement) – 'that's Schubert, not Beethoven.' '*Staccato*, flute – like whistling boys.' 'Gentlemen, give me your heart for this symphony – not so classical, the audience must dance – and now we make Johann Strauss – that's not so easy.'

*

5 March 1949.   Kingsway Hall.
Krips – Decca. Recording.

Mozart, 'Jupiter' Symphony.

The second oboe coming in with a rush at 10.5 a.m. and sitting down next to Mac (first oboe) and E. Walker (first flute).

Jupiter I – entry of second subject. 'Sh, sh, *pianissimo*, we start that – it's a new country – the heights of Mozart.' Letter B: 'First violins, you must feel a *crescendo* – but a *crescendo* of the soul.'

Speaking of cricket during the interval E. Walker and Nicholson said they had fixed up a match with Claygate in October, remarking that if you hadn't won the game by the time the 'Swan' opened, you had had it!

Second side = end of 1st movement, 2 before letter D. 'Gentlemen, please, I will not feel the bars – the whole phrase.'

The morning the 1st movement only was recorded – on two sides: there is no doubt that after the gaieties of Schubert and Strauss or the over-well-known Beethoven and Tchaikovsky, the apparent simplicities of Mozart are extremely difficult.

*

14 April 1949.   Kingsway Hall.
Recording.

Jupiter, 3rd Movement: 'Whole movement, one bar.'

By the way, at the lunch the other day Krips bore out exactly the analysis by Vaughan Williams of the history of English Music. The coming of

Handel and Haydn – the two great disasters – the rediscovery of Purcell, the going back to the roots of the tradition, the source of today's strength: Krips quoting especially Vaughan Williams himself and Britten – '*Sancta Civitas* is with Bach'. Also quoting the *Tallis Fantasia*. Vaughan Williams not well known abroad. Full of praise for LSO discipline – idealists, who do not make enough propaganda, not enough notices in the papers.

At the end of a sparkling performance of the last movement, George Eskdale puts down his trumpet and says, 'Very dull'. 'Those parts get me down – pa hum, pa hum. Very nice music but not this' (i.e. the trumpet part).

Earlier, Krips to the firsts: 'Too *timide* – timid – you are frightful.' End of 1st side last movement, *Jupiter*. Taking up bassoon parts again and again: 'That was too early', 'pa, pa, – *pa'*. '*That* was too early.' '*That* was right, *that* was nice.'

*

20 April 1949.   Royal Albert Hall.
Susskind.   Menuhin.

Borodin, Polovtsian Dances.

The big brass and timp. entry before letter E. 'By the way, harp, when you have the chord, play a little bit louder than the rest. The notes are not so important as the octave': stopping after E: 'and so on and so on. Letter G.' 'Now letter I' – beautiful timp. entry. Susskind talks very little; workmanlike, stops them rarely, conducts in shirt-sleeves. Cutting certain sections, begining the finale at U.

On the last beat he says, '*Bartered Bride* Overture; thank you, percussion.' Short discussion of 'cut-off' with brass. 'Now.' Begin again at the beginning. Discussion of the rhythm; 'da da dum, da da dum.' Stop on the long violin passage, for the seconds to complain they can't see his beat if he sits. Susskind: 'I am sorry', and stands. They go into N again, and then he says, 'and so on'. '2 before 2 on the up beat, and I only want the first and second violins.'

Menuhin comes in in shirt-sleeves and old pullover; quickly, waving left hand, looking very young, shakes hands with the conductor.

Tchaikovsky, *Violin Concerto*: short remarks from Susskind – a cut of nine bars after letter F ('this is the only cut in 1st movement'). Several stoppings at opening; 'no, no, someone's playing *legato*, no, I say *non legato*.' '*Pianissimo* but *vibrato*' in first violin entry. Stopping in full flight – turning to Menuhin, 'I am so sorry'. After letter E, orchestral entry: 'For these two we really play as in a symphony.' 'I would be grateful if you wouldn't play such short notes in the ta ta tá cantabile.'

Menuhin very little fussy – very little turning and listening and fidgeting, one sees. 'Cut cadenza – all right – end of cadenza.'

During the whole of this first movement, two managerial types sitting in Block H talk loudly, so as to ruin the study or enjoyment of the twenty-odd people who are listening to Menuhin.

Allegro near end. 'Hold back – yum pum pum – so that we can hear the double-stop there.'

Cuts in 2nd and 3rd movements.

T. *2nd Movement and 3rd Movement:* Restart the opening bars. There seems this morning to be an extra clatter of cleaners, noise of people sorting crockery, vacuum cleaners – perhaps more noticeable because of the intimate 2nd-movement opening. One cannot again help thinking with Menuhin of the music as Danubian. He makes it, someone said next to me, a 'cry coming through the general noise of the orchestra'.

After the first sweep and opening emotion Susskind stops and discusses several points. Letter H, discussion of 'cut' problem with the winds. Men in blue boiler-suits with pipes in their mouths discussing something up in the roof – I mean, standing down in Block J, looking up. Man with string as usual straightening arena seats. 'K, for the *pizzicato*, including first violins, do a little *crescendo* and *diminuendo* in the *pizzicato*.' Rattle of applause at end. Query from double bass leader. 'Now, begin the last movement once more, begin the last movement.' After a few bars, 'and so on'. Menuhin modulates into next orchestral entry.

After the break – in which the Walkers are discussing a holiday in Majorca ('It's about three miles from the sea') and a player regrets having to go to Denham for a film session next three days ('I wanted to go to the Zoo – perhaps I am!') – swing right into the Bach Violin Concerto. One has immediately the overwhelming sensation of *music*. Strings only, and yet what power and majesty! Here Menuhin is transformed, no longer the Danubian: the plaintiveness of the solo instrument is changed like the composer.

2nd Movement: Reduced strings; at least half a dozen of the non-playing strings walk out into the auditorium to listen. The trolley with cups rattling along under the gas-light during the most delicate solo moment. The huge size and emptiness and staring seats of the Albert Hall are reduced to a little German room – a solo violin supported by four 'cellos, one double-bass, six violas, six firsts, and six seconds. Following Bach we are in the real country of music – the conductor quietly talking little scraps: 'I shouldn't use too much *vibrato*.' 'D sharp, D sharp.' 'Take your time.' 'No *diminuendo*.'

The flower: 'Last movement.' From the start, straight through. Clapping for Menuhin at end.

*

10 May 1949.   Royal Albert Hall.
José Iturbi conducting and playing.

> Weber, *Oberon* Overture.
> Strauss, *Don Juan.*
> *Marche Burlesque.*
> Mozart Piano Concerto.
> Arias (Soloist, Consuelo Rubio).
> Liszt, *Hungarian Rhapsody.*

Began late, with moving of pianos – the one from last night's Donald Peers's concert off and the one for Iturbi on. Until the piano is in position the string desks can't be set, so they drink coffee (is this the interval?) or stand about in Block H, while Iturbi, with a huge cigarette-holder in his mouth, tries the piano, surrounded by men in uniform, movers, assistants.

'Good morning, gentleman...the *Oberon*.' Coat off, short-sleeved Hollywood vest. There is an incredulous look on the first horn's face watching his beat. Conducting without score. 'Tonight we make it *together*, yes?' to the wood-winds, not stopping for a ragged entry.

To begin with at least, the worlds of music and film (or is it Albert Hall and Hollywood?) are not mixing. As so often, this is my feeling (or is it my recollection of the time and care spent on the 'elves' by Krips earlier this season?). Maybe it just is he is in a hurry and so not going to bother. The overture never ends. Before the last beat, '*Don Juan*, gen'l'men, please.' 'Have you the right time, please, Mr Stratton?' After a few bars, stop. 'Gen'l'men, after the intermission, would it be trouble to move first trumpet next to first trombone, please?' George Eskdale moves immediately now. Iturbi comes right out of another culture, so he is partly very deferential to ours ('I leave it up to your judgment'), and partly unable to restrain wisecracks and winks. In *Oberon* the gap between Spain and the first-trumpet-calls of 1820 romanticism is too great to be bridged. In Strauss the gap is at least not so great.

Marche Burlesque (anonymous, ? by Iturbi). 'Trumpets short as possible – *pizzicato* – here' pointing to forehead. 'The *crescendo* – of bad taste on purpose – bad taste *crescendo*.' First trombone: 'Mr Iturbi, 4 after 2, is it C sharp or C natural?' Iturbi: 'C natural. The first trumpet is C natural, and to make it more modern is C sharp' (i.e. the first trombone). The laughter that follows this reply breaks down the gap, and has the orchestra laughing with him. 'Follow me – I am the *soloiste* supposed to be tonight – same place.' This he is conducting with score. A great part of the time the winds spend staring at their parts with amusement.

For the Mozart Piano Concerto, Iturbi conducts from the piano stool and plays the solos himself – an arrangement probably much nearer to that of Mozart's time than the separate modern conductors and soloists. The result, with the reduced orchestra, is a sort of party on the platform, Iturbi's bare arms waving above the keyboard when he is not actually playing.

One interesting thing appears, Iturbi, of course, *at* the piano, instead of saying 2 before G, or la-la-ing or singing the phrases, plays them on the keyboard and sorts out note problems in the same way (momentary return of the Kapellmeister). It must be said that the orchestra, or most of them, adore this rehearsal atmosphere. They admire his touch as a pianist, his sense of rhythm, and his personality – 'so easy to work with'. 'This is the time when we enjoy rehearsing.'

Aria from *Le Nozze di Figaro*: Consuelo Rubio: first appearance in U.K. 'Gen'l'men, as in the concerto, every time you come to the *topic* (is that how you put it in English?) a slight *diminuendo*: do you mark it – I leave it to your good judgment.'

Soloist is a beautiful girl with flowing dark hair, in grey beret with dark wine-colour flowing coat. Now the rehearsal has a pleasant informal air, and the sympathetic personality which affects the orchestra has this morning another effect. Workmen are sitting on the steps of the amphitheatre listening. Of course, there is the name, too, but you know who has a great name also and does not attract men in overalls, listening to arias from Wagner and Falla. At the end of the Arias her manager comes to take the soloist away; she is given a good round of applause by the orchestra, and then on to the platform comes Harold Holt.

The Liszt. Now here, of course, Iturbi is in his element, and starts straight away describing *phrasing* of the work, by playing the phrases on the piano – has the orchestra really with him. The simultaneous conducting, and then his playing with George Eskdale, have them really happy and on their toes. The morning ends with the final chords of the Liszt and a general appreciation of happiness.

1949

In the summer of 1949, Jennings was commissioned by John Grierson and the Festival of Britain Committee to make a film about British achievements. After severe differences of opinion between Jennings and Grierson, *Family Portrait* eventually emerged.

Rough research notes for 'Festival of Britain'

28 June [1949]
Notes on discussion with Dr Green
MRC [Medical Reseach Council]

Fleming the original discoverer of penicillin was a friend of Wilson Steer and an amateur painter. At precisely the time of the first discovery (1928-9) he showed Green some 'paintings' which he had made on laboratory plates with colour-forming cultures (i.e. moulds) similar to the broth in which the action [of] penicillin was observed... Green himself pointed out later that the accidental discovery of penicillin, was likely to be influenced by Fleming's interest in the colours of cultures... [...]

This took place at St Mary's Hospital. Academic work. The antibiotic properties were not appreciated at the time – principally because chemotherapy was not yet in being. Realize that at that time there were no specific treatments for majority of diseases. (Exceptions quinine, mercury). In general the aim was to 'let nature effect a cure' In the 1930s a complete change of outlook came about as a result of German work at I.G. labs on sulpha drugs (M & B 693 and so on) – [...]

On another subject – electronic calculator – note that we have now taken up & developed American work – both at Manchester and Cambridge – and developed inventions originating in Manhattan Project – this would appear to be a reverse case to the normal one of American or German development of a British discovery. See Lord Halsbury on this –

TO CICELY JENNINGS   *8 Regent's Park Terrace,*
Saturday [no date, 1949]   *NW1*

[...] We seem at last to be reaching sense over the Festival of Britain – I am now dealing with them direct – including Ian Cox who is the secretary of the Science section. [...] Ian very sweet and helpful as always. My! is Grierson unpopular everywhere you go – the first [time] I had a row with him I thought perhaps it was *me* – but everyone says the same – anyway I think we are straightening things out and getting well *in* the festival which is the principal thing. […]

TO CICELY JENNINGS   *as from The George Hotel,*
Wednesday morning [postmarked 20 July 1949]   *Edinburgh*

My darling Pip –
After York we swept up across to Manchester in pouring rain. Spent a night there – peeped into the spine-chilling ICI chemical labs. – had a look at the industrial past – railways and canals still working from the 18th-19th centuries – then went down to near Crewe to look at daylight astronomy – the new science – tracking meteors by radar – that was yesterday morning – and many other things as well – and then left for here – driving all day – the sun coming out at last as we got into the Lakes. Wonderful evening near Carlisle – spent the night at Hawick on the border and arrived here at 10 this morning – going to see a Professor of Agriculture at 11. […]
Very good trip for the things we were looking for – far too much material of course as usual – the main problem though, being able to talk chemistry one moment, jet engines the next, radar the next, and so on – I mean enough to follow what is said! […]

TO CICELY JENNINGS   *Hotel du Danube, Rue Jacob,*
Tuesday [postmarked 18 August 1949]   *Paris 6e*

[…] Violently hot – almost too hot during the day but very beautiful in the evening. The left bank over-run by American students – would-be writers, painters. Give me the impression of fitting in fairly well – but living nostalgically on their mail all the same.
Have not yet made up my mind exactly what to do as there is a possibility of my attaching myself to a film-unit (this sounds very stupid as I write it) who are going to visit Gide and Picasso – but not certain. In any case only for a few days. […] Café life has of course definitely shifted from Montparnasse down to St Germain & the river – still pestered by street singers and Algerian rug-sellers – […]

TO CICELY JENNINGS   *Hotel du Danube,*
[Postmarked 25 August 1949]   *Rue Jacob*

[...] I don't seem to have *done* very much except one or two museums
including the re-opened Cluny to which Papa took me in the 20s and
which is really wonderful – mediaeval tapestries and carvings – much of
the time I seem to have spent talking to Frenchmen in cafés – they all have
the greatest hopes of England and you can't imagine the absolute worship
of Churchill – except I suppose by the Communists of whom I haven't
seen anything – but of course among the average middle-class intelligent
people the most violent passions are liable to flare up – people's war-
records being the usual subject – on which they will insult each other in
the most terrifying manner and then go & have a drink together! Anglo-
French Union is a very real subject here.

I also met a fascinating American scientist – originally Lithuanian
emigrant and now back in Europe looking at it as an American – looking
through his eyes was really enlightening. [...]

Enormously impressed by Matisse's recent paintings and book-
illustrations and depressed by every other sort of painting – except some
of Max Ernst's. Have done a few watercolours – [...] Oh and to my
astonishment (or did I tell you this?) found my name on a poster and discovered they were running *Spare Time, Listen to Britain* and *Timothy* at an
Experimental Film Festival – but in September!

This, I am afraid, is just a list and not a proper letter – The question
most often asked: 'Is it really true – vraiment vrai – that Sir Stafford Cripps
only drinks water –' They shake their heads wistfully over the puritanism
of the English – [...]

TO IAN DALRYMPLE   [No sender's address]
Wednesday, 31 August 1949

PRIVATE AND CONFIDENTIAL

I. Dalrymple Esq.,
Meyn's Hotel,
Soltau, Germany

My dear Ian,
I am sorry to have to bother you from this distance with a list of troubles, but I see no way of avoiding it. I returned on Monday from my holiday to find a letter from Gordon Smith, addressed to me privately, in
which he indicated in a sort of dully incomprehensible way that the C.O.I.

or at any rate Grierson, while they appreciated the amount of work which had gone into it, considered the treatment insufficient or incomplete. The fact that the Festival people liked it, was, he said, beside the point, since – if you please – they had not been present at the original discussions with Grierson. Grierson required a two page précis of a 'story line' – of what I had in my head as the shape of the film – which would, no doubt, be little trouble to write and which would, if added to the draft treatment, in some way complete it, and bring us a stage nearer to the famous commissioning letter. This faintly insulting document of Gordon Smith's I immediately showed to Derek, who suggested I put down some sort of statement of the way in which I proposed to shoot and construct the film, and he in the meantime would ask the C.O.I. what exactly they expected in their 'two page précis'.

As a result we were both bidden to see Grierson at 5 p.m. yesterday. Whereupon, after the usual delays, we were taken to his flat – given an exposé of his relations with Dr Malan (he is proceeding on leave of absence to South Africa for a few weeks in the near future) and then Derek, who quite rightly proposed to let Grierson do the talking, asked what was required. Grierson pretended to be astonished that we, and I in particular did not see it – '*but a story line*' by which he meant apparently not a story line but a statement of philosophy cum '*purposive*' intention of the film – or something of that sort. Well, clearly that was not impossible. What it came down to was this: that Grierson, in view particularly of my supposed bad record with the Treasury, could not – would not – pass the present piece of writing – he would not even call it a draft treatment – without a clear statement of aims.

Agreed. Reasonable enough if annoying. Ah, but – much more important – this was also to be done for *my* benefit – to help me get wise to myself – and then out paved a mass of personal insults laced with insensibilities and backhanded compliments such as I have never been treated to even by Grierson. Derek was there at the time; had his share of insults and will no doubt bear me out. This piece of writing of mine – full, no doubt, of clever literary allusions – but no shape – no form – no beginning middle or end – such philosophy as it had was 'fascist' – its scholarship thoroughly second-hand – its politics amateur – the confused product of a neurasthenic who had been living in the luxury of the feature world and who had now trailed his impracticability, desire to overspend, and self-pity across twenty-odd pages which would run to ten reels of film and £60,000 of production costs!

And, Ian, I am understating. But, Jesuit-like, there was still hope. I had only to write this two, nay, one page of clarity, purity, form and philosophy – which, I give him his due, he said he would not necessarily insist on agreeing with – and I could save myself from the fleshpots of the feature world. Everything was brought in; the high standards of the past from which I had fallen was [*sic:* 'thus'?] ignobly – *Listen to Britain*, for example (I had the momentary pleasure of quoting what his stooge Anstey had said of it at the time). Both Wessex and you personally were, I regret to say, castigated. Of course, there was no inkling of connection between you as Producer and *Listen to Britain*! The great men of the past – Leonardo and Michael Angelo were dragged into it as examples of artists working *with* Governments – but when I, in a moment of pride no doubt, suggested that a nearer analogy might be to imagine someone asking Cézanne to design a poster in twenty-four hours – there was an explosion in which really we feared for the furniture. How dare I mention Cézanne or even the sacred word 'artist'? To think that Cézanne had toiled in poverty (not true by the way) and to think that his name should be soiled by a hireling (like me) of 'bums' (that was the word) like Wessex – no no that was too much! The sacred shrines of Art watched over by Abnegation and Toil, were in his hands who had just served us with absinthe from the cocktail bar in his flat, and which in his passion for order and discipline he upset all over the table...

However at the end all was to be forgiven – I would have all the freedom I wanted – why I had only to go home and sit down for an hour and write this little précis and he would never disturb me again. That, from a practical point of view, all this rampaging might have the effect of muddling one, was never considered. No, the thing was to be tough. Nobody, least of all you, Ian, was tough enough (you after all do not scream and shout in the name of law and order). The plain fact however is, that if I went into that session unclear I came out of it really bewildered, and I regret to say *hurt*. It is, no doubt, silly to be hurt, particularly by a charlatan. But I find twenty-four hours later that I am still incapable of writing this précis or anything else for Grierson – even if I wished to. And nobody knows better than I do the short-comings of the draft treatment – I have been at perhaps too many pains to point it out – but I know it has something which I cannot stand by and see destroyed in this way. Grierson's ravings not only muddle – they undermine one's own faith in one's work. I have compromised on former occasions when I thought it really necessary and many of these occasions were flung at me yesterday evening. So I do not propose to do so again.

I am therefore writing, all the more regretful because my heart is deeply engaged in the project, to say that I cannot see any way in which we can usefully proceed. To say that, as I understand it, this will automatically terminate my employment by Wessex at the end of September – and that I can't express sufficiently my sense of your kindness and forebearance towards me all this time. After the fleshpots we will see what Abnegation and Toil will do. If there is any way – my dear Ian – in which past indebtedness can be repaid, you are to say so. If you think I am taking the completely wrong line, I know you will tell me.

I have consulted my own conscience (I must not use the words 'Artistic Sensibility'!) – I have discussed the matter with Cicely. I feel morally that I cannot give in to Grierson in this way, and in any case practically it can't be done. Derek has suggested playing with him so far just as to get the commissioning letter and then shut the door on him. I confess I have fears for the future of such a scheme and do not feel I can undertake it. There would always be a moment when Grierson rushes in to help – dictator-like – produce trouble and then say I told you so. No, it is better as it is.

With regard to the Festival – [Sir] Paul Wright [of the Festival of Britain] is away till the 3rd. No doubt they will be cut-up but a collision between them and Grierson has been inevitable for months now, and it may be as well to take place, I suppose. I finished the rewrite of the 2nd half of the treatment before going away – so that our promises to the Festival have been kept.

Well there it is – I hope all is going well in Germany –

My very best wishes to you

Yours ever, [No signature]

FAMILY PORTRAIT

[Working title: *Festival of Britain*]

Analysis of Draft Treatment, 14.9.49

Humphrey Jennings
Wessex Film Productions,
146 Piccadilly,
London, W.1.

Preliminary Note

In general I would say that the existing Draft Treatment is too long, that the opening sections are over-literary, and the later ones too diffuse. It could I think be condensed into 15 pages instead of 20 and its 40 odd paragraphs into about 25. It is with this in mind that I have made the following analysis. In it the film is presented as approximately 20 sequences, each of which, for purposes of clarity, I have given a cross-head, indicating not the argument but the content.

I think of the average length of these sequences as round about a minute, but of course they would not all be the same – the earlier ones for example dealing with atmosphere would be shorter and the later scientific and industrial sequences longer. I have also indicated what seem to me to be the principal climaxes of effect so that some idea of the film shape on *the screen* can be judged. It will be appreciated that part of the following analysis is technical and part more general as its purpose is to indicate the way in which the picture should be made, as well as its total impression.

Visuals, Commentary, Music

There is one important thing about the visual construction of the film which I must make clear. A certain number of images will have a recurring value. I mean that they will appear more than once in the picture in different circumstances (as for example references to the Armada, Greenwich, The Battle of Britain...) and also that the same locations and people may very well appear in different sizes, aspects, throughout the length of the picture instead of in only one sequence.

With regard to Commentary I envisage at the moment something like 3 layers of voices:

(a) A rather official voice or voices representing the Festival and making the basic authority to statement on history and perhaps science – something like the voice of Leo Genn in the current BBC 'History of the War'.

(b) An 'average man' voice of the order of Wilfred Pickles representing *us*. Actually Pickles himself would be very good for this because he would bring warmth and humour to the film (which it badly needs) – could write his own material – and would in general act *for* the audience against official pomposity. Remember this contrast of official and non-official is itself one of the theses of the film

(c) There would also be, used much more sparingly, the voices of actual people alive and dead e.g. Churchill and Constable. These last should be kept down to the minimum and we should not forget the possibility of translating the more essential statement of the official voice for foreign versions.

No doubt there would be moments in the picture in which we would like to use existing music more or less as a sound effect. e.g. quotations from Elgar. But first of all we want a musical theme for the picture, as the basis for an actual score. What I envisage here is our finding an existing British theme which could be adapted by a young composer. Without going into details it must obviously be a good open air march tune which can be made to represent the movement of a whole people. The following possibilities occur to me at the moment:

Handel's March from Rinaldo (which appears in *The Beggars' Opera*
as 'Let Us Take the Road').

Or the Handelian treatment of 'O God Our Help in Ages Past'
which occurs in one of the Chandos Anthems (and might very
well tie-up with Cup Final Community singing).

Or something out of Purcell – not the hackneyed Trumpet tune but
something from his 'Yorkshire Feast'.

List of Sequences

To make matters clearer I list straightaway the cross-headings or titles
of the main sequences and their relations to the pages of the existing treatment.

A. *The Festival Itself* – covering the first two paragraphs of page 3.

B. *The Island and the People* – page 3 paragraph 3.

C. *The Battles of Britain* – page 3 paragraph 4 running over to page
4. This is the first climax.

D. *Sea-Power and Silence* – page 4.

E. *The English Bible* – pages 4, 5.

F. *Earth and Sky* – (that is to say, Land and Weather) – covering
pages 5 and the beginning of page 6.

G. *Experiment and Industry* – this covers the first two paragraphs on
page 6 and brings us to the second climax in the picture: the Industrial Revolution.

H. *The Individual at Home* – this begins at the bottom of page 6 and
runs over to roughly the second paragraph of page 8.

I. *Poetry and Action* – The remainder of page 8 running over to the
first paragraph of page 9.

J. *The Patterns of British Life* – pages 9, 10 – to the middle of page
11. (This section of the treatment certainly needs condensing.)

K. *The British Across the Seas* – this runs from the middle of page
11 to the middle of page 12, and brings us to the third climax: the
celebration of British achievement at the Festival, and 'The End of
an Epoch'.

L. *The Wizard War* – this begins with the Churchill quotation on
page 12 and takes us roughly to the first paragraph of page 14.

M. *The New Spirit in Science* – this would cover the reference to the
status of the Scientist in pages 14 to 18 and would lead without a
break to

N. *The Laboratory of the World* – This (the heaviest sequence in the whole film) would cover the contemporary developments of applied science and industry – pages 15 to 18 and give us the fourth climax – the middle of page 18.

O. *Town and Country Today* – the middle of page 18 to the top of page 21. This of course covers the problems of population and food and authority and individual as in the treatment.

P. *New Lines Across the World* – page 21 and part of page 22 down to 'We have been there before'.

Q. *The Age of Radar* – page 22 to the end – obviously corresponding to 'Science and Sea-Power' above and leading to the final climax – the statement of the faith of 1951.

Notes on Presentation

A. *The Festival Itself* – The idea of the Festival should be introduced with the titles and should link up with any actual visual Festival propaganda e.g. flags, emblems, blue-prints, lay-outs or whatever. The March which would be the title music of the film would obviously carry the visuals of the people as in the opening paragraph. All this should be allowed to have its effect before the entrance of the first commentary which forms a link between the opening and the introduction of the island in the second sequence.

B. *The Island and the People* – This starts with a blank screen and silence and it is the real beginning of the picture. Let me here give some indications of style. The blank screen is really the sky – the camera drops down to the sea. Breakers. And the sea sound. And then figures and faces out of the past. The first of them The Long Man cut in the chalk on the Downs (and here begins Wilfred Pickles' voice: 'Our ancestors...') and then other figures such as the Roman Centurion at York and so on. And again and again the sea and the coast-line. The White Cliffs are obvious. The sands of the East Coast. The Pembrokeshire cliffs. The Western Isles. (One shot each and each of them is an image which will reappear later.) And then with the population figures ('...two million...six...ten or twelve...forty-seven million...') back to the opening crowds which we saw at the beginning of the picture. And the opening musical theme for a moment.

I am not prepared at this moment to give similar details on every sequence but quote this particular one to suggest the method of approach and the essentially three-dimensional quality of this kind of film.

C. *The Battles of Britain* – Here of course the trick is to bring the White

Cliffs up to date by placing radar masts and Ack Ack on them and to suggest
the eternal invasion and survival problems by playing, as it were, two Battles of Britain simultaneously. I mean for example cross-cut C.U.s of Gun-
ners and girls in tin hats with Elizabethan faces in Armada helmets (from
engravings) and playing the sound of Spitfires and so on over the Armada
itself. Another point of course is to give us the two limits – beginning and
end – of the epoch of seapower which we are going to deal with in the next
sequence. This Battle Sequence also of course looks forward to sequence
L. 'The Wizard War' and should form something of a first climax, building up from the silence and the sea at the beginning of sequence B.

D. *Seapower and Science* – This would begin with a so-called 'montage' of
four centuries of British sea-power. Obviously using the main musical
theme. Images (real one and pictures) of big and little ships from the *Golden Hind* to the *Victory*, to the *Great Eastern* to the *Queen Elizabeth*. And
then a 17th-century map of the world and the meridian of Greenwich O
in C.U. and here the beginning of a scientific commentary. I mean that the
voice should suggest the quiet calculator – the scientific attitude. Annotat-
ing as it were the pictures of the magnet, telescope, chronometer (the scientific and political background to the ships) and of course Greenwich
itself. Ending on the famous figure of Newton in Trinity Chapel, Cambridge – and the stars.

E. *The English Bible* – in the Chapel the lectern and on the lectern the
Bible. These interior images repeated on other sites. The plain church and
chapel interiors of Protestantism. The Bible opens and a voice begins:
'Where wast thou when I laid the foundation of the earth...' Back of
course to Newton. 'Who hath stretched the line upon it –' Back to Greenwich and so on. Linking the 'foundations' and 'cornerstones' with the geology of the next sequence.

F. *Earth and Sky* – here for the first time we see the land of Britain – an
early morning sequence coming out of the words 'morning stars' from the
Bible above – the shapes and shadows of creation. In practice the visuals
have already been set out in the books of the geologists such as Dudley
Stamp. The commentary again the scientific voice, simple and factual.
The earlier images in the sequence should be without people – the later
ones introducing the solitary figures of the farmer, miner, in and under the
landscape. These are in fact the introductory long-shots of people and
places seen later in C.U. This develops into the most lyrical sequence in
the film. Let me explain it in more detail. Among these solitary figures are
the Miller and also the Landscape Artist (not of course seen in C.U.)
Above them the moving clouds. Around them the movements of the wind
in the grass, on the leaves, and the face of the streams. This is East Anglia.

We should suggest the brush dipping into the painting water like the leaves of the willow in the stream. For a moment it should be difficult to distinguish brush marks from reality. Cloud studies from real clouds. The essence of this sequence is *that it should flow* for contrast to the industrial sequence which comes next. Such commentary as there is divided between the scientific voice used earlier and a Suffolk voice representing the words of Constable himself. At the end of the sequence the images broaden out to pick up men at work whenever necessary 'no two men handle a boat alike...' here the sound of the sea comes back and there should be a sense of stress – of man struggling with nature.

G. *Experiment and Industry*. Here (if you except the Ack Ack and radar faces) are the first big close-ups of people in the picture, covering the twin ideas of observation and experiment: 'Clear proofs are afforded by trust-worthy experiments –' These images of course also represent the scientific work necessary to make possible the Industrial Revolution. Here there is something of a visual problem. Of course the material should be actual present-day reality, but at the same time the industrial images should not be representative of the latest developments of 20th century British indus-try. They must look like history. The emphasis is, of course, on power. It will be seen that we have touched on indigenous raw materials (the farmer, the miner), on craftsmanship ('no two men...' etc), on scientific experiment, and now their application from one to another give us a build-up to the Industrial Revolution which is the second climax of the picture.

H. *The Individual at Home*. Begin with traditional images from industry to the individual. I mean the characteristically British lay-out of home and gardens and allotments which form the suburbs of the great industrial towns. Example: In the background the mill chimneys, in the foreground the man tending the rose. Here the Wilfred Pickles 'average man' voice comes into its own. Beginning with the idea of spare-time – hobbies – (the visual contrast of the machine tool and the rose). Thence to the idea of the amateur. And then from the unnamed to actual amateurs, eccentrics, double-lives, as suggested in the treatment (but less literary) and thence to the basic contrast of reality and imagination. This is one of the few points in the film where the commentary should lead the visuals. And there should be no real break between it and the next sequence.

I. *Poetry and Action*. Here clearly we look back for a moment to the sea-power images of sequence D and lay over them (as it were) the quotations from Gray and Kipling.

J. *The Patterns of British Life*. Clearly in these sequences we are building up a kind of slow March. Here is the moment for Elgar's music. One visual point is important. The images of events and ceremonies should not just be newsreel long-shots but specifically laid-on closer shooting to emphasize the individual in the pattern: e.g. the faces of the men rowing in the eights, the faces of the Miners' March and so on. The top moment of this slow March sequence is clearly the introduction of Royalty which, in turn, will lead us naturally to Westminster, to the idea of Parliament and the political importance of compromise etc. as indicated in the treatment. I suspect that somewhere here, as in the Stephenson episode, there is an opportunity for a kind of commentary dialogue between the official and non-official voices.

K. *The British Across the Seas* – here comes the second world map in the picture. The visual point of the sequence is that we contrast the home images – streets, allotments and so on which we have already seen – with those of the outside world: desert, veldt, bush . . . on the map we should see the explorers' tracks and the shipping-lanes. Emotionally the repeat of Kipling (page 9) gives us the third climax.

   And here also is the main pause for the audience to take breath in the whole film. We then open up again in

I. *The Wizard War* with the average man claiming 'we survived as we did in 1588' – so that audiences can really feel that they have been living history. I very much hope that it will be possible to get Mr Churchill to record the paragraph from his memoirs which I have quoted in the treatment. It will give authenticity in a way which nothing else can. It would be left to the scientific voice used earlier to make the point 'the war brought the wizards together in a way never before achieved'. It will thus be clearly seen how important, particularly in the second half of the film, is the play between the three layers of voices – official, man-in-the-street, and authentic which I suggested to begin with. Thus the conflicts of life in Britain are carried by the commentary as well as the visuals.

M. *The New Spirit in Science* – this sequence and the next one

N. *The Laboratory of the World* should form a whole. That is to say we should begin with the new status of the scientist, examples of teamwork, backed up if necessary with quotations from Florey, Appleton and so on and then lead to the really exciting contemporary developments of applied science and industry. The obvious examples have been given in the treatment but it is not easy at this point to give the final order in which they should appear in the film. That is to say, for example, it is not easy to estimate whether the turbo-jet is or is not the most impressive from a film point of view. This is basically a cutting-room job. The essential things being that all the scientific and industrial material could be laid out in an almost childishly simple form – the order being dictated simply so as to give us the maximum climax at the end of the sequence, which, after all, represents the scientific power of Britain today.

1. Still from *Fires Were Started* (1943)

2. Jennings (right) acting as one of the Weird Sisters in *Macbeth* for the GPO Film Unit production *BBC – The Voice of Britain* (Stuart Legg *et al*, 1935)

3. Photograph of Jennings by Walter Bird, *c.*1944

4. Jennings working on *Pandaemonium*, *c.*1946, photograph by Beiny

5. Still from *Words for Battle* (1941)

6. Still from *Spare Time* (1939); the Kazoo Band sequence

7. & 8. *Listen to Britain* (1942); steel works scenes

9. Jennings: photograph of a Bolton street scene (1939)

10. Christmas still from *A Diary for Timothy* (1944)

11. Jennings: collage, c.1935

12. Jennings: oil painting of a locomotive, c.1936-8

13. Jennings: photograph of studio with portrait of Byron, *c*.1939

14. Jennings: oil painting of Bolton allotments, *c*.1944-5

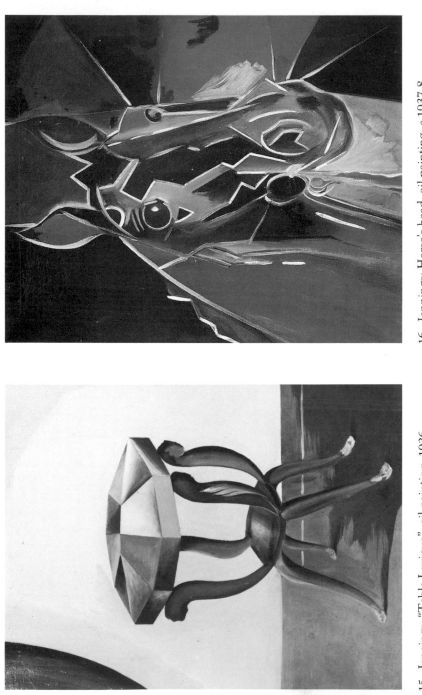

16. Jennings: Horse's head, oil painting, c.1937-8

15. Jennings: "Table Lyrique", oil painting, 1936

O. Town and Country Today – under this innocuous title, I mean of course that we should look back for a moment at the age-old survival problems of food and population, and political problems of the freedom of the individual in their new forms. During all the scientific sequences we will have heard nothing but the voices of experts. Now we should hear Pickles again introducing the farmer. This sequence is a final statement of all the contrasts and paradoxes which we have hinted at earlier. If you understand me, the rose and the lathe reappear as the ear of corn and the turbine blade.

The last two sequences form a kind of coda to the whole. The first one

P. New Lines Across the World – looks back for a moment from 1951 to the Great Exhibition and its ideals, and then restates – with an air-map of the world – the island's new relations to the outside world – to the earlier images of 'desert, veldt, bush . . .' the new contrasts and relationships of the Manchester Laboratory and the African rain-forests – the sheep-stations of Scotland and Australia – linked physically by air as well as sea – but also linked by the free exchange of information across the Commonwealth – which was begun right back in the days of Newton and the Royal Society . . . so the images lead naturally to Greenwich and the newest thing in science – the new radar observatories of which the most important has been described in some detail in the treatment . . . this with all its implications forms the material for the last sequence

Q. The Age of Radar – which would of course end with some sort of envoi taking us back to the festival and the mood of Britain in 1951.

The above analysis should of course be read with the existing treatment which it is not meant to supersede. With regard to shooting certain things can be laid down now. To all intents and purposes the whole picture will be shot on location – as near as possible in the actual place with the actual people – interiors and exteriors. Again the whole or nearly the whole of the shooting would be silent. The total shooting time is likely to be of the order of three months – but spread over at least four. Since we have now lost the summer the more we can shoot in the spring the better. It would however be useful to be in a position to pick up even at this late date some autumn material. For the scientific and industrial material there is still a great deal of research and checking work to be done. So that – apart from any autumn shooting – we should spend October and part of November on research and writing shooting script, shoot from December to March – leaving perhaps a few scenes as late as we dare to delivery date – the main cutting taking place February-May . . . All of this is of course assuming that a decision is taken in the immediate future – without which from a time point of view alone the film becomes impossible to deliver in early summer . . .

TO IAN DALRYMPLE   *Wessex Film Productions Ltd,*
[undated]   *Pinewood Studios,*
                                                Iver Heath, Bucks

My dear Ian,

I am extremely sorry that you feel at all left out of it – but the fact is it
was agreed with Derek that he would keep you posted and I would keep
quiet so as not to worry you. He has I believe explained to you the present
set-up. It remains for me to fill in the background.

After your original wire it became clear that we were asking the Festival
people to take sides in the matter of Grierson, which surprisingly enough
they did – and agreed to revise the original scheme of making all film
moneys from through [*sic*] the COI. This was really quite a diplomatic victory for us – but of course it didn't produce the necessary cheque or contract. However, from then on we were dealing with [Sir] Paul Wright and
[Sir] Gerald Barry [Director of the Festival of Britain] only. They then
agreed in writing to the draft treatment and also indicated that the money
when finally sanctioned would be nearer £11,000 than £12,500. We then
worked out production figures including recouping *all* moneys paid out by
Wessex – salaries etc since May 1949. Made an estimate of the next (pre-
shooting) stage – and made it clear to Paul Wright that we could not go
on even under the new agreement without cash.

At this moment the Government axe began to fall on the Festival as
elsewhere and it became for a short time extremely difficult for them to
commit themselves. However they did agree to £1,000 for current
expenses including salaries if actually incurred – to which Rosser [accoun-
tant member of the board of Wessex Films] very sensibly said we were
already owed £1100 (i.e. salaries etc since May) – and I understand they
have agreed to pay this. From a production point of view of course it had
become clear to me that we had lost any real hope of exteriors this autumn
– and moreover it was agreed with Derek that it would be folly to waste
driblets of our precious money in odd days' shooting. I am determined,
Ian, that you shall recoup everything out of the £11000.

It became clear therefore that the best way to use the present time
would be in writing a final script – mainly in commentary form – i.e. to
reverse the usual – or my usual – procedure of shooting first and commentating after, which would eat up too much money (shooting unit spread
over too long a period in particular). In agreement with Derek and Paul
Wright I am therefore writing this final treatment – and endeavouring to
do so with the minimum of expenses.

This will be ready by the time you are back. We should under this
scheme do no shooting until the spring – i.e. February – and then have a

concentrated spell at it. McAllister (whom I saw again last night) will I think be available mid-January but not before. He seems keen on it – is in good form – & wants to talk to you. Let me say also how much I need your help at this stage.

Now (i.e. about three days ago) it became clear that the Festival has scrapped *all* its other documentary-projects and is relying on this one alone for *home* as well as *overseas* – ! this in turn confirms my feelings that it can be an important document – or that at least it is likely to be very widely shown & discussed and that we have got to be absolute experts in what we say. All the more reason for very careful writing at this stage.

I hope this covers everything you want to know. Longing to see you.

Yours ever

Humphrey.

Work on *Family Portrait* continued until the summer of 1950.

1950

A FAMILY PORTRAIT
FOR
THE FESTIVAL OF BRITAIN
1951

Final Commentary
'...the rainbow bridge that connects the
prose in us with the passion...'
E.M. Forster

Humphrey Jennings
Wessex Film Productions
June, 1950

Perhaps because we in Britain live on a group of small islands, we like to
think of ourselves as a family (and of course with the unspoken affection
and outspoken words that all families have). And so the Festival of Britain
is a kind of family reunion. To let us take a look at ourselves...to let the
young and old, the past and the future meet and discuss. To give thanks
that we are still a family. To voice our hopes and fears...our faith...for
our children...

Where to begin?

Here...this is Beachy Head...there's the channel – joining and dividing...that's the remains of radar station here during the war...('Air
Ministry Property – keep out')...

When Drake was fighting the Armada (this is part of family history) the
Spaniards said he had a magic mirror in his cabin which revealed enemy
ships to him. What we should call marine-radar...

You could have seen the Armada from here...and the Normans too –
over there (other side of Eastbourne)...and the Romans.

Fact is our ancestors nearly all came as invaders (and they had to be
enterprising chaps and good sailors to do it)...early Bronze Age – late
Bronze Age – different layers of Celts – shiploads of Jutes and Vikings and
Saxons. Remember Kipling, where the Long Man of Wilmington 'looks
naked to the shires...' Saxon probably...

A very mixed family as you see. But who together have resisted further
invasion for nearly a thousand years.

Then the extraordinary diversity of nature in this small space; the variety of land structure...the local variations of soil and climate...the rapid
exchanges in the weather above...the jumble of coal and rock underground...all somehow match the diversity of the people.

You can see it in Shakespeare...

Today it's all wharves, cranes, warehouses, imports, exports – but the place is still called Bankside...

It was here that Shakespeare created Hamlet and Lady Macbeth and Falstaff and all the rest...'to hold as 'twere the mirror up to Nature...' ...not classical gods or heroic figures but individual people with souls of their own...and the small parts – the comics and hangers-on...all different from each other...as we feel ourselves to be!

As for the wharves and warehouses...we have to eat, don't we?

'Sweet Thames run softly till I end my song...' You see, for centuries the family's mixed poetry and prose together.

Stand up above the Thames by the Observatory at Greenwich...there is the great city of trade...down in the river, the sails (as they were) of her merchantmen. We had to learn (we had almost to create) the art...the science of navigation...Study the magnetism of the earth...the path of the moon...the position of the stars. We began in a matter of fact way – keeping our eyes on the object.

But at the same time that we were making these observations to help ships find the longitude at sea, we produced Newton whose genius saw that they in fact describe the structure of the universe itself...

Today Greenwich gives the longitude to the world...and the telescope still checks the time on the meridian...if the weather and the smoke permits...

But the smoke that blinds the modern astronomer is also the emblem of invention...because something like a quarter of the family live right on top of coal...power for the winning of it.

But again it needed two sides of the family to meet...James Watt, crossing Glasgow Common one Sunday morning, suddenly to see the 'separate condenser' in his mind's eye...and the skill of the John Wilkinsons, the iron masters of the time...to get the steam-engine made at all...

The meeting of scientific imagination and engineering skill...a new kind of poetry and a new kind of prose...

In work and play alike we began to hear the march of the machine...

And then came Trevithick building the first locomotives in the world at a Welsh steam-foundry to take the place of horses...and calling one of them *Catch Me Who Can* and backing it to run against any horse at Newmarket...

And then Stephenson from Newcastle saying he could drive a rail-road straight across Chatmoss which won't bear the weight of a man...

Local lads who used their wits and had a good laugh and then (like Shakespeare and Newton and Watt) started something at home that went right round the globe...

But to be honest our matter-of-fact way can get the better of us...often (as the towns and population grew) the practical gifts never met the imaginative ones and one part of us lost sight of the other (rifts in the family we're still having to repair)...

We can only thank heaven we produced a Blake, a Shaftesbury, a Dickens to proclaim love and health and light:

What a mixture of muddle and orderliness, dinginess and open air we are...

How to reconcile the farm and the factory?...

Stand here by the Oak. That is the most celebrated strip of farmland in the world; Broadbalk Field, Rothampstead... known in the outback and middle-west... where we first began to bring the land and the laboratory together... this was in 1843. The 'Hungry Forties' they were called – and they were the reason for Rothampstead; every day we had more and more mouths to feed...

And it was now that the mind of Darwin began turning over what the eye had seen in the forests of Brazil and the hedgerows at home – the minute variations of nature – the hunger of all living things – and began to imagine... to deduce from them – the laws of our own origin and being ... in the struggle for existence.

And in this struggle we are helped, saved perhaps, by our very paradoxes.

So the most eccentric among us has discipline (we think) inside him somewhere; remember Lewis Carroll and Edward Lear...

So we admire innovations (and need and produce them) and also love tradition...

So we like sitting quiet at home and we like pageantry...

But then, pageantry in Britain (believe it or not) isn't put on by a sinister power to impress anyone – nor just to have fun... it's part of the pattern of life...

The year itself swings round in a pattern of events...

The secret is that we created these things ourselves, gradually... but, as Milton warned us, 'not without dust and heat'...

The banks of Runnymede – the heights of Edinburgh – the Palace of Westminster itself – were once battlegrounds where the burning ideas of other civilizations were bitterly adapted to the climate of home...

We were lucky to learn the trick of voluntary discipline – of 'dining with the Opposition'... of calling meetings which would end purposely in compromise...

But for the most paradoxical thing compare Britain herself with the rest of the world... no eternal snow... no unending forest or drenching jungle ... small and varied and restrained... and yet our history has taken us precisely into the vast and violent areas of the globe...

Captain Cook going to the South Seas with the new chronometer for guide... Livingstone taking the Bible from the falls of Clyde to the falls of the Zambesi...

'The Earth is the Lord's and the fulness thereof...'

The skill of Sheffield and Swansea and Belfast... going the road to Mandalay and Capetown and Cairo... the crack of the village bat heard on Australian plains... the skirl of the pipes in Canadian snows...

The idea of Parliament itself spreading from the Thames to the Indus and the Ganges...

Four hundred years ago Gilbert told the Queen that 'the earth itself is a great magnet...'

And all the time the return voyage has brought us back food and foods for machines... brought us back genius (Rutherford from New Zealand to Manchester and Cambridge)... brought us experience and responsibility on a world scale...

All this we inherit and celebrate, but we know that the times have changed... 'Great men have been among us'... When we admire the sunset we are using the eyes of Turner, when we switch on the light we are tapping the mind of Faraday... But the very genius of Clerk Maxwell, Thompson and Rutherford shook the foundations of matter itself...

The Elizabethan journey ended with the Battle of Britain...

And then, as the battle raged, out of the fragments and tracks of matter we made the magic mirror that the Spaniards dreamt of... Radar. The meeting of fundamental research and radio engineering... the new navigation... prose and poetry again but put together in a new way.

At the time of Nelson Australia was five months' sail from home – but already in 1800 a Yorkshire squire called Cayley had written down the laws by which the aeroplane flies...

And now we – with the turbo-jet and propeller-turbine – we are talking about making Sydney in 36 hours – Capetown in 18 – New York non-stop in 6...

But what a wealth of family brain and eye and hand are helping the planes into the air! This is the new thing...

So in the making of penicillin, biologists, biochemists, crystallographers working together, did it.

Solitary shade of Cayley! Look at the teams of designers and draughtsmen doing your job today!

Shades of the iron masters of old! Listen to your hammers stamping the steel discs of the jet...

The skill that put the first steam-engines together now fits the delicate turbin-blades into the disc...

How eagerly the eyes of Stephenson and Watt would have followed the tests of an aero-engine!

14,000 revolutions a minute...

The science that spies into the inside of things – the industry that gives them shape – which is the poetry? which is the prose?

'The Earth is the Lord's and the fulness thereof...'

But at the end of all this, no less than half the family are living on food from abroad...

At the Norman invasion there were about two million of us... By the defeat of the Armada, five... and by Trafalgar, fifteen... but today there are more than fifty millions of us on the same stretch of land...

So we must try and plan the use of the small space we have – where to live and where to work – where to draw power from water as well as coal – where and how to plant new forests – what to preserve – what to exploit ...and learn to compromise again between one use and another...

And how does the individual fit into all this? The countryman for example with his local wisdom – his human doubts and silences – his sense of the living thing.

Can you really treat John Barleycorn as you do the blades of a turbine... two sides of the family again... farmer, scientist... the farmer learning to trust... the scientist learning to accept... accept the fact that the land varies from yard to yard... accept the richness and subtely of nature not as errors to be corrected but as part of the truth to be understood...

We should pray for these two to agree – our bread and butter depend on it...

But it goes deeper than that...

Under the surface of the practical world lies the insatiable curiosity of the human spirit...

Tonight there are new shapes on the skylines of home... the fantastic antennae of modern science, reaching oujt to the unknown... Peacetime versions of radar picking up radio waves coming in from the blank spaces in the Milky Way – or plotting the tracks of meteors as they rush through the sky...

That's a meteor there...

But this in turn depends on the free exchange of knowledge (begun in the days of Newton and Pepys at the meetings of the Royal Society) and this exchange itself is in danger... for it's not science that tyrannizes but the pride of man. Tolerance in Britain is linked to the Royal Society's defence of free enquiry...

Remember Newton saying he felt like a little boy playing on the shore of the great ocean of truth: –

> Canst thou bind the sweet influences of the Pleiades?
> Or loose the bands of Orion?

Knowest thou the ordinances of heaven?
Canst thou set the dominion thereof in the earth?'

We were lucky again science began here at the very time of the great translation of the Bible into English...

In the end, most of the family faces look back to Scandinavia, Germany,
France...our ideas...our faith...have their roots in Italy, Greece, Israel
...we have just had the knack of putting prose and poetry together.

And now we also belong to a communion across the Atlantic and the
South Seas...we are too small...too crowded...to stand alone...We
have to come both inside the family of Europe and the pattern overseas
...we are the link between them...

For all we have received from them and from our native land, what can
we return? Perhaps the very things that make the family, the pattern possible: tolerance, courage, faith – the will to be disciplined and free together...

> With *Family Portrait* completed, Jennings was asked by the US
> Economic Co-operation Administration to direct one of a series of six
> films to be presented under the general title *The Changing Face of
> Europe.* Jennings chose 'The Good Life', on the subject of health, and set
> off for location shooting in Greece.

TO CICELY JENNINGS   *Hotel Baur au Lac,*
Sunday morning 3 Sept [1950]   *Zurich*

My dearest Pip –

A line to you all to wish you a very happy birthday [it was in fact Mary-
Lou's birthday] and to show that I have got this far. The weather is fortunately improving – the white sails are crowding the lake and the Police-
band are blowing their way through Bizet [...]

Paris was rather a rush – but I saw the celebrated Lady Allen [of
Hurtwood] – expert on children who had just been to Greece. Remarkable
and imaginative person. I also gathered that at the Antibes festival they
were running a programme of films of mine – among the 'masters' –
there's glory for you! [...]

TO CICELY JENNINGS   *Hotel Delphi,*
Wednesday [no date or postmark]   *Athens*

Dearest Pip

You seem not to have had my letter from Zurich. I spent a couple of
days there on the way to Rome where I received your long Mary-Lou
birthday letter. It was very noisy and hot in the city itself – very changed

from the little I remember of it – but not really looking like *Bicycle Thieves* either although I saw many of the locations where it was shot. [...]

The customs & other official stuff was so complicated that we decided not to try and shoot in Italy to begin with but to come on here ... here everything has been going very smoothly thanks to the magic of working for ECA – [...]

Athens is also fantastically noisy hooters and bells – there is a huge Orthodox church just opposite my room here whose bells wake me at 6 every morning – but the hills beyond the Parthenon are fresh and green & smell of pine – a particular resin which they mix with the white wine *rhezina* – the colours exactly Cézanne's palette – orange rocks – blue sky & sea – light blue – dark blue – fresh yellow greens in the young trees – olive greens & darker greens too but less of them. Behind all the fundamental fresh colours – blue & white – the marble & the sea – the white wash of the houses & the sky – the national flag – blue & white –

The Greeks I have met friendly & cultured & enthusiastic beyond anything I have ever seen – without the cynicism of Paris or the suspicion of Burma – All the doctors – newspaper people & suchlike speak French excellently & some English – and we are learning a few words of Greek –

So far – except for a little toothache I feel fine – the sun shines solidly every day – we have not seen more than half a dozen tiny clouds in the last 5 days – The Greeks themselves are 'working like beavers' – stripped of everything in the villages – but with a colossally high morale – laughing and singing over everything –

Last night I went to the Greek press-show of *The Third Man*! and met the Athens critics & cinema people – who thought the picture fine – they had heard the Harry Lime theme but had not seen the picture itself till now –

From your letter it sounds as though Marylou has found herself some work?

Give them all my love

Bless you   Humphrey

On the morning of Sunday 24 September 1950, Jennings set off from Athens on a reconnaissance trip to the island of Poros. 'At about 2.15 we started to climb the cliff,' his assistant, Dillon Barry, reported, 'as Mr Jennings wished to see the view of the islands from the top for a possible shot.' As he reached the top, Jennings slipped and fell on to the rocks. Dillon Barry found a boat and took him to Poros Military Hospital; treatment proved useless, and he died later that afternoon. His body is buried in Athens.

Critical Writings

Design and the Theatre

All the family agreed in disliking the baby. The theatrical manager thought that Art was all very well in museums but likely to cause trouble in the theatre. The producer said he might want a spectacular set now and again but he could always hire the costumes. The author said that the play was the thing and that any way with his stage directions you wouldn't want a designer. The actor said he had got along pretty well so far and wasn't going to wear talc dresses now. The public didn't say anything, and the baby sat in the corner drawing. ·

And of course everybody except the public was in the right. Art does cause trouble: you don't want spectacular sets for every play: the body *is* more than the raiment: and Garrick *would* look silly in a talc dress (though Serge Lifar looks admirable). To put it another way, everybody has agreed in distrusting somebody who seems likely to come between them and the great heart of the public. The great heart itself sits on the fence: it naturally likes designers when it gets them, but doesn't notice when it doesn't get them; and there the real trouble begins.

It may be that the public like the theatrical manager connects the idea of stage-design with modern art, and as a result distrusts it. 'Quite right, too,' says the producer (here backed up by the critics), 'look at the continental production, all art and no play!' And once again the producer is in the right, and the baby sits in the corner drawing. Let us then take no notice of continental productions: let us turn the accursed word Art out of the theatre: but there is still one question to be answered. Is it necessary, because the designer rules the German roost, that he should be hunted out of the English farmyard? Charles B. Chanticlere is rightly suspicious of Reinhart the Fox: but the unfortunate result of this is that the theatrical lion will not (as Mr Sheringham wittily says) lie down with the designing lamb because he is afraid every lamb is a wolf in sheep's clothing.

At the same time a few designers do get jobs in London: 'Of course,' says the producer, 'I agreed that there were occasions when a spectacular set is useful, but at the present I am producing modern comedy...' *There* is the vital confession: that for modern comedy no designer is wanted[1]. Let us by all means agree that modern comedy should be played in an unobtrusive manner, that here above all nobody must come between the author, the actor, the producer, and their audiences. Very well then – tarry a little, there is something else. Suppose the hired costumes and the undesigned scenery – the baronial sets – were to come between!

[1] I am well aware that Mr George Harris for instance has designed admirable sets for unspectacular plays, but the baronial sets continue overwhelmingly.

So far the designer has been (with a great deal of justice) regarded and denounced either as a substitute for the producer – 'the fox's case must help when the lion's skin is out at the elbows' – or as a luxury, 'the spoilt child of the theatre'. For our baby in the corner to become a spoilt child would be a pity, but in the present state of affairs a designer must either be spoilt or say with the boy in *Coriolanus*:

I'll run away till I am bigger, but then I'll fight.

Mr Gordon Craig fights, but can hardly alter the situation: troubles in the theatre like other troubles are

Not by might mastered, but by special grace.

Last winter *The Studio* published a selection of modern designs for sets and dresses which it is hoped may stimulate English audiences to clamour for design in the theatre – in all the theatres. At the same time the selection was for students a poor one[2], and was for designers a dangerous publication altogether. Dangerous because it insists on the designs themselves rather than the finished scenery and costumes 'in action'. For we derive very definite pleasure from the designs of Gontcharova, Andreenko, etc., as pictures complete in themselves and without any reference to their fitness as projects for scenery. That there *is* a danger in this is proved in the same volume by Mr Cecil Beaton's 'design for a backcloth', and Mrs Vera Willoughby's designs 'for eighteenth-century costumes': these pictures may or may not be charming in themselves, but they are not connected with the working theatre. A backcloth for which scene of what play? dresses for which characters?

Moreover, the whole idea of producing a design as a complete work of art is entirely wrong: a backcloth or a dress are parts of a while and must not be satisfying unities in themselves. Mr Cochran has put this admirably: 'If our stage artist provides a scene which is fundamentally a single stated entity, he endangers the whole dramatic concept which it should be his function to assist in making plain.'

Thus we are brought to a new situation. There is room in the theatre for our baby, but the pictures which he has been drawing in the corner are likely to be quite useless as projects for scenery and dresses. At the same time sketches for scenery *are* necessary, since the designer cannot paint all his sets by himself; and if professional dressmakers are going to make the

---

[2] It omitted Picasso completely, gave nothing like an idea of the work of Larionow, and Jean Victor Hugo, and took up the space they might have had with projects for a film of *The Divine Comedy*, and the work of Pollock of Hoxton. The drop curtain at the King's Theatre, Edinburgh, got next to a ballet scene by Duncan Grant!

dresses sketches will be necessary. [Here again, most of the designs for dresses in Mr Sheringham's collection would be quite useless to the average dressmaker.]

Lately Mr Granville Barker has once again insisted on the necessity of a repertory company for intelligent production and acting[3]: and here is the solution of our problem. In a repertory company a designer could work with the same painters and dressmakers week after week: for it is with the painters and dressmakers that his real business lies, and not with museums or exhibitions. With amateur dressmakers whom one has worked with for a few weeks, it is perfectly possible to eliminate all sketches: as regards the painting I suggest the designer should do some himself and employ his painters as the sixteenth-century masters employed their pupils, to put in the background. This assumes a high level of intelligence in dressmakers and painters, but that will be found more among amateurs than in Wardour Street.

There is, however, one other reason why pictures are made: to convince the producer that the designer knows his business. 'After all' (says the producer) 'I want to know what scenery I am going to get.' But the scenery surely depends on the producer: he knows or should know where he wants the chairs and tables for his modern comedy, or the balconies and pillars for his poetic drama. If the designer wants to crowd the stage with more chairs than the producer needs, or put his balcony too high for Romeo, then he is breaking our first rule of 'coming between'. '*But*' (say the designer and producer simultaneously) 'that is not our idea of design! We had never thought of chairs and tables as scenery: we always hire *them*.' More confessions!

If a room has its necessary furniture and the characters apt costumes, what more is wanted? It is precisely in these little things, in choosing the colour of the hero's socks, in seeing that the furniture is painted in the studios and not hired – and at the same time keeping his eye on the audience and the author, and the actor and the manager's purse; it is here that the designer's real job lies.[4] Of course a complicated backcloth is sometimes wanted to give 'atmosphere', but the costumes are infinitely more important because drama deals with 'men and women doing things', which brings us paradoxically back to the producer's first remark that he could hire the costumes: nothing should ever by hired by anybody.

Last July *The Gods Go A-Begging* was produced at His Majesty's: the dresses and scenery were not in the least novel or exciting. They were

---

[3] In his *Prefaces to Shakespeare: First Series*.

[4] Hence Gordon Craig's little sketches for his actual production of *The Pretenders* are infinitely more interesting than his vague etchings.

confined to two or three colours: there was a noticeable use of black and white, and the colour of the baskets used in the *fête champêtre* was matched by the lining of the gentleman's hats. In a word, it was just such a piece of work as we have been advocating. The name of the designer was omitted from the programme.

Experiment No. 1, November 1928

Odd Thoughts at the Fitzwilliam

The hideous new wing of the Fitzwilliam Museum is nearly finished: the many people therefore who to their shame have never been to the old building as it now is should go immediately, and old friends must pay their adieus. For it cannot be that the present glorious mix-up will remain; there will be a tidying-up and a sorting-out, a re-arranging and a re-hanging, and that muddle of sculpture, old-clothes and superb water-colours which is the Fitzwilliam will have departed for ever.

The very badness of some exhibits (Victorian copies of insipid Dutch pictures, and insipid Victorian pictures themselves) is a restful contrast to the excellence and interest of others. That oppression of masterpieces which one feels at the Uffizi, for instance, is delightfully absent here. Yet the MS of *Jude the Obscure*, and some splendid Nottingham alabaster-work, and Samuel Palmer's *The Magic Apple Tree*, are all within ten yards of each other. From *The Magic Apple Tree* one can cross to Palmer's etchings, thence to Blake's Illustrations for *The Georgics*, and to complete the pastoral atmosphere, there is a delicious early Gainsborough above the hot-water pipes. And downstairs all the time there are two thundering pieces of Assyrian bas-relief in an overheated room of white match-boarding which looks out on to Peterhouse Fellows' Garden.

The Fitzwilliam is always warm: the over-opulent entrance-hall with its endless marble and pink walls and gilt carving and peacocks and hangings and painted glass, gives you a sense of palatial comfort that will not be denied whatever you may think of the peacocks and painted glass themselves. And in a case of English Delft ware between two particularly silly marble deities is a jug dated 1691 with the magic words 'Bee Merry' written across it.

Among the Miniatures and Music MSS is a Breughel: a village fête, with a procession, dances to the bagpipes, surreptitious embracings, and much drinking out of those three-handled stone-ware jugs that could still be bought in pre-war Bavaria. In the centre there is a play on a rough platform stage in front of a single curtain; the stage is built upon tubs, and the stage-manager is lifting a chair up from the gaping audience for the actors' use. Someone is in a basket and a woman is sitting on a man's knee at a breakfast table: domestic farce obviously. There is a similar scene in a Breughel at Avignon, and in a sketch by him which was at the Flemish Exhibition, but none of the handbooks or histories of the Theatre have reproduced any of them. How many earnest students of early drama have passed the Fitzwilliam and missed this?

On going down the dark stairs to what I can only call the basement you pass drawings from the antique by Legros, marble busts of nineteenth-century worthies, and then enter the classical section. Here there are two things to look at; not the vast Fragmentum Cereris nor the masses of black and red vases, but a group of Corinthian pottery tucked away in a corner, and better still a *Male Head from Eski Shehr: Phrygia* which is almost lost among Roman portraits. This brings us to the new gallery where everything is laid out in exquisite precision and one hardly dare tread. The real trouble is this: the appreciation of anything, aesthetically or archaeologically, is essentially a discovery. And if everything is set out in perfect order half the joy of discovering it is lost. It is not nearly so exciting to walk up and down the row of Rembrandt etchings in this room as it is to hunt for a Jan Steen upstairs.

But assuming the necessity for a new wing, it seems unfortunate that while its interior is so admirably lighted and so clean compared to the old, its exterior should be so atrocious. The connecting gallery was a success precisely because it went with the old building. But the wing itself doesn't go. The whole thing is so timid: and is put to shame by an average Dutch power-station. The architect has made a well-meaning attempt at 'good manners in architecture': the old building is classical, so the new building must be vaguely classical to go with it; but obviously it cannot be in exactly the same style. Now this sounds all very well in theory, but in practice I begin to doubt its success. For the Fitzwilliam is not the only example of a building spoilt by compromise: the new building at King's is frankly a hopeless jumble. Why can't we be whole-heartedly modern? Will anybody seriously maintain that the neo-Gothic west door to Great St Mary's is better than the classical doorway which is to be seen in Ackermann's print? Or that the façade of the University Library should have been Gothic to go with the main building and King's Chapel?

The Fitzwilliam, however, continues to house a representative collection of English water-colours from Towne's notebooks to the latest splashings of Wilson Steer. For this we are extremely grateful. We can only hope that the family circle will not as in *The Man of Property* be broken when an architect crosses the threshold. But what a place it is for suggestions! Downstairs in the new gallery are two eighteenth-century Chinese figures with their hair done so exactly in the manner of the tall men's wigs (*toupées*) worn *circa* 1770 that I feel there must be some connection. If Mr Kenneth Clark would follow his admirable book, *The Gothic Revival*, with a history of Chinoiserie in England, one might be certain.

Experiment No. 2, February 1929

Notes on Marvell 'To His Coy Mistress'

I

These notes are intended to be to the 'Coy Mistress' very much what Mr Eliot's own notes are to *The Waste Land*: suggestions for further interpretation of thought and for a fuller development of visual imagery. The question of what notes are relevant or irrelevant cannot be dogmatically stated, as it obviously differs from reader to reader with their experiences; at certain points however to explain fully is to destroy. Thus to insist on a fuller visual image of 'the Indian Ganges side' would be destructive rather than helpful: at the moment it is as happily vague as Horace's 'fabulosus Hydaspes', 'The tide of Humber' is distinctly more vivid though perhaps not more visual than the other: the word 'tide', and the facts of Humber being in England and that Marvell lived at Hull, give the second phrase freshness contrasting with the dreaminess of the first.[1] Once, by this contrast, the sense of space is established, the words have done their work. At the same time, it is important to realize that Marvell's Ganges is the Ganges of the Ptolemaic and Dantesque geographies, and is the furthest point East, the point of sunrise. To imagine China stretching out beyond it is to spoil among other things its remoteness and the corresponding remoteness of the Coy Mistress, so suited to her character.

In connection with the word 'Indian', consider these two lines: 'both the Indias of spice and Mine' and 'Her bed is India: there she lies, a pearl'. Donne is insisting on the range of the Sun's travels, and the richness of the countries visited, leading up to 'All here in one bed lay'. Shakespeare's use of 'bed' in the second quotation is of course connected with oyster beds, and again suggests richness: but also Troilus is describing Cressida, and to the audience purity and constancy are the question: hence the pearl,

[1] cf Du Bellay: 'Plus mon Loire gaulois que le Tibre latin'.

symbol of spotlessness (see the fourteenth-century poem 'Pearl'). Marvell's 'Indian' combines both these uses, only he brings in neither spice nor pearls; neither the Coy Mistress's purity nor her richness are in question: she is seated by the Ganges appropriately finding rubies. Appropriately geographically, as has been noted by Miss Sackville-West, but also symbolically:

> Look here, what tributes wounded fancies sent me,
> Of pallid pearls and rubies red as blood;
> Figuring that they their passions likewise lent me
> Of grief and blushes, aptly understood
> In bloodless white and the encrimson'd mood:
> Effects of terror and dear modesty,
> Encamp'd in hearts, but fighting outwardly.
> > (Shakespeare: 'A Lover's Complaint')

Ganges we said was the point of sunrise: look at

> Even as the sun with purple-coloured face
> Had ta'en his last leave of the weeping morn,
> Rose-cheeked Adonis hied him to the chase:
> Hunting he loved, but love he laughed to scorn

and (of Adonis speaking)

> Once more the ruby-coloured portal opened
> Which to his speech did honey passage yield

These serve to show the intricate symbolism that Marvell inherited: and adds still more point to the Coy Mistress' being by the Ganges

Pearls we have seen belong to the sea and to grief as well as to purity: and the next phrase not only balances the first with its river nearer home, but presents a complete piece of symbolism balancing the other. The forlorn lover stands like the weeping willow, his emblem, by the waterside complaining, 'Augmenting it with tears.' And these tears are pearls, and the pearl and the ruby as we have seen are opposed.[2] By the waterside also, fallen greatness and empire have traditionally been lamented: the work of Time. With this in his mind Marvell moves gracefully from his lament to a consideration of limitless Time, where

> My vegetable Love should grow
> Vaster than Empires, and more slow.

---

[2] cf Marvell: 'The brotherless Heliades / Melt in such amber tears as these.'

II

The *Triumphs* of Petrarch are a series of poems showing the relation of
Man to the rest of the Ptolemaic cosmology, on the analogy of Roman
Triumphal Entries. Love triumphs over Man, Chastity over Love, Death
over Chastity, Fame over Death, Time over Fame, and Eternity or
Divinity over Time. Each of these Triumphs involves a combat, some of
which combats are familiar enough to us as single motifs without our
having realized their context. For instance, the combats of Love and Chastity and of Time and Fame are obvious in Shakespeare's Poems and Son-
nets. The sequence of Triumphs is clearly showin in 'Lycidas':
ll.64-84:

> To sport with Amaryllis in the shade
> Or with the tangles of Neaera's hair

is the Triumph of Love.

> To tend the homely slighted Shepherd's trade,
> And strictly meditate the thankless Muse

is the Triumph of Chastity over Love.

> Comes the blind Fury with the abhorred shears

is the Triumph of Death over Chastity (and over the apparent results of
Chastity: 'the fair Guerdon').

> Fame is no plant that grows on mortal soil

is the Triumph of Fame over Death.

> The perfect witness of all-judging Jove

suggests a Last Judgement, the dividing of the mortal and immortal, and
hence, the Triumph of Time over Fame.

> So much Fame in Heav'n

is the final step, the Triumph of Divinity over Time.

The 'Coy Mistress' is not a statement either of the sequence of
Triumphs alone, or of one of the combats alone. It is based on the limitations implicit in the sequence: how Chastity limits Love, Death Beauty,
and so on. And it is with a statement of limitations that the poem opens
'Had we but World enough, and Time' and the ideas of Space and Time
run through the first section as we have seen.

> But at my back I always hear
> Time's winged Chariot hurrying near:
> And yonder all before us lie
> Desarts of vast Eternity.

The Triumphant figures in Petrarch and in later Renaissance art and symbolism make their progress in chariots or cars: it is therefore not to be supposed that Marvell invented the idea of Time having a chariot, or that it was anything other than a commonplace when written. More important, the phrase 'winged chariot' does not mean that the chariot is propelled by wings, that it is anything like a Pegasus. Chariots were drawn by appropriate animals and had wheels; cars, for aerial or marine deities were boat-like affairs, but again drawn by some animal. The look of the chariot need not concern us as the whole phrase gains strength precisely from its vagueness, from its being at one's back, a sensation rather than an image: it must however be considered to be travelling on the ground – 'hurrying near' shows that – to lead on to the deserts to be crossed two lines later. The momentary feeling I think is of a man on the road being overtaken by a coach, which is also the Triumphal Pageant of Time, and it is Time who is winged.

As the coach is Time, so the deserts are Space, looking back to 'Had we but World enough, and Time'. Time and Eternity are, as has been said, two parts of the sequence of Triumphs: Love and Chastity we have already had: the Triumph of Death over Chastity comes in the next lines:

> Thy beauty shall no more be found:
> Nor, in thy marble Vault, shall sound
> My echoing Song: then Worms shall try
> That long preserved Virginity.

It may be fanciful to find a hint of Fame in 'marble Vault' and 'echoing Song'. 'Echoing' has the curious effect of getting attached in one's mind to 'Vault', only for one to find that it shall not sound there: like Milton's description of Mulciber, followed by 'thus they relate Erring'.

III

The third section of this poem is admittedly the most difficult, and I only propose to tackle one part of it, the lines

> And tear our pleasures with rough strife
> Thorough the Iron gates of Life

with such of the preceding lines as are indivisible from these. For 'gates' Tennyson suggested, or wished that Marvell had written, 'grates': a remark which indicates roughly how he interpreted the phrase. The idea is of wild beasts in a cage tearing their meat through the bars: this is reasonably consistent with the lines earlier

> And now, like amorous birds of prey,
> Rather at once our Time devour,
> Than languish in his slow chapt power.

Only one might imagine from this that they were not beasts tearing their pleasures, but vultures, except for the intervening couplet

> Let us roll all our Strength, and all
> Our Sweetness, up into one Ball

which, whatever the total meaning, refers obviously to 'Out of strength came forth sweetness': lions. Possibly Marvell had in mind the heraldic lion with his paw on the globe. The word 'strife' also seems to fit the lion: compare Shakespeare's use of it, although from the mouth of Snug, 'For if I should as lion come in strife'.

The transference from vulture to lion may have been suggested by Time's 'slow chapt power': certainly it is helped by it. This brings us back to 'Iron gates', which is a heavy description of an aviary and sounds more in keeping with lions. At the same time, the 'gates of Life' can stand as a phrase by itself, especially considering the insistence on Death and Time in this poem. Let us first get clear what in Marvell's experience both gates and cages (or grates) would be.

> When Love with unconfined wings
> Hovers within my gates,
> And my divine Althea brings
> To whisper at the grates.

Here 'the grates' refers obviously to the grating in the door of his cell: the gates to the outside prison entrance. Consider this entrance for a moment. When in *Paradise Lost* Book II, the gates of Hell are opened, Milton thus describes it:

> Thus saying, from her side the fatal Key,
> Sad instrument of all our woe, she took:
> And towards the Gate rolling her bestial train,
> Forthwith the huge Portcullis high updrew,
> Which but herself not all the Stygian powers
> Could once have moved; then in the keyhole turns
> Th' intricate wards, and every Bolt and Bar
> Of massy Iron or solid Rock with ease
> Unfastens: on a sudden open fly
> With impetous recoil and jarring sound
> Th' infernal doors.

This means that there is a portcullis in front of the doors: as for instance, is to be found at the Tower, forming an enormous grating between the stone sides of the gateway. Inigo Jones has a drawing of 'The Prison of Night' which shows this exactly. Again, the lions' dens in the Tower were made on precisely the same principle, and looked far more like gates than our circus cages.

> Stone walls do not a prison make
> Nor iron bars a cage –

there are the two essentials of the prison: add to these Shakespeare's 'gates of steel so strong', and it is obvious that there was for Marvell no difficulty in reconciling the two ideas of gateway and cage: the visual image is almost the same for both.

Experiment No. 2, February 1929

Rock-Painting and La Jeune Peinture

This article is prompted by a vital exhibition recently held in Paris, whose vitality derives from its co-incidence with the contemporary situation of painting, a coincidence which is to our generation what the discovery of Negro art was to the generation of Cubists. This is not essentially a coincidence of technique, but rather of directional feeling.

The cubists soon left behind their superficial likeness to Negro work, which was only a confirmation of their feelings, not a source of inspiration. A profound confirmation of the feeling in *la jeune peinture* and its suppor-ters is to be found in the rock paintings of South Africa. The importance of this has been emphasized by an exhibition at the Salle Playel, where copies of rock paintings from all parts of South Africa have been on view. These were made by Prof. Frobenius on his last expedition (1928-30) and were exhibited mainly owing to the energy of M. Christian Zervos, the editor of *Cahiers d'Art*, who devoted a double number of his paper to the subject.

The significance of this exhibition is overwhelming to people who have followed the course of modern painting beyond Cubism. It included copies of work from different localities and ages, but an indisputable sameness of feeling and constancy of power made themselves felt throughout. South African painting is both unified and profound. (How far Prof. Frobenius has departed from the originals in these copies is merely a matter for archaeology. For us his results only are of importance.

It should be noted, however, that it is improbable, judging from other copies of similar work, that he has exactly rendered the colours of the originals. However, there is no reason to suspect his rendering of relative tones.)

A fundamental difference between these works and practically all other painting lies in the different conceptions of time and space evidently natural to the African mind. A single work may have been painted at different times by different men with no apparent consciousness of the consequences of superimposition. Figures overlay, definite planes are abandoned, rhythms intersect and above all, scale is widely varied.

Space in these paintings is not bounded; they have no frames, but this does in no way exclude depth.

Despite all this diversity there is extraordinary unity; a unity new to us because it does not depend upon a frame-induced composition. The African pictorial cosmos is cellular in structure; when you look at the largest of these copies (forty or fifty feet long), you are impressed by the fact that however small or large an area is considered, that area is itself a unity and at the same time is organically related to the surrounding work. The copy of a detail, even of a single figure from a surrounding area, is superbly self-sufficient, so passionately is it stated.

Depth, as we have said, is not excluded from these works, despite the fact that modelling is almost entirely absent: nor is it dependent upon observance of natural recession, or upon any substitute for perspective, such as those used in Chinese and Egyptian art. The effect is of what can only be called mental depth. It is obtained by the process of superimposition above described, by the conflict of scales remarked on, and especially by the quality of light issuing from their acute feeling for tonal values which are established by the process of superimposition. Their use of white is particularly striking in this connection.

Their stupendous sense of rhythm, exercised on their subjects from contemporary life (one naturally full of movement) produces the most violent and the most satisfying distortions. It is most important to remark that these distortions do not reduce the paintings to mere patterns, nor are they naturalist or surrealist works. The African scale of values induces a new proportional interpretation of the human body. The spiritual significance of these distortions is on a parallel to the significance of the heroic distortions in Western art. The latter depends for depth primarily upon modelling, as in the heroic paintings of Rubens, while the former substitutes its own peculiar effect of mental depth. African painting is thus possessed of its own proper and particular mythology.

Where our comparison of the African paintings to *la jeune peinture* begins is at the acknowledged death of Cubism about 1925. A cubist picture is primarily a construction of wedges. By the above date all possible wedges had been driven home. The resulting tightness caused Cubism to degenerate into mere pattern-making, dictated by a preconceived composition. Freedom had to be regained, both technically and mentally, and we can now see how this was done.

To take a few obvious examples: Miro shook the flat areas of Cubism into movement; Borès and Cossio revived brushwork on a large scale; Masson contributed spontaneous quality of line, Viñes new ideas of space and light. Vigorous rhythms, both of areas and line, light and grace interrelated, revolt against architectural composition: precisely the qualities of the rock-paintings. Smaller points may be noticed: superimposition and the corresponding transparency of planes, are to be found especially in Borès and Masson. But in this revolt these qualities have come to be not so much characteristics of new discoveries in painting, as to be the discoveries themselves: the fundamental effects of actual technique have been used for their emotive qualities.

Cubism not only enslaved technique but practically killed the naturalist myths (landscape, still-life, portrait) upon which painting has for the most part relied since Poussin.[1] The want of myths following on Cubism has been filled from various sources, pre-eminently by Surrealism. Of Surrealist paintings two things can at once be said: their principle of construction is that of dreams and their unity depends, not upon demonstrable composition, but upon mental reconstruction of elements which are in themselves pictorial unities; and not, as in cubist pictures, wedge-like fragments. The one follows from the other; a dream has two aspects: its obvious shapes and the impulses these shapes represent. So that, for example, a picture by Dali has in it a group of recognizable objects, which by arrangement, lighting, and so on, form a piece of phallic symbolism. It is a kind of pictorial pun.

Evidently the Surrealist myth may be constructed of anything, and the scope of myth-construction is by this almost infinitely widened. (Léger has arrived at the same position in a different way, by breaking up the cubist still-life.) But at the present moment the Surrealists (especially Ernst) are exploiting the rather temporary emotive qualities of incongruity provided by the juxtaposition of objects as objects (with literary associations). There are other pieces of myth-construction in *la jeune peinture*, related to Surrealism: dream-suggestion has been used by Sima, metamorphoses and animal combats by Masson, and Roux has extended the idea of metamorphosis into a complete world-reconstruction by

---

[1] Delacroix is the obvious exception: his influence in Paris lately has been enormous.

symbolism. The work of these painters also relies greatly on the actual shock of following the literary metamorphosis. Thus, both technique and myth are at present using our associations for their power; a state of affairs which by its nature cannot last. A new solidity as firm as Cubism, but fluid, not static, is required. Precisely such a solidity both of technique and myth we find in South African rock painting; we are not for a moment suggesting that the solution of modern problems lies in the copying of African painting, but that in it may be seen a solution of similar problems.

Of the qualities present in African work, *la jeune peinture* does (as we have indicated) possess many, but the contribution of each painter is limited to a few only whereas the present position demands their collection in one man.[2]

Painting stands between Fear and Nature: between Surrealism and Realism. By Realism we mean both the more obvious return to nature of (say) Léonide, and the much subtler imaginative treatment of nature employed by Borès and Cossio. The work of Masson and the Surrealists is based on fear primarily, and is correspondingly limited. In a sense these two classes cancel out: each possessing the virtues lacking in the other. This is not to disparage the painters we have mentioned for a moment: in spite of contrary opinions in this country, painting in Paris has more promise and energy now than at any time since the first period of Cubism. By its qualities it challenges comparison with the African painting we have described, and compared to the finest, the 'classical style' of South Rhodesia, it naturally looks rather fragmentary. That it will find solutions to its problems as complete and satisfying as the solutions of similar problems in the rock paintings we feel confident and suggest that it is through the fusion of the different elements of technique and myth here analysed that it may do so. We look for a slow regaining of the heroic sense. By heroic we mean the co-ordination of a greater number of emotions than painting has for some time managed to use; a grasp of problems as complete as that which Rubens had of the muddle of sixteenth-century painting, and as in Rubens, the use of technique as technique, to create mutations in the subject, and the subject thereby to be in its proper place, as the basis of a metamorphosis by paint and not by literary substitution: producing a world of heroic mutations parallel to the heroic proportions of African painting.

HUMPHREY JENNINGS
G.F. NOXON

Experiment No. 7, Spring 1931

---

[2] Perhaps Beaudin is the nearest young painter to this ideal.

A Reconsideration of Herrick

Herrick's *Hesperides* was first published in 1648, failed, and was rediscovered in the last years of the eighteenth century, though not reprinted entire until 1823. But the popularity of Herrick in the nineteenth century was evidently inaugurated by a selection published in 1810. This popularity may be judged from the following representative passages.

> His poems resemble a luxuriant meadow, full of king-cups and wild flowers, or a July firmament sparkling with a myriad of stars. His fancy fed upon all the fair and sweet things of nature; it is redolent of roses and geraniums; it is as bright and airy as the thistledown, or the bubbles which laughing boys blow into the air, where they float in a waving line of beauty. *Retrospective Review*, 1822

Sir Edmund Gosse (*Cornhill*, 1875) found the *Hesperides*

> a storehouse of lovely things, full of tiny beauties of varied kind and workmanship.... What is so very precious about the book is the originality and versatility of the versification.... Those delicate warbles that Herrick piped out when the sun shone on him and the flowers were fresh.... Our gentle and luxurious babbler of the flowery brooks.

Similarly, Grosart (1876) wrote:

> The book is full of all those pleasant things of Spring and Summer, full of young love, happy nature, and the joy of mere existence.... Herrick's sun might be that stray Venus of Botticelli's, which rises, rosy and dewy, from a sparkling sea, blown at by the little laughing winds, and showered upon with violets and lilies of no earthly growth.... It matters not what Herrick describes – he gives you its very 'form and pressure,' and over it, as the seven-fold rainbow breaking into ineffable fragments under its load of rain, or before the blast of the wind; and better than saint's nimbus, you have the 'final touch' in epithet or in break of music, that differentiates the Poet from the Versifier.

And this is the last word of Mr Humbert Wolfe (1926) on the situation. Quoting the end of *Corinna*, he declares:

> All of us who read this will in the end be a fable, song, or fleeting shade. But Herrick is none of these things. It is early Spring with him. The dew is on the grass. The larks are up, and, as we take our leave, we hear him, as the centuries after us will hear him, calling on a note of immortal laughter –
>
> Come, my Corinna, come, let's goe a Maying.

And they are going.

We do not quote these passages primarily for the sake of amusement; they represent the serious judgments of a century upon Herrick's poetry, and show Herrick reconstructed according to the perversities and propensities of a taste formed by the two principles of the Romantic Revival, its return to nature, and its undirected romance. Further not only has Herrick been the especial victim of the concentrated fatuity of a hundred years, but our possibilities of experience from his poetry have been seriously inhibited by an attitude such as that of Dr Moorman, who (1910) said that

> Burns and Shelley and Heine are of necessity more to us than Herrick can ever be.... But there are times when, feeling that the world is too much with us, we try to free our minds from the burden of modernity; and then it is that, in holiday mood, we turn to the *Hesperides*, and find refreshment of soul in the contemplation of an age that knew little of misgiving or disillusion.

Herrick, it is true, never experienced misgiving or disillusion as profoundly as Donne and Webster. At the same time he was not the simple poet of escape that the critics have found him: the poet of escape is one who, like William Morris, fails either to recognize reality or to complete a system which is for both a self-defence and a positive statement.

The anthology method of reading Herrick – gathering rosebuds in holiday mood – has obscured the complexity of imagery in the *Hesperides*. For an investigation of the totality of Herrick's work reveals that one poem explains another, that the imagery is interrelated, and hence that to isolate poems and then to be aware only of the qualities retained or acquired in isolation is to make his experience appear fragmentary and his imagery casual. In other words, Herrick has been reduced to the level of, and acclaimed in terms of, the Romantics: but since not unnaturally, after the reduction, Dr Moorman has to find Herrick unsatisfactory by these standards, no course is left to him but finally to reverse the positions; to elevate Shelley to the level of 'high-seriousness' ('O world! O life! O time!') from which Herrick has just been debased. That is to say, Romantic standards have impoverished Herrick by emphasizing his apparent affinities with their own poets of escape.

The nineteenth century, Matthew Arnold excepted, failed to realize the nature of the experiences that can produce poetry, limiting them by a demand for naturalist statement: that philosophical poetry should sound like philosophy and natural description like nature. They found Herrick merely decorative because his experience fell outside their definition. Arnold (1865) formed a wider conception of poetic experience:

> In literature, the elements with which the creative power works are ideas; the best ideas on every matter which literature touches, current

at the time.... The grand work of literary genius is a work of synthesis and exposition, not of analysis and discovery; its gift lies in the faculty of being happily inspired by a certain intellectual and spiritual atmosphere, by a certain order of ideas, when it finds itself in them; of dealing with these ideas, presenting them in the most effective and attractive combinations – making beautiful works with them, in short... It has long seemed to me that the burst of creative activity in our literature, through the first quarter of this century, had about it something premature... and this prematureness comes from its having proceeded without its proper date, without sufficient materials to work with. In other words, the English poetry of the first quarter of this century, with plenty of energy, plenty of creative force, did not know enough.... In the England of Shakespeare, the poet lived in a current of ideas in the highest degree animating and nourishing to the creative power; society was, in the fullest measure, permeated by fresh thought, intelligent and alive.

It was in terms of this thought, this knowledge, that Herrick conceived and directed his experience. Renaissance England used the collected ideas of antiquity, of revived mediaeval cosmology, and of the outside world in general, to give dignity and significance to its life. Such a synthesis of impressions through the agency of exotic ideas implied the equation of native experience with foreign ritual.

If you will bee good Scholars, and profite well in the Arte of Musicke, shutte your Fidels in their cases, and looke up to Heaven: the order of the Spheres, the unfallible motion of the Planets, the iuste course of the Yeere, and varietie of seasons, the concorde of the Elementes and their qualyties, Fyre, Water, Ayre, Earth, Heate, Colde, Moysture and Drought concurring together to the constitution of earthly bodies and sustenance of every creature.

The politike Lawes in well governed common wealthes, that treade downe the prowde, and upholde the meeke, the love of the King and his subiectes, the Father and his childe, the Lorde and his Slave, the Maister and his Man, The *Trophees* and *Triumphes* of our auncestours, which pursued vertue at the harde heeles, and shunned vyce as a rocke for feare of shipwracke, are excellent maisters too shewe you that this is right Musicke, this perfecte harmony.

Gosson: *The School of Abuse*, 1579

Gosson is speaking not of the ordering of life itself, but of the position of the artist, and the nature of his ideal experience, which is, he insists, to be derived from a ritualist conception both of the universe and of man's

activities. Critics have noted Herrick's 'delight' and 'interest' in folk-lore
and ancient ceremony, but they have failed to see that, delight and interest
apart, ritual in a wider sense was integral to Herrick's way of thinking.

By 'integral' we mean that Herrick possesses a subtler kind of unity than
that which critics have looked for, or than he claimed for his book. For
instance, the title *Hesperides* places a conscious unity on the book. This
word has been mainly interpreted 'poems written in the West', 'children
of the West', 'golden apples of Devonshire': naturalist interpretations
which by no means state all the implications of the word. *Hesperides* is not
simply a playful way of describing products of the West; following the
Renaissance methods discussed above, Herrick actually identifies his
golden apples with the famous Golden Apples, and so on. And the book,
thus dignified, becomes Herrick's weapon against time:

> Pillars let some set up,
> (If so they please)
> Here is my hope,
> And my *Pyramides*.

The word 'hope' suggests another meaning of *Hesperides* evident from the
Dedication: 'To the Most Illustrious, and Most Hopefull Prince, CHARLES,
Prince of Wales.'

> Well may my Book come forth like Publique Day
> When such a *Light* as *You* are leads the way:
> Who are my Works *Creator*, and alone
> The *Flame* of it, and the *Expansion*.
> And look how all those heavenly Lamps acquire
> Light from the Sun, that *inexhausted Fire*:
> So all my *Morne*, and *Evening Stars* from You
> Have their *Existence*, and their *Influence* too.
> Full is my Book of Glories; but all These
> By You become *Immortal Substances*.

The *illustrious* and *hopeful* Charles is the sun, which brings light and hope:
giving light to the stars, that is, inspiring the poems as Apollo ('all my
Morne, and *Evening Stars*', children of Hesper) and bringing hope of
immortality to Herrick, since the dedication has related the personal (and
therefore mortal) life of the poems to the central ritual of his time and
country, the life of royalty.

Such a conscious attempt to make his poems '*Immortal Substances*'
through relating them to ritual, is extremely interesting in itself, but does
not give a unity to his poems in the way that his poetic experience based
on that ritual does. (Gosson's instructions will not make an Elizabethan

artist, but *King Lear* evidently contains experience of the ideas described by Gosson.) Again, in *The Argument of his Book*, Herrick catalogues everything that it contains except his epigrams and some poems addressed to friends and patrons. This catalogue should be taken not so much as the list of subjects it purports to be, as an indication of the nature and scope of the imagery Herrick uses. Thus, without making a definite statement, the lines

> I write of *Youth*, of *Love*, and have *Accesse*
> By these to sing of cleanly-*Wantonnesse*.
> I sing of *Dewes*, of *Raines*, and piece by piece
> Of *Balme*, of *Oyle*, of *Spice*, and *Amber-Greece*

suggest and cover the poems whose imagery is from clothes and perfumes. These are, incidentally, more numerous than the flower-poems with which Herrick has usually been associated, and contain a big percentage of his best work. Herrick the flower-poet is largely the invention of people who like flowers and wish Herrick to have liked them too, because he mentions them. Delight in the emotive imagery of Wordsworth leads to making the imagery of the Elizabethans emotive also. But the question of Herrick's likes and dislikes is irrelevant since for him as a poet imagery has no intrinsic significance: an image is one element of a metaphor, and Herrick's poetry is a structure of metaphors; the *Argument* is a catalogue of elements. It is the interchangeability of these elements that is the basis of Herrick's cosmos.

Both times and things are interchangeable. Times, for instance, in the bringing together of customs of different ages in his Epithalamia: from the Song of Solomon, from Catullus, from English folk-lore. The most obvious examples of interchangeability of things are to be found in the many short poems which record actual metamorphoses:

> How Marigolds Came Yellow
> *Jealous Girles* these sometimes were,
> While they liv'd, or lasted here:
> Turn'd to *Flowers*, still they be
> Yellow, markt for Jealousie.

This interchangeability derives from the ritualist attitude we have insisted on; in ritual there is no waste, everything has a symbolic, as opposed to naturalist, existence: it is related to something else by more than fortuitous resemblance, and at the supreme moment of the ritual becomes the thing symbolized.

Herrick, of course, makes continual use of simile in its simplest form (superficial likeness), but more often his similes involve metaphor (organic relation) which in turn leads to ritual (systematic identification). Transition from simile to metaphor is well illustrated in the lines *To Virgins*.

> Heare ye Virgins, and Ile teach,
> What the times of old did preach.
> *Rosamund* was in a Bower
> Kept, as *Danae* in a Tower:
> But yet Love (who subtile is)
> Crept to that, and came to this.
> Be ye lockt up like to these.
> Or the rich *Hesperides;*
> Or those Babies in your eyes,
> In their Christall Nunneries;
> Notwithstanding Love will win,
> Or else force a passage in;
> And as coy be, as you can,
> Gifts will get ye, or the man.

What appears to begin as a succession of similes is made a closely inter-related structure by the metaphors contained in the last simile: the word 'Babies' translates a pun on the meanings of *puella*, and the continued metaphor of 'Nunneries' looks back to 'Bower' and 'Tower', giving them increased definition. Again, since Love is said to enter at the eye and the Virgins are compared to the pupils of their own eyes, metaphor becomes ritual: the eye as a whole is symbolic of the Virgins in a nunnery, and at the moment, in life, of Love's entrance into bower and tower the eye will actually be entered too. This suggestion in Herrick of a leap from meta-phor into life is naturally connected with his interest in actual scenes of ritual where life seems to make a leap into metaphor, not only in his descriptions of '*May-poles, Hock-carts, Wassails, Wakes*', but also (as in his Epithalamia) where the poem describing the event can be used as part of the event itself.

> In sober mornings, doe not thou reherse
> The holy incantation of a verse;
> But when that men have both well drunke, and fed,
> Let my Enchantments then be sung, or read.

These lines, from *Where he would have his verses read*, are designed as a bridge between the reader (the outside world) and the cosmos of the poems: they describe the transformation of normal circumstances of reading into the ideal magical conditions necessary for the success of his 'enchant-ments'; and to these magical conditions the poem is itself an initiation.

Thus, not only is Herrick's method of writing magical, but also the materials of his transformations are often remains from the systems of the Magical World,[1] and by this derivation suited to his purpose. Among the poems so constructed is his most important work, *Corinna's going a Maying*. 'The dew is on the grass' (says Mr Wolfe) 'The larks are up.' But consider the actual passage in Herrick:

> Get up, sweet-Slug-a-bed, and see
> The Dew-bespangling Herbe and Tree.
> Each Flower has wept, and bow'd toward the East,
> Above an houre since; yet you not drest,
>   Nay! not so much as out of bed?
> When all the Birds have Mattens seyd,
> And sung their thankfull Hymnes; 'tis sin,
>   Nay, profanation to keep in,
> When as a thousand Virgins on this day,
> Spring, sooner then the Lark, to fetch in May.

It is admittedly essential to know what dew and larks are, and that they are to be seen in the early morning; as, indeed, it is necessary to know that the background of the poem is the actual rite of bringing in may (which was sophisticated at least as early as the time of Henry VIII). But to this background, and to Mr Wolfe's realistic dew and larks are brought associations, quotations, suggestions, 'to make of impressionism something solid and lasting.' The dew becomes pearls for decoration at the rite, tears for lost maidenheads; the lark in Renaissance literature appears with the morning to praise the sun (*l'alouette, louer*).

It should be realized that this symbolism was Herrick's inheritance, not his invention: from the mass of ancient symbolism extant at the time he made a selection which it was his problem to present 'in the most effective and attractive combinations'. Herrick's cosmos was constituted according to the mutations effected by his process. With what complete control Herrick ordered his materials can be seen in *The Lilly in a Christal*, where the images are not, as in *Corinna*, related by their derivation:

> Thus Lillie, Rose, Grape, Cherry, Creame,
>   And Straw-berry do stir
>   More love, when they transfer
> A weak, a soft, a broken beame;
>   Then if they sho'd discover
> At full their proper excellence;

---

[1] See, in this connection, the very important chapter on 'The Neutralization of Nature', in Mr I.A. Richards's *Science and Poetry*.

Without some Scean cast over,
To juggle with the sense.

These objects have by nature only the slightest imagic connection;
symbolically they are not inter-related at all. But by an extremely delicate
suggestion (in the earlier stanzas) of the likeness of the changes they
undergo in certain conditions, Herrick effects a relationship between them
which gives them an importance parallel to that derived from a magical
connection. The poem is thus a cosmos constructed on the analogy of the
Magical World: and is as highly organized.

HUMPHREY JENNINGS
J.M. REEVES

Experiment No. 7, Spring 1931

The Theatre Today

I

'What this school needs is co-operation; that means working with me.' – *A Headmaster*

At the height of his triumph the returning Roman conqueror was invested
with the robes and insignia of Jupiter and was identified by the crowd with
the god himself: (Pompey as Jupiter). In the theatre Roscius *plays the part
of* the conqueror (Roscius as Alexander) and at the moment of Tamburlaine's triumph in the theatre we have the series: Alleyn (the actor),
Tamburlaine, Alexander, Jupiter:

Where Belus, Ninus, and great Alexander
Have rode in triumph triumphs Tamburlaine....

Marlowe, *Tamburlaine*, II, 4181.

and

Then in my coach like Saturnes royal son.
Mounting his shining chariot gilt with fire,
And drawn with princely Eagles through the path,
Pav'd with bright Christall and enchac'd with starres,
When all the Gods stand gazing in his pomp,
So will I ride through Samarcanda streets....

Marlowe, *Tamburlaine*, II, 4104.

When, in poetry, for example, in *The Progress of Poesy* (1754), the poet has substituted himself for his patron,[1] the actor substitutes himself for his part; that is, he is no longer identified with the hero by the audience: Mr Garrick as Mr Garrick as Macbeth, or (more complete) Mr Kean as Mr Kean as Richard II as God.[2] (The player scenes in *Hamlet* produce further perspectives: Burbage as Hamlet as an actor,[3] or Mr Irving as Mr Irving as Hamlet as an actor (or one of the children of the Chapel Royal[4]) as Æneas.) Again, when the poet substitutes himself for the King we get Alleyn as Richard II as Shakespeare. The rhetoric of Shakespeare's heroes at 'moments of emotion' Mr T.S. Eliot has already dealt with.[5] Add that at these moments –

> For God's sake let us sit upon the ground
> And tell sad stories of the death of Kings....[6]

and

> Who can control his fate?[7]

the king or hero is literally changed into a poet, into the Poet.

By the nineteenth century these two metamorphoses, of the poet and the actor, have produced:

(a) Messrs. A, B, C, etc., in the parts of Mrs Alving, her son, the maid, etc., all together making up an expression of Ibsen,[8] and

(b) Type-casting – Mr Fishooks as Romeo played by Mr Fishooks, leading finally to the film of Mr Douglas Fairbanks' tour round the world in which we have Mr Fairbanks as Mr Fairbanks as Mr Fairbanks, and where all possibility of drama ends.

---

[1] Yet oft before his infant eyes would run
Such forms, as glitter in the Muse's ray
With Orient hues, unborrowed of the Sun.
          – Gray, *The Progress of Poesy*, 118.

[2] The breath of worldly men cannot depose
The deputy elected by the Lord.
          – Shakespeare, *Richard II*, III. ii. 56.

[3] – This is one Lucianus, nephew to the King.
– You are as good as a chorus, my Lord.
          – Shakespeare, *Hamlet*, III. ii. 238-9.

[4] In Marlowe's *Dido, Queen of Carthage*, the original of Hamlet's 'Æneas' tale to Dido' (II. ii. 444).

[5] T.S. Eliot, in *Selected Essays*, Faber.

[6] *Richard II*, III. ii. 155-6.

[7] *Othello*, V. ii. 267.

[8] 'In every new play I have aimed at my own spiritual emancipation and purification.'
– Ibsen.

The extreme displacement of the traditional central figure by Ibsen (continued in France by Roussel) has in England led to the assumption that one can be a playwright without being a poet. The immediate result has been a 'theatre renascence,' a 'new movement': 'art'-theatredom: all methods of presenting or cloaking a new metamorphosis exalted in village-green drama, praise-god repertory, and other leagues, guilds, and love of the theatre-hoods: the metamorphosis of Jupiter into Pompey into Roscius into Crummles into The Producer, under whose leaden sceptre, etc....

The producer is one of the great English group which includes parents, commanding officers, headmasters and magistrates, all of whom *cannot be answered back*. (The mantle of Jupiter is on all of their shoulders.) The producer is a lion, the roaring king of actors, scenic artists, electrics, and of long dead authors: his opinion (opinion not knowledge or certainty) is sacred and final. Historically he is the inevitable result of secondary education: that is, he has been taught that one thing is better than another, that anything can and should be improved. He has *ideas*. His ideas come from his opinion and are therefore not in any sense invention. They are distinguished by their arbitrariness, which is only natural since they do not derive from any constant interior source but from whatever the producer has happened to notice or pick up in his educational rambles. The current ideas of any art-producer simply date back to his last ramble, which may have been ten minutes ago (reading *Hours in the National Gallery* on his way to the theatre) or years back, in which case it will by this time have become a habit with him to refer back to it on every occasion: so there will be the producer who begins every conference on scenery with the question, 'Did you ever see a film called *The Cabinet of Dr Caligari?*'

His opinion is made up of these ideas and, as a wild coachman to them, of the celebrated modern phantom, 'Unity'. By a natural jumble (that is, proceeding naturally from the miraculous circumstances of his birth – above) he will claim, in lectures on 'Producing a Play', in 'A Note' in his programme, and so on, that the Producer is the person who gives to the otherwise jarring work of the actors, designer, etc. that Unity without which.... And so it is towards this Unity that the producer's passion for improvement (already mentioned) is directed.

Indeed the popularisation of æsthetic theories corresponds with the appearance of the producer and they are his self-justification. For they all depend on the same phantom Unity. Unity has become in poetry what loyalty is in the State: that is, the substitution of the poet for the king which should in fact represent the substitution of freedom for tyranny, has been disgustingly perverted by the culture-thirsty to provide a new tyranny in whose name Baudelaire and Rimbaud are declared to be traditional 'after all', and thanks to which we can all snuggle under once more and forget.

But in the theatre before it became an 'art' there simply was no producer. The play was written by the poet, acted by the actors, decorated by the designer, regulated by the manager and the stage-manager and so on. To have another guy hanging round 'producing' is simply providing the widest possible opportunities for the local busybody. And so, apart, for example, from the infinitely painful rehearsals which become 'talks on the theatre', you will find him dabbling with a little scene-paint immediately before the first-night curtain, altering lighting cues during the performance, and running round behind to annoy actors with notes on intonation. But Dionysius is not taken in.

The producer's position is, of course, infinitely strengthened by the fact that most of the plays which he produces are 'revivals': no horrid live author to deal with, and a play which is known (in one circle or another) to be a 'good' play, even to be a classic! The dreams of the adolescent producer gulping down a mixture of Arthur Rackham, Gordon Craig, and *A Midsummer Night's Dream* can be realized at last! And since the audience know the play already, continuity and intelligibility can be swept away for 'treatment' to take their place; which is where the great 'ideas' come in. And so it becomes possible to produce *Everyman* (such a beautiful play) with the flagellation-scene cut, and to spare 'modern sensibility' the shocking sight of such maso...introducing at the same time exquisite mediæval tableaux constructed out of hessian and the company's electric light – to make up for it.

That is to say, the 'Art theatre' is simply the producer's (Jupiter's) method of indulging in 'self-expression'. Being an 'artist' he cannot of course sully his paws dealing with the 'trade' theatre: so the extra money (don't imagine an art-theatre pays for itself) comes from benevolence, direct and indirect. Indirect benevolence: 'When' (here the Higher Powers speak for themselves) 'when the History of the English Theatre in the twentieth century comes to be written, no small place will have to be given to the boy- and girl-students working in Art- and Repertory-theatres. Like the chimney-sweeps of former ages they performed arduous tasks which have sometimes been thought to be too onerous for their years, but of which it may be said that their work gave them valuable experience, allayed their too impulsive animal spirits, and developed their rational powers: in a word fitted them for life in their profession. They had the benefit of strict supervision from their superiors who at the same time allowed the enthusiasm of youth to have full scope in the long hours which theatre work demands. They were also often taken without a premium and as they improved were sometimes paid a small wage. Tribute also must be paid to the high-mindedness of the students' parents on whom in the end the burden of keeping their children in board, lodging, and clothing usually fell. But we are always to remember that the cause of Art was at the same time being constantly forwarded. . . .'

II

'England, Home, and Beauty'

Consider the opinions of Pepys, whom one would at least have expected to like 'musicals', on *A Midsummer Night's Dream*,[1] and of Lamb, who is always supposed to have understood the Elizabethans so well, on *Tamburlaine*;[2] but Pepys and Lamb (being typical English theatre-goers) are among the favourite authors of Alethea Campstool, who living as she does 'within seventeen minutes of Charing Cross' and having apparently no household cares and endless three-and-sixpences manages to see the matinées of *The Grey Cuckoo* (or *Heartsease* or *March Winds* . . .) any afternoon when her sister, who runs a home-made tea-shop, is also free. You will find them on their sixpenny folding seats reading as I say Pepys or Lamb or one of the Montaigne-and-water essayists of the present day, because they love what Alethea calls 'good' literature, and 'good' plays; with 'sensitively drawn characterizations' and 'entirely beautiful performances'. They find Chekhov 'a little morbid, but then the world is disillusioned nowadays, isn't it?' They also love music: *Nymphs and Shepherds* is Agatha's favourite. Of Shakespeare they prefer *As You Like It* and *The Merry Wives*. But among authors of 'good' plays they remember particularly Euripides ('*Our* Euripides the human'): happy is he who belongs to the Church of England and the League of Nations Union: or alternatively for those who are not regular churchgoers, the difficulties of *The Bacchae* have long been explained away as 'glorious poetry' by Macaulay. In either case the word 'good' will cover the gaps and the Englishman's profound

---

[1] 'To the King's theatre, where we saw *Midsummer Night's Dream*, which I had never seen before, nor shall ever again, for it is the most insipid, ridiculous play that ever I saw in my life.'

[2] 'The lunes of Tamburlaine are perfect midsummer madness. Nebuchadnezzar's are mere modest pretensions compared with the thundering vaunts of the Scythian Shepherd. He comes in drawn by conquered Kings, and reproaches these *pampered jades of Asia* that they can *draw but twenty miles a day*. Till I saw this passage with my own eyes, I never believed it was anything more than a pleasant burlesque of mine ancient's. But I can assure my readers that it is soberly set down in a play which their ancestors took to be serious.'

belief that Greek poetry and Italian Art and the Bible[3] were all really produced by Englishmen will be further deepened; and in turn further power will be given to the patron saint of speech days: the Christian militarist with a classical education.

Behind the performance of *Iphigenia* that the Campstool sisters so enjoyed are the ranged powers of Church, State, and University, of the Societies for this and the Associations for that – manifesting through correspondence columns and vouched for by banks – whose directors are also governors of schools, trustees of collections, organizers of charities …all, whether they are aware of it or not, using this performance of Euripides for their own ends – the solidification of their own interlocking positions: the 'corporate life of the Nation' and what a body! And it is they who in their lives and actions ultimately define the word 'good'. In England rackets are rarely called rackets even by their victims because those who are running them are not aware (native imbecility) of the racket themselves: they only become aware if something is not running as smoothly as usual (what they call 'unrest'). This curious blindness does not in any way lessen the effectiveness of the racket: on the contrary it makes it far more difficult to oppose.

Types of rackets: (*a*) park your car in a garage or get it punctured by the garage-hands (simple or American racket). (*b*) Reasonably similar is the speech day racket noticed above: in which, for example, there is a certain amount of money invested in India – in order to ensure dividends on this military control in India is necessary – in order to ensure military control officers are necessary – in order to ensure the training of officers a brass hat distributes the prizes on speech day, and is doubly welcomed by staff and parents since after all they are paid out of those dividends. (*c*) But often substituted for the speech day racket is the Culture racket which bears directly on the theatre: in order to protect dividends as before, the utmost docility ('Citizenship') is desirable; this is procured by investing, through the opinions of apparently disinterested critics, professors, etc. (from whose translations the word 'Citizenship' has already been borrowed) a Greek tragedy or whatever it may be with certain virtues (truth, beauty, goodness, invented by those critics or their forerunners), and which, on a moral plane make for 'Citizenship', and by then contrasting the excellence (i.e. production of docility) of the Greek tragedy with the badness (since the critics have not invested it with the virtues) of

---

[3] 'This was the earliest manuscript of the New Testament in the world. Was it not right that the Government should have the courage to say that this was a thing which England ought to possess when it was for sale?' Mr Duff Cooper on The Sinai Codex in the House of Commons, 31 July 1934 (reported in *The Times*).

whatever work is chosen as a foil. The audience is thus deluded into admiring and imitating the virtues and not considering the work itself at all. So that every Campstool who thinks that Euripides is so beautiful so good and so true (and who even has the illusion of discovering these virtues for herself) is playing into the hands of 'safety-first'-ism in the simplest because obscurest way.

And Alethea herself (also unaware) uses the performance as a sacrifice to atone for her self-frustrated destiny: she says she has been to 'something worth while'. And the performers themselves will be all the more applauded because they are known through magazines to lead beautiful home-lives (as distinct from ordinary theatre-folk) and to subscribe to the philosophy of 'after all': the classics they will tell you have something the others haven't got, and when in later years they come to write the history of their stage life in a little thatched cottage in the country (hollyhocks and pewter and old French songs) they will remember that these performances were an inspiration to them and helped them to forget the Russian and German atrocities and so on. In that history also you will read how they took *The Grey Cuckoo* (or *Heartsease* or *March Winds*...) on tour to Canada, Australia, and South Africa, how the 'Aussies' loved it, how the author of *Heartsease* had himself come down to the later rehearsals of it, how after all they are glad to have lived their lives giving the joy of the theatre to others and if life were to be lived over again.... So wide is the provinciality of the Theatre in the British Empire.

III

'They do but jest; poison in jest: no offence i' the world.' – Hamlet

The 'theatre which is a trade' – that is to say the ordinary theatre – is curiously parallel to the dress business, and the two are connected by the audience. Thus it is the shop-girls (very many from the dress business itself), their shoulders still faintly Schiaparelli-ish, who throng to see the picture-postcard star (who on tour has his fan mail card-indexed, for next time) in a morning-coat song and dance show, and the leading lady attended to by a male chorus of newly-scrubbed shop-walkers. It is the rather 'better class' wearers of the eternal 'period dresses' who will adore anything about Old Vienna, the Tyrol, or beautified scraps of Tudor history, while Society itself in *original* models adorns those revues which begin to overlap the remnants of the Russian Ballet, and those chic first-nights where we all go to see each other, where the gallery applauds arrival of the theatre people in the stalls, and the stalls applaud the appearance

of Society people on the stage, and all of which is in any case only preparatory to everybody's meeting afterwards for supper.

As a trade the theatre is no doubt worse run than the corresponding
dress business at each 'level'.[1] At all 'levels' the idea (like that of Estate
Agents) is to present the perfect picture of the world in which the audience
already fancies it moves. But here without appealing to Art or to Culture.
Here the magic words are 'good entertainment' and 'good theatre'.

The 'entertainment-' and 'theatre-rackets' are similarly run to the
others, but if possible even less recognized as rackets, at any rate by the
victims. Here the necessary opinions come not from professors but from
theatrical critics, Sunday papers, Society magazines and general gossip
columns. The criticisms are, of course, directed first by the momentary
policy of the paper concerned, but also, inside the limited field dictated by
the proprietor of the paper and his advertisers, it is in the simple use of the
terms 'entertainment' and 'theatre' that another racket becomes possible.

(*a*) 'Good entertainment': with these words the critic not only boosts
any particular production he is told to, but also produces in his readers the
required feeling that 'after all' one goes to the theatre to be entertained and
not to be instructed (an apposition dragged from the classics in order to
support only one term of it) that there is nothing like a good laugh, that
to have a sense of humour is to have a sense of God (that pulpit chestnut),
that we are all good fellows here, and so on in series of deception and self-
deception, to the conclusion that life on this right little tight little island
is fine as it is, etc. (A conclusion resulting incidentally in their voting
national, buying the canned goods advertised in the same paper, and so
on.)

This exercise in debauchery is, of course, stimulated most strongly by
the actual performance in question,[2] but it is also stimulated to some
extent *every time* (see current circulation figures) that the term 'good
entertainment' is read in a paper. The term is primarily used by critics as
a method of saying something for a show which is obviously pretty grim.
Do not imagine that the public on going to a show labelled 'good entertainment' will notice that it isn't even that. They have paid their money
to be entertained and entertained they will be. Do not think that they are
going to come home and tell everybody that they have been taken in by
going to a poor play: vanity and pride alone won't allow that. They may

[1] The incredible shortsightedness of people with money in the theatre is taken as
known.

[2] Particularly by certain apparently innocent details, such as the introduction of an
animal on to the stage, farmhouse windows with pretty check curtains, the endless
butlers and references to cocktails.

get as far as scenting that something is not quite 'up to' what they expected
– and it is just here that the critics' words do their damnedest: the audience
is able to explain anything and everything away to itself and friends by the
grand covering remark, 'Oh well, of course it isn't highbrow, I dare say,
or this or that, but it's jolly good entertainment!' – and so the wheels spin.

They will have come home from the playwright's theatre: the theatre
still pathetically used for masculine story-telling: stories of Life on the
Ocean Wave, smart life, club life and country life, life behind the scenes
in big business: plays called *Old Mysore, Dead Men, At Heaven's Command*. . . . Meet the author of *Dead Men*. He lives abroad part of the year
or writes plays on Mediterranean cruises. He is a quiet man, but usually
manages to make friends with fellow-passengers who have noticed his
slow walk round the deck and his curly pipe. He is so good too with the
kiddies. He began life as a doctor or lawyer and in his London house he
has a comfy study where he works, with club-chairs and water-colours and
whisky and *Punch*, really very much like real doctors and lawyers: he likes
dogs too, and golf and fishing: he works methodically from nine to twelve
and from two to five, and believes hard work to be the only real kind of
genius. But he is too well-bred to take his plays completely seriously. He
is in fact very *human*, very much like an ordinary man – there is nothing
to be afraid of. Very much indeed – he positively *is* an ordinary man and
his plays read and act like it also – and there is just that to be afraid of.
(Apollo as Mr Blank.) *His* plays more than any 'art' productions are perfect
'self-expression'. The lives, mentalities and infinitely boring adventures of
his characters are portrayed by one who knows, since Mr Blank knows
about nothing else. Play-writing is a game: producing jolly good exciting
stuff. How deadly the influence of his 'stuff' can be has just no idea; since
it is in the assumptions he makes and not in any direct statement that the
deadliness lies: in his and in his audience's satisfaction with a world
composed of white bosses and Oh yes 'emancipated' 'niggers', of pretty
girls and their young men in the Services: existences distributed between
baronial halls (armour and decanters) lonely tarns and doctors' waiting-
rooms. Of course it is only entertainment and I am taking the whole thing
too seriously. . . that label again.

(*b*) 'Good theatre': with these words the 'theatrical profession' itself
boosts up a job of work – acting, writing, producing or whatever it may be
– which it knows very well to be outside its wishes. Meet an actor and ask
him what show he is in and at any question of quality out comes the reply:
'Oh! but it's terribly good theatre': pride again. It is also the only word of
criticism an actor has because as a race they are easily the worst educated
and least capable of *seeing* anything, existent, even beating English *nature-
mortistes* and coroners:

Il serait sans doute injuste de chercher parmi les artistes du jour des philosophes, des poètes et des savants; mais il serait légitime d'éxiger d'eux qu'ils s'intéressassent, un peu plus qu'ils ne font, à la religion, à la poésie et à la science.

Hors de leurs ateliers que savent-ils? qu'aiment-ils? qu'expriment-ils? Or Eugène Delacroix était, en meme temps qu'un peintre épris de son metier, un homme d'éducation générale, au contraire des autres artistes modernes qui, pour la plupart, ne sont guère qui d'illustres ou d'obscurs rapins, de tristes spécialistes, vieux ou jeunes; de purs ouvriers, les uns sachant fabriquer des figures academiques, les autres des fruits, les autres des bestiaux. Eugène Delacroix aimait tout, savait tout peindre, et savait gouter tous les talents. C'était l'esprit le plus ouvert à toutes les notions et à toutes les impressions, le jouisseur le plus éclecticque et le plus impartial.[3]

(The solitary serious 'cultured' actress who reads D.H. Lawrence at rehearsals does not manage to be the least better actress for it.) Absolute professionals in apparently any business have a special fury which sweeps up a blinding dust into their own eyes. So a well-known Shakespearean actor will reply to his producer: 'You know, old man, it's no good telling me what the lines mean because Shakespeare just means nothing to me whatever.'

Actors are principally unobservant and clumsy – they cannot open windows or undo knots or step down two steps instead of one: partly because they do not know how things are done and partly because for some reason it is an affront to expect them to do anything except move from position to position and of course, 'act'. (Try the carpet-scene in *Cæsar and Cleopatra*). Equally they are totally unaware of the simplest or commonest 'stock responses': hence the success of the Marx Brothers. The audience is amazed to see actors who really appear to understand (i) ordinary human thoughts and actions, and (ii) who realize and use the difference between these and stock theatrical behaviour. (Remember Groucho's 'You're a mother: you'll understand.') The audience is in fact so amazed and delighted that there is a sudden *danger* of them recognizing these thoughts as their own, and so the Marx Brothers are camouflaged as 'crazy week', just as Ibsen has been camouflaged as 'sociological' and *Life's a Dream* as a 'fantasy'. And so (second abuse of the word) Sandy Powell singing *Underneath the Arches* is explained away as 'entertainment for the masses' or a good substitute for slumming parties. If there does appear anyone on the English halls with something to say the audience has been

---

[3] Baudelaire *L'Œuvre et la vie D'Eugène Delacroix*, II, in *L'Art Romantique*.

so trained to regard him as 'entertainment' only, and he has been so trained to regard his work as 'theatre' only, and to be unaware of what it might be, that the possibilities of his touching anybody's *existence* (neither entertainment nor education) are snuffed right out.... Example of someone getting away with and putting over a good proportion (say 50 per cent.) of what he really has to say: Eddie Cantor, who isn't an *actor*, or a *comedian*, or a *film star*: those are all *shapes* like ready-made suits, to look at: but Eddie on the contrary comes right *out*, at *you*: and literally alters behaviour.

IV

Enslav'd, the Daughters of Albion weep; a trembling lamentation
Upon their mountains; in their valleys, sighs toward America.   – Blake

Now I mention Eddie Cantor not to begin a film and theatre argument (anyway he comes from the stage and 'good cinema' or not, his pictures show it) but because he has something England lost centuries ago and which America in general has still got (went there with the pilgrim fathers) and which Ireland has still got also.[1]

Since the seventeenth century, in England poetry and the theatre have gone in opposite directions: the poets producing rather cloudy attempts at play-writing: *Agrippina, Otho, The Cenci, Harold, The Dynasts*, while theatre-writers have managed to turn out some 'perennial successes': *The Way of the World, She Stoops to Conquer, The School for Scandal, The Importance of being Earnest*, showing the possibilities of exploiting oneself and of making one's fortune by writing for the English (and satisfying their stock ideas about the Irish being so paradoxical and so on) to several other Irishmen. But from before the seventeenth century the native Irish have been utterly unquellable. If the days when 'Good Queen Bess' did her utmost to kill the wildness of Ireland, produced in despite of her[2] such English drama as there is, the days when Ireland finally freed herself from us, have produced an Irish theatre in which the work of three poets – Synge, Yeats, O'Casey (but especially Yeats) – is at least acted not for anybody's exploitation but with the poet actually in the position of King,

[1] Read immediately Yeats's introduction to his selection of Spenser's poems.
[2] See her attempts to stop the playing of *Richard II*: read the life of Marlowe: Tamburlaine was a gangster.

and poetry realizing free desires.[3] The handbooks of course already try to drag the 'Irish School' into the history of English Drama. The work of these three poets has nothing to do with 'English Literature' courses or drama schools or the rest of that junk, because it is something that nobody living has seen in England: poetry *in action*, and derived from the following series:

(a) Direct realization of desires in war, conquest and the apotheosis of the conqueror, which was once the action of Kingship.

(b) 'Imitation' of above through the medium of the theatre by the poet (his desires not free) of which the degeneration has already been traced.

(c) Realization of free desires through the medium of words only: regal action of poetry (Rimbaud).

(d) Realization of free desires through the medium of the theatre: poetry *in action*.

But don't hope that I am going to write a panegyric on the Irish theatre 'to make up' for what I have said about the English one; so that it could be silently transferred from one to the other 'because after all Dr Yeats writes in English' or 'because Ireland is still in the British Isles' or 'will come back to the fold in the end' or any other such ambiguity. I mention the Irish theatre precisely because such *evasions* have already been made and because the Irish theatre retains the freedom ours has swamped in safety.

What is meant by 'But especially Yeats'? In Yeats the revelation of wishes is less alloyed by circumstances (quaint Irish peasant stuff, theatrical conventions, etc.) and he is therefore more completely the poet-king and less the poet-subject than others. But at the same time his theatrical writing is less and not more *realizable* as techniques are at present, purely and simply because Yeats having got his poetry on to the stage has been cheated of *further* realization. We arrive here at the supposed necessity (c.1900) for a new theatre: meaning to Yeats (see his *Essays*) a new technique for the realization of poetry in action. Now all the people responsible for the new techniquery (designers and so on) seized of course on the Celtic twilight (Tara's Halls and Green Erin) side of Yeats's poetry (and invented parallel 'blasted heath' and 'Cotswold' and 'Shakespeare's England' sides of Shakespeare – about as historical as James A. Fitzpatrick's delightful 'Old Madrid') i.e., just those sides which are incapable

---

[3] The reference, if you must have it, is Blake's *Garden of Love*:
And priests in black gowns were walking their rounds
And binding with briars my joys and desires.

of being further or fully realized in three dimensions, and proceeded to
make a new 'theatre art' ultimately leading to the merely disgusting Art-
racket as described above.

Q. And what in heaven is this *realization* stuff anyway? A. In *Horse-
feathers* there was a scene where the frog in someone's throat was seriously
searched for. In *King Lear* (III, vii) Regan says 'Pluck out his eyes' (ordinarily equals 'I would like to pluck his eyes out'): Gloster turns the wish
into an image:

> Because I would not see thy cruel nails
> Pluck out his poor old eyes

the image leaps into poetry:

> The sea with such a storm as his bare head
> In hell-black night endured would have buoyed up
> And quench'd the stelled fires

and poetry into action: Gloster's *eyes are plucked out* and in full view of the
audience and as terrifyingly as possible.

Again, every schoolmistress knows the line: 'To ride in triumph
through Persepolis' and every producer with a large enough stage can
bring on a horse or a camel (cf. Crummles: 'My chaise-pony goes on in
Timour the Tartar.') But the stage direction in *Tamburlaine* which amazed
Lamb so much is this: 'Tamburlaine drawen in his chariot by Trebizon
and Soria with bittes in their mouthes, reines in his left hand, in his right
hand a whip, with which he scourgeth them.' Marlowe did not invent
this: Sesostris (Rameses II) was said to have been drawn thus by captive
kings (see *Diodorus Siculus*). In life this was a piece of Egyptian mega-
lomania (Rameses is to men as men are to horses); but on the stage
Tamburlaine and the Kings are still actors all the time, and so this action
so far from being a pre-arranged piece of vulgarity and outrageousness (as
Lamb thought it was, and as the original action of Rameses was) is completely *inside* the medium of the theatre (actors), as horses and camels are
not.

This is not only poetry in action but also metaphor in action and the *solidification* of imagery. 'But,' you should complain, 'precisely in Yeats the
imagery is least of all solidifiable.' Yep; and this just *owing* to the gerlorious
new theatre art failing (in simple courage among other things) to produce
any means of solidification, even plain borrowings from the circus like
Cocteau's. The conflict of twilightery and solidification is in fact the
purported 'subject' of several of Yeats's later poems: 'Ego Dominus Tuus',
for example. Read also (I am not going to quote) the long arguments of
Forgael and Aibric in *The Shadowy Waters*. In this play there are the two

following stage directions: 'The deck of an ancient ship. At the right of the stage is the mast with a large square sail hiding a great deal of the sky and sea on that side. . . .' and 'Voices and the clashing of swords are heard from the other ship, which cannot be seen because of the sail.' This 'other ship' which has come alongside remains completely unreal: and I am perfectly aware that as things are it is even meant to be unreal and to present simply a starting point for the audience's wretched imagination, which is not imagination at all but only the raking up of one stock mood or another. So that criticism apart, *The Shadowy Waters*, for example, presents poetry *on the stage* but not *realized through the medium of the theatre*. Without any passion for the Baroque it may one day be discovered that the scenic machines of the Italian theatre (including ships which came on to the stage) had some *reason* behind them. Even the completely provincial Inigo Jones produced in England definite and active scenery which had an influence on the imagery of seventeenth-century poetry. And Yeats's imagery is twilightish because the theatre he was working in aimed at twilights, in turn because his poetry was full of them.

V

> – Or heap the shrine of Luxury and Pride
>   With incense kindled at the Muse's flame.
>
> – Gray

But now, now that a nation of busybodies like the English is positively invited to telephone the police when they see anything that they consider *queer* going on, now that we buy art-petrol, and National-mark the fruits of Neptune, what place has so vulgar (so vulgar because so free) a thing as a poet in England,[1] let alone for him to be a dramatist or an actor (for actors and dancers have been poets)? The eighteenth-century Italian Ballet, the Russian Imperial Ballet, and the short, passionate, black and chestnut existence of pre-War Paris all met in Nijinsky; of whom we have still some photographs as made-up for *Spectre de la Rose*: and the story of him sitting for Rodin. But now, late even in pettiness, it is England's turn to make charming nineteenth-century tableaux, of which the following might be the history:

---

[1] So I have heard an English Art critic complain that Picasso's colour is sometimes rather vulgar! In case anyone still believes England has treated her poets well, there is a passage on this subject in Moore's life of Byron.

(1) Lautrec painting a Café-Concert in the nineties includes some dancers and the lights and boards of the stage.

(2) The picture presents in the directest possible way the 'vulgarest possible' existence of the time in absolute *hatred* of Art and Connoisseurs and Rue La Boétie-ism, and of public romantic perspectives.

(3) The picture is now (1934) exhibited at a select exhibition to an adoring audience of *Art-Lovers*, Connoisseurs, and wives of financiers, who have already made a romantic perspective running back to the nineties and to Lautrec in particular.

(4) In the wash of this crowd (and ultimately depending on them for existence) are 'young people' who are running a 'Ballet' (as if Sonnie Hale had not superbly made even the word unbearable).

(5) In their baths the next morning they suddenly have a *wonderful* idea: Why not make a Ballet of Lautrec's picture....

There are still certain things in England that have just not been culturised; examples: beer ads., steam railways, Woolworths, clairvoyantes (the backs of playing-cards having been adorned with 'good' patterns lately, someone wanted the faces beautified also). When the life has been finally veneered out of these it really will be the end.

I am aware that this continued defence of the poet is regarded as very dilettante by the now politically minded English. Art must now be social and useful. Alas! we have been all over that ground only such a very short time ago and in the theatre too. But Fabianism and Bernard Shaw and the social dramas of Mr Granville Barker are already so unreadable – simply from sheer dullness – that it is difficult to work up any enthusiasm for yet another political drama. Mr Shaw's little tricks for becoming the 'greatest living playwright' were described by Coleridge as long ago as 1817:

> the whole secret of the modern Jacobinical drama and of its popularity, consists in the confusion and subversion of the natural order of things in their causes and effects: namely, in the excitement of surprise by representing the qualities of liberality, refined feeling, and a nice sense of honour, (those things rather which pass amongst us for such) in persons and in classes where experience teaches us least to expect them; and by rewarding with all the sympathies which are the due of virtue, those criminals whom law, reason, and religion have excommunicated from our esteem.
>
> *Biographia Literaria*: II, 193.

Compare with this description the 'Russian' opening of *Heartbreak House*: the romanticising of Doolittle in *Pygmalion*, the sentimentalising of the English priest in *Saint Joan*. The work of Ibsen from which the work of Mr Shaw is supposed to descend (and who was the 'figure behind' the drama-movement of the 1900s) is neither 'social drama', nor politics, nor 'Art', nor 'entertainment', but from it any or all of these can be and have been extracted. The spectacle of the great 'Socialist' playwright paying super-tax is not so remarkable after all, since the tax is on what the English public have agreed to pay Mr Shaw for giving them harmless mouthfuls of a politico-philosophical mixture (Ibsen and water) marked 'dangerous' (but that is part of the plan) with which to put off the terrible moment of Existence a little further.

England hasn't got It and doesn't want to have: she is deadly afraid: she wraps herself up in every kind of blanket – Art, Culture, Entertainment – against the explosion of the terrible bomb. Her capacity for turning any fragments or news of foreign passions (themselves explosions) which may have strayed into this country into blankets is really astonishing:[2] that is what she wanted from this article. But the bomb, dear Englishmen, is inside and not outside – you need a different type of blanket – but there, Freud is already labelled 'Foreign', 'Scientific', 'Interesting',[3] and it's no good talking.

The English have certainly got the theatre they want (even including me: I don't want it altered or 'improved': I am simply describing it and its surroundings): and also, to use their own phrase, the theatre 'they deserve'.

'But, but, but...' you cry.... Of course you hoped I was going to come forward with heavyweight pronouncements on the value ('value!') of the Irish theatre or of Meyerhold or Strobach or Pirandello or Mr James Bridie or 'mime' or wherever else you happen to think the 'future of the theatre' lies. Now all such labelling with adhesive values is simply a method of avoiding the consequences of attack from the work in question and utilising it thus weakened to confirm satisfaction with habitual behaviour. And this satisfaction is all the pleasanter when the labelling is done for one. You had expected no doubt that I was going to do the old conjuring trick: that I had a new theatre connected in some vague way with 'modern art' and 'suntrap houses' howling with rebirth in my pocket.

For a short period at the end of the sixteenth century and at the beginning of the seventeenth several Englishmen used 'the theatre' as they found it, for their own purposes of poetry and analysis of behaviour – *connaissance* – we have no word for it – naturally. That these may still be constructed by Englishmen there seems just a possibility, but that they can or will use the theatre as a means is hardly possible since in one way or another it is precisely against these things (seeing in them its own

[2] She is even managing to use Communism as one.
[3] And the paintings of Dali 'Pathology'.

downfall) that the present theatre's activity is directed (if one can use the word 'directed' of cottonwool). Nor (*here the speaker addressed himself more particularly to those who were or were about to become parents*) do I see any likelihood of the motives behind this activity altering in any relevant way.

The Arts Today. edited by Geoffrey Grigson, 1935

'Colour Won't Stand Dignity'

The Trail of the Lonesome Pine definitely establishes the following points, which are presented not as highbrow speculation, but as part of the urgent problem of how to use colour.

Colour is hopelessly revealing. It reveals not only new physical aspects and properties of objects, but becomes a devastatingly accurate index of the mentality of the film-maker, and of his approach to his material in the smallest details; and anything faked – faked sets or faked situations – shriek in colour where they could be got away with in black-and-white. This is because *Colour* and *Ideas* are fundamentally opposed; the black-and-white film has always lived on ideas; but colour depends upon *sensations*. It is an instinct for this that has sent people out of doors to make colour films. In *The Lonesome Pine* horses, rifles and trees look grand – the small-part players look pretty good – the 'stars' look definitely not so hot.

Far greater care has been taken in shooting Sylvia Sidney and Macmurray than with the extras and log cabins. But that's just it; all that care shows – little touches of blue back-lighting and dabs of powder look terrible, because you can feel 'the experts' putting them there. Again, on people the definition *seems* less good than on machines and dogs. It isn't. But one is satisfied with a sensation of dog; one is not so satisfied with a sensation in place of a *star*; and colour is a sensation. Hence by far the best parts of this film are scenes of a camp on fire, stampeding horses and rough-house scenes, where the action has got out of the Director's and Art Director's control. And unutterably awful are the smart hotel interiors with Sylvia Sidney telephoning in her negligée: they smell of arcs and plaster, simply because they are in colour and because the colour has been put there on purpose to look good. Of course, real interior locations should have been chosen.

There is one exception. When Sylvia Sidney has mud all over her face, and Macmurray has a swollen jaw, they look good. They have been knocked off their dignity and have become human beings. And this, in fact. is the secret of the business. Colour won't stand dignity. And the scenes of fire and rapid action do show what a whopping film will be made in Technicolor when everybody has come off the high horse. In the meantime, it should be said that the colour printing and Technicolor lab. work are as good as ever.

World Film News, No. 3, June 1936

Surrealism

How can one open this book,[1] so expensive, so *well* produced, so conformistly printed, with so many and such mixed illustrations, so assorted a set of articles, containing so *protesting* a number of English statements and so stiffly pathetic a presentation of French ones, and compare it even for a moment with the passion terror and excitement, dictated by absolute integrity and produced with all the poetry of bare necessity, which emanated from *La Révolution Surréaliste* and *Le Surréalisme au Service de la Révolution*, without facing a great wave of nostalgia, and bringing up a nauseating memory of the mixed atmosphere of cultural hysteria and amateur-theatricality which combined to make the Surrealist Exhibition of June so peculiar a 'success'.

Mr Sykes Davies assures us that there is no need to worry ourselves with such comparisons. The course of historical development will justify blind faith. Mr Read simply resolves all difficulties by the dissolution of the 'universal truths of classicism'. That is to say, they find writing articles on Surrealism an excuse for another affirmation of their favourite theses: Mr Davies' article becomes a lecture on Coleridge, and Mr Read's a defence of Romanticism.

A Romanticism, however, which can only pity Michelangelo (p.45) even if not patronisingly, which still imagines Pope to have been just a classical wit (p.78) and lumps Hardy with Dickens in opposition to the Black Novel (p.56), can hardly be said to have a dialectic grip on the human situation. Mr Read does not venture to commit himself about Homer.

Now a special attachment to certain sides of Surrealism may be defendable, but the elevation of definite 'universal truths of romanticism' (pp.27-8) in place of the 'universal truths' of classicism is not only a

---

[1] *Surrealism*: edited, with an introduction, by Herbert Read; articles by André Breton, Hugh Sykes Davies, Georges Hugnet and Paul Eluard (Faber & Faber).

short-sighted horror, but immediately corroborates really grave doubts already existent about the *use* of Surrealism in this country. We all agree with Mr Read that the eternally fabricated 'eternal truths of classicism' constantly appear as the symbols and tools of a classical-military-capitalist-ecclesiastical racket. But then we remember a recent query in a film-paper: 'Is it possible that the business of national education is passing, by default, from the offices of Whitehall to the public relations departments of the great corporations?'

Is it possible that in place of a classical-military-capitalist-ecclesiastical racket there has come into being a romantic-cultural-*soi-disant* co-operative-new uplift racket ready and delighted to use the 'universal truths of romanticism – co-eval with the evolving consciousness of mankind' as symbols and tools for its own ends? Our 'advanced' poster designers and 'emancipated' business men – what a gift Surrealism is to them when it is presented in the auras of 'necessity', 'culture' and 'truth' with which Read and Sykes Davies invest it.

To the real poet the front of the Bank of England may be as excellent a site for the appearance of poetry as the depths of the sea. Note the careful distinction made by Breton in his article (pp.112-13): 'Human psychism in its most universal aspect has found in the Gothic castle and its accessories a point of fixation so precise that it becomes *essential to discover what would be the equivalent for our own period*' (my italics – H.J.). He continues to say that Surrealism has replaced the 'coincidence' for the 'apparition', and that we must 'allow ourselves to be guided towards the unknown by this newest *promise*.' Now that is talking; and to settle Surrealism down as Romanticism only is to deny this promise. It is to cling to the apparition with its special 'haunt'. It is to look for ghosts only on battlements, and on battlements only for ghosts. 'Coincidences' have the infinite freedom of appearing anywhere, anytime, to anyone: in broad daylight to those whom we most despise in places we have most loathed: not even to *us* at all: probably least to petty seekers after mystery and poetry on deserted sea-shores and in misty junk-shops.

'Imagination' says Eluard (p.173) 'lacks the imitative instinct.' Its mysteries are not mysterious. 'It is the spring and torrent which we do not re-ascend.' (ibid). Creation is *not* the re-presentation of 'the truth', however much it may at times look like it. But at those times (the 'Greek' drawings of Picasso are instances) the eruptions of doubt and the magic of treachery are precisely at their greatest. It is the next generation that *believes* in the results. So it is that the enduring statements of Picasso, early Chirico, Duchamp, Klee, Magritte, and of certain Dalis, are due to their unquestioning acceptance of *all* the conditions of the moment: forgetting all 'beliefs' preceding the picture, which would deny the promise of the

unknown. But so deadly agile is man's mind that it is possible, even easy
to form a series of 'truths' and 'loyalties' which produce imitations of the
creative powers of non-selectivity; forgetting that Surrealism is only a
means and believing in the 'universal truth' of it; or again, still relying on
aestheticism (as admitted by Read p.63) to the rules of which Surrealism
has now been added. 'To the poet everything is the object of sensations
and consequently of sentiments. Everything becomes food for his imagination.' (Eluard p.174). But for the English to awaken from the sleep of
selectivity, what a task. And to be *already* a 'painter', a 'writer', an 'artist',
a 'surrealist', what a handicap.

Contemporary Poetry and Prose No. 8, December 1936

'*Do Not Lean Out Of The Window!*'

> The following texts are presented not in any sense as a picture of the
> development of Machinery itself, but to suggest rapidly some of the
> varying situations of MAN in this country in having to *adapt himself*
> rapidly to a world altered by the INDUSTRIAL REVOLUTION, and
> in particular to THE IMPACT OF MACHINES on everyday life.
>
> H.J.

1. *1797*

Luvah & Vala trembling and shrinking beheld the great Work master
And heard his Word: 'Divide, ye bands, influence by influence.
Build we a Bower for heaven's darling in the grizly deep:
Build we the Mundane Shell around the Rock of Albion.'
The Bands of Heaven flew thro' the air singing & shouting to Urizen.
Some fix'd the anvil, some the loom erected, some the plow
And harrow form'd & fram'd the harness of silver & ivory,
The golden compasses, the quadrant, & the rule & balance.
They erected the furnaces, they form'd the anvils of gold beaten in mills
Where winter beats incessant, fixing them firm on their base.
The bellows began to blow, & the Lions of Urizen stood round the anvil
And the leopards cover'd with skins of beasts tended the roaring fires,
Sublime, distinct, their lineaments divine of human beauty.

(Blake – *Vala*: Night the Second)

2. c.1835

We were introduced to the little engine which was to drag us along the rails. She (for they make these curious little fire horses all mares) consisted of a boiler, a stove, a small platform, a bench, and behind the bench a barrel containing enough water to prevent her being thirsty for 15 miles – the whole not bigger than a common fire engine. She goes upon ten wheels, which are her feet, and are moved by bright steel legs called pistons; these are propelled by steam, and in proportion as more steam is applied to the upper extremities (the hip joints, I suppose) of these pistons, the faster they move the wheels, and when it is desirable to diminish the speed, the steam (which unless suffered to escape would burst the boiler) evaporates through a safety-valve into the air. The reins, bit, and bridle of this wonderful beast is a small steel handle, which applies or withdraws the steam for the legs or pistons, so that a child might manage it.... There is a chimney to the stove, but as they burn coke there is none of that dreadful black smoke which accompanies the progress of a steam vessel. This snorting little animal, which I felt rather inclined to pat, was then harnessed to our carriage, and Mr. Stephenson having taken me on the bench of the engine with him, we started at about 10 miles an hour. You can't imagine how strange it seemed to be journeying on thus, without any visible cause of progress other than the magical machine with the flying white breath and rhythmical, unvarying pace, between these rocky walls, which are already clothed with moss and ferns and grasses, and when I reflected that these great masses of stone had been cut asunder to allow our passage thus far below the surface of the earth, I felt as if no fairy vale was half so wonderful as what I saw.

(Letter by FANNY KEMBLE –
From Steele's *History of the L.N.W.R.*)

3.   1844

If we cross Blackstone Edge or penetrate it with the railroad, we enter upon that classic soil on which English manufacture has achieved its masterwork and from which all labour movements emanate, namely South Lancashire with its central city Manchester. Again we have beauti-ful hill country, sloping gently from the watershed westwards towards the Irish Sea, with the charming green valleys of the Ribble, the Irwell, the Mersey, and their tributaries, a country which, a hundred years ago chiefly swamp land, thinly populated, is now sown with towns and villages, and is the most densely populated strip of country in England. In Lancashire, and especially in Manchester, English manufacture finds at once its

starting point and its centre. The Manchester Exchange is the thermo-
meter for all the fluctuations of trade. The modern art of manufacture has
reached its perfection in Manchester. In the cotton industry of South
Lancashire, the application of the forces of Nature, the superseding of
hand labour by machinery (especially by the power-loom and the self-
acting mule), and the division of labour, are seen at the highest point; and,
if we recognise in these three elements that which is characteristic of
modern manufacture, we must confess at once that the cotton industry
has remained in advance of all other branches of industry from the
beginning down to the present day. The effects of modern manufacture
upon the working-class must necessarily develop here most freely and
perfectly, and the manufacturing proletariat present itself in its fullest
classic perfection. The degradation to which the application of steam-
power, machinery and the division of labour reduce the working-man and
the attempts of the proletariat to rise above this abasement, must likewise
be carried to the highest point and with the fullest consciousness.

(ENGELS: *Condition of The Working Class in England*)

4. *1863*

Notwithstanding the losses and suffering occasioned by strikes, Mr.
Nasmyth holds the opinion that they have on the whole produced much
more good than evil. They have served to stimulate invention in an
extraordinary degree. Some of the most important labour-saving processes now in common use are directly traceable to them. In the case of
many of our most potent self-acting tools and machines, manufacturers
could not be induced to adopt them until compelled to do so by strikes.
This was the case with the self-acting mule, the wool-combing machine,
the planing machine, the slotting machine, Nasmyth's steam arm, and
many others. Thus even in the mechanical world, there may be 'a soul of
goodness in things evil'.

Mr. Nasmyth retired from business in December, 1856. He had the
moral courage to come out of the groove which he had so laboriously
made for himself, and to leave a large and prosperous business, saying,
'I have now enough of this world's goods; let younger men have their
chance.' He settled down at his rural retreat in Kent, but not to lead a life
of idle ease. Industry had become his habit, and active occupation was
necessary to his happiness. He fell back upon the cultivation of those
artistic tastes which are the heritage of his family. When a boy at the High
School of Edinburgh, he was so skilful in making pen and ink illustrations
on the margins of the classics, that he thus often purchased from his
monitors exemption from the lessons of the day. Nor had he ceased to

cultivate the art during his residence at Patricroft, but was accustomed to fall back upon it for relaxation and enjoyment amid the exploits of trade. That he possesses remarkable fertility of imagination, and great skill in architectural and landscape drawing, as well as in the much more difficult art of delineating the human figure, will be obvious to anyone who has seen his works, – more particularly his 'City of St. Ann's', 'The Fairies', and 'Everybody for ever!' which last was exhibited in Pall Mall, among the recent collection of works of Art by amateurs and others, for the relief of the Lancashire distress.

(SAMUEL SMILES: *Industrial Biography* Ch. XV)

5. 1865

You have despised Nature; that is to say, all the deep and sacred sensations of natural scenery. The French revolution made stables of the cathedrals of France; you have made race-courses of the cathedrals of the earth. Your *one* conception of pleasure is to drive railroad carriages round their aisles, and eat off their altars. You have put a railroad-bridge over the falls of Schaffhausen. You have tunnelled the cliffs of Lucerne by Tell's chapel; you have destroyed the Clarens shore of the Lake of Geneva; there is not a quiet valley in England that you have not filled with bellowing fire; there is not a particle left of English land which you have not trampled coal ashes into...

(RUSKIN – *Sesame and Lilies* I)

6. 1871

...Just then a shriek was heard to issue from a female throat, and a stout elderly woman was observed in the act of dashing wildly across the line in the midst of moving engines, trucks and vans. Even in these unwonted circumstances no one who knew her could have mistaken Mrs. Durby's ponderous person for a moment. She had come upon the station at the wrong side, and, in defiance of all printed regulations to the contrary – none of which she could read, being short sighted – she had made a bold venture to gain her desired position by the most direct route. This involved crossing a part of the line where there were several sidings and branch lines, on which a good deal of pushing of trucks and carriages to and fro – that is 'shunting' – was going on.

Like a reckless warrior, who by a bold and sudden push sometimes gains single-handed the centre of an enemy's position before he is discovered and assailed on every side, straight forward Mrs. Durby ran into the very midst of a brisk traffic before any one discovered her. Suddenly a passenger train came up with the usual caution in such circumstances, nevertheless at a smart rattling pace, for 'usual caution' does not take into account or provide for the apparition of stout elderly females on the line. The driver of the passenger engine saw her, shut off steam, shouted, applied the brakes and whistled furiously.

We have already hinted that the weather was not fine. Mrs. Durby's umbrella being up, hid the approaching train. As for the screaming steam-whistles, the worthy woman had come to regard intermittent whistling as a normal condition of railways, which like the crying of cross babies, meant little or nothing, and had only to be endured. She paid no attention to the alarm. In despair the driver reversed his engine; fire flew from the wheels, and the engine was brought to a stand, but not until the buffers were within three feet of the nurse's shoulder. At that moment she became aware of her danger, uttered a shriek, as we have said, that would have done credit to the whistle of a small engine, and bending her head with her umbrella before her, rushed frantically away on another line of rails. She did not observe, poor soul, that a goods train was coming straight down that line towards her – partly because her mental vision was turned in terror to the rear, and partly because the umbrella obscured all in advance. In vain the driver of the goods train repeated the warnings and actions of the passenger engine. His had more speed and was heavier; besides, Mrs. Durby charged it at the full rate of five miles an hour, with the umbrella steadily in front, and a brown paper parcel swinging wildly on her arm, as if her sole desire on earth was to meet that goods engine in single combat and beat its brains out at the first blow...

(R.M. BALLANTINE – The Iron Horse)

London Bulletin No. 4, July 1938

In Magritte's Paintings...

In Magritte's paintings beauty and terror meet. But their poetry is not necessarily derived from the known regions of romance – a plate of ham will become as frightening as a lion – a brick wall as mysterious as night. His painting is thus essentially *modern* in the sense required by Baudelaire. Simultaneously Magritte never allows himself to be seduced by the immediate pleasures of imitation. Precisely his passionate interest in the concrete world has made him remember that a painting itself is only an *image*.

Poetry, according to Aristotle, implies a 'bringing together'. But the elements in a picture by Magritte are not *forced* together. Their 'bringing together' *occurs* in a passive sense in the painter's imagination. Hence their simultaneous irrationality – since nothing is chosen 'on purpose' – and their evident truth – since their 'bringing together' is in fact an 'event' beyond choice. It is of the likenesses and discrepancies between the image and the reality that these events are composed, and it is in the relentless logic of these likenesses and discrepancies that Magritte sees the central human situation: *La Condition Humaine.*

London Bulletin No. 1, April 1938

The Iron Horse*

I

Machines are animals created by man. In recognition of this many machines have been given animals' names by him – 'mule', 'throstle', 'basilisk', 'puss-moth', 'taube', and so on. (Cp. also such phrases as 'donkey-engine', 'iron horse', and for an animal regarded as a machine at the time of the industrial revolution see Blake's *Tiger*:

>   And what shoulder, and what art,
>   Could twist the sinews of thy heart?
>   And when thy heart began to beat,
>   What dread hand? and what dread feet?

>   What the hammer? what the chain?
>   In what furnace was thy brain?
>   What the anvil? what dread grasp
>   Dare its deadly terrors clasp?)

The idea of a machine which would go *by itself* (automatically – without the help of an animal) has long obsessed man because then it could be considered to have a life of its own – to have become a complete pseudo-animal. Cp. Milton's *Paradise Lost* VI:

>   And the third sacred Morn began to shine
>   Dawning through Heav'n: forth rush'd with whirlwind sound

---

* In July the London Gallery will present an exhibition of 19th Century Drawings and Engravings of Machines; also a complementary show of Cubist, Dadaist and Surrealist paintings.

The Chariot of Paternal Deitie,
Flashing thick flames, Wheele within Wheele undrawn,
It self instinct with Spirit...

And as man is related to the real animals so every machine has a latent *human* content.

II

In the past poets and painters often identified themselves or their heroes with animals: *e.g.* Gray's translation from the Welsh:

Have ye see the tusky boar,
Or the bull, with sullen roar,
On surrounding foes advance?
So Caradoc bore his lance.

and the Darwinian passage in *Hamlet* (I.5.):

Thy knotted and combined locks to part
And each particular hair to stand an end
Like quills upon the fretful porpentine.

The so-called 'abstract' painter identifies himself or the person in his picture with a machine. (Cp. Baumeister: 'Nous savons que la croute terrestre a reçu un humus nouveau: les machines' etc.) Note how the sailing ship – a non-automatic machine: dependant on wind and water – has in face of competition with later machines become an 'artistic' obsession – 'Homeward Bound', 'In the Tropics' and so on. At the moment (1938) there is exactly one English-owned topsail schooner still plying without an auxiliary engine. Not to be confused with abstract painting is the anti-artistic creation of pseudo-machines by Duchamp, Picabia, Ernst, Baargeldt, Man Ray: *e.g.* the painting by Ernst: 'Petite machine construite par minimax dadamax en personne'. Compare the two following passages:

Machine

The new condenser consists of 2 sets of pipes 8 in each sett. They are each ¾ inch diameter & 18 inch long, 16 inch of which will be evacuated each stroke of the pump. They are to be ½ inch distant from one another in all directions. Each set is to be surrounded at ½ inch distant in a box of wood thro' which cold water can be made to run at pleasure. They are joined at top by a thin cast iron box thro' which they communicate with the steam. It is made sloping at the ends that as little useless water as possible may be in circulation...

(Watt. Letter on the Kinneil Engine, 1769)

Pseudo-
Machine

L'aiguille pouls en plus du mt. vibratoire est montée sur une caisse de vagabondage. Elle a la liberté des animaux en cage – à condition qu'elle soufflera (par son mt. vibratoire actionnant le cylindre sexe) la ventilation sur la Lampe (au tympan). Cette aiguille pouls promènera donc en équilibre le cylindre sexe qui crache au tympan la rosée qui doit alimenter les vaisseaux de la pâte à filaments et en même temps imprime au Pendu son balancement selon les 4 pts. cardinaux.

(Duchamp. Note for 'La Mariée mise à nu')

III

The pre-eminent example of the automatic machine – the steam railway – developed at precisely the same time as the realism of Gericault, Daumier, and Courbet. (Cp. Chirico on Courbet.) And also at the same time as the researches of Cuvier and Lyell. So that for example Courbet's 'Cliffs of Entretat' is practically a large coloured illustration to Lyell's *Manual of Elementary Geology*. The development of the steam engine and of railways increased the mining, tunnelling, and excavation of the earth's crust. The principle of Stratification was proposed by William Smith, a mechanical engineer, from observations in cuttings and pits. Courbet's paintings represent the world just before the excavation begins – with suggestions of it in 'inland cliffs', outcrops, pictures of stonecutters – photos of a condemned house. Bourne's lithographs of the construction of the Great Western Railway present the excavation, the work itself. The sectional elevation of an express locomotive is precisely an *anatomical drawing* of a machine.

The unresolved meeting of all these currents is to be found in Ruskin – geologist, realistic water-colourist and at the same time the forlorn defender of the 'cathedrals of earth' against the profanation of the engineers. With Ruskin compare Cézanne:

Un beau matin, le lendemain, lentement les bases géologiques m'apparaissent, des couches s'etablissent, les grands plans de ma toile, j'en dessine mentalement le squelette pierrex, je vois affleurer les roches sous l'eau, peser le ciel. Tout tombe d'aplomb. Une pâle palpitation enveloppe les aspects lineaires. Les terres rouges sortent d'un abime. Je commence à me separer du paysage, à le voir. Je m'en dégage avec cette première esquisse, ces lignes géologiques. Le géometrie, mesure de la terre.

So Cubism looks straight back to the surveyor's level and telemeter that Watt was improving at the same time that he was working on the separate condenser. So also Chirico's 'Nostalgie du depart.' The point of creating pseudo-machines was not as an exploitation of machinery but as a 'profanation' of 'Art' parallel to the engineers' 'profanation' of the primitive 'sacred places' of the earth. 'Only in one field has the omnipotence of thought been retained in our own civilization, namely in art. In art alone it still happens that man, consumed by his wishes, produces something similar to the gratification of these wishes, and this playing, thanks to artistic illusion, calls forth effects as if it were something real.' (Freud, *Totem and Taboo*.)

London Bulletin No. 3, June 1938

A Determination not to Dream

In 'Peterborough's' column of the *Daily Telegraph* ('London Day by Day') for June 8th appeared a reproduction of Paul Nash's *Landscape from a Dream* (reproduced in the May number of the *London Bulletin*). Discussing the likelihood of the picture's finding 'a home in the Tate Gallery' the columnist says:

> Mr Nash disclaims the idea that it portrays an authentic dream. It is merely a landscape treated in a special way... Mr Nash has been described as a surrealist. This eccentricity is not of his own designation. He is content to be an acclimatised Dorset man.

Passing over the facts that Nash was an exhibiting member of the Committee of the International Surrealist Exhibition of 1936, has signed surrealist manifestoes, written articles such as 'Swanage, or Seaside Surrealism' and so on, it is worth while to note the curious opposition of dreams and Dorsetshire. It must after all be disturbing to think that one can't stop oneself dreaming. But we know of humanity's efforts to forget their dreams. A parallel symptom evidently is the columnist's almost desperate attempt to free a picture, a gallery, even a county, from 'authentic' dreams.

H.J.

London Bulletin No. 4, July 1938

Who Does That Remind You Of?

Two or three years ago there seems to have been a plan for taking the glass off the pictures in the National Gallery, so that you could see *them* instead of a reflection of yourself. Also important as breaking down a barrier between the public and the 'sacredness' of the images they are allowed to peer at. The glass having in fact been taken off a Honthorst (a big Dutch picture) I asked the attendant if they were seriously going to take the glass off all the pictures. He said he certainly hoped *not*. Why? Because he'd have a terrible time: 'Do you know what they do? They come in here and put their hands over the mouth and nose of a Rembrandt, and then say "Who does *that* remind you of?".'

No doubt the appearance of Rembrandt in this kind of story (rather than say Titian) is due to his connections with photography: – 'Rembrandt lighting', sepia prints (in imitation of Rembrandt's colouring), his etchings (the photography of his time) – exploited as competition with nineteenth-century photography by Whistler), the suburban photographer's studio called 'Rembrandt House' (fact) – *i.e.* portrait photography ('Who does that remind you of?'), etc. Then lately we have had Mr Laughton as Rembrandt philosophically reading the Old Testament – before that as Ruggles as Lincoln, and since as a beachcomber – in fact it is clear that Rembrandt (particularly in his pictures of 'Philosophers') was one of the first people to exploit the 'Old Curiosity Shop' motif, and with it all the different ideas coming under the heading of 'a brown study'.

Photography itself – 'photogenic drawing' – began simply as the mechanization of realism, and it remains *the* system with which the people can be pictured by the people for the people: simple to operate, results capable of mass reproduction and circulation, effects generally considered truthful ('the camera cannot lie') and so on. But intellectually the importance of the camera lies clearly in the way in which it deals with problems of choice – choice and avoidance of choice. Freud (*Psychopathology of Everyday Life* p.203) says that the feeling of *déja vu* ('Who does that remind you of?') 'corresponds to the memory of an unconscious fantasy'. The camera is precisely an instrument for recording the object or image that prompted that memory. Hence the rush to see 'how they came out'.

In the same book Freud insists on the impossibility of a voluntarily 'arbitrary' choice or association of objects. Below is an unfinished (or incomplete) chart of certain words and images (evidently a personal list) with dotted-line indications of the relationships ordinarily assumed to exist between them (between 'sea' and 'blue' for instance). Clearly it is a problem just how far these 'common sense' relationships differ from or overlap the relationships (between 'prism' and 'fir tree' for example), established in a painting, or dictated by 'unconscious fantasy'.

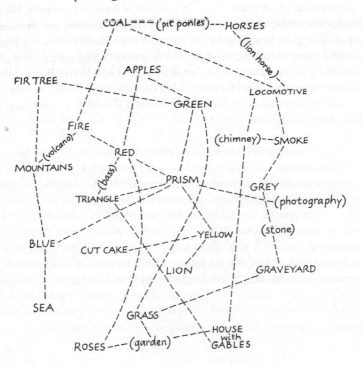

Review of *The Anatomy of the Horse* by George Stubbs
with a modern paraphrase by Prof. J.C. McGunn,
assisted by C.W. Ottaway (Heywood Hill).

The excitement of handling a full-size reprint of the original edition of Stubbs' *Anatomy of the Horse* cannot stop one feeling a little disappointed with it. The physical make-up of the book is pleasant enough and it may be that horsemen will be satisfied with the plates as anatomy and with the translation of Stubbs' text into modern veterinary terms. But it seems a pity that such an undertaking could not have been planned a little more completely. Thus it is usual in this type of semi-facsimile reprint to indicate the original from which it has been made and to give some account of early editions and states. There is a reproduction from the statuette of St Simon by Sir Edgar Boehm but no list of contents, no index and no proper pagination. Stubbs' text curiously enough comes second to the transcription. Again the short anonymous biographical note does not present us with anything new or give the source of its statements. The prospectus for this volume did indeed give some 'Authoritative Opinions of Yesterday' – quotations from *The Sporting Magazine* and so on. There are certainly some pages of 'Authoritative Opinions of Today' but one is not impressed by criticism of the standard of Mr Lionel Edwards' opinion that 'There is a terrific gap in skilled representational art between the Parthenon Frieze and Van Dyck'... Even supposing Mr Edwards cannot stomach *The Rout of San Romano* he seems to have forgotten Leonardo.

In other words admirable in idea as this reprint is and thrilling as Stubbs' plates remain, the book as a whole has not really been *edited* – and one may legitimately demand that such a work should be edited by modern standards as that it should be reproduced by modern methods. After all 'George Stubbs, Painter' is emphatically not the property of riders to hounds only. The passionate attack upon reality which in fact this book represents is far closer to the so-called atheist science of Leonardo than to the conservatism of the English Country gentleman.

Undated typescript, c. 1939

Colorado Claro

Thoughts on the 'Cleaned Pictures'

Aged 40, Humphrey Jennings is a film director and painter. He was with the GPO and Crown Film Units from 1934 to 1947, and is now working for Wessex Film Productions. He has also painted continuously since 1930. Home ground: East Anglia. Politics: Those of William Cobbett.

As you approach the rooms containing the 'Cleaned Pictures', between the National Gallery entrance and the rooms themselves, you mount a flight of steps flanked by two balconies or wings, on whose walls are hung six pictures which are not strictly part of the Exhibition: two Renoirs (*Les Parapluies* and *La Première Sortie*), a Manet (*La Servante de Bocks*), a Van

Gogh landscape, a Degas oil of an intense brick-orange-red, and a large Delacroix. Even so, the choice and placing of these paintings is adroit to say the least of it. Five of them represent a moment in European painting when the artist's passion for life – for the world around him and for his own craft, had a directness of vision and method singularly unencumbered by official or theoretical trappings – religious, mythological, political, or of his own making. So while these pictures are placed like trumpeters to herald the Exhibition, they have also a very practical use in leading our vision from the grey and nervous landscape of Trafalgar Square to the earlier Bacchanalia of Rubens and Poussin.

More than that. Renoir and the rest (except perhaps the Delacroix) have not been misted over by the dirt of Time or man's 'Gallery Varnish', and they are still close enough to us not to have become 'sacred'. In front of them a painter still thinks he sees *how* they were painted. But through what distorting fogs have we till now admired the 'Old Masters'. Most obvious of all – glass. The 'Cleaned Pictures' are now hung without glass. A Rembrandt portrait no longer presents the peering visitor with his own reflection. Then the pictures have been hung on newly decorated walls or backgrounds of curtain, with the possessive pedantry of gallery numbers, dates, and so on rendered as unobtrusive as possible, and altogether in an air of luxe and style which make the other parts of the Gallery (if you go back to them) feel more than ever like a station waiting room.

The cleaning itself consists of the removal of old varnish (some of it yellow from passage of time, some of it coloured on purpose to alter the tones of pictures when they came into the Gallery) the removal of dirt and of some earlier patches of 'restoration'. Between us and the paint surface there is today only the air we breathe and a thin coating of colourless modern varnish...that at least is the ideal. The weave of the canvas and El Greco's delicate layers of paint are no further away from us – if you understand me – than the canvas and paint of the Degas on the balcony. Among the crowds at the Exhibition (and there are crowds) there are, of course, those who with a fanatical look point to the two Velasquez portraits of Philip IV and cry out aloud: 'Velasquez never painted....' Of course they don't really mean that they were looking over the artist's shoulder in Madrid three centuries ago, though it sounds like it. They mean that the *idea* – the *myth* if you like – of Velasquez on which they have been brought up and nourished, and to which maybe their own painting is related, has been attacked and seriously damaged. They are men defending vested interests. Of course, many *ideas* are damaged by this exhibition. The idea, for example, of Rubens and Claude as painters of *golden* landscapes. The colours of Poussin, even of Veronese (whose work seems most of all to gain from 'cleaning') are seen to be as *bright* (to leave aside for the moment subtler questions) as that of Van Gogh and Renoir. Vollard has reported Renoir's visit to the tobacconist's where he noticed the words *Colorado Claro* on a box of cigars, and saw in them (or in his mistranslation of them) the slogan of his ideal in painting: COLORE CLAIR.... And looking at the 'Cleaned Pictures' those are just the words.

Then again one can begin to glimpse how some of these older paintings were made. I mean you can watch Rubens and Velasquez making altera-tions: they too were mortal men and liable to troubles and second thoughts in their work. The idea of the 'Old Masters' as a sacred mystery – which like the holy relics of a religion had to be kept in semi-darkness, behind the altar-rail and away from the vulgar[1] – until the darkness and railings came to be connected with the power of God... this has gone. Of course it was self-protection, too. To what emotions, to what springs of action might not the unshrouded God appeal? And some of the objections we have heard before in other fields: that this is a wicked materialist age from which all reverence, all romance, have departed.

More plausible is the Liberal cry: 'But are you not as bigoted as the 19th Century with its Gallery Varnish? Have you not got a preconception of what Chardin should look like, from Georges Braque?' To which the answer is that every age remakes the classics, and of course remakes them in its own image. The question is, in *what* image, *for what purpose* we remake them?

Do not let us delude ourselves that we know 'what the artist originally intended'. The majority of the Old Masters can have had little idea of the use to which their pictures are put today, clean or dirty. Little idea indeed of the smoke-trailing city, the island of machines, the atom-haunted world from whose walls their children now look out. The essential thing about the cleaning is that we have now removed the things they did *not* intend – dirt, yellow varnish, and glass. (How remarkable that the know-alls did not tell us long ago that Van Eyck did not, could not, have intended glass in front of Jan Arnolfini.) But if we approve that the cleaners of the National Gallery under enlightened direction have cleared away so much fake mystery, we must say also that what they have revealed is a thousand times more marvellous, more poetic, and in another sense mysterious.

Agreed we can now see the paint and the canvas and visualize the man at work – we can watch Poussin's brush decorate with blue leaf-strokes the white porcelain bowl as it catches the falling juice of the grape. Leaf-strokes like those with which the girls in the Potteries decorate export china... and then, not like. The more we gaze (as now we may) – the

[1] As indeed they were absolutely unavailable to 'the working classes' before the coming of *spare time* with the Ten Hours' Bill.

deeper we look – the more the 'mystery of the craft' affects us. Paint and not paint, simultaneously. Decoration (*colorée, claire*) but containing like a signature the character, the emotions, the wishes and regrets of a human lifetime. (Renoir, you remember, began by painting porcelain.)

Take a more complex example: the Velasquez full-length portrait of Philip, whose cleaning first and most of all enraged the Old Guard:

> In its reconditioned state, it looks to me as if it might have been painted today, in preparation for next year's Academy. Along with the dirt, which a simpler method of cleaning could have removed, the patina of natural age has disappeared, and, I think, the touch of the master with it.... The canvas now shows through the thin texture to which the paint has been reduced. It is probable that Velasquez mixed paint with the varnish, and that in removing the latter the upper layer of the work has been destroyed.
>
> (*Daily Telegraph*, 19.12.36)

In other words, what we now see is underpainting. There is no doubt that this is the one picture in the whole exhibition which nearly all visitors find disturbing in its present state. I certainly do. But I do not see any necessity to attribute this to overcleaning. I should be more inclined to attribute it to Velasquez himself. Of course, if you have always accepted him as a kind of super-de Laszlo, I don't know what can be done. But a serious study of the reflection-problems in *Las Meninas*, of the shape-problems in *Las Hilanderas*, of the extraordinary mixture of mythology and everyday life in *The Forge of Vulcan* and even in *The Drinkers*, should have suggested that the portraits might contain more than the observations of an acute psychologist and court photographer.

So looking at the cleaned 'Philip' one must either say that the picture has been ruined – or that Velasquez was incompetent in precisely the domain for which he is renowned – how could those thick dabs and squiggles of white on a thin flat brown ground be meant for an *accurate* representation of Philip's breeches? – or that Velasquez is in fact 'having a game' with his audiences past and present. Why now we look again there actually seems to be air lying between the white and the brown – between the *fond* and the decoration. There is light *in* the paint – the white handwriting glows, has movement and dimension. It was to represent the embroidery on Philip's breeches and ends up by talking to us about the artist's interior life – nay, about our own. No doubt if you re-covered the picture with yellow varnish and dirtied it down a little, and put a glass on it, and hung it in a dark room – then no doubt this disturbing effect would disappear. But as it is we must either dislike it or find new terms to describe what we see, and what we think Velasquez saw:

For double the vision my Eyes do see,
And a double vision is always with me.
With my inward Eye 'tis an old Man grey;
With my outward, a Thistle across my way.

Double vision. Of course we know Van Gogh was like that (after all, he was mad!) but Velasquez....

We are used to hearing that such and such a modern artist is really 'in the tradition'. This Exhibition illuminates the path of tradition the other way round. In it we see the Old Masters as youthful, visionary creators, whose pictures do indeed look as though they 'have been painted today', who, like Renoir and Degas and Van Gogh enjoyed life, savoured it with passion, and who (no less than more 'political' names) can teach us to transform it.

Our Time, December 1947

The English

Review of *The Character of England*, edited by Ernest Barker (Oxford: Clarendon Press).

An Indian, reviewing, in the Third Programme, British rule in India, recently said: 'The most remarkable thing about the character of the English is their zeal for writing essays about the English character.' He did not stop there. 'This,' he said, 'launches me straight away into the melancholy conjecture that self-admiration is the primary English failing.... The British have made it clear in their frequent moments of frankness that they want hypocrisy to be enthroned as their characteristic error....I must insist on putting first things first. The root and beginning, I suggest, is self-admiration, and hypocrisy is only its most distinguished product.'

So be it. But then, no other nation has so much in itself to admire. This is not saying a great deal. *Homo sapiens* is not doing so tremendously well just now, either in India or elsewhere, that any of his branches can be superior about any of the others. As for the English, it is what they are going to do which will require to excite admiration. There is only one occasion when admiration for past deeds may be given full rein, and that is in an epitaph. It is a dangerous tendency for the living. Narcissus was very beautiful and quite rightly spent a very long time admiring himself; but he died of it. However good our characters are, they all can stand a great deal of improvement.

It is probable that all books about national character should be written by foreigners. A man, or a nation, cannot truly appreciate his own character any more than he can correctly hear his own voice. The reproduction of one's own voice, either by a gramophone record or by a broadcast, is well known to be one of life's most startling experiences.

Character is even more intimate than voice, and must be reflected preferably by a frontier, to be known. There is a frontier in this island, or at the very least an ex-frontier: that which runs between England and Scotland. Descriptions of the Scots by English investigators have often differed most remarkably from the Scots' conception of themselves. So a Scot, reading a book by the English on the English compares it with his own mental picture of that great race. The two do not at all coincide; but here, as elsewhere, the onlooker may be seeing most of the game.

Looking at the English from outside, one or two obvious facts stand out which the English themselves ignore completely. Their ruthlessness, for example. The English in America exterminated one race, the Red Indians, almost completely, and imported another race, the Negroes, as slaves, on whom they inflicted unspeakable brutalities. The English in Australia carried extermination even further than in America. They accomplished a good deal of it by the simple use of arsenic, though there were other ways, more horrible and straightforward, which the Australians themselves have chronicled. This characteristic has not passed away. Some of the English achievements in the late war, notably the burning of Hamburg, make the blood run cold.

There is also the English habit of buccaneering, of dropping honest work and taking to simple, bluff, hearty plunder. A buccaneer was originally a man in the West Indies who boucaned, that is, who cured meat by drying it in the sun. But the English knew a trick worth two of that. They took to piracy. Very few people nowadays associate buccaneers with honest toil; indeed, its termination has passed into an acknowledged suffix of disreputableness.

There are other characteristics of the English, well known to their neighbours, but altogether unmentioned by themselves. Their propensity for endless aggressive war, for example. The Hundred Years' War looks quite different from the French side of the Channel. Let those who think it simply a piece of medieval romanticism ask the Scots – or the Welsh – about their experiences. It would be inadvisable to ask the Irish.

But these are very necessary traits nowadays; very desirable; not at all to be apologized for. There is nothing more dangerous than the current cant phrase, 'We must gather together all the peace-loving nations.' Unless the peace-loving nations can induce one or two war-loving nations to join the club it is simply an invitation to be plundered. The larger the assembly of sheep the more it appeals to the wolves.

Now, for some strange reason, the Englishman likes to think of him-self as a sheep; and so great is his artistry, so thoroughly does he see him-self in any part which he has assumed, that he frequently deceives not only himself, but others. This mild, beneficent, benevolent, trustful creature, easily imposed upon, unmindful of injury, is a pose. But, like all the best poses, it takes in its author as well. The English are not hypocritical. They are sincere. In that lies their deadly danger to others.

The English are in fact a violent, savage race; passionately artistic, enormously addicted to pattern, with a faculty beyond all other people of ignoring their neighbours, their surroundings, or in the last resort, them-selves. They have a power of poetry which is the despair of all the rest of the world. They produce from time to time personalities transcending ordinary human limitations. Then they drive other nations to a frenzy by patronizing these archangels who have come among them, and by indi-cating that any ordinary Englishman could do better if he liked to take the trouble. As exemplified in Ben Jonson's insufferable appreciation of Shakespeare.

An exasperated opponent said of Gladstone that he did not mind the Grand Old Man having aces up his sleeve; what he resented was the assumption that God put them there. This exemplifies another habit of the English: a belief that the story is meant to end happily – that is to say, with an English victory; moral or material. Bernard Shaw draws attention to it in *Saint Joan*. The attitude has not weakened in the passage of time. Nobody can make out whether the English believe they will overcome their enemies because they have looked up the answer at the end of the book, or whether it comes out that way by accident. No doubt it was one of the problems that embittered Hitler's last hours in his bunker. It remains a question-mark still, to the new challengers.

There are other things the English have done besides riding their luck and making poetry, but they are not so important. Poetry certainly appears in *The Character of England*. There is a scholarly essay on this subject by James Sutherland. But there is no chapter on the Englishman's Luck. That is what we should like to know about. Can they do it again?

Because they are hard pressed just now. The English have been a Great Power for quite a long time, and the adjustments necessary if they are to remain in that class are profound. They will require to people continents from their loins, as they did after the discovery of America; but at the same time they will have to recreate the Anglo-French State of the Angevins, and add to it the conquests of Charlemagne. This is an exten-sive programme. It is certainly worth while for them to take stock. What sort of people are they, the oldest of the Old Powers, the youngest – indeed the unborn – of the Newest Powers, starting to challenge Fate again?

The formidable volume before us sets out in 575 pages to answer this question. Yet it balks completely at the threshold of the problem. What relation to Old England is Newest England, the England of the streets? In the index you will find under the heading 'City Life' two pages only – pages 4 and 5 – where this, the essence of modern England, is sandwiched between a few words on the Pleistocene age and a description of the 'dry Boreal period... when pine forests grew over much of the country and the North Sea was still advancing for its final isolation.' There is, it is true, a chapter on Town Life. But that is not the same thing at all.

The furious industrial epoch, of which England was the pioneer, and of which she is still much the most extreme example, cannot be so put aside. There is no country so urbanized as England. There is no country with so small a percentage of its population engaged upon the land. There is no country with such an energy of horse-power heaped and crammed into so small a space. In spite of the fact that a grocer's calendar will carry the picture of a cottage in the snow, or that the frontispiece of *The Listener* may show a village spire, England, modern England, is a series of city streets. The streets of London are paralleled by the streets of the Midlands, by the streets of Yorkshire and Lancashire. Nine out of every ten Englishmen anywhere are born in the towns and bred in the streets. Yet out of those streets came the men who could outlast the Arabs in the desert, who could outfight the Japanese in the forests, who flew above the birds and dived below the whales.

It is true that Lord Kennet has written a chapter on Town Life, just as Miss Sackville-West has written a chapter on Country Life. But read these two chapters, side by side, and you will see that Country Life is described from the inside, and Town Life from the outside. This is not surprising. Miss Sackville-West lives in the country, loves the country, and only with reluctance comes to town, for as short a period as she can possibly arrange. Nobody ever said the converse about Lord Kennet. As for the intense appreciation of city life, such as that possessed, for example, by Dr Johnson, or by Damon Runyon, it would be to him simply incomprehensible. Even his title is drawn from the loneliest and loveliest of little English rivers, famous for the most solitary of sports; and his delight is in watching birds – which, unlike horses, or pigs, or even rats, all of which have their devotees, are positively repelled by cities.

The English carry into almost every department of modern life their great unwillingness to admit facts, their power of pretending that things are not so. Only in their unconscious literature do they reveal themselves. The chapter on English city life, that is to say, on the life of nine-tenths of the English who make up the present nation, ought in logic to have been written by someone who could and would write, sing, whistle, dance and watch for his or her own personal pleasure, 'The Lambeth Walk'.

The chapter on Recreation and Games comes nearer to the mark, because no Englishman could possibly write an uninteresting chapter on this subject. Mr I.J. Pitman comes to the core of the matter when he directs our attention to the part which teamwork plays in the attraction which games have for the Englishman. 'An eight going perfectly on the tideway, English figure-skating perfectly called and executed with precision and timing, the reverse pass with which a stand-off half sends his centre three-quarter racing for a clearly certain try, carry a satisfaction in corporate human relationships which can be felt but not described.' This is the English love of pattern, of order, referred to above, one of their fundamental qualities. It is responsible for their delight in ships, the supreme example of a patterned life, for their fame abroad as troupe-dancers ('les Girls'), for the spectacle of Trooping the Colour. The most extreme example is that of bell-ringing. Give a Continental campanologist a spire full of great bells, and he will begin to play a tune on them. Only the English will undertake an endless series of ringing-the-changes; pulling sally after sally, for hour after hour, with no other purpose than to pursue some intricate rhythm in company, through peal after peal, clanging over a countryside, to the grave admiration of the whole parish.

This absorption in pattern is one aspect of the general power of absorption, of concentration, which the Englishman so specially enjoys. It is possible that this has enabled him to pass into a civilization of the streets without becoming a part of it. So the English travel in trains; not a company, but a collection of individuals; first turning each carriage into a row of cottages – the word compartment is a word of praise – and then sitting in each corner with the same blank denial of any other presence that the lovers show in the parks. The English live in cities, but they are not citified; they very seldom produce, for example, that characteristic symptom of a city, the mob. They are urbane without being urban; creating their own environment within their own being, they can dwell in the midst of twenty miles of paving stones and pretend, with the aid of a back green or even of a flower-pot, that they are in a hamlet on the Downs. Or so it seems to the outsider. Perhaps the English have something completely different in their heads.

Because they are also very inscrutable. Don Salvador de Madariaga has said that the wisdom of the English is so far above that of other races as to be of no use to them. This is horribly true. They cannot communicate their fine flowers – cricket, for instance – to other nations. They are unaware that among their supreme achievements in the transmission of culture – something not forced upon foreigners, but sought out by them –

is Association Football. They cannot communicate – perhaps it is incommunicable – their angelic mastery of lyric poetry. They do not know that the art-form which they have perfected and launched upon the modern world is not what the common man regards as the pretentious nonsense of their *avant-garde* poets, or the gibberish, to him intentionally unintelligible, of Joyce and the followers of Joyce, but Sherlock Holmes and all that has flowed from him.

In the detective story the English lose their self-consciousness; they move easily and naturally in the world which they normally inhabit. The world recognizes this and takes them to its heart. Sherlock Holmes in lodgings in Baker Street, Sherlock Holmes going to classical concerts on Saturday afternoons, Sherlock Holmes discussing with his brother, the great civil servant, the affairs of the Diogenes Club, Sherlock Holmes displaying, as naturally as a courting blackcock, the whole naïve, intimate, enraging – and strengthening – snobbery of the English – here is a description of contemporary manners in the vein of the everyday passages of Chaucer or of Shakespeare. Edgar Wallace, the English Dumas, pouring out an endless succession of ephemeridae, Jack London in America, knocking off thrillers with the power and enjoyment of a blacksmith fettling for the great grey dray-horse his bright and battering sandal – these are the authors whose works are studied and appreciated abroad – along with Milton, Byron and the romances of Oscar Wilde. These current authors are not mentioned, let alone analysed, in this volume.

The English are deserting Kipling, but the French are discovering him; the Russians, weary of Dostoevsky and Tolstoy, want to be able to write like Miss Dorothy Sayers or Miss Agatha Christie. None of this the English know. They certainly will not learn it from the pages before us.

They will find a great number of very charming and well-informed essays. They will find Miss Rebecca West on the Englishman Abroad (it is always worth while reading anything that Miss West writes). They will find a chapter on England and the Sea, and another on England at War. But they will not find that the authors have laid hold, singly or collectively, of the inner genius of this extraordinary people. In particular, the essays do not emphasize their singular originality of thought. The chapter on the sea, for instance, omits mention of the fact that the English invented, in Elizabethan times, the fore-and-aft rig, an invention almost as revolutionary as that of the internal combustion engine. The chapter on war omits mention of either the long-bow or of the tank, and though it mentions the Spitfires, leaves out radar, on which the whole strategy of air defence and the short-range fighter pivoted. It does not mention the inland voyage of Marlborough, *via* the Rhine, to the Danube, or Wavell's switch backwards and forwards of his Indian Division, from the Mediterranean to the

Central African mountains and – only just in time – back to the Mediterranean again. The feat of holding a quarter of the world together for so
many long years 'with twelve battleships', as Hitler querulously remarked,
and a corporal's guard, merits greater consideration. The boldness, the
presumptuous quality of English thought is seen as well in their conduct
of war as in any of their other exploits.

This quality was outstandingly demonstrated in the last war. But no
doubt the authors are right to lay little stress on this portion of English
history. For one thing it is too near to have any real knowledge of the facts
or any proper perspective upon them. For another, the English were at
bay and staking everything they had. If they won, all would be well. If they
lost, nothing would greatly matter. Yet for all that, the decision to fight in
the Levant at all, in 1940, is a decision so arrogant that it is not easy to see
where history will rank it. Some of Hitler's decisions will seem inexplicable
to history; but that was because they failed. The decision to fight in the
Levant succeeded. Otherwise history would have found it just as inapplic-
able to any reasoned appreciation of the facts.

The chapter on the Universities by Sir Maurice Powicke, mentions the
strange division between Oxford and Cambridge and 'the eight other
English universities whose history begins with the foundation of the
Owen's College at Manchester in 1851.'(!) 'Foreigners,' he says, 'find our
universities very English. There is nothing like them in the world. This
perhaps is the only generalization about them to which nobody would
demur.' It is very true. If one could understand the English universities,
one would understand at least half of England. But here also the mystery
is withheld from us.

Perhaps the most revealing of all the essays, because the least assuming,
is that of Lady Violet Bonham-Carter, on the subject of Children and
Education. Anyone reading it will learn a great deal of the English view
of children and a great deal more besides. An essayist who can discern and
describe that characteristic English contribution to social life 'the Nannie',
and who has the courage to assert, of one of the unrecognized peaks of
English literature, the nonsense rhymes, that for sheer poetry *The Dong
with the Luminous Nose* can hold its own with *Kubla Khan*, is not only an
author; she is the very thing of which she writes; she is no less than the
English character itself.

All these considerations, all these essays, have a very practical and
immediate bearing on our present times. The most important political
and economic fact of the day is the break-up of the British Empire. The
question is whether, and, if so, in what shape, it will re-form. It has already
broken up twice. Once when the Anglo-French State, so necessary, so
impossible, so nearly achieved, collapsed under the stroke of Saint Joan.

After that, the English State abandoned the Channel and reformed upon the ocean. Then the Atlantic commonwealth, also so necessary, split under the impact of General Washington. Very few societies have done this trick twice. None, except perhaps the Greek, with Athens, Alexandria and Byzantium to its credit, has done it a third time. The English have to do it a third time; or perish.

Or perish. There is no middle way. The structure is too tall, too boldly conceived to be dismantled arch by arch and beam after beam. It must stand, or crash. We are watching one small corner cracking – in Palestine; we recognize with horror how great a series of stresses will be opened by the buckling of even a single girder.

The English at present are sleeping, as a sailor sleeps after a storm, cast up on a beach, in the sun. But in their dreams they know very well that they will have to rise and go forth. There are traces of this in their current light writing, in their action, even in their thought. Miss Rebecca West, an outside observer, suddenly breaks into it – *à propos de bottes* – at the end of her essay. 'We were to know again,' she says, 'the conflict of continental faith and local genius: there came back into life something of a Tudor strength and richness: the hammer was striking on the anvil again.'

These quick, tremendous, inventive, bold people are to be tested once more. They will have to move suddenly from the period of Racine to the period of Villon. One of the great epics of the world is to be played out before us, and played out now.

Times Literary Supplement, 7 August 1948

Paule Vezelay

because she uses clear colours and simple shapes – because her paintings neither look like what we think we see when we look out of the window – nor picture the terrible dramas which we suppose to belong specially to the twentieth century – Paule Vezelay will be labelled 'abstract'

but she has little in common with the friends of 'functional' architecture, pretentious builders of worlds of light, decorators of uninhabitable 'machines-to-live-in', who call themselves abstract painters

Paule Vezelay lived for many years in paris, and her technique is certainly french – that is to say, her expression is clear & direct . but her paintings are also homely . she chooses & arranges shapes & harmonies as she lays a table or arranges the mantelpiece: with care and with affection . that is why her pictures aren't really abstract – the affection is for real objects . you can't see the objects 'in the picture itself'? no . she learnt in paris not to make the old mistake of confusing the origin of her feelings with the final expression of it

she is, I would say, a contemplative artist . her pictures sometimes remind me of those refreshing letters & diaries written by retiring people in the last century, recording their thoughts & emotions without apparent reference to the industrial pandemonium, the banging & clattering of bridge building and rail roading, which we know to have been going on around them

there is a line of Mallarmé, which, I think, suits her well: *musicienne du silence*

Catalogue note for an exhibition at
St George's Gallery London W1, 1949

Selected Broadcasts

Plagiarism in Poetry

There are various dictionary definitions of plagiarism, which make it look like some sort of crime. The New English Dictionary, for example, calls it 'the wrongful appropriation or purloining, and publication as one's own, of the ideas (literary, artistic, musical, mechanical, etc.) of another.'

Well – that takes a view of literature which is, I think, very narrow, and which is certainly not based on experience of poetry. It makes the peculiar assumption that certain ideas in literature belong to particular people, and also it suggests that in a definite statement – like Shakespeare's 'To be or not to be', for example – each of these words belongs somehow to Shakespeare. To me that really is not so – they're simply part of the English language, and had been used before by literally millions of people.

In the early eighteenth century there appeared a book called Bysshe's *Art of English Poetry* in two volumes. One volume consisted of recipes for making poems, just as you can buy books on how to take photographs or how to paint watercolours. The second volume consisted of excerpts from existing poetry arranged under headings such as Death, Love, Trees, Colours, Paradise, etc. So that when you proposed to make a poem you just looked under the heading in question and found out what the great poets (principally Shakespeare, Milton and Dryden) and a certain number of smaller poets had already said about it.

Now Gray's 'Elegy' has been, I suppose, the most constantly popular English poem. Dr Johnson said of it: 'The Churchyard abounds with images which find a mirror in every mind, and with sentiments to which every bosom returns an echo.' At the beginning of the 'Elegy' there are two lines which run: 'The breezy call of incense breathing morn, / The swallow twittering from the strawbuilt shed.' It has been pointed out that part of the line – 'the breezy call of incense breathing morn' – was taken by Gray from Milton's 'The humid flowers that breathed their morning incense'. Then, some three or four years ago, a reviewer made the point that anybody could feel, as he said, the artificiality of the first line – 'breezy call of incense breathing morn' – and the naturalness of 'the swallow twittering from the strawbuilt shed.'

Well – that's called reading poetry according to one's knowledge, instead of according to one's heart, because it so happens that part of the second line was also taken by Gray from Milton, who speaks of the bees in 'their strawbuilt citadel'. Look at what has happened: a distinction is being made between naturalness and artificiality parallel to that dictionary's idea that words can belong to a person, so that ultimately, borrowed words, artificiality and bad poetry are all supposed to be the same thing.

Look at the first line of the 'Elegy': 'The curfew tolls the knell of parting day'. Gray himself admitted plagiarism of the idea from Dante. Now Milton has a line, 'I hear the far-off curfew sound': Dryden has a line, 'That tolls the knell of their departed sense': Pope in his translation of Homer has a line, 'Hail the rising, close the parting day': Young, in his 'Night Thoughts', says 'It is the knell of my departed hours'. All these poems were perfectly well known to Gray, and I suggest not that he had all the books open in front of him, or that he worked it out in a laborious way, but that he certainly had all these things at the back of his mind.

What happened was that he did in actual fact stand in a country churchyard, that he noticed a certain set of sensations coming over him at dusk, and that instead of taking out his pencil and writing out what he felt in colloquial language – he himself, by the way, said that 'the language of poetry is never the language of contemporary life' and therefore it was a problem for him to find out (if he could) what was the language of poetry – he constructed poetry from poetry, in a way very similar to that recommended as we've seen in Bysshe's *Art of English Poetry*.

The really remarkable thing – and this is why these points are not so academic – is that he does not make them appear as though they had been constructed from poetry. They correspond exactly to our feelings in similar circumstances – in fact as Johnson says, 'Sentiments to which every bosom returns an echo.'

The second line's exactly the same: 'The lowing herd winds slowly o'er the lea.' Now in Pope's translation of the *Odyssey*, we have the line, 'As from fresh fields the lowing herds return', and in Thomson's 'Castle of Indolence': 'Joined to the prattle of the purling rills / We heard the lowing herds.' Then in Dryden's translation of Horace: 'The lowing herd walked o'er the plain'. Again from Thomson: 'Or where old Cam soft paces o'er the lea'; and in John Gay's 'Rural Sports' we have: 'The ploughman leaves the task of day / And trudges homeward on the way.' There are many more quotations I could give, but it is obvious from this small bunch that they've all contributed something to Gray's statement: 'The curfew tolls the knell of parting day, / The lowing herd wind slowly o'er the lea'; and yet we think of *Gray* as the inventor of this statement. But Gray had this particular feeling and constructed his poetry in this particular way.

There are some very beautiful and famous lines near the end of the 'Elegy' which begin: 'Yet ev'n these bones from insult to protect / Some frail memorial still erected nigh.' Johnson remarks: 'The four stanzas beginning: "Yet even these bones" are to me original: I have never seen the notions in any other place; yet he that reads them here, persuades himself that he has always felt them.' We know that in Homer and Virgil there is an insistence on the necessity of saving the corpse killed in battle from mutilation and saving it for proper burial. We also know of Gray's admiration for Dryden and Pope and for their translations of Virgil and Homer. Suppose we look for a moment at Dryden's translation of the tenth book of the *Aeneid*, and these lines:

> ...But let my body have
> 'The last retreat of human kind, a grave.
> Too well I know th'insulting people's hate;
> Protect me from their vengeance after fate.

Well – from these words Gray has, I believe, constructed his phrase 'from insult to protect'.

Two stanzas further down in the 'Elegy' we have:

> For who to dumb Forgetfulness a prey,
> This pleasing anxious being e'er resigned,
> Left the warm precincts of the cheerful day...

It's well known that the ghosts in Homer, Virgil and Dante have an intense longing for light, and so in Pope's translation of Homer we have the question – 'Why mortal, wanderest thou from the cheerful day'.

Similarly, I suggest, behind Gray's lines, 'For thee, who mindful of th'unhonoured Dead / Dost in these lines their artless tale relate...' are lying statements from Pope's Homer, such as: 'Nor must thy corpse lie honoured on the bier, / Nor spouse nor mother grace thee with a tear.'

You see, the thing I really want to bring out is that Johnson says 'he has seen the ideas nowhere, but everybody persuades themselves that they have felt these ideas'. They are therefore taken to be original by Johnson, or felt by other people (such as a reviewer) to be natural. In fact, the moment you look into it you find that practically all the combinations of words have been taken from somewhere or other – particularly the key phrases, such as 'cheerful day'.

But why do I quote particularly from Gray's 'Elegy'? Well, I should say this: the change in social conditions between 1580 (when Spenser began to write)'and 1740 (when Gray began to write) divorced the poet more and more from contemporary life. We know that Spenser was right in the thick of the Irish troubles of his time. We know that Shakespeare was a countryman who made good in London and worked in the theatre as an actor and a shareholder as well as a playwright. But with Milton we begin to get some hint of difficulty. He was too busy as one of Cromwell's secretaries writing propaganda to write poetry, with the result that instead of his poetry being part of the revolution it came rather pathetically after it.

We know the battles that Pope and Swift had with contemporary poets and journalists and patrons. And we know, finally, that by Gray's time there was no social place for a poet. It's a notable fact that Gray's mother actually did not know that he wrote poetry. In fact, it is curious to think that the 'Elegy' was not written to be published and only became known through an indiscretion of Horace Walpole. It was simply written because Gray was a person of tremendous integrity as well as being a natural poet and a scholar, and he wrote poems for the sake of poetry, which he connected with liberty and freedom.

He tended more and more to fall back on books, and particularly on poetry – the one thing he felt he understood. The result of all this was to make a distinction between everyday life and poetry. He lived his everyday life as he could, and he wrote his poetry as he could. But nobody (however much of a recluse) can cut everyday life out of his existence – everyday life will still exist.

In the 'Elegy', Gray gives a view of the end of feudal England, of a churchyard tower, of the groves, of the oldest inhabitant – and the sensitive poet mooning over them in the evening, with the people returning from their work: a perfectly contemporary scene, but in the language of poetry.

You have, at the same time, passing through Gray's mind, his reading, his reminiscences, his memories of the ritual of life and death of the heroic age as recorded by Homer and as translated again by Pope, and he sees some connection between this ritual and the contemporary ritual of life and death in a small country churchyard. But it's by balancing one with the other that he creates naturalness; not the naturalness which is supposed to depend on the originality of words or ideas, but on human emotion – the common factor between the strange and dark and stirring memories and pictures he had himself extracted from Homer and Virgil and Dante and his own musings in the country. And then because you have both these elements welded together in Gray's 'Elegy', you have the reason for the poem still continuing to be read, and still continuing to emanate human emotion.

Therefore there is, I think, a certain amount of service in pointing out that Gray's 'Elegy' was written in a highly artificial manner, because I am reminding people that poetry does not consist of naturalness on the one hand and artificiality on the other, but in a fusion of the two. If, simply by the gift of being a poet, a poet manages to get into words (and to let out of words) real human emotions, we shall always call them natural, as indeed we must, because it's the most natural thing in the world to us as human beings to recognize human emotion, and we must allow our poet to write his poetry just as he wishes. Gray wished to employ plagiarism as a method of writing poetry.

Broadcast on the BBC National Programme, 8 December 1937

The Disappearance of Ghosts

After lunch last Saturday I was sitting quietly in a London club discussing with an eminent Conservative various problems of reality and hallucination, and without my suggesting anything he brought out a story about some female relation of his.

At the end of the last century they were living in a cottage in the wilds in the Midlands. One afternoon, just after lunch, in a moment's silence, they heard noises upstairs as of something heavy falling to the ground. They went out: there was nothing. Months later they heard that a relation of theirs – a young man on a windjammer at sea – had at that time, on that day, fallen from the yards on to the deck and been killed. This to them was the explanation of the disturbance upstairs in their cottage. 'But,' said my friend, 'how could there be any connection? In those days there was no wireless.'

Well, it's a terribly flat story – but it's the comment that's the interesting thing. I mean the comment about the wireless.

Now hold that for a moment and go back nearly three thousand years to the adventures of Ulysses – the *Odyssey* of Homer. In the *Odyssey* there is a moment when Ulysses is leaving the island of Circe to sail north to the edge of the world to summon Tiresias, the prophet from the dead, at the entrance of the underworld to ask what is going to happen to him. Homer notes that the ship left the island with all her crew except one who, being suddenly woken up in the middle of the night, fell headlong from the roof and broke his neck.

It took them a day's sail to get to the edge of the world. On the beach Ulysses performs a thrilling ritual to summon up the dead. With his sword he carved out a kind of grave on the shore and poured into it wine and milk and water and flour and blood. And then

> ...lo! appeared along the dusky coasts,
> Thin, airy shoals of visionary ghosts;
> Fair, pensive youths and soft-enamour'd maids,
> And wither'd elders, pale and wrinkled shades...
> Round the black trench the gore untasted flows,
> 'Till awful, from the shades Tiresias rose.
>   There, wand'ring thro' the gloom to first survey'd,
> New to the realms of death, Elpenor's shade.

Elpenor was the sailor who'd broken his neck on the night before they left: 'His cold remains all naked to the sky / On distant shores unwept, unburied lie.' As thrilling as this is, the *point* of the story (as far as we're concerned) is the question which Ulysses immediately asks him. 'How,' he says, 'did

you come here over the unfooted sea?' How could he have got to the edge
of the world so quickly and *without a boat*?

The point of the question doesn't lie in the attempt to get an accurate
answer as to whether the ghost exists or not (or whether it could or could
not go by ship or by any other means), but simply the peculiar poetic thrill
of raising doubts and asking questions about the supernatural problem
without necessarily giving an answer. In other words, it is in the raising of
doubts that the thrill lies, and not in the flat assertion that a ghost can walk
over the sea or cannot walk over the sea, for example, which has no poetic
value. The poetic effect and the human effect, because of the doubts
which exist in human beings, are brought out when you ask a certain
question of which this is an example. The question is not merely poetical
in a romantic sense. It is thrilling in a human sense. 'How could you have
come so quickly over the unfooted sea?' is absolutely the right question to
ask, because we all identify with the difference between the labour of
sailing over a long stretch of sea and the immediate telegraphic achievement of the ghost in flashing from one place to greet Ulysses when he
arrives in another, thus gratifying all our human wishes not to be bound
by the laws of Nature.

Now listen to this question – only three hundred years ago – from Hamlet:

> What may this mean
> That thou, dead corse, again in complete steel,
> Revisits thus the glimpses of the moon,
> Making night hideous, and we fools of nature
> So horridly to shake our disposition
> With thoughts beyond the reaches of our souls?
> Say why is this? wherefore? what should we do?
>
> [*Text amended*]

Ulysses went to the edge of the world to look for ghosts but now the ghost
has come to look for Hamlet. Hamlet is very far from going to consult
ghosts about what is going to happen to him; it is the *ghost* that is dictating
to Hamlet, and the whole question of the play becomes whether Hamlet
can stand the impact of the ghost on his everyday life.

This impact is clearest and most terrifying at the moment when the
ghost's voice is heard under the stage telling Horatio and Marcellus to
swear. The effect is so peculiar that Hamlet, to withstand the peculiarity,
has to say in an almost jocular way, 'You hear this fellow in the cellarage.
Consent to swear.' Note that *Hamlet* being a play, the ghost (in order to
say the word 'Swear') has in actual fact to go under the stage into the
cellarage. In other words, Hamlet is calling the ghost an actor – which he
is – and immediately after, when the ghost shifts ground, he calls him a

mole – 'Well said, old mole! Canst work i' th' earth so fast?' [*Text amended*]
Hamlet is determined not to call the Ghost a ghost.

So we see that whereas Ulysses had only to perform a ritual to summon
the ghosts, in *Hamlet* the whole play opens with Horatio's doubts ('Tush,
tush, 'twill not appear') and at the most dramatic moment of all the ghost
has in fact *disappeared* and has become an actor under the stage or a mole
under the ground.

These are steps in a long sequence – the disappearance of ghosts.

Now in the long campaign of rationalism in the eighteenth century, it
was only natural that the ghost should disappear even further. But natural
also that there should appear a counter-attack: the black novel, the ghost
story, and the intensely romantic poetry of the 'Ancient Mariner'. Obviously once you have created a special type of book or story in which ghosts
are *expected* to appear they *will* appear, because the writer has only to *make*
them appear.

So I don't propose to deal with ghosts in the ordinary ghost story. The
writer of a ghost story is like Ulysses: he sets out on purpose to find ghosts.
I suggest that there are other places in the prose and poetry of the nineteenth century in which the ghost, like the ghost in *Hamlet*, is trying to
make itself understood. For example, in the opening scene of *Great
Expectations* the hero (as a little boy) is looking at his mother's grave in a
churchyard by the flat shore of the Thames near Gravesend. In the river
fog are lying convict ships bound for Botany Bay. Suddenly, from behind
his mother's gravestone, there appears a figure. The scene itself, the terror
of the little boy, the effect on the reader – these without any possible doubt
are due to an unspoken suggestion, if only for a moment, that the figure
is a *ghost*. The place is right – a churchyard – the ships in the fog – the
suddenness of the appearance – and the fact that the little boy was thinking of the past – his own past – which, since ghosts are ancestors, has
always been the mood to evoke them. Everything is right.

I would put it this way: that in order to appear in this thoroughly
realistic novel, the ghost has had to become an ordinary figure – in this
case a convict – and his appearance as a ghost (if you see what I mean) is
limited to that half-second in which we and the little boy are most
frightened. As soon as he is recognized to be a man, as soon as the curious
reason for his being there at all – that he was an escaped convict – as soon
as these things are clear, he is *no longer* a ghost.

There is another example of what I might call the difficult appearance
of a ghost in a supremely beautiful poem of Tennyson's:

> Now sleeps the crimson petal, now the white;
> Nor waves the cypress in the palace walk;

Nor winks the gold fin in the porphyry font:
The fire-fly wakens: waken thou with me.

Now droops the milkwhite peacock like a ghost,
And like a ghost she glimmers on to me.

You see Tennyson *doesn't* (perhaps *can't*) allow the ghost as a ghost, but
it can and does make a momentary appearance as a white peacock. We
have seen that the ghost was an actor, a mole, a convict, and now he is a
peacock.

No doubt you will object that this is only a matter of words. Well it *is*
only a matter of words. The ghosts has in fact become a word. This is what
is meant by 'The disappearance of ghosts'. It is perhaps *we* who are determined that the ghost shall not appear, but it does its best – it still appears
in the language as a word, 'ghost'. It appears in a poem as a milk-white
peacock, and I am even going so far as to suggest that it appears less
embodied than ever, if possible, in a single title of another book, *The
White Peacock* by D.H. Lawrence.

I know this may sound ridiculous but what in fact is the appeal of the
title *The White Peacock* – and what is the business of the white peacock
itself in the actual novel by Lawrence? If it were only a question of having
a house with a peacock in the garden – well, you would have a *peacock*. If
it were only a question of having a house – well, the house was *deserted*,
and that was all there was to it. Why introduce a peacock? Why talk about
a *deserted* house at all?

Now you talk about a deserted house in Lawrence's case because he and
the people in his novel were struggling with the past. To symbolise their
struggle with the past Lawrence brings in a deserted house and garden,
and in order to give that deserted house a special distinctiveness (which
corresponds to his feelings about the past), he introduces into the garden
a peacock. And in order to give that peacock special distinctiveness in
relation to the *house* and the *past* and his *feelings*, he made the peacock a
white peacock.

Now what other single being can we think of which is at once:

    (a)   related to the past
    (b)   related to a deserted house
    (c)   which walks up and down the garden
and   (d)   which is white?

Well, the answer is a ghost, of course. And if you want further proof that
it *is* a ghost, you've only got to turn up Tennyson's poem in which he's
talking about a garden and about a peacock in the garden and in which he
says, 'Now droops the milkwhite peacock like a ghost.'

It has been made clear, I hope, that the use and power of the ghost as a poetic symbol has declined from Homer's day – when to all intents and purposes there were such things as ghosts – down to Lawrence's and our own time. The power and efficacy of the ghost as a symbol has declined. The ghosts have tended more and more to disappear. In a poem of Swinburne's we have the line, "The ghost of a garden fronts the sea". Here there is actually no ghost in the garden – the Forsaken Garden itself has replaced the ghost.

Now the *obvious* question is, 'What is the future of ghosts in poetry?' But I suggest that the proper question to ask is, 'What is the future of poetry without ghosts?' We have spent three hundred years or more in the position of Hamlet – increasingly terrified of the possible impact of ghosts on existence. What our poets have to do is to find the modern equivalent of the sword, wine, water, flour and blood that Ulysses used to ask the *past* about the future.

Broadcast on the BBC National Programme, 11 February 1938

From
The Poet and the Public

1   The Modern Poet and the Public

I think it's generally agreed that the poet today has somehow got himself out of touch with the public. If this is true, it means that the public is missing something that I think would be of use to it, and it's to try and turn up some of the difficulties that lie between the poet and the public that this series of talks is aiming at.

The two things that have got out of touch with each other are modern poetry and everyday life. The modern poet certainly has his or *her* own little public, but they're not representative of the public at large. The great big public thinks of poetry, particularly modern poetry, as something highbrow.

First of all, what is this public's everyday life like? Well, for a glimpse of it I don't think I can do better than read you a description, by a railwayman from the Midlands, of the world in which he lives and works.

> I live in a street [he says] practically closed in, the backs of one row of houses face our back, and the fronts of another row of houses face our front, across the bottom there is a Methodist Sunday School

and at the top an open meadow; across the meadow is the public maternity hospital. Where I work is in the railway coal yard, very dreary and dull. It is situated in the lowest part of the town. As I look out of my office window, to my left I see coal waggons, beyond them on the hillside a row of rather dirty looking houses, and beyond them a hillside of green fields, very drab and steep, with a pylon for electricity top and bottom. In front, more waggons, the fruit shed, and two mill chimneys to the right, the yards gates at the bottom of the main street which I can see about half of, with a hotel at the bottom, shops, a garage and a cinema as if goes up to a left turn. At my back there is some spare ground on which travelling fairs stay, a few dirty shops, with the passenger station which I cannot see to the back.

Well, that may sound a bit grim to some of you, but I don't think it's unfair as a picture of a modern town – and after all it's the townsmen who're the most modern part of the public.

Hang on to that for a minute while I read a few lines by Miss Edith Sitwell – which I think are quite a fair example of what the public calls 'modern' poetry. She's giving a sort of romantic picture of her childhood:

> There in a land, austere and elegant,
> The castle seemed an arabesque in music;
> We moved in an hallucination born
> Of silence, which like music gave us lotus
> To eat, perfuming lips and our long eyelids
> As we trailed over the sad summer grass,
> Or sat beneath a smooth and mournful tree.
>
> And Time passed, suavely, imperceptibly.
>
> But Dagobert and Peregrine and I
> Were children then; we walked like shy gazelles
> Among the music of the thin flower-bells.
> And life still held some promise – never ask
> Of what – but life seemed less a stranger, then,
> Than ever after in this cold existence.

Now you couldn't have two worlds more different than that. I wouldn't say that the railwayman would necessarily read poetry if it were about railways, but I think the poetess is making her stuff almost unusable from the point of the railwayman because it's about such a *tiny little bit* of the world – *most* of the world has simply got left out, and even that little bit is one that he hasn't got any experience of.

How does Miss Sitwell come to be writing this kind of thing? In fact, how has poetry managed to become highbrow? To be quite frank, I don't think the ordinary literary explanations are much good. I think the easiest way to tackle it is this:

Look at a butterfly. It usually has very bright colours on its upper pair of wings and darker and softer colours on its under-wings. This was once explained by Darwin as follows: when the butterfly has its wings shut it merges automatically into its surroundings – the dull colour of the under-wings gives it protection. On the other hand, when it opens its wings to fly, it *shows itself off* and attracts other butterflies.

Well now, man also needs to protect himself and to show himself off. And indeed Darwin went so far as to suggest that man has evolved his language in the same way as the butterfly its colouring – to protect himself and to show himself off.

Since the invention of printing, reading has become very nearly as important as talking and today (for the first time in our history) there are forty million people in England who not only talk but *read*. *What* do they read? Well, they read notices like 'Don't Cross', they read advertisements like 'Keep Fit', and they read newspapers. And I suggest we read notices, advertisements and newspapers as a protection (just as the butterfly with its wings shut is protecting itself), because it's through the newspaper that we can watch other people's lives and we can try and distinguish between friends and enemies – from politicians to burglars.

At the newspaper office the news comes ticking in over a tape machine like this:

> 4.32 p.m. Laundry explosion – two dead.
> Two men were killed and three men and nine women were injured in an explosion at a steam laundry this afternoon.

That actually happened last week. When the sub-editor got that message, his instinct was to make what he calls a 'human' story out of it, to get *inside* the bare news. This is part of what the sub-editor made of it:

> Most of the girls who rushed from the building collapsed in a state of hysterics on the lawn in front of the laundry, and were powerless to move, owing to fright. Residents from neighbouring houses, in spite of their own alarm and the fact that their own houses had been damaged, helped the panic-stricken girls into their homes, and allowed them to rest and recover there. According to one of the girls, the force of the explosion blew most of them off their feet.

It's *exciting*, isn't it? Why? Because that's exactly the sort of thing that might happen to any one of us at any moment – of course it mightn't happen in Miss Sitwell's little bit of world, but it certainly might happen to the railwayman, and *he knows it*.

That was a bit of *straight* news, but straight news is not the only thing you find in a newspaper. The office girl going to work in the morning takes her morning paper with her. She reads it in the train, she reads it at lunchtime, and in London, at least, you can still see her reading it on the evening train home. She reads a lot more than the headlines. She reads the woman's page, the horoscope, the gossip columns, short stories. You wouldn't call a short story news – take this for example:

> Day after day, all through the long, hot summer, the two old women sat together at one end of the green-painted shelter facing the sea, sharing the small luxuries, a few sweets maybe, an orange or a soft bit of cake, which one or the other brought, and enjoying the laughing briskness of the holiday crowds, forgetful of their own sorry age and ailments.

That paragraph actually came out of a newspaper short story last week, and its style isn't the brisk style of a reporter either. What's a short story doing in a newspaper, anyway? I suggest it is there because all of us have a longing for romance – even in newspapers; in fact, it is romance that is the top half of the butterfly's wings. We've seen that in reading *news* you can imagine yourself in a real explosion; in romance, you can imagine yourself taking part in things that have *never* happened. And the reader can turn himself into an actor and take parts, which are invented *for* him by the author: he can dress himself up in other people's clothes, he can show off. It's like the cinema, where the office girl and the railwayman can turn themselves into Scarface or Garbo.

The newspaper presents its readers with both these things: news and romance. But you've got to admit that neither of them has got much staying power. The news shifts from one day to another, and when we buy tomorrow's newspaper we get a new short story with it.

So much for news. How about poetry? Well, when printing came in in the fifteenth century, it was bound to help journalists rather than poets, because the journalists rely on the rapid printing of news, and that's just what printing can do. Over the last three hundred years we have language going two ways: it's used for *news*, real news and romantic news, and it's used for *poetry*. What happens to poetry? Well, let's look at a poem that was written at the time when printing first came to England. A poem written by a man who was Poet Laureate to Henry VIII, John Skelton, called 'Speak Parrot'. It begins like this:

My name is Parrot, a byrd of paradyse
  By nature devysed of a wonderous kynde,
Dyntely dyeted with dyvers dylycate spyce
  Till Euphrates, that flode, dryveth me into Inde
  Where men of that countrye by fortune me fynd,
And send me to great laydes of estate:
Then Parrot must have an almon or date.

First, note that instead of being about an abstract subject or a difficult subject, it's a poem about a bird. After all, a bird is a simple everyday thing (we still have birds, even in towns), but this was a *special* bird – a bird of Paradise; and a bird which, he says, has been constructed in a special way ('By nature devised of a wond'rous kind'); and it's fed on special things ('Daintily dieted with divers delicate spice'). Best of all, it comes from a romantic and distant part of the world; it sails down the Euphrates to India, where it is captured and brought from India to England. By the time the parrot gets to England, it's really a piece of news.

At the same time the fantastic mixture of Paradise and Euphrates and India (all of which, even to a well-educated Englishman in 1500, must have been equally vague sorts of places) keep the story pretty romantic. So that parrot makes news, makes romance and makes poetry, all at once. That was in 1500.

Now take a poem at the end of the eighteenth century, at a time when newspapers were getting into full swing and when men's ideas of geography were a bit clearer.

Tyger Tyger, burning bright
In the forests of the night;
What immortal hand or eye,
Could frame thy fearful symmetry?

In what distant deeps or skies
Burnt the fire of thine eyes?
On what wings dare he aspire?
What the hand dare seize the fire?

[Text amended]

Nobody will disagree I think that that's pretty crack-a-jack poetry and it has romance – but does it have *news*? Did it ever have news? Blake's Tiger doesn't prowl about in the Indian jungle – we shall have to wait for Kipling for that; it *burns* in the forests of the night. And readers of poetry still find 'the forests of the night', and 'distant deeps and skies' not only romantic and thrilling, but *moving*. But if they don't exist (if it's all romance) why *do they* move anybody? Is there any *difference* between romance and poetry?

Let us go back to Darwin again. Darwin would say that the superb and terrifying look of the real tiger has been specially cultivated in the tiger to frighten its enemies and to show itself off to the tigresses. Now *Darwin* asks, 'Why did the Tiger get itself its look and its colouring?' but *Blake* asks, '*How* did it get it?' and 'Where did it get it *from*?' and this brings up the question, 'How are *we* going to protect ourselves?' and so on.

We've seen the way in which newspapers and short stories help us to deal with the *outside* world, but what about our lives by *ourselves*? You see newspapers don't give us news about *ourselves*. Who is going to help us to show off ourselves to ourselves? – because that is what we need. In fact what sort of language has man invented to deal with *himself*? Why, *poetry*, of course. When we repeat 'Tyger Tyger, burning bright', we're not talking about a *real* tiger, we're talking about ourselves, because with the poem we frighten ourselves – almost mesmerise ourselves – and at the same time we end up feeling as strong as a tiger. And that's what we mean when we say that the poem *moves* us.

But for all that, if the average Englishman is going to be able to use poetry in this sort of way (I mean to deal with what's going on inside his own head), the things in the poem have got to be as simple and as familiar as the things that he already *has* in his head. Birds and tigers and so on.

But very *complicated* subjects will obviously only work for people with very complicated things in their heads.

Once upon a time, it may be poetry and romance and news all managed to tie up together – and the poet was a kind of reporter. But since we've had newspapers, the reading public has been able to choose between reading news about other people (such as the newspaper gives them) and news about themselves such as the poet tries to give them. The newspapers keep things simple, and anyway people's instinct is to read about other people, so the poor old poet stopped becoming a reporter and got left to himself.

As the poet was an expert precisely at thinking about himself, the things inside his head naturally got more complicated than the things inside other people's, with the result now that they just can't *follow* him. And that's why the railwayman is bound to find Miss Sitwell highbrow.

Just what happened to the poet during the last three centuries when he found newspaper news was slipping away from him is another part of the story, which I will try and describe next week.

Broadcast on the BBC National Programme, 26 April 1938

2   The Poet and the Public in the Past

Last week I suggested that, in the last two or three hundred years, as news-papers became more and more popular, so the poet became more and more of a recluse. Now I want to look rapidly at three poets in the past, Shakespeare, Gray and Shelley, and see how far they were in or out of touch with the poetry of their time.

It's so difficult for us to think of Shakespeare ever having been a real live person. We think of him as a 'subject' – a *school* subject, an examination subject, as a public institution that provides tags for after dinner speeches and advertisements. In other words we think of him as a *book* instead of as a man – as a human being.

Even so, if we're going to think of him as a human being we mustn't think of him as having been a favourite poet, a *bard* writing for a gaping public. His plays were printed, certainly, but they were only printed after they'd been acted and *because* they'd been acted. In *actual fact* Shakespeare started off in the theatre in a pretty humble sort of way, namely by re-writing (or patching up) other people's plays just as, for example, old silent films are now re-made into talkies to keep them up to date.

I suppose that at the time of Shakespeare about thirty per cent of the population of Great Britain could read. Obviously only a very small percentage of these could afford to *buy* books, even if they wanted to, and so the people who wanted exciting stories went to the theatre just as we go to the cinema. In the earliest plays the action of the story was con-sidered so important that you often saw it twice over: once in a dumb show and once with the words. The point about Shakespeare was that he was so good at writing *the words*. When a play had been a success, if you could read and if you could afford it and if you wanted to, you bought the book of the words.

You remember that the old silent films always had plenty of thrills and action, and we put up with uncomfy seats and a flickery screen and a piano. Nowadays the usherette shows us to superbly comfortable *fauteuil* and we lean back and criticize the dialogue and the music and the colour in a thoroughly sophisticated sort of way. Well, it was just the same during Shakespeare's lifetime: the theatre public seems to have got more and more interested in the words and have taken the action (the story) more and more for granted. As a matter of fact this is exactly what suited Shakespeare, because he was a *wizard* with *words*.

I don't mean just beautiful sing-song stuff; the words were important for a very practical reason. You know when you see a revival of an old film the people on the screen seem to be such sticks; every time you re-make it, you have to make them far more human. That's what Shakespeare

found, and that's why the play of *Hamlet* (which started off as a melodrama about a Prince of Denmark revenging his father's murder) ended
up in Shakespeare's hands as the character study of a *human* being – of a
man who (when it came to the point) found the killing, the revenge, just
so difficult. And every time he finds it difficult the action stops. And what
does Hamlet do? He talks, he argues, he goes over it and over it ... just like
the human beings in the audience. 'How all occasions do inform against
me / And spur my dull revenge!' ... 'Words, words, words.' And as he talks
he walks up and down the stage surrounded (on the Elizabethan stage
literally surrounded) by the public. When you come to think of it, there's
something peculiar here because Hamlet talks like Hamlet yet it was
Shakespeare who wrote the words – or another way round, it's Shakespeare talking but dressed up as Hamlet.

So we get a figure on the stage, who is a character in a play, who is the
poet himself and who is a human being like the audience – all at once ...
And how does he manage to be all these three things at the same time?
Why – *through the words!* It's through all the talk on the stage at Shakespeare reached the public.

Just about the time when Shakespeare died, people started writing sort
of descriptive prose sketches called 'characters'. They're not like a short
story because they don't have any action. They simply describe a typical
English person of the time, such as a countryman, a soldier, a politician,
the way they behave, the kind of things they wear, the kind of things they
think about. This realistic kind of writing was obviously very important at
a time of civil war – because everybody wanted to know what their
neighbours were like – and it was this sort of writing and this kind of
public interest that in the end produced the novel.

It was the *novel* that the public at the beginning of the eighteenth
century wanted, because it presented to them a simple picture of a new
sort of life, what we call the modern world, the industrial revolution which
was just starting.

Look at *Gulliver's Travels*. We think of *Gulliver's Travels* as a sort of
fairy story for children *now*, but if you look at the first paragraph of the
first voyage you think it's going to be a real description of somebody's
travels: 'Travels into several remote nations of the world – by Lemuel
Gulliver. Part 1 – a Voyage to Lilliput. Chapter 1':

> My father had a small estate in Nottinghamshire; I was the third of
> five sons. He sent me to Emmanuel-College in Cambridge, at four-
> teen years old, where I resided three years, and applied myself close
> to my studies: but the charge of maintaining me (although I had a
> very scanty allowance) being too great for a narrow fortune; I was

bound apprentice to Mr James Bates, an eminent surgeon in London, with whom I continued four years; and my father now and then sending me small sums of money, I laid them out in learning navigation, and other parts of the mathematicks, useful to those who intend to travel, as I always believed it would be some time or other my fortune to do. [*Text amended*]

Just as with Shakespeare, so here we must get out of our heads the idea that *Gulliver's Travels*, that *Robinson Crusoe*, and that *Joseph Andrews* were written as *literature*. On the contrary, they were making an almost desperate effort to hang on to *life* at all costs. And in the background to all this (that's to say, in the 1740s) a new kind of *poet* – a literary poet – was emerging.

> The Curfew tolls the knell of parting day,
> The lowing herd wind slowly o'er the lea,
> The plowman homeward plods his weary way,
> And leaves the world to darkness and to me.

Now Gray's *Elegy* was written *entirely* for his own *personal satisfaction*. It was never meant to be published, in fact it was published by mistake and Gray himself regarded the publication as a *disaster*. It was putting his private life in the hands of the public.

You see, while the realistic novel was a professional kind of writing, which people made money out of, the only person who ever made any money out of Gray's poetry was his publisher, Dodsley. Gray himself never made a *penny* out of it – not because he couldn't, but because he didn't want to. He was an absolutely non-professional poet. This doesn't mean that he was a dilettante – on the contrary, it was because he regarded poetry so seriously that he felt it was hopeless to put it in front of a public who were getting more and more interested in horse-racing and steam-engines. And how did Gray manage to live? By dividends, of course, South Sea stock (among other things) – in fact on the world described by the novelists, that world that I think he was actually pretty frightened of.

Listen to a short passage from one of his letters about a walking-tour in the North.

> The gloom of these ancient cells, the shade and verdure of the land-scape, the glittering and murmur of the stream, the lofty towers and long perspectives of the Church, in the midst of a clear bright day, detain'd me for many hours and were the truest subjects for my glass I have yet met with anywhere.
>
> But as I lay at that smoky ugly busy town of Leedes, I dropp'd all farther thoughts of my journal. [See the extract from Gray's *Journal of a Tour of the Lakes*, 1769, 'Daemons at Work', in *Pandaemonium*, p.64]

I think that that is a kind of admission by Gray of how *frightened* the poet is becoming in front of the great industrial world ('The smoky ugly busy town of Leeds').

This conflict between the commercial world and the single individual poet became most *bitter* in the famous battles of Shelley, first with his university, then with his father about money, and finally with Lord Eldon, the Lord Chancellor of England. Shelley was sent down from Oxford for writing a pamphlet, his father threw him out of the house, and his children were taken away from him by the state because he was supposed to be unfit to look after them. Ultimately his father gave him an allowance (more dividends, you see) and he went to live by the sea in Italy.

In the summer of 1819 he was living at Leghorn, opposite the Gulf of Spezia, where he was drowned three years later. It was during this summer that the famous Peterloo massacre occurred in Manchester. On the 16th of August a public meeting was called there to petition Parliament for reform and for the repeal of the Corn Laws. This meeting was held in a big open space in the middle of the city called St Peter's Field. There were about sixty thousand people there. The local magistrates seem to have been specially instructed from London by the Castlereagh government. The Chief Speaker (I'm quoting an eyewitness) made his appearance in an open barouche. On reaching the hustings, he was received with enthusiastic applause – the waving of hats and flags, the blowing of trumpets, and the playing of music.

> Then an alarm arose, and I heard the sound of a horn, and immediately the Manchester Yeomanry appeared, coming from Peter Street. I heard the order to form three deep, and then the Trumpeter led the way and galloped towards the hustings, followed by the Yeomanry.
>
> Whilst this was passing, my attention was called to another movement coming from the opposite side of the meeting. A troop of soldiers, the Fifteenth Hussars, turned round the corner of the house where we stood and galloped forwards amongst the people creating frightful alarm and disorder. The people ran helter-skelter in every direction.
>
> Clouds of dust arose which obscured the view. When it had subsided a startling scene was presented. Numbers of men, women, and children were lying on the ground who had been knocked down and run over by the soldiers. I noticed one woman lying face downwards, apparently lifeless. [See 'Peterloo', *Pandaemonium* pp.146-52]

This disgraceful affair, in which six hundred were killed or wounded, produced the most enormous indignation all over the country.

When the news got to Italy it made Shelley white with anger, but it also filled him with compassion and stirred him into writing almost the only straightforward popular poem he wrote – I mean *The Mask of Anarchy*. He meant it to be read by the whole country and he wrote it almost like a ballad. It begins like this:

> As I lay asleep in Italy
> There came a voice from over the Sea,
> And with great power it forth led me
> To walk in the visions of Poesy.
>
> I met Murder on the way –
> He had a mask like Castlereagh –
> Very smooth he looked, yet grim;
> Seven blood-hounds followed him: [...]
>
> Next came Fraud, and he had on,
> Like Eldon, an ermined gown;
> His big tears, for he wept well,
> Turned to mill-stones as they fell.
>
> And the little children, who
> Round his feet played to and fro,
> Thinking every tear a gem,
> Had their brains knocked out by them.

And then a direct appeal to the people:

> Men of England, heirs of Glory,
> Heroes of unwritten story,
> Nurslings of one mighty Mother,
> Hopes of her, and one another;
>
> Rise like Lions after slumber
> In unvanquishable number,
> Shake your chains to earth like dew
> Which in sleep had fallen on you –
> Ye are many – they are few.
> [See *Pandaemonium* pp.152-5, and *Words For Battle*]

Shelley sent this poem to Leigh Hunt for him to publish it in his magazine. Hunt didn't put it in because, he says, 'I thought that the public at large had not become sufficiently discerning to do justice to the sincerity and kind-heartedness of the spirit that walked in this flaming robe of verse.'

So you see even when the poet tried to get directly in touch with the public, there was an editor there already dividing the crowd into highbrow and lowbrow.

Now I don't want to draw any *general* conclusions from what I've said; I've just tried to present three pictures. First, Shakespeare reaching the public through the characters in his plays; second, Gray working right outside it – scared of it and at the same time writing the most popular poem in the language; and last, Shelley making a rather hopeless attempt to reach *back* to the public, failing to do so, and remaining the specimen of the exiled poet asleep in Italy.

Next week, with the help of a member of the public, I want to try and see where the public stands – because up to now we've been talking mainly about the poet.

Broadcast on the BBC National Programme, 3 May 1938

4 *Understanding Modern Poetry*

A few weeks ago I tried to answer the question, 'How has poetry become highbrow?' This is not the same question as the one I want to ask now – namely, how has it become obscure or difficult? You know you can have poetry which most people would call highbrow (that's to say, remote from the everyday world), but which needn't necessarily be difficult. A good example of this sort of poem is one by Tennyson out of 'The Princess'. It starts off like this:

> The splendour falls on castle walls
>   And snowy summits old in story:
> The long light shakes across the lakes,
>   And the wild cataract leaps in glory.
> Blow, bugle, blow, set the wild echoes flying,
> Blow, bugle; answer, echoes, dying, dying, dying.

[*Deleted:* That poem was written in the 1860s and I quote it because it was at the time of Tennyson that tonight's subject (that's to say 'understanding modern poetry') first became a real problem. I say this because I think that Browning (who lived at exactly the same time as Tennyson) was probably the first English poet who was considered by the reading public to be difficult – obscure and so on.]

Now these lines – 'The splendour falls on castle walls' – aren't, when you come to think of it, very difficult to understand. Some of the phrases are a bit up in the air perhaps – 'The splendour falls' and 'The long light shakes'. But even so, that's the sort of thing that, whether we like it or not, we expect in poetry. That's to say it's highbrow (it belongs to a romantic world like the Middle Ages), but it's not obscure.

But compare Tennyson with Browning, because Browning was probably the first English poet who was considered by the reading public to be obscure. Tennyson we generally think of as the bard with long hair and a black cloak and a big hat, who lived right away from the crowd, a man who wrote about beauty and romance. On the other hand, Browning was (and he said it himself about himself) 'always a fighter'. This being a fighter did not, as one might expect, mean taking a very active part in public life. He was not a politician or a soldier, as well as being a poet, in the way that, say, Byron was. I think the point about Browning is this. He was a poet who regretted seeing that first the novel (Dickens, Thackeray and so on) and then the newspapers were taking away from poetry the excitement of action and hence the poet's touch with his public. And he tried by one method or another (and this, I think, is the point; even though it may sound like rather a quibble) to get some sort of new life into his work, and not let his poems only be about the Middle Ages or only become sing-song.

The first thing he did was to introduce to the general public of poetry readers (of whom there was a considerable number at that period, more of 'em than there are today) the rhythms and words of something like conversation, something like ordinary, middle-class speech. I suppose that this is at its most noticeable in a poem of which even the title itself (however you look at it) is not very romantic: 'Mr Sludge, the Medium'.

'Mr Sludge, the Medium' begins like this:

> "Now, don't Sir! Don't expose me! Just this once:
> "This was the first and only time, I'll swear –
> "Look at me, – see, I kneel – the only time,
> "I swear, I ever cheated – Yes, by the soul
> "Of her who hears – (Your sainted mother, Sir!)
> "All, except this last accident, was truth!"

That was published in 1864. Even to us in 1938, it doesn't sound very much like the rhythms and charms of 'beautiful poetry', does it? But there are other troubles in Browning besides this conversational way of talking. He starts you slap in the middle of the story, and the story itself is not very uplifting.

Instead of having a sort of prologue, such as, 'Once upon a time there was a Mr Sludge, who was a spiritualistic medium', and then going on to tell you that owing to one thing and another he was accused of trying to fake the result of one of his seances – in other words turning the whole thing into a soul's tragedy – instead of that, Browning takes the situation by the scruff of the neck, and starts off with a squeal from Mr Sludge: 'Now, don't Sir! Don't expose me! Just this once.' And Mr Sludge himself, as one gathers even from these few lines, is a slightly vulgar person – not altogether the kind of noble figure which would appear in, shall we say, Lord Tennyson's poetry.

All the odd things that we've noticed about this poem – that's to say, the direct conversational tone, the fact that we don't really know what is going on, and the fact that the persons and actions in the poem are just slightly contemptuous [sic] from the point of view of the upper-middle-class reader – all those things have a reason. And this is the interesting thing: they all have the same reason. They're all there as a kind of protest against the lyrical poetry which we connect (as I said last week) with knights and fair ladies of the Middle Ages – romantic things like castles, bugles, wild cataracts – all of which, of course, have produced extraordinarily beautiful and extraordinarily moving poetry from time to time. But this sort of poetry, Browning, at any rate, felt had become overdone; not merely unusable from the point of view of art, but really and totally out of touch with life and out of touch with the public. That's the point.

Browning wasn't the only person in the nineteenth century to try to get new life into his poetry. Among other people there were Thomas Hardy and Gerard Manley Hopkins. Hopkins's poems were only published in 1918, but they were written in the 1870s and the 1880s. Hopkins, like Browning, has been accused of obscurity, of being difficult to understand. You remember I made a comparison of Tennyson with Browning. Now I'm going to make another comparison, this time between the eighteenth-century poet Cowper and Hopkins.

Perhaps you remember two very simple and very beautiful lines by Cowper, describing the cutting down of a row of poplar trees at Olney, where he lived most of his life. The lines are these: 'The poplars are fell'd, farewell to the shade / And the whispering sound of the cool colonnade.' Now Cowper was eminently a poet who retired from the world and didn't attempt to fight it or to introduce the fights of the world into his poetry. The two lines I've quoted are easy to understand, with a pleasant rhythm and musical vowels ('cool colonnade'); the whole thing is rather soothing, slightly sad.

Among Hopkins's poems there are some lines on a similar subject. The title is 'Binsey Poplars – felled 1879', and they open like this:

> My aspens dear, whose airy cages quelled
> Quelled, or quenched in leaves the leaping sun,
> Are felled, felled; are all felled;

[Text amended]

It's obvious that Hopkins is using the same theme as Cowper (the cutting down of some favourite trees) and he is even using for his central word the same word, 'felled'. And he produces a series of energetic variations (so to speak) on that theme.

We start off quite simply with 'My aspens dear'. But then – 'whose airy cages quelled'. Airy cages! The trees, within five words of being trees, have become *cages*. Why are they, how are they cages? They're cages evidently (if one looks at it very carefully) which are made of the leaves, cages inside which the sun is an animal jumping about ('the leaping sun'). The poplar trees, as the sunlight went through them, seemed to Hopkins to have a sort of movement like a jumping animal inside a cage.

Then, as if that wasn't enough for one gulp, the poet is off on another track: 'Quelled, or quenched in leaves the leaping sun.' Well it's difficult, one feels, to have a cage which quenches or quells. Cages don't quench – water quenches. But, says Hopkins, water quenches fire, and the sun is made of fire, the leaves cage the sun, and the cage quells fire. But we've seen that water also quells fire – it quenches it. So we have the curious statement that leaves quench the sun. Hopkins presents the sunlight in poplar leaves as a battle between an animal and its cage, between fire and water. So we have the lines:

> My aspens dear, whose airy cages quelled,
> Quelled or quenched in leaves the leaping sun,
> Are felled, felled, are all felled;

There's just one other point. What is Hopkins's idea in making all this fuss about sunlight and green leaves? What makes one talk about it as a battle?

It's not because of the sun and the leaves by themselves (that's just a pretty picture), it's because of the contrast between the life of the trees when they were standing and the blankness (the nothingness) of the landscape (and of his feelings) when they're all cut down: 'Are felled, felled, are all felled'. It's the contrast between life and death, and that really is a battle and worth making a fuss about. In presenting this battle it isn't enough for Hopkins simply to say the trees were cut down; it's not enough to say, as Cowper did, that the poplars are felled. No, Hopkins has to say: 'Are felled, felled, are all felled'. Why? Because to cut down those poplars you've got to have the energy of the strokes of the axe, and it's through this queer, nervous use of words that he tries to get the movement of the trees, and the dead weight of the axe into the poem itself. So we have two sorts of energy, the energy of the sun – the 'leaping sun' – representing all the play of Nature on a hot day, and the destroying of that energy by another kind of energy, the blows of the axe.

Now I've quoted these two pieces from Browning and from Hopkins not merely because they're two good examples of the appearance of difficulty and obscurity in poetry in the second half of the nineteenth century, leading up to poetry as it is written today, but because they also represent two different sorts of obscurity or difficulty. In Browning, in 'Mr Sludge, the Medium', the poet, in order to get life into his poem, is using a piece of life itself – a perfectly commonplace, rather grubby sort of incident, and illustrating it and presenting it in, as nearly as possible, ordinary conversational language.

On the other hand we have Hopkins, who is also intensely interested in getting life and energy into his poems, but he is not doing it by dealing with ordinary existence. No person, no peculiar thing, no unpoetic person occurs in his poem. The subject of his poem is the cutting down of a row of poplars, which by itself is an old-fashioned subject. Nor is he attempting to present some peculiar incident: the poplars are simply cut down. Nor is he attempting to use conversational or ordinary, everyday language. His language *is* poetic: 'The leaping sun', 'airy cages' – those taken by themselves are the kind of things we expect in lyrical poetry. They're highbrow but not very obscure. He's trying to put new life into an old-fashioned subject, and he does it by the re-arrangement of ideas and words which by themselves aren't difficult. It's the re-arrangement that makes them difficult, and it's through this re-arrangement that your train of thought is continually being interrupted and held up, and so you find it difficult.

[*Several pages have been deleted here, probably by the producer: the cover page of the script is marked 'Too long cut to 8pp'*]

These two poets were worried simply about how to get more 'life' into their poetry. But (and as I've said before, it's not a quibble) it wasn't the life of the public, not a life that the public could sympathize with or understand, but life simply in the sense of energy, in the sense of making words do a lot of new things that they'd never done before.

Precisely during this last fifty years, so far from making old words do a lot of new things, universal education and newspapers and radio and so have steam-rollered the language out, so as to try to get some one way of speaking and reading and writing which is absolutely understandable from Land's End to John O'Groats.

We have seen that some poets try to get away from old-world poetry like the lyrical poetry of Tennyson, and because they do this they have been called at any one moment 'modern'. But you can't say that means they're close to modern life, because in order to get away from Tennyson they've neglected the very first thing which is absolutely essential for keeping in touch with the public – namely, being intelligible, being understandable.

However there are some ordinary people (very few it must be admitted) who, without being professors or critics, have managed to follow poetry into the jungle of incomprehensibility and who've come back convinced that after all it was really quite worth it. It's with one of these hard-working readers that I hope to discuss 'Understanding Modern Poetry' next week.

Broadcast on the BBC National Programme, 17 May 1938

8   The Poet Laureateship

Now, this business of the Poet Laureateship. Well, I'm not going to worry you by giving a long historical account of all the Poet Laureates who've ever lived. I think it's much more important to get as clear as we can the original idea of what the Poet Laureate was supposed to stand for and then to see how, in fact, that idea works in the modern world.

One of the main ideas behind the Poet Laureateship was very well explained by Sir Philip Sidney, the Elizabethan soldier and poet. He says: 'I think and think (I think) rightly, the laurel crown appointed for triumphing captains, doth worthily (of all other learnings) honour the *poet's* triumph.' What he means is this: in the old times the victorious general was given a crown of laurel as a sign of his victory, and Sidney (who was both a poet and a soldier) points out that the poet for his successes was also given a laurel crown. In other words, we have the poet being crowned just like the conqueror.

Now the other main idea about the Poet Laureateship (which of course everybody knows) is that the Poet Laureate's business has always been to celebrate royal events and special occasions connected with the king. There once was a time when the king led his armies into battle himself, and so he had a chance of coming home and being crowned as the conqueror, and then, presumably, the poet wrote up a special account of the conquest and he, in turn, was crowned for that.

All that's very nice as an idea, but only last week Herbert Read – who was a soldier and a poet in 1918 – was emphatic that modern warfare, whatever Sir Philip Sidney may have said of war in the past, is not very amenable to the poet, nor does the king lead his armies into battle himself today, and hasn't done so for a couple of hundred years. The king became more and more of a private person, and you can follow the same change in poetry.

Let's go back to Sidney for a moment. He says 'The laurel crown appointed for triumphing captains.' Now 'triumphing' didn't just mean 'victorious', it meant a real gala show, with flags and music and prisoners and a crown and a chariot. It was a Show – like a Lord Mayor's Show – and you could have a triumph for any special figure: the triumph of Neptune, or the triumph of Love, for instance. And this triumph stuff was one of the stock-in-trades of the poets at the time of Sidney. Look at the lines of Ben Jonson:

> See the Chariot at hand here of Love,
> Wherein my Lady rideth!
> Each that drawes, is a Swan, or a Dove,
> And well the Carre Love guideth.

> [*Text amended*]

Notice in this poem that it's one person (the poet) talking about one person – the figure of the lady on the chariot. That poem was written at the beginning of the seventeenth century. You'll notice that Jonson is talking about 'my love'; he's not describing Queen Elizabeth or James I whom you might expect to be celebrated in this way. It was with the restoration of the monarchy (that's to say under Charles II and James II) that the Poet Laureate came into his own as a figure. But I think you'll agree that his poetry was not so hot.

I don't suppose you've heard of most of the eighteenth-century Laureates: Theobald, Cibber, a man called Whitehead and a man called Pye – they certainly didn't make a success of it. Now they're just names. Their stock-production was the birthday ode, that is, a piece of poetry intended to rouse the public to enthusiasm on the occasion of the king's birthday. Let's have a look at one of the more passable birthday odes. Here's Colley Cibber's birthday ode for 1723, addressed to George II and Queen Caroline:

> Let there be light:
> Such was at once the word and work of heav'n,
> > When from the void of universal night
> > Free nature sprung to the Creator's sight,
> And day to glad the new-born world was giv'n.

> Succeeding days to ages roll'd,
> And every age some wonder told:
> At length arose this glorious morn!
> > When to extend his bounteous pow'r,
> > High heav'n announced this instant hour
> The best of monarchs shall be born!

Born to protect and bless the land!
And while the laws his people form,
His scepter glories to confirm
    Their wishes are his sole command.

The word that form'd the world
    In vain did make mankind
Unless, his passions to restrain,
    Almighty wisdom had design'd
Sometimes a WILLIAM or a GEORGE should reign.
Yet farther, *Britons*, cast your eyes,
Behold a long succession rise
Of future fair felicities.

Around the royal table spread,
See how the beauteous branches shine!
    Sprung from the fertile genial bed
Of glorious GEORGE and CAROLINE.

So far I've been trying to keep any ideas I may have as to what's good or bad poetry out of this series, but you can't help your feelings creeping in sometimes, and just as I said a few weeks ago that I thought Blake's 'Tiger' a smackingly good poem, so I must say I don't think this ode of Cibber's is a particularly good one. If you ask me why, I can only say that I suppose it's because those people (Cibber, Whitehead and so on) went on writing their poetry precisely about triumphs and chariots and so on as though nothing were happening in the outside world. What was happening in the outside world round about 1732? Well, I'll tell you one thing – there was a boy called Humphrey Potter who was employed on a low-pressure steam engine to open the cocks to let the steam into the cylinder and one morning he had the bright idea of tying the cocks to the moving beam so that they opened themselves automatically. You may think that hadn't got a lot to do with poetry, and Cibber didn't think so either – but that was just the trouble. That little incident was actually part of the Industrial Revolution, and it was the Industrial Revolution that in 1732 was the future for the vast majority of mankind. But look at Cibber's idea of the future:

Yet, farther, *Britons*, cast your eyes
Behold a long succession rise
Of future fair felicities.

That is, the children of George II and Queen Caroline.

You may ask why the Poet Laureate should bother about the public as well as about the king. One very good reason is that it is the public he's trying to rouse to enthusiasm about their king – notice in this poem Cibber appeals to them as 'Britons'. You might also ask why he should be concerned with the future, but Day Lewis was saying only a couple of weeks ago that the poet has always been concerned with prophecy, and this is true whether he's a Laureate or not. [*Deleted:* 'Hear the voice of the bard / Who present past and future sees.']

I've already shown how some poets (Shelley, for example) tried to keep up with the Industrial Revolution once it really got going. And I think it's fair to say that one Poet Laureate at least really had a shot at it. I'm thinking of Tennyson's 'Ode Sung at the Opening of the International Exhibition' of 1851, which incidentally was the culmination of the Industrial Revolution of the eighteenth century.

> ... lo! the long laborious miles
> Of Palace; lo! the giant aisles,
> Rich in model and design;
> Harvest-tool and husbandry,
> Loom and wheel and enginery,
> Secrets of the sullen mine,
> Steel and gold, and corn and wine,
> Fabric rough, or fairy-fine,
> Sunny tokens of the Line,
> Polar marvels, and a feast
> Of wonder, out of West and East.

And so on. If those lines are better than Colley Cibber's – and certainly I think they are – it's entirely because the poet is dealing with a series of things (looms and wheels and mines) which the public really were in contact with. But you'll notice that the people who work all these things aren't mentioned at all.

In fact, we come back to Walt Whitman again; you remember his complaint that there weren't any poets at his time who interested themselves in the mass of the people and in individuals, in their idiosyncrasies and so on. [*Several paragraphs deleted*] I've been complaining through these talks that even the poets since Whitman haven't done anything about this. On the whole I think that's true, but there's a short modern poem written in about 1915 or 1916 I want to read you. It was written by a poet who was at that time American, and who does seem to me to be going the way Whitman [*deleted:* and Henry Ford (also American)] suggested. This poem is by T.S. Eliot, and it's called 'The Boston Evening Transcript'. It goes like this:

The readers of the *Boston Evening Transcript*
Sway in the wind like a field of ripe corn.

When evening quickens faintly in the street,
Wakening the appetites of life in some
And to others bringing the *Boston Evening Transcript*,
I mount the steps and ring the bell, turning
Wearily, as one would turn to nod goodbye to La Rochefoucauld,
If the street were time and he at the end of the street,
And I say, 'Cousin Harriet, here is the *Boston Evening Transcript*.'

Now I don't say that the poem was written for the readers of the *Boston Evening Transcript*. It wasn't. But the poet is at any rate beginning to describe them, to take an interest in them, and when he talks about himself in the poem – I mean the lines: 'I mount the steps and ring the bell...' – he is representing himself as one of the readers instead of a poet aloof from the world with a big hat or a laurel crown. And in the last line – 'And I say, "Cousin Harriet, here is the *Boston Evening Transcript*."' – the *Boston Evening Transcript* (that's to say, just an ordinary newspaper) has taken the place of the swans and the doves drawing Jonson's chariot. In other words, poetry in this poem of Eliot's is beginning to do what I have for weeks and weeks been asking poetry to do – namely, to talk about something fairly ordinary, fairly up-to-date, in a fairly straightforward way.

[*Paragraph deleted*] But somehow the relating of the modern world to royalty or to official occasions seems to have beaten the Laureates so far. [*Paragraph deleted*] Today royalty has not only ceased to lead troops into battle, it has been extraordinarily successful in making itself democratic. It has been able to do this – to appeal in a human way direct to the people – thanks not to poetry but to modern transport (the motor-car particularly), thanks to newspapers (especially picture papers), to radio (the king's own voice), to newsreels and so on. What is the result? I think of one or two things in particular. To me, one of the newsreels of the funeral procession of George V was one of the most moving pieces of film ever: I remember the presentation of the slow movement of the cortège, the eerie effect of the minute guns and the sailor's music, the rain, the *people* – the faces of the people. The film captured in a peculiar way the emotion of the people at this event, and re-presented it *to* the people. Their emotion was the result of a human appeal to them, and the picture was another human appeal.

Why I mention all this is because it shows (1) why I've been insisting on the importance of a Poet Laureate's thinking of the people; (2) because it shows the competition from the cinema, for example, that the Poet

Laureate has to face; (3) because it shows that the direct way of presentation by the camera so far from losing the 'feel' of an occasion like the king's
funeral succeeds in catching it; and that therefore the Poet Laureate
cannot in fact afford to ignore this directness.

Now I don't suggest that the Poet Laureate should write a kind of
newsreel. I suggest what he can do is to make an analysis of this emotion
which the camera photographs, an analysis of the 'feel' of an event like the
Coronation when people sat by their radio sets and suddenly burst into
tears *and didn't know why*, and to make this kind of poetic analysis, I
suggest, he would have to begin somewhere near those lines of Eliot's I've
just quoted: 'When evening quickens faintly in the street, / Wakening the
appetites of life in some' because that is an analysis of *everyday* emotion.
The Poet Laureate's would be an analysis of a special emotion of a special
Day, when the chariot reappears for a short time.

Next week we shall have here a poet who does write for this everyday,
newspaper-reading public, in a newspaper. She is Patience Strong. And I
hope we shall get from her some idea of the effect newspaper writing (if
I may call it that) has on poetry.

Broadcast on the BBC National Programme, 14 June 1938

10   *Poetry and National Life*

I think the simplest thing to begin with, in dealing with this subject of
poetry and national life, is a small piece of poetry from a part of the world
where not simply in the past, as we so often have to say, but *at this very
moment* poetry is definitely a part of national life; where it's never been
considered as a special thing and therefore hasn't had the opportunity of
getting cut away from the public. The part of the world I am thinking
about is the South Seas.

There's a group of islands in the South Seas called the Trobriand
Islands. Now the Trobriand Islanders spend a great deal of their time
cultivating rather exotic gardens, and in doing so they have a series of
magical rituals for promoting the growth of their plants and so on. And
the gardeners, instead of being called Head Gardeners, are called Garden
Magicians. These Garden Magicians aren't merely gardeners and they're
not merely magicians, they're also poets – that's to say, they conduct, they
recite or lead the recitation of traditional incantations which are, in fact,
poems, and which find themselves right in the middle of a very important
part of the national life. This garden ritual is related not merely to making

the plants grow, but also to the ancestors of the Trobriand Islanders. Let
me quote you a passage that's part of the central ritual for making the
plants grow:

> Show the way, show the way.
> Show the way groundwards, into the deep ground.
> Show the way, show the way.
> Show the way firmly, show the way to the firm moorings.
> O grandfathers of the name of Polu, O grandfathers
> of the name of Koleko... and thou, new spirit,
> my grandfather Mwakenuwa, and thou my father Yowana.
>
> The belly of my garden leavens,
> The belly of my garden rises,
> The belly of my garden grows to the size of a bush-hen's nest,
> The belly of my garden rises like the iron-wood palm,
> The belly of my garden lies down,
> The belly of my garden swells,
> The belly of my garden swells as with a child.
> I sweep, I sweep, I sweep away!

Now I think there's no objection to considering that as poetry. But it has
with it – not to make a long analysis – two things. It's poetry in action; it's
poetry which is doing something. It's not in a book (it is in a book now, of
course, but only because an ethnologist – Malinowski – has put it in a
book). And secondly it's dealing with things which are well-known to the
Islanders. It's dealing with the range of the Trobriand Islanders' life, from
the mysteries of ancestor worship on the one side, to the simplest, most
practical business of digging in the ground ('Show the way groundwards')
on the other side. In other words, it fulfils the requisites that we might ask
of poetry at a time when the poet and the public really are in agreement
with each other instead of being divided from each other.

Now the two things that I want to stress in this final talk are just those
two that've turned up in this Trobriand poem. One – bringing practical,
everyday things into poetry, and two – the relating of these simple things
to whatever it is in *our* life that corresponds to the ancestors (the mysteries
of ancestor worship) in the South Seas.

Many talks back I said that if you read the first paragraph of *Gulliver's
Travels* you might think you were off on a real voyage, but the more you
get into the voyage the queerer it becomes. There's another voyage in
English poetry in which very much the same thing happens. I mean the
'Rhyme of the Ancient mariner'. Take the Argument introducing the
whole poem:

> How a ship, having first sailed to the Equator, was driven by Storms
> to the cold Country towards the South Pole; how the Ancient
> Mariner cruelly and in contempt of the laws of hospitality killed a
> Sea-bird and how he was followed by many and strange Judge-
> ments: and in what manner he came back to his own Country.

In both of these voyages it's difficult to say which strikes one most – the
real bits or the queer bits. It really is the way in which out of the real – the
simple, the everyday – bits, the poet manages to extract the queer, the
terrifying, the beautiful. After all the ship itself is a perfectly ordinary
eighteenth-century barque. But listen to this:

> Beyond the shadow of the ship,
> I watched the water-snakes:
> They moved in tracks of shining white,
> And when they reared, the elfish light
> Fell off in hoary flakes.
>
> Within the shadow of the ship
> I watched their rich attire:
> Blue, glossy green, and velvet black,
> They coiled and swam; and every track
> Was a flash of golden fire.

It's out of this flash of fire with the snakes that life comes back to the
Ancient Mariner himself:

> O happy living things! no tongue
> Their beauty might declare:
> A spring of love gushed from my heart,
> And I blessed them unaware:
> Sure my kind saint took pity on me,
> And I blessed them unaware.

Why does the Ancient Mariner 'bless' the water snakes? You will remember he'd killed the albatross and got himself into a sort of mental tangle.
I think he blesses them because the peculiar sight of them hits him in a
vivid way and undoes the tangle. Don't ask me why – it simply does, the
poem says so. Exactly how it happens, of course, is a mystery just as the
way in which the ancestors of the Trobriand Islanders are able to help the
gardeners. The water snakes in Coleridge play the same part as the ancestors in the Trobriand poem.
   But the two poems aren't quite parallel because the Trobriand poem is
about a social ritual (digging in the ground) and the 'Ancient Mariner' is

about a fairy story – something that never happened, doesn't exist. Now does this mean that the 'Ancient Mariner' hasn't a social use? I say quite definitely that it has got a social use. The effect of the 'Ancient Mariner' on its readers is a social action. How is it a social action? Because each reader – let us admit this – finds himself (today particularly) in a mental tangle just as the Ancient Mariner did. We spend a long long time turning it all over and worrying about it. The Ancient Mariner looked over the side of the ship and looked at the water snakes. What we do is to read the poem of the Ancient Mariner and the description of him looking over the side at the water snakes. He follows the track of the snakes and so do we. And when his tangle unties itself that has an effect on us – we feel better for it. Just how or why we feel better for it is another mystery.

The poet is the person who corresponds to the garden magicians in the Trobriand Islands. He is the person who's responsible for seeing that this mystery reaches us, that we're aware of it. This is all the more difficult because whereas the Trobriand Islanders really want their gardens to grow, we're not at all sure that we want to face the mysteries that the poet's discovering.

What's more, there's a practical problem for the reader. It's a problem that doesn't arise for the Trobriand Islanders. You see, at the time when their poem's being recited, they're at work – they're actually digging in a garden. But we're not in that state when we read poetry. We read poetry after work, or instead of work, and so we have a tendency to regard the reading of poetry as a sort of specialized activity. An activity that most people are rather ashamed of, as we saw last week. But I don't think this being ashamed of poetry is just a social trick. I think it's profounder than that; and I think it's because it ties up with what I've already been saying. We've been so much brought up with the idea that with all our science we've conquered nature and grown into adults, and that now there's no necessity for us to indulge in any curious primitive practices such as the Trobriand Islanders talking to their ancestors, or to indulge in the sort of communication with the mysteries of existence that the poet brings up. And so we're ashamed of admitting that there are still bits of life that we don't understand.

I think we can say that it's precisely one of the principal functions of the poet to remind the community of two things. One is not to be so [*several lines deleted*] proud. By pride I don't mean that we're over happy because we can cross the Atlantic in an aeroplane, I mean something that is nearer to our hearts than this. I mean by pride the way in which the industrialization of the world has (so to speak) hardened our hearts. I've brought an admirable letter I've just had from a labouring man that expresses this better than I could: 'Can the large mass of people, who today are more and more dependent on a routine system for a livelihood – can they, being dependent, feel sympathy?'

He says: 'I think they can't. In this dependency for a living, their own fear and anxiety allows of none for their fellow-workers. What I mean is – poetry asks for that warm sympathy that doesn't weigh up the pros and cons of a situation, but sees a human being suffering. But today he must needs consider his dignity, his self-consciousness, his unwillingness to lose face or be different.' The man who wrote this letter speaks about a human being suffering. That's an exact description of the Ancient Mariner. He says that poetry doesn't weight the pros and cons of a situation – so again the Ancient Mariner doesn't bother whether the water snakes are beautiful or ugly, whether he's to catch them or whom they belong to; he just looks at them and loves them.

Now the second of the poet's functions I want to note is that he can remind us that there are still mysteries – we haven't discovered everything – and that these mysteries reside in the humblest everyday things. I mentioned just now that the sailing ship in the 'Ancient Mariner' was at the time of Coleridge a perfectly everyday thing – I say that because we now think of sailing ships as part of romance. You see now why I've been making such a fuss in these talks about the Industrial Revolution, when, for example, sails were gradually replaced by turbines. Because it's the Industrial Revolution that has created this pride in the conquest of nature. So the poet has to start with the thing that's produced this pride – a steamship or a train – and relate that to the unexplored mysteries that I've been suggesting.

In past talks I know I've been complaining that the poet has ignored most of these developments. Yes, but I quoted Shelley at the beginning of the nineteenth century as at least keeping his eye on them and I think that Thomas Hardy at the end of the century did so too. I'm thinking of a poem of his called 'Midnight on the Great Western'. It starts like this:

> In the third-class seat sat the journeying boy,
>   And the roof-lamp's oily flame
> Played down on his listless form and face,
> Bewrapt past knowing to what he was going,
>   Or whence he came.
>
> In the band of his hat the journeying boy
>   Had a ticket stuck; and a string
> Around his neck bore the key of his box,
> That twinkled gleams of the lamp's sad beams
>   Like a living thing.

Now there I think you have the joining of an everyday thing – a small boy in a railway train – with just that queer twist which reveals mysteries and questionings about human destiny ('Bewrapt past knowing to what he was going / Or whence he came'). Look at the way in which the key of the child's box hangs round his neck, and the light of the lamp on it 'gleams' (Hardy says) 'like a living thing'. Isn't that exactly like one of the lines I quoted from the 'Ancient Mariner'?

> They coiled and swam; and every track
> Was a flash of golden fire.

> O happy living things!...

This idea of the juxtaposition of very ordinary things with something mysterious turns up again nearer to us in a passage of T.S. Eliot's in *The Waste Land*. I'm sorry I can't read some of the poem to you, but the word that I'm thinking of is the word 'inexplicable' – 'inexplicable splendour', he says. He uses this image to describe the inside of one of Christopher Wren's city churches near the Thames. The poet pictures himself just outside a pub in Lower Thames Street with the usual noise of the bar and the melancholy sound of a mandolin playing. These are the part of life which is explicable – the rational, everyday part of life which we think we have complete control over. But then the poet brings up the 'inexplicable splendour' of the church – the inexplicable part of life, those parts which we have no control over.

I don't think Eliot brings in the church only because he happens to like the decoration. No! As compared with the modern part of the City – the industrial buildings, the banks, the wharves – Wren's churches are sort of ancestors, and Eliot's known attachment to them is really a kind of ancestor worship. For example when he's talking about the Thames with its barges and its oil, he suddenly brings in Queen Elizabeth and Leicester sailing down it in a state barge. I think you'll find again and again in *The Waste Land* he's talking about figures and monuments from the past in just the way that the Trobriand Island poet invokes his ancestors ('O grandfathers of the name of Polu, O grandfathers of the name of Koleko'). But just as the Trobriand Islander invokes his ancestors as part of his digging in the garden, so the bits of the past that turn up in *The Waste Land* are necessary to give the present its meaning. You see, however industrialized we may be, we have ancestors whether we like them or not, and how they come in here is best expressed by the French poet, Apollinaire, who said that unlike other men he didn't stand with his back to the past and face the future; on the contrary, he stood with his back to the future, because he was unable to see it, and with his face to the past, because it was in the past that he could discover who he was and how he had come to be him.

That idea of extracting an idea of 'what I am' from the past is a thing that the poet does for himself and especially it is a thing that he can do for the community; I mean he can try and tell them who they are. Now he can't tell the community who they are unless he does two things: unless he talks about the things that the community knows about, the things that they're interested in, and unless he also looks on the community's past – at the figures, the monuments, the achievements, the defeats, or whatever it may be, that have made the community what it is.

In order for the poet to be able to write this kind of poetry, and in order for the community to be able to accept it, it isn't enough for it to be in terms that both poet and community agree on. There must be something added to that, but something which is not so easily definable (I'm thinking of the 'warmth' that was mentioned in my labourer's letter). In Eliot's case it's the love of a certain place. I don't mean patriotism, because patriotism weighs the pros and cons; I mean simply the love of this poet for two completely different sides of a place like London – the pub side of it and the classical (the City church) side of it. You see it's on a love of, a passion-ate attachment to the things round us, both the easy things and the inexplicable things, that poetry depends. It depends on it because this warmth, this attachment, is the only medium through which we can really get near either to things or to people; everything else is snobbery.

So far in these talks we've had various recommendations as to how the poet and the public are to come together – for example, that we should have a special sort of social movement to do it, that we must slip poetry over through a special medium of entertainment. Personally I think that it's with the poet himself that the answer lies. These two sides of life that I've been talking about – the mysteries and the everyday – simply repre-sent the poet and the public. I've already said that the poet is the person who is in touch with mysteries, mysteries like the Trobriand Islanders' ancestors; well, the bar in Lower Thames Street is part of the life of 'the public'.

If you look at The Waste Land again you'll see that Eliot relates the bits of London's past (our ancestors) to the bar in Lower Thames Street – that is the social use of poetry, and to me that is relating poetry to the public. In other words, the poet and the public can only be related by poetry – and that's why I say it's up to the poet.

Broadcast on the BBC National Programme, 28 June 1938

Science Review No. 10

A hundred years ago a Scotsman called James Nasmyth invented the steam-hammer. To show the importance of the steam-hammer to the engineering world, here is a short passage from an engineering paper in the 1860s: 'It is not too much to say that without Nasmyth's steam-hammer we must have stopped short in many of those gigantic engineering works which but for the decay of all wonder in us, would be the perpetual wonder of the age, and would have enabled our modern engineers to take rank above the gods of all mythologies'. But the history of Nasmyth shows that nineteenth-century engineering and the 'gods of all mythologies' weren't necessarily so far separated as that.

According to Nasmyth, his name had a peculiar origin. Some time during the Middle Ages one of his ancestors was fleeing a party of Douglases and ran into a smithy where he persuaded the smith to disguise him. But when one of the Douglases came into the smithy to look round, the disguised hammer-man was so agitated that he struck a false blow with his hammer and broke the shaft in two. The Douglas man spotted him and said to him 'You're nae smith'. But in the end the Douglases were beaten and the family took over the name of Nasmyth with armorial bearings consisting of a dagger and two broken hammer shafts to remind them of the incident. And the family motto was 'Non arte sed marte' – 'not by art but by war'. After James Nasmyth had invented the steam hammer he had this motto altered to 'Not by war but by art', and instead of the two broken hammer shafts he put the steam-hammer itself, which he described as the 'most potent form of mechanical art'. Here begins a series of connections between art and war and art and science in this man's life. His father was a well-known Scots landscape painter, and when James was only a child, his mechanical turn of mind was already well developed and he invented machines for grinding his father's paints. Later, when he was looking for work as an engineer, he journeyed on foot across the Black Country and in a description of this journey he says: 'The grass had been parched and killed by the vapours of sulphurious acid thrown out by the chimneys and every herbaceous object was of a ghastly grey, the emblem of vegetable death in its saddest aspect. Vulcan had driven out Ceres'. Today, steel works in the North are still called by classical names: Atlas works, Hecla works, Vulcan works, after mythological engineering.

By the 1840s Nasmyth had become extremely successful as an engineer and inventor; and he built a foundry for himself near Manchester (called the Bridgewater Foundry) for making steam-hammers and other inventions of his. The steam-hammer was taken up abroad first of all by the Creusot Armament Works in France, then by Woolwich Arsenal in this

country, and then by the Kronstadt Arsenal in Russia. With this foreign
business of his, Nasmyth made a series of tours abroad to keep an eye on
what was being done with his patents. Returning from Russia he stopped
at old Uppsala in Sweden: 'I went down', he says, 'into a cottage near the
tumuli and drank a bumper of mead to the memory of Thor from a very
antique wooden vessel. I made a special reverential obeisance to Thor,
because I had a great respect for him as being the great hammer-man and
one of our own craft – the Scandinavian Vulcan'.

Then on a tour to Egypt he stopped at Naples and visited Vesuvius.
Here he performed another ritual of homage, which he describes like this:
'I went down to the very edge of the crater, stood close to its mouth, and
watched the intermittent belching of the blasts of vapour of sulphurious
gases. I rolled as big a mass of cool lava as I could to the edge of the crater
and heaved it down, but I heard no sound. . . . On leaving this horrible pit
edge I tied the card of the Bridgewater Foundry to a bit of lava and threw
it in as a token of respectful civility to Vulcan, the head of our craft'.

At Manchester he lived in a house called 'Fireside', where he built himself a telescope and spent much of his leisure looking at the moon. Here
is part of his description:

> While earnestly studying the details of the moon's surface, it was a
> source of great additional interest to me to endeavour to realise in
> the mind's eye the possible *landscape effect* of their marvellous
> elevations and depressions. Here my artistic faculty came into
> operation. I endeavoured to illustrate the landscape scenery of the
> Moon, in like manner as we illustrate the landscape scenery of the
> Earth. The telescope revealed to me distinctly the volcanoes, the
> craters, the cracks, the projections, the hollows – in short, the light
> and shade of the moon's surface. One of the most prominent con-
> ditions of the awful grandeur of lunar scenery is the brilliant light of
> the sun, far transcending that which we experience upon the earth.
> It is enhanced by the contrast with the jet-black background of the
> lunar heavens – the result of the total absence of atmosphere. One
> portion of the moon, on which the sun is shining, is brilliantly
> illuminated, while all in shade is dark. While the disc of the sun
> appears a vast electric light of overpowering rayless brilliancy, every
> star and planet in the black vault of the lunar heavens is shining with
> *steady* brightness at all times; as, whether the Sun be present or
> absent during the long fourteen days' length of the lunar day or
> night, no difference on the absolutely black aspect of the lunar
> heavens will appear.

I suspect that the moon to him was a sort of endless Black Country.

Nasmyth believed that industrial strikes were at least beneficial in one way – they stimulated invention to take the place of man. At the same time as this astronomical work he produced a series of etchings – one a picture of Manchester called 'City of St Annes', another called 'The Fairies' – a sort of Barriesque idyll of little people crowding round a huge fireplace and peering into the fire – and another called 'Everybody for Ever!' which was shown at a Pall Mall art gallery in an exhibition of which the proceeds went to help the unemployed cotton workers in Lancashire.

It looks as though the Nasmyths, in putting the words 'art and war' into their motto, were remarkably prescient at least about James Nasmyth. In his history, as in the history of Leonardo, we see the crossing of the two currents of science and of art. But that altering of the family motto to 'Not by war but by art' doesn't, when you come to think of it, seem to have been so well upheld by the man responsible for the steam-hammers of the Creusot Factory, of Woolwich, and of Kronstadt. So the next time you see a news-reel of the launching of a battleship, think for a moment of James Nasmyth – the man who sat at the edge of the crater of Vesuvius and threw in the visiting card of the Bridgewater Foundry.

Broadcast on the BBC National Programme, May 1939;
published, with a few alterations, as 'Homage to Vulcan'
in *The Listener*, 8 June 1939

'Pourquoi j'aime la France'

Il y a 120 ans, a peu près, une dictature dans la peinture francaise donnait naissance à la question-slogan suivante: 'Qui nous délivra des Grecs et des Romains?' Question étrange et a laquelle la réponse était assez imprévue: 'Qui nous délivra des Grecs et des Romains?' – 'Les Anglais.'

Oui, il y avait un moment òu les yeux de quelques romantiques – de Géricault, de Delacroix – se tournaient vers nos côtes. En particulier Géricault venait ici où il dessinait les courses à Epsom et la vie quotidienne dans les rues de Londres que devait célébrer plus tard Gustave Doré. Et la peinture anglaise – la peinture de moeurs de Hogarth, les paysages de Constable, les marines de Turner – influencait profondément les Français soit à Londres, soit dans les salons de Paris.

Qu'apportait l'Angleterre en effet? Mais un grand souffle d'air frais aux ateliers trop opprimés d'idées périmées de dieux classiques: une lumière nouvelle – la lumiere du soleil, du jour lui-même: le réalisme: l'amour des objets, des êtres tels qu'ils sont dans la vie, dans la rue: le sens du bien-être. Et c'est [*illegible*] ce réalisme anglais qu'est né le réalisme français de Daumier, de Courbet, de 1848.

Après ça la peinture francaise n'avait plus besoin d'apport anglais. Au contraire Londres et nos grands quartiers industriels sombraient de plus en plus dans les brumes et les brouillards.

Mais en France cette lumière nouvellement acquise produisait, après le réalisme, l'impressionisme et la peinture de la joie de vivre de Renoir: elle saisit l'opportunité de fixer sur toile la grande vie populaire.

Pour moi c'est à cette époque-lá – pendant les vingt dernières annés du 19ième que la vie française s'est exprimée plus que jamais dans les arts: ou tout ce qu'ici nous aimons dans la France, sol, soleil, vigne, se concretisait pour toujours: et la femme francaise incarnait la beauté du siècle.

Renoir, Monet, Seurat, le douanier Rousseau, nous rendaient tout ce qu'ils nous avaient emprunté, et avec intérêt.

Et maintenant que nous voici tous opprimés par le blackout (obscurité) et les brouillards de guerre – c'est à la peinture française que je fais appel. Images de Paris – cité de la lumière – images du Midi, visages d'enfants aux temps de cérises, images des objets les plus humbles, les plus essentiels – bouts de pain, couteaux, verres de vin – jamais les Allemands ne sauraient les detruire, tels qu'ils sont sur nos murs dans nos coeurs.

Ailleurs, comme on sait, les Nazis ont tout fait pour anéantir tout ce qui est vivant, créateur, joyeux, dans la peinture, comme dans les autres domaines de la vie. Je suis persuadé qu'ils ne réussiront pas à detruire ce qui constitue une des plus grandes gloires de la France – sa peinture: parce qu'il ne faut pas que ça arrive: il ne faut pas qu'on laisse porter atteinte à la culture française.

Souvenez-vous la France a toujour été un foyer international de la culture. C'est pour ça que j'aime le France, et que je ne peux qu'attendre le jour où nous serions tous libres de retrouver les choses que maintenant je ne goût qu'en image.

Broadcast on the BBC French Service, 23 February 1941

Selected Poems

REPORTS

1

He was then resident, and afterwards envoy extraordinary at the Court of Tuscany. Music, painting, and statuary occupied him chiefly, and his unpublished catalogues, not less strikingly than his copious printed notes, show the care and assiduity of his research. In the mountains of Calabria, where Salvator painted, the chestnut flourished. There he studied it in all its forms, breaking and disposing it in a thousand beautiful shapes, as the exigencies of his composition required. We find it nearly always forming a prominent feature in his bold and rugged landscapes, many of his most striking scenes being drawn from the wild haunts and natural fastnesses of that romantic country, wherein he passed so many of his youthful days. 1934

2

The front windows on the ground floor were entirely closed with inside shutters and the premises appeared as if altogether deserted. In a minute the front door was opened and Mr. Kellerman presented himself. His manner was extremely polite and graceful. His complexion was deeply sallow and his eyes large, black and rolling. He conducted me into a parlour with a window looking backward, and having locked the door and put the key in his pocket he desired me to be seated. The floor was covered with retorts, crucibles, alembics, bottles in various sizes, intermingled with old books piled one upon another. In a corner, somewhat shaded from the light, I beheld two heads, and entertained no doubt that among other fancies he was engaged in remaking the brazen speaking head of Roger Bacon and Albertus. 1935

3

When the horse is impassioned with love, desire, or appetite, he shows his teeth, twinkles his coloured eyes, and seems to laugh.

He shows them also when he is angry and would bite; and volumes of smoke come from his ears.

He sometimes puts out his tongue to lick. His mouth consists of the two rays of the eternal twins, cool as a sea breeze.

1936

Contemporary Poetry and Prose No. 1, June 1936

THREE REPORTS

1

The conditions for this race, the most important of the Classic races for three-year-old fillies, were ideal, for the weather was fine and cool. About one o'clock the Aurora again appeared over the hills in a south direction presenting a brilliant mass of light. Once again Captain Allison made a perfect start, for the field was sent away well for the first time that they approached the tapes. It was always evident that the most attenuated light of the Aurora sensibly dimmed the stars, like a thin veil drawn over them. We frequently listened for any sound proceeding from this phenomenon, but never heard any.   1935

2   (From a long narrative)

The race-course is a tract of ground extending to the distance of four miles over a spacious and level meadow, covered with short grass and marked out by tall wooden posts, painted white. These are continued the whole way, placed at regular intervals from one another; the last is distinguished by a flag mounted upon it, to designate the termination of the course. The horses intended for this exercise in order to render them the more swift are kept always girt that their bellies may not drop; and when the time of the races draws near they feed them with the greatest care and very sparingly, giving them, for the most part, beverages composed of soaked bread and fresh eggs. Two horses only started on this occasion. They left Newmarket saddled in a simple and light manner led by the hand and at a slow pace by the men who were to ride them, dressed in taffeta of different colours, that of Howard being white, and that of Eliot green. When they reached the place where they were to start, they mounted, and loosening the reins, let the horses go, keeping them in at the beginning, that they might not be too eager at first setting off, and their strength fail them in consequence at the most important part of the race. And the more they advanced in the course, the more they urged them, forcing them to continue at full speed to the goal, where trumpets and drums, which were in readiness for that purpose, sounded in applause of the conqueror.

But whosoever imagines that the victories and praises of the conquerors are the proper subjects of the Odes inscribed to them will find himself mistaken. These victories indeed gave occasion to these songs and are therefore taken notice of by the poet, but as such circumstances could scarcely furnish out matter for an Ode of any length, so would it have been an indecency unknown to the civil equality and freedom as well as to the simplicity of the age, to have filled a poem intended to be sung in public and even at the altars of the Gods, with the praises of one man only:

'Il avait la passion des chevaux: les aima comme des incarnations de mouvement, de force, et d'élégance. Il les élut pour porteurs et messagers favoris de ses rêves. Il fit le cheval femme et le cheval fée.'

The flower-laden horse that figured in this ceremony was the symbol of the Divine Mind or Reason, and resolves itself into the light of EK HU – the great mind, soul, or spirit.

When the king returned into the castle, the company soon dispersed; the setting sun also was rapidly withdrawing its rays and the face of nature was about to be enveloped in the shades of darkness.   1935-36

3   THE FUNERAL OF A NOBLEMAN

This nobleman's career may be likened to a wintry sun, which shines between storms and sets suddenly in gloom.

The apartment in which he expired is distinguished by an awning in front of the window.

It was a delightful sunny day. The enthusiasm was immense. At Parkside the engines stopped to take water. Mr. Huskisson having got down from his carriage, the Duke beckoned him to his side and they were just shaking hands when a cry went up from the horrified spectators who perceived that the body was that of Lord Byron being carried to Newstead. Reason never recovered from the hideous coincidence. The journey was completed amidst a deluge of hostile rain and thunder, missiles being hurled at the coach in which the Duke was riding.

From the tomb seawards may be seen Brighton afar off. Worthing nearer, and closer in, in the valley, the village of Salvington.   1936

Contemporary Poetry and Prose No. 4/5, August/September 1936

REPORT ON THE INDUSTRIAL REVOLUTION

The material transformer of the world had just been born. It was trotted out in its skeleton, to the music of a mineral train from the black country, with heart and lungs and muscles exposed to view in complex hideosity. It once ranged wild in the marshy forests of the Netherlands, where the electrical phenomenon and the pale blue eyes connected it with apparitions, demons, wizards and divinities.

Contemporary Poetry and Prose No. 10, Spring 1937

THE BOYHOOD OF BYRON

The labours of the antiquary, the verbal critic, the collator of mouldering manuscripts, may be preparing the way for the achievements of some splendid genius, who may combine their minute details into a magnificent system, or evolve from a multitude of particulars some general principle destined to illuminate the career of future ages.

Observe the horses of Spanish America, that live wild; their gait, their running, their leaping, seem neither constrained nor regular. Proud of their independence, they wander about in immense meads, where they feed on the fresh productions of eternal spring.

Can we suppose that so gifted a race as the Greeks remained insensible to the forest-crowned cliffs and the deep-indented shores of the moving Mediterranean? Landscape however appears among them as the background of a picture of human passions. Thus Oedipus approaching the grove of the Eumenides, the nightingale loves to tarry, and the repose of Nature heightens the pain called forth by the blind image.

The Aberdonian epoch of Lord Byron's life spans the black stream with a single arch just where it falls down from a narrow defile overhung with trees:

'The awful proverb made me pause to cross, and yet lean over with a childish wonder, being a wife's one son, and a mare's ae foal.'

It is certain that one of the poet's feet was, either at birth or at an early period, so seriously clubbed or twisted as to affect his gait.

Creeping still further down he came into what seemed a subterranean hall, arched as it were with cupolas of crystal, divided into aisles by columns of glittering spar – in some parts spread into wide chambers, in others terminated by the dark mouths of deep abysses receding into the interior. The huge locomotive, the more gigantic for being under cover, was already quivering with that artificial life which rendered it so useful and so powerful a servant. Its brasses shone with golden lustre, its iron cranks and pistons glittered with a silvery sheen, while the oblong pit over which it stood glowed with the light of its intense furnace.

If we shut ourselves up in a perfectly dark room, if the sea-water be slashed with an oar in the darkest night, through the window-shutter which intercepts the illuminated landscape from the internal dark chamber, an inverted cone of light will enter the apartment, and depict on the white wall opposite a living representation of external objects:

'The slavery of these creatures is universal. They are never wholly free from their bonds: the flying white breath of education, the coals which are its oats, the unvarying pace between rocky walls, already covered with moss and grasses.'   1936-38

Contemporary Poetry and Prose No. 8, December 1936;
This text from *London Bulletin* No. 12, April 1939

PROSE POEM

As the sun declined the snow at our feet reflected the most delicate peach-blossom.

As it sank the peaks to the right assumed more definite, darker and more gigantic forms.

The hat was over the forehead, the mouth and chin buried in the brown velvet collar of the greatcoat. I looked at him wondering if my grandfather's eyes had been like those.

While the luminary was vanishing the horizon glowed like copper from a smelting furnace.

When it had disappeared the ragged edges of the mist shone like the inequalities of a volcano.

Down goes the window and out go the old gentleman's head and shoulders, and there they stay for I suppose nearly nine minutes.

Such a sight, such a chaos of elemental and artificial lights I never saw nor expect to see. In some pictures I have recognized similar effects. Such are *The Fleeting House of Ice* and *The Fire* which we fear to touch.

1937

London Bulletin No. 2, May 1938

TWO AMERICAN POEMS

The hills are like the open downs of England – the peaceful herds upon the grassy slopes, the broken sea-washed cliffs, the beach with ever-tumbling surf, the wrecks that strew the shore in pitiful reminder, the crisp air from the sea, the long superb stretch of blue waters – the Grave-yard.

*

As we journey up the valley
Of the Connecticut
The swift thought of the locomotive
Recovers the old footprints.

1938

London Bulletin No. 11, March 1939;
reprinted with corrections, No. 12, April 1939

TWO AMERICAN POEMS

I

The Procession

Let us in imagination turn our faces westward

The green cars of the Union line running out Ninth Street
The red cars of the Second running out Third Street
The yellow cars of the Eastern Penitentiary
The white marble of the pure Methodist
The rich brown of the First Baptist
The splendid Episcopal church of the Incarnation
The pioneers of the piano business
The pleasant spots in which repose the dead of this great city.

[May 1939]

II

'Were You Disappointed in the First View of Niagara?'

This love of the gigantesque reminded me of the earlier stages of art, where inferior persons are represented as pigmies –
Niagara! fearful word, ominous and overwhelming:
We lie down at night, we wake in the morning, and still we are rushing on.

[Autumn 1939]

AUTUMN 1939

A derelict cart with dead grass entwined in its great wheels: plants and grasses which had climbed up in the spring-time and been upheld by the spokes, flowered in the summer and now died in October. The cart unmoved all the year round – the wheels unmoved and unmoving – lit and unlit with the daily light of the great sun....

SUMMER 1940

Along plain streets of working-class houses, where industrial Lancashire veils her deepest wishes and untold regrets, pours the level sunlight of an evening in August. For an hour the hard edges of the mill-tied town alter and begin to open like a rose. The deformed become sculpture, and the Gods themselves, whose eyes have for so long peered out of letter-boxes, come out in the street again and reveal themselves to Man.

A PICTURE IN THE VICTORIA AND ALBERT MUSEUM

On the left side of the picture the corn has been cut and lies low in the sun. Up the path in the cornfield comes a woman in blue with a blue parasol. Behind her stretches the chalk-blue sea. On the other side of the path where the corn is in stooks sits another woman in blue and behind her the white cliffs of the Isle of Wight.

What minutiae of music lie in the blue of the breathless channel, in the dazzlingly white fossil fish, in the depths of the yellow corn, on the cheeks of the woman under the blue parasol, in the heart of the woman under the shadow of noon!

[July 1940]

I SEE LONDON

I

I see London

I see the dome of Saint Paul's like the forehead of Darwin

I see London stretching away North and North-East, along dockside roads and balloon-haunted allotments

Where the black plumes of the horses precede and the white helmets of the rescue-squad follow.

I see London

I see the grey waters of Thames, like a loving nurse, unchanged, unruffled, flooding between bridges and washing up wharf steps – an endlessly flowing eternity that smooths away the sorrows of beautiful churches – the pains of time – the wrecks of artistry along her divine banks – to whom the strongest towers are but a moment's mark and the deepest-cleaving bomb an untold regret.

II

I see London at night.

I look up in the moon and see the visible moving vapour-trails of invisible night-fliers

I see a luminous glow beyond Covent Garden

I see in mind's eye the statue of Charles the First riding in double darkness of night and corrugated iron

On the corrugated iron I see wreaths of fresh flowers

I see the black-helmeted night and the blue-helmeted morning

I see the rise of the red-helmeted sun

And at last, at the end of Gerrard Street, I see the white-helmeted day, like a rescue man, searching out of the bottomless dust the secrets of another life.

[March-April 1941]

III

I see a thousand strange sights in the streets of London

I see the clock on Bow Church burning in daytime

I see a one-legged man crossing the fire on crutches

I see three negroes and a woman with white face-powder reading music at half-past three in the morning

I see an ambulance girl with her arms full of roses

I see the burnt drums of the Philharmonic

I see the green leaves of Lincolnshire carried through London on the wrecked body of an aircraft.

[May 1941]

WAR AND CHILDHOOD

I remember as a child by the ferry watching the soldiers testing horses for France. Farm-horses – chasing them naked down to the river while the men on the banks hallooed and shot off guns in the air. I remember the Scots fisher-girls on Blackshore gutting the herring and singing in Gaelic. Scaly hands running in fish-blood, the last vessel dropping her sail at the pier's end, the last fish kicking the net. But to-day there is nothing – nothing of the girls or the boats or the nets or the songs or even the fishmarket itself. Utterly gone – only the wind and broken glass and rough tiles made smooth by the sea. Only still visions of bloodshot eyes brimming over with fear. Nothing. War. Childhood.

[1943]

AS THE SIRENS 1944

As the sirens were sounding
The children were singing
'Run along, little Tishy, run along!'
As the sirens were sounding
The eyes were brimming
Wind on water breathing
Heart stirring and leaf lilting
As the sirens were sounding.
And across Bedford Square
A woman was walking
In black cloak and black bonnet
And black scarf blowing
As the sirens were sounding.
And by Camden
A man was marching
A London street-barrow
Not cauliflowers calling
Or fine French beans
Or spuds nice and brown
But on the bare barrow
Funeral wreaths with tender inscriptions

Marching them along
As the sirens were sounding
And the eyes were brimming
And the children in the street singing
'Run along little Tishy, run along!'

[rewritten 1947]

WALES IN SNOW

Have you seen snow in Wales?
I don't mean on the hills or farms
Or photographs of Snowdon.
I mean on Dowlais Top and the Merthyr Road –
I mean the shift that went down in starlight and worked
in the darkness and came up in the pale fleece of the afternoon.
I mean this man with thumbs in his belt and jack in his
pocket, and grey mac blowing.
With the black earth on his face and the white sky on his
boots.
With only his teeth and eyes whiter than Wales in
Snow.

[1948]

THE PLOUGH

The gallows, the vine, the gang, the beet, the subsoil, the
hoe,
The Norfolk wheel,
Whether in Tull's tune-book, Jefferson's design, on the
Illinois prairie or pagoda ground,
All, all I see reflected in the giant shadow plough;
The gallows coloured green, the vine coloured red, the
gang-plough lemon yellow, sombre purples and browns,
And the Norfolk wheel itself deep blue, standing alone
in the snow.

[1948]

AS I LOOK

As I look out of the window on the roofscape of smoke
The factory chimneys standing up as rocks stand in the sea
The glistening slates lying along what would be the shore
As I look into the mist and let my vision dive
    (As Corot in Campagna when the sun descended mixed
    the paints together)
I perceive in the grey picture all the colours that were once there
Not only the simple divisions of the prism
Brilliant orange iron ore peacock coloured coal
I perceive also the hues of the men who built the city
The quarrymen cutting the slate, the furnace men, men under-
    ground, men felling timber
Each a brain, a peculiar skill, a knot of passions, breathing being,
    living soul
Each slate in its place, every one put there by a man
The smoke itself which swirls and settles like flakes of snow
All got out of the earth under the earth by men
And all this work coloured with men's blood men's ideas men's
    fancies and regrets
Coloured with love friendships hates unspoken wishes outspoken
    words
And now like the sea each individual wave individual work
Washes and mixes in with the rest
And the exact day fades and the exact man
Yet to the mind's eye that looks out this evening and dives into
    the depths
Every single colour is still there nothing lost
Not one of the things done not one man whose cunning produced
    the littlest part of what I see in the whole
But is represented by some stroke of brush flake of snow speck
    of soot
In a picture of how many million touches.

                                [1949]

Filmography

1934:

Post Haste
GPO Film Unit
Producer: John Grierson
Director: Humphrey Jennings
Length: 10 minutes

Pett and Pott
GPO Film Unit
Producer: John Grierson
Director/Script/Writer/Editor:
    A. Cavalcanti
Associate Directors:
    Basil Wright, Stuart Legg
Sets: Humphrey Jennings
Sound recording: John Cox
Music: Walter Leigh
Length: 33 minutes

Locomotives
GPO Film Unit
Director: Humphrey Jennings
Musical Direction: John Foulds
Music: Schubert, arr. Foulds
Length: 10 minutes

The Story of the Wheel
GPO Film Unit
Editor: Humphrey Jennings
Length: 12 minutes

1936:

The Birth of the Robot
Shell-Mex BP
Gasparcolor
Producer/director: Len Lye
Script: C.H. David
Photography: Alex Strasser
Colour decor and production:
    Humphrey Jennings

Models: John Banting,
    Alan Fanner
Sound recording: Jack Ellit
Music: Gustav Holst
Length: 7 minutes

1938:

Penny Journey
GPO Film Unit
Director: Humphrey Jennings
Photography: H.E. (Chick) Fowle,
    W.B. Pollard
Length: 8 minutes

Design for Spring
Distributor: ABFD
Dufaycolor
Director: Humphrey Jennings
Length: 20 minutes
Made with the dress designer
    Norman Hartnell

Speaking from America
GPO Film Unit
Producer: A. Cavalcanti
Director: Humphrey Jennings
Photography: W.B. Pollard,
    Fred Gamage
Commentator: Robin Duff
Diagrams: J. Chambers
Sound: Ken Cameron
Length: 10 minutes

1939:

Spare Time
(Working title: *British Workers*)
GPO Film Unit
Producer: A. Cavalcanti

Director/Scriptwriter:
    Humphrey Jennings
Assistant Director: D.V. Knight
Photography: Chick Fowle
Commentator: Laurie Lee
Sound: Yorke Scarlett
Music: Steel, Peach and Tozer
    Phoenix Works Band,
    Manchester Victorians'
    Carnival Band,
    Handel Male Voice Choir
Length: 18 minutes

The First Days
(Alternative title:
A City Prepares)
GPO Film Unit/ABPC
Producer: A. Cavalcanti
Directors: Humphrey Jennings,
    Harry Watt, Pat Jackson
Editor: R.Q. McNaughton
Commentary: Robert Sinclair
Length: 23 minutes

English Harvest
Dufaycolor
Director: Humphrey Jennings
Length: 9 minutes

S.S. Ionian
(Alternative title: *Her Last Trip*)
GPO Film Unit
Director: Humphrey Jennings
Length: 20 minutes

1940:

Spring Offensive
(Alternative title:
An Unrecorded Victory)
GPO Film Unit
Producer: A. Cavalcanti
Director: Humphrey Jennings

Photography: Chick Fowle,
    Eric Cross
Script: Hugh Gray
Writer of Commentary: A.G. Street
Designer: Edward Carrick
Editor: Geoff Foot
Sound: Ken Cameron
Length: 20 minutes

Welfare of the Workers
GPO Film Unit for
    the Ministry of Information
Producer: Harry Watt
Director: Humphrey Jennings
Photography: Jonah Jones
Editor: Jack Lee
Sound: Ken Cameron
Commentary: Ritchie Calder
Length: 10 minutes

London Can Take It
(Alternative title of shorter film
for domestic distribution:
Britain Can Take It)
GPO Film Unit for
    Ministry of Information
Directors: Humphrey Jennings/
    Harry Watt
Photography: Jonah Jones,
    Chick Fowle
Commentary: Quentin Reynolds
Length: 10 minutes

1941:

Heart of Britain
(Alternative title of
slightly longer export version:
This is England
Eire title: *Undaunted*)
Production: Ian Dalrymple for
    Ministry of Information

Director: Humphrey Jennings
Photography: Chick Fowle
Editor: Stewart McAllister
Sound: Ken Cameron
Commentary: Jack Holmes
Length: 9 minutes

Words for Battle
Production: Ian Dalrymple for
    Crown Film Unit
Director: Humphrey Jennings
Editor: Stewart McAllister
Sound: Ken Cameron
Commentary spoken by:
    Laurence Olivier
Length: 8 minutes

1942:

Listen to Britain
Production: Ian Dalrymple for
    Crown Film Unit
Directed and Edited:
    Humphrey Jennings/
    Stewart McAllister
Photography: Chick Fowle
Sound: Ken Cameron
Length: 20 minutes

1943:

Fires Were Started
(Alternative Title:
    I Was a Fireman)
Production: Ian Dalrymple for
    Crown Film Unit
Director/Script:
    Humphrey Jennings
Photography:
    C. Pennington-Richards
Editor: Stewart McAllister

Story collaboration:
    Maurice Richardson
Music: William Alwyn
Length: 80 minutes

The Silent Village
Production: Humphrey Jennings
    for Crown Film Unit
Director/Script:
    Humphrey Jennings
Photography: Chick Fowle
Editor: Stewart McAllister
Sound: Jock May
Length: 36 minutes

1944:

The True Story of Lili Marlene
Production: J.B. Holmes for
    Crown Film Unit
Director/Script:
    Humphrey Jennings
Photography: Chick Fowle
Editor: Sid Stone
Music: Denis Blood
Length: 30 minutes

The 80 Days
Production: Humphrey Jennings
    for Crown Film Unit
Director: Humphrey Jennings
Commentary: Ed Murrow
Length: 14 minutes

V1
(Made wholly for overseas use
with same material as *The 80 Days*
but re-edited and with a new
commentary)
Production: Humphrey Jennings
    for Crown Film Unit
Commentary: Fletcher Markle
Length: 10 minutes

1944-45:

A Diary for Timothy
(Released 1946)
Production: Basil Wright for
  Crown Film Unit
Director/Script:
  Humphrey Jennings
Photography: Fred Gamage
Editors: Alan Osbiston, Jenny Hutt
Sound: Ken Cameron, Jock May
Music: Richard Addinsell
Commentary: E.M. Forster
Spoken by: Michael Redgrave
Length: 38 minutes

1945:

A Defeated People
Production: Basil Wright for
  Crown Film Unit
(for Directorate of Army
  Kinematography)
Director/Script:
  Humphrey Jennings
Photography: Army Film Unit
Commentary spoken by
  William Hartnell
Music: Guy Warrack
Length: 19 minutes

1947:

The Cumberland Story
Production: Alexander Shaw for
  Crown Film Unit (COI for
  Ministry of Fuel and Power)

Director/Script:
  Humphrey Jennings
Photography: Chick Fowle
Editor: Jocelyn Jackson
Music: Arthur Benjamin
Length: 39 minutes

1949:

Dim Little Island
Production: Wessex Films
for Central Office of Information
Producer/Director:
  Humphrey Jennings
Photography: Martin Curtis
Editor: Bill Megarry
Music: Ralph Vaughan Williams
Commentary: Osbert Lancaster,
  John Ormston, James Fisher,
  Ralph Vaughan Williams
Length: 11 minutes

1950:

Family Portrait
Production: Ian Dalrymple for
  Wessex Films
Director/Script:
  Humphrey Jennings
Photography: Martin Curtis
Editor: Stewart McAllister
Sound: Ken Cameron
Music: John Greenwood
Commentary spoken by:
  Michael Goodliffe
Length: 25 minutes

Index of Names

Index of Humphrey Jennings's Films